Dance History

Originally published in 1983, the first edition of *Dance History* rapidly established itself as a core student text. Now fully revised and updated it remains the only book to address the rationale, processes and methodologies specific to the study of dance history.

For the main body of the text, which covers historical studies of dance in its traditional, social and theatrical contexts, the editors have brought together a team of internationally known dance historians. Roger Copeland and Deborah Jowitt each take a controversial look at American modern dance; Kenneth Archer and Millicent Hodson explain the processes they go through when reconstructing 'lost' ballets, and Theresa Buckland and Georgina Gore examine traditional dance in England and West Africa respectively. With other contributions on social dance, ballet, early European modern dance and feminist perspectives on dance history this book offers a multitude of starting points for studying dance as well as presenting examples of dance writing at its very best.

Professor Janet Adshead-Landsdale is now Head of the Dance Department at the University of Surrey, a post previously held by Professor June Layson until her retirement.

In 1992 **Professor Layson** was awarded the title of Emeritus Professor in acknowledgement of her contribution to the study of dance.

Dance History

An introduction

Second edition

Edited by Janet Adshead-Lansdale and June Layson

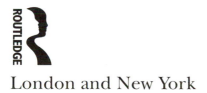

London and New York

GV
1589
D38
1994

First published 1983
by Dance Books, London, as
Dance History. A methodology for study,
edited by Janet Adshead and June Layson

Second edition, revised and updated, published 1994
by Routledge
11 New Fetter Lane, London EC4P 4EE

Simultaneously published in the USA and Canada
by Routledge
29 West 35th Street, New York, NY 10001

Typeset in Baskerville by
Ponting–Green Publishing Services, Chesham, Bucks
Printed and bound in Great Britain by
Biddles Ltd, Guildford and Kings Lynn

British Library Cataloguing in Publication Data
A catalogue record for this book is available from the
British Library.

Library of Congress Cataloging-in-Publication Data
Applied for

ISBN 0-415-09020-6 (hbk)
      0-415-09030-X (pbk)

Contents

Illustrations

Notes on contributors

Professor Janet Adshead-Lansdale is Head of the Department of Dance Studies at the University of Surrey, UK. Her publications include *The Study of Dance* (1981), *Choreography: Principles and Practice* (1987), and *Dance Analysis: Theory and Practice* (1988). Her research in the field of dance analysis and theoretical issues in the structure of the discipline of dance studies follows on from her Ph.D. work in the late 1970s. She has lectured extensively in mainland Europe and in Australasia and N. America.

Dr Kenneth Archer, English scenic consultant, and *Dr Millicent Hodson*, American choreographer, have reconstructed modern masterpieces with the Joffrey Ballet, the Paris Opéra, Les Grands Ballets Canadiens and the Finnish National Ballet and have created ballets for Carla Fracci in Naples, Milan, Vicenza and Palermo. Featured in the Arte film *Les Printemps du Sacre* (1993) and WNET/BBC film *The Search for Nijinsky's Rite of Spring* (1989), they broadcast and lecture internationally and write for various dance periodicals.

Carol Brown is a dancer, choreographer and researcher. She was educated in New Zealand and trained initially in the Bodenweiser system. She has won awards for choreography and toured professionally. She is currently studying for a Ph.D. in Dance at the University of Surrey. Her research area concerns feminist issues in dance.

Dr Theresa Buckland has recently been appointed Senior Lecturer and MA Course Director of Dance Studies at the University of Surrey. Formerly she was Head of the Department of Arts, Design and Performance, Manchester Metropolitan University. Her research interests lie in the areas of popular dance culture and dance anthropology and she has had articles published in folk and traditional dance journals.

Judith Chapman is Manager of the National Resource Centre for Dance (NRCD), University of Surrey, and lectures at the University of Surrey. She edits the *Dance Current Awareness Bulletin*, has compiled two dance, film and video directories and has devised and edited several resource packs and videos for dance education.

Professor Roger Copeland lectures at Oberlin College in the USA. He has published articles about dance, theatre and film in periodicals including *The New York Times, The New Republic, The Drama Review, Dance Theatre Journal,* and *The Village Voice.* His books include *What is Dance?* (1983) and the forthcoming *Cunningham's Legacy.* He has worked as an adviser for the 'Dance in America' series on American public television and for the US Government's National Endowment for the Arts.

Dr Georgiana Gore is based in France as a freelance lecturer and writer in dance anthropology. She established the dance section in the Department of Theatre Arts, University of Benin, Nigeria, and also taught at the University of Surrey, where she initiated a Master's degree course in dance anthropology. Her research interests include southern Nigerian performance traditions, theoretical issues in dance anthropology, and the politics of the body and dance.

Michael Huxley is Acting Head of Performing Arts at De Montfort University, Leicester, where he was formerly Head of Dance. He has been published in a variety of journals including *International Working Papers in Dance, Journal of Aesthetic Education, Ballet International,* and *New Dance.* He has held positions with various national dance organisations including The Society for Dance Research, East Midlands Arts and, currently, Dance Four.

Deborah Jowitt has written a weekly dance column for *The Village Voice* since 1967 and published articles in numerous other newspapers, journals, and anthologies in the USA. Her books include *Dance Beat* (1977), *The Dance in Mind* (1985), and *Time and the Dancing Image,* which won the de la Torre Bueno Prize for 1988. In 1985, she was the recipient of a citation from the Dance Perspectives Foundation, and a 'Bessie' for her contributions to dance criticism.

Professor June Layson established the first UK postgraduate courses in dance at the University of Leeds. Her appointment to the University of Surrey in 1981 was to establish the first Dance Department in a British University where she was responsible for the development of full undergraduate, postgraduate and research degree programmes. She has been a member of several national and regional arts bodies including the Arts Council of Great Britain. Currently she sits on the Victoria and Albert Museum's Theatre Museum Committee. She has lectured extensively abroad and published widely. Her Ph.D. research was on Isadora Duncan and her current work is on the development of British early modern dance.

Patricia Mitchinson is a freelance lecturer in dance and a Moderator in Performing Arts for the Business Technology and Education Council (BTEC). She is an assessor for the Yorkshire and Humberside Arts Association and Chairperson of Friends of Dance North. She is the author of several published articles and a contributor to the Yorkshire Oral History Dance Project. She has worked as an adviser for a number of UK arts and educational organisations.

Dr Giannandrea Poesio has contributed to Italian magazines and newspapers such as *La republica, La danza, La nazione* and *Danza & danza* for which he is London editor. He has worked as Artistic Consultant and Director of the Dance Courses at Teatro Verdi in Pisa and has taught Dance History at the Sarah Lawrence Program in Florence. Since 1990 he has been a regular contributor to *Dancing Times* and teacher of Dance Studies at the English National Ballet School in London.

Jane Pritchard is archivist for Rambert Dance Company and English National Ballet.

Preface

What is dance history and how does it relate both to history generally and to the study of dance? If dance history can be regarded as a worthwhile academic activity how might it best be studied, engaged in and communicated? This text is written in response to such questions.

It is based on an earlier publication *Dance History: A methodology for study* published in 1983 by Dance Books. Then the need was to provide a theoretical basis for dance history as a burgeoning area of academic study, to offer examples of good history writing and to outline various curriculum development strategies. In the ensuing decade dance history, particularly at university and college level, has become well-established worldwide and a wealth of dance history writing and other forms of communication is beginning to accumulate. However, new theoretical positions, innovative technologies and an ever-growing concern to understand the present in the light of the past confront dance historians. There is a need to re-conceptualize, to re-tool and to re-appraise the study of dance history if it is to move into the second millenium in a healthy, vigorous and confident manner.

The three-part format of the original text proved successful and has been retained but the chapters have been re-written and several new contributions included. Part 1 now focuses more directly on specific theoretical and methodological matters. Part 2 provides examples of good historical writing which range across many dance genres and style in both place and time. The authors in this section are distinguished dance historians drawn from five different countries and across three continents and they bring a wealth of experience and varied historical stances and expertise to the text. In Part 3 the two chapters are concerned with new ways of studying dance history and writing about it. The three appendices form a valuable source base to the whole as well as providing complementary sources for dance history study generally. This new publication is written with university and college students and their teachers in mind.

Unlike other subjects, which might be hampered by a long tradition, it is possible to be flexible in methodology and adaptable in technique in dance history practice. To be free from entrenched positions about what dance history should do and how it should do it can be an advantage in developing a discipline that is responsive to the activity being studied.

This text aims to play some part in the continuing evolution of the subject, to bring dance history scholars together and, especially, to enhance student education in the field of dance history.

Janet Adshead-Lansdale
June Layson
August 1993

Acknowledgements

As Editors we wish to thank our twelve contributors for bringing their subject specialisms to the text and thereby adding expertise, variety and some controversy. As always, we are indebted to our postgraduate and research students whose questioning, critical responses and, above all, delight in and commitment to furthering the study of dance create an exciting climate in which to put forward and develop our ideas. Our grateful thanks, too, to Amanda Lillie whose word-processing skills and general support services have proved invaluable in the production of this book.

Part I

A rationale and methodology for dance history

Chapter 1

Historical perspectives in the study of dance

June Layson

1.1 INTRODUCTION

Chapter 1 provides the foundation line for the rest of this book in outlining and discussing the nature of history generally and, more particularly, dance history. It is acknowledged that at a basic level it is possible to study dance history, write about it and be involved in other forms of dance history communication without addressing such epistemological questions as what constitutes dance history, what purposes it serves, what roles are available to the dance historian and so on. However, it is contended here that any study of dance history, in whatever form and for whatever purpose, can be enlightened and enriched by an understanding of the nature of the dance history enterprise. To apprehend and appreciate the field of operation is a vital preliminary to acquiring knowledge and understanding in any area and dance history is no exception to this.

In section 1.2 the general historical perspective is outlined as the forerunner to a more detailed consideration in section 1.3 of dance in its historical perspective. Together these two sections reflect relatively well established perceptions of both general history and dance history. In section 1.4 the discussion is opened up to include reference to the current challenges being made to traditional approaches in the form of radical perceptual shifts and in the introduction of highly innovative practices. In the light of this discussion, section 1.5 identifies selected areas of dance history as an academic discipline requiring strategic reconsideration and redevelopment, and the chapter is summarized in section 1.6.

1.2 THE GENERAL HISTORICAL PERSPECTIVE.

As an academic discipline history is often justified on the grounds of inherent worthwhileness since the past of any group of people is regarded as a cultural legacy to be valued. In addition, history is seen to provide links between the past and the present so that, through its study, the here and now can be informed.

These particular notions of history serve to emphasize its chronological core and its linearity. Nevertheless, this does not imply that such ideas can be conflated with a teleological stance which would promote the identification of 'natural' chronological progressions and beginnings and endings. Indeed, history may be diachronic in its study of particular thematic developments over time or synchronic in its study of a specific time-span devoid of reference to its historical antecedents, but it is, nevertheless, fundamentally concerned with the character of continuity and the nature of changes through time.

The historian's role in this is traditionally seen as one of both chronicler and interpreter. Even so, in the quest to establish what happened in the past it is impossible to retrieve everything. Therefore, the historian is, inevitably, also a selector with the responsibility for distinguishing the important from the trivial, the central from the peripheral. Such selection, though, is always from the relative position of the researcher, whether declared or otherwise, and invariably reflects the demands of the project in hand, further external requirements and so on.

The working methods employed by the historian are based on sources, the residue or traces of the past, which more often than not are fragmentary and incomplete. These are critically appraised, assembled into logical relationships and structures and then used as the basis for historical communication, the commonest form of which is the written word, sometimes termed 'historiography'. Historical writing is concerned both with recreating the past, and thus relies on description and connecting narrative, and interpreting the past, by means of analytical techniques.

From this necessarily brief outline of the domain of history and the role of the historian it is evident that it is far from being an exact science. Indeed the very idea of history being at all related to the sciences is vigorously challenged by the 'new' historians. Its grouping with the humanities and/or the social sciences acknowledges that characteristically it not only involves high degrees of technical skills but also requires abilities to synthesize, to make inferences, to interpret and to offer judgements and evaluations. This in turn means that history is essentially 'open', that is, always amenable to reinterpretation.

The essentially contested nature of history gives the discipline the potential for instability and creativity. The subject is periodically seen to be in a state of flux and there is an ongoing debate to determine its scope and rationale, to devise new methods and appropriate approaches and, more recently, to question the role of the historian. One of the implications of this openness is that to study history can involve engagement in an exciting and challenging area. Similarly, historical communication, in whatever form it takes, can engender imaginative and creative work with the real possibility of contributing to the knowledge base of the subject.

1.3   DANCE IN ITS HISTORICAL PERSPECTIVES

In dance history all that has been touched upon in the preceding section applies, the crucial difference being that, instead of a general concern with the past, dance is now foregrounded. Dance history, as a body of knowledge, and the study of dance history, as a scholarly activity, constitute in some respects a hybrid discipline. This discipline shares many characteristics with history in general but, more importantly, forms one of the central methodologies of dance studies. The main contribution of dance history to the study of dance is that it reveals a highly complex human activity serving many purposes and developing a multiplicity of types which proliferate, prosper, decline and otherwise change through time.

A convenient way of characterizing dance history as a body of knowledge and as a disciplined activity is by means of a simple three-dimensional model.[1] Here it is used to explore different modes of engaging in dance history (Figure 1.1).

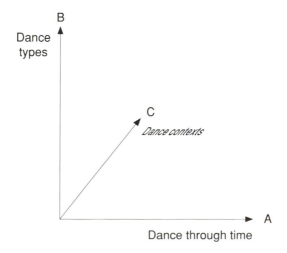

Figure 1.1

1.3.1   Dimension A – Dance through time

This is the fundamental dimension and defining characteristic for the area of study and it allows many different approaches (Figure 1.2).

The traditional approach is by means of a systematic study which

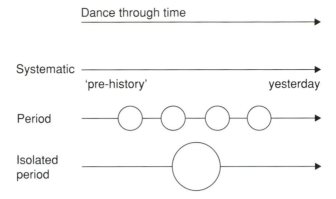

Figure 1.2

attempts to cover all aspects of dance and either starts with 'pre-history' and concludes with the dance of yesterday or selects a sizeable portion of the whole, such as several centuries. This mode of study has the merit of moving steadily through time so that broad features, as in the growth and development of dance styles, can easily be historically situated.[2] However, the disadvantages are considerable. Even if the dance of 'pre-history' can be studied, and, given the lack of evidence, this is clearly in doubt, or the dance of many centuries considered as a unified whole, which is also problematic, the attempt to encompass such a wide time-span inevitably leads to superficiality. Furthermore, in such study there is always the danger of succumbing to the notion that dance, like human activity in general, has evolved into ever more advanced states and is, in some way, 'better' as time progresses.

A period-based study may solve some of these problems because eras can be chosen which are highlights in the history of dance and offer opportunities for in-depth enquiry. Nevertheless, this may well be at the expense of identifying causes and effects, discerning longer term trends and understanding the reasons for the growth or decline in dance in preceding and subsequent eras.

By concentrating the study of dance on one isolated period it is possible to work in detail and to pay attention to single events and their relation to the time-span of the selected area. Here, though, the potential to note subtle shifts through several time periods in dance, and in attitudes towards it, is in jeopardy.

The 'dance through time' dimension serves a useful purpose because it ensures that events are placed in chronological order and it gives a temporal structure to dance history. However, the source base available for dance study is not uniform but increases rapidly as the twentieth century progresses and it is unsurprising that there are more materials extant for the twentieth than for any other century. This means that the opportunities for studying pre-twentieth-century dance are hampered by the lack of a comprehensive dance source base. Such a factor reflects the ephemerality of dance and the comparatively recent establishment of dance studies as an academic discipline as much as the normal loss of material evidence through time. Even so the 'silences' concerning dance in the extant pre- and early-twentieth-century sources are telling.[3]

The use of a left-to-right arrow to denote the historical dimension of dance might give the impression that the logical and only way to study dance history is to proceed through time, from 'then' to 'now'. In practice, though, there are several instances where this is not the case. Oral history and oral tradition are both important elements in studying specific types of dance,[4] as are oral sources generally. In such cases the 'here' and 'now' is seen to provide access to 'before' and 'then' and, consequently, historical study is conducted 'backwards' through time.[5]

1.3.2 Dimension B – Dance types

Figure 1.3

This model (Figure 1.3) allows all types of dance to be identified and subsequently subdivided into their constituent parts (Figure 1.4).

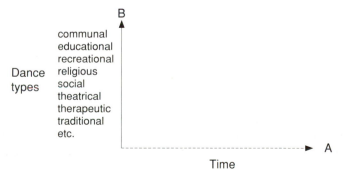

Figure 1.4

The notion of dance types is at the macrocosmic level and derived from their function and context. For example, a distinction can be made between traditional dances, which usually have a ceremonial, celebratory function, are popular, that is, 'of the people', and tend to endure, and social dances which, too, are popular but are more concerned with reinforcing individual and group relationships, are a form of entertainment and are liable to rapid changes in fashion.

In moving towards the microcosmic level it is possible to subdivide a dance type in several ways. For example, theatre dance can initially be divided on one of several geographical bases and subsequently by genre, style and 'organizing concepts' (Adshead 1988) (Figure 1.5).

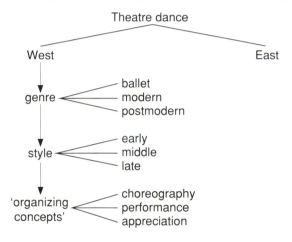

Figure 1.5

Simply by combining the time and type dimensions the immensity of the area encompassed by dance history is partially revealed as any one or more of the sub-sets, in various combinations, can be studied within appropriately selected periods of time.

1.3.3   Dimension C – Dance contexts

Dance is ultimately defined by its contexts (Figure 1.6). The consideration of, for example, place, location, artistic or social contexts has traditionally been the concern of dance historians, though often only in a perfunctory manner. However, the need to study dance within its appropriate circumstances and in relation to prevailing ideas and attitudes is vital if dance is to be understood both in its own terms and that of the many contexts in which it exists (Figure 1.7).

Because the contexts in which dance exists are manifold there is a

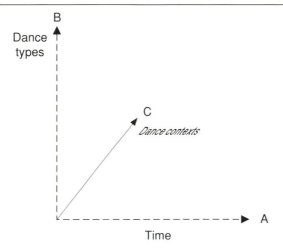

Figure 1.6

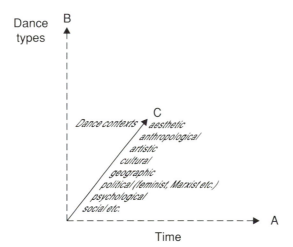

Figure 1.7

potential tension between studying the dance itself in depth and studying it within its immediate and wider contexts. A detailed examination and analysis of dance devoid of its contiguous and contemporaneous contexts is likely to be seriously flawed since the dance is both part of and derived from its contexts. Similarly, a multidisciplinary contextual approach taken to extremes may, instead of informing the study of dance, merely reduce it to the status of exemplar. There may be occasions when either extreme approach is justified but generally the need is to find a balance between these polarities. Even so, such problems are likely to persist since, as the study of dance gains

momentum, the development of, for example, highly detailed choreographic analyses and, coexistently, the recognition of the crucial nature
of contextual concerns, will need to be reconciled.

With the third dimension articulated, the vastness and complexity of
the area of dance history, hinted at earlier, is now clearly evident. While
its subject boundaries can barely be glimpsed it is probably the case that
only a very small percentage of dance history worldwide has been
studied to date. This may appear daunting but it also presents exciting
challenges to future dance historians.

A model of the subject area for dance history is shown in Figure 1.8.

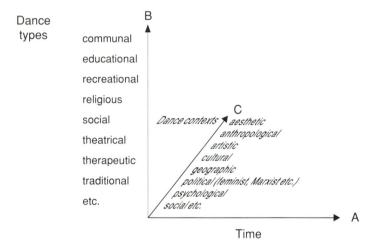

Figure 1.8

1.4   THE TRADITIONAL AND THE NEW: CHANGING
PERSPECTIVES IN DANCE HISTORY

Although it is impossible in this text to do justice to both traditional and
'new history' orthodoxies in relation to their rationale, perceived terms
of reference and prevailing ideologies, it is profitable at this juncture to
identify those concerns which currently have an impact upon dance
history or have the potential to do so. In fact the debate concerning
'new' dance history is, as yet, in its infancy.

What might be termed the traditional approach to history originated
in central Europe and 'by the second half of the nineteenth century
was beginning to establish itself throughout the Western world as an
autonomous academic discipline' (Marwick 1989: 43). Nevertheless,
during the early twentieth century and subsequently, the fundamental
bases of the subject as an area of study were still a matter for debate.

Notions such as the 'proper' focus of history (either the political state or a wider concern with economic, social and other factors), the objectivity of the historian (either an ideal to be attained or the explicit acknowledgement of subjective involvement) and the methodologies to be employed (ranging from support for the 'scientific' to embracing techniques from new disciplines such as psychology and statistics) were raised as various schools of thought held sway.[6]

The current challenges to traditional history stem from the broadly-based postmodern movement and, in particular, the work of the French philosopher/historian Michel Foucault (1926–85). In his seminal attack on the status quo of history Foucault (1972) endeavours to expose its inherent fault-lines. He, too, regards the still evident preoccupation with political events as misplaced but, more fundamentally, points to the manner in which historians implicitly promote notions of deep-rooted and long-lasting structures as if

> beneath the shifts and changes of political events, they were trying to reveal the stable, almost indestructible system of checks and balances, the irreversible processes, the constant readjustments, the underlying tendencies that gather force, and are then suddenly reversed after centuries of continuity, the movements of accumulation and slow saturation, the great silent, motionless bases that traditional history has covered with a thick layer of events.
>
> (Foucault 1972: 3)

In addition to criticism emanating from the application of postmodern theories, traditional history has for some time had an uneasy relationship with Marxist approaches to the subject and, more recently, has similarly tried to accommodate feminist theoretical positions.[7] Thus the state of flux alluded to in section 1.2 prevails.

The current situation and debate are important to dance history and its protagonists not only because there is a need to keep abreast with new thinking but also because a crucial stage has been reached in the development of the area as a subject of study. Since its inception as an academic discipline in the USA in the first quarter of the twentieth century, the drive to establish dance history has been fuelled by the need for documentation. Much has been achieved in this respect, and dance history is now on the verge of a new era in its development. It can, unlike the longer-established general history discipline, respond, adapt to and even embrace radical modes of thought in an immediate manner. In these special circumstances it is worthwhile probing further the postmodern and parallel approaches in order to explore their implications for dance history even though it puts this text at risk of presenting an over-simplistic account which fails to do justice to highly sophisticated theoretical positions. Specific aspects are selected which relate to the model presented earlier in section 1.3, and the use of technical terms has been avoided.

Both the traditional and the new approaches to history acknowledge the crucial concept of time and the central concern with the past, but the manner in which this is perceived and the outcomes it gives rise to are very different. To the traditionalists time is seen as a seamless, linear phenomenon providing the link between otherwise disparate events. In contrast, the new and other schools of historical thought regard time as a series of surges, with interruptions and dislocations. Therefore, while traditional historical accounts tend towards or seek continuity and give causal, time-based explanations, new approaches highlight disjunctions and tolerate temporal ambiguities. In dance history this means, for example, that instead of regarding the history of ballet as one of gradual development to be described in terms of incremental growth, with successive improvements and clearly identifiable points of innovation, in a radical approach the genre would also be studied for its capricious, even haphazard existence through time. A new perspective to a history of ballet would not ignore seemingly atypical events or demote irregularities in order to present a unified whole but would divert attention to the contradictions, culs-de-sac, failures as well as achievements, with the intent of revealing the genre in all its historical manifestations.

In the historical study of types of activities and groups the new thinking would abhor the hierarchical labelling structures that traditionalists might use. Traditionalists regard category by type to be a necessary process towards clarification since naming can provide useful 'pegs' on which to 'hang' ideas. The postmodern stance would treat such work with extreme caution because to categorize is to exclude as well as include. It also calls into question the construction of any grouping since groupings, thus created, carry hierarchical significance. In this instance theatre dance would be cited as having acquired supreme importance in western dance history even though, for example, it could be argued that far more people are engaged in social and traditional dance, and certainly these are the most widespread dance activities.

The traditional and new notions of history both recognize the significance of context but, again, the manner in which this is acknowledged differs. In traditional history contextualization is often likened to an onion and its many skins or layers. The historian starts at the centre and gradually works outwards through ever-widening layers or contexts so that systematically the event or activity which is the focus of the study is placed within its relevant contexts. These contexts are often more political and economic in orientation than social and psychological, particularly in history written before the second half of the twentieth century. In contrast the new history would eschew any ideas of separate, impermeable contexts and certainly distrust any hierarchical notions.

In its place the new thrust would be towards articulating the whole context as a dynamic entity and neither separating nor implying priorities. There is no doubt that the absence of dance in traditional general history texts is a direct result of the bias towards certain prized contexts and the demotion or exclusion of others, such as artistic and social considerations, where dance might feature. However, by the same token dance historians have similarly been guilty of prioritizing certain contexts and ignoring others since it is rare to find a dance history book in which, for example, the economic or political factors relevant to a particular dance concern are acknowledged.[8]

As well as criticizing many of the basic concepts of traditional history, advocates of new history attack the long-established methodologies by which the historian proceeds. At its most extreme the criticism focuses on the traditional modes of dealing with sources. It is claimed that procedures which entail selection, re-arranging and re-ordering can lead to misreading and misrepresentation in the overriding quest for unity and continuity. Furthermore, the need to establish facts is seen to have driven historians to claims of a quasi-scientific objectively verifiable position. The new historians would claim that sources are representations or re-presentations, the latter carrying the force of a current and creative reading, or even construction, of an event. Therefore, the same events may be interpreted in various, even contradictory, modes each of which has validity for the specific purposes it serves. The manner in which history has traditionally been written is similarly criticized. For example, the notion of history as narrative is questioned since, of necessity, it creates both a structure and a meaning.

Such assaults on the role and nature of traditional history have been rebutted on several grounds. One main argument is that current research and writing is already moving in the direction some of the new approaches advocate and a major criticism is that the radical questioning has remained at the ideological stage and has yet to produce either alternative working models or outcomes.

In this text no ideological position is taken concerning traditional and alternative approaches but rather the emphasis is to characterize dance history in terms of current practice and thought and to explore ways in which it might be studied, engaged in and communicated. However, as the subject-identity debate continues in general history circles, so implications for dance history are beginning to emerge. Clearly feminist perspectives are highly relevant as are Marxist-derived notions such as 'cultural theory'. The postmodernist scepticism of the nature of history and its working methods also offers dance history many new and potentially fruitful avenues to explore. All this is taking place at a time when, as indicated earlier, dance history is itself approaching a new threshold in its development. Therefore, given the opportunities and pressures from both within and outside the subject area, it seems pertinent to look briefly towards a new conception of the dance history discipline and to propose some areas and strategies for action.

1.5   TOWARDS A NEW CONCEPTION OF THE DISCIPLINE OF DANCE HISTORY

The current attack on the status quo, the posing of fundamental questions and the attempts to find answers have crucial implications for dance history and its future. There is no denying or avoiding such challenges and ultimately dance history should profit from radical scrutiny and a deep probing search for a new validity.

Dance history is at a stage where, instead of clinging to the coat-tails of general history, it can take steps to establish its own rationale. Logically, many of the features of general history will be retained as it, too, passes through another period of metamorphosis. However, since dance is a cultural phenomenon of major import, in terms of the resources that have been invested in it worldwide and throughout time, dance history needs to claim a place as an eminently important and worthwhile area of study. Such a claim will necessarily be founded on the particular nature of dance history and be supported by fully fledged arguments concerning its basic tenets, its organizing frameworks and its relationship to the study of dance as a whole.

This will in turn require a reappraisal of procedures and method-ologies. To date, working practices adopted from traditional history have enabled dance historians to articulate many aspects of the dance of the past. Inevitably, though, the current predominant need for docu-mentation and the prime dependence on written sources will give way to more conceptually-based concerns as new thinking and new techno-logies become available. In addition postmodern, feminist and other late-twentieth-century theories point to different and, for dance, poten-tially more productive ways of reclaiming the past. Therefore, the need is to rethink and recast the manner in which dance history proceeds. This will entail a move from the position in which the ephemeral nature of dance is offered as the sole excuse for a partial dance history to one where a worldwide dance history is regarded as accessible and amenable to study.

The reappraisal of the 'what', 'why' and 'how' of dance history can be accomplished only by dance historians in an open and public debate. Projections into the future may be either intimidating or irrelevant to those who do not regard themselves as in a position to question, let alone alter, dance history as it now exists. However, striving towards a new dance history is the province of all engaged in the area. Such work may be initiated at national and regional levels through conferences, colloquia and the publication of seminal texts. In parallel, rethinking and reconceptualizing can also begin at the personal and local level. One specific area for scrutiny and action is identified here.

The study of dance has yet to develop the consistent and detailed terminology and thesauri that characterize the more established academic disciplines. In dance history this is particularly so and there is an urgent need to address the problem in order for the area of study to mature and to realize its potential.

The most glaring example, not only of the lack of accepted nomenclature but also of the inappropriateness of current jargon, is the use of the title 'historical dance'. The preceding discussion in this chapter and, indeed, the whole tenor of this text, is based on the premise that all the dance of the past, placed within its time perspectives, is historical dance. Yet this phrase has been appropriated by some to characterize just the seventeenth- and eighteenth-century court and theatre dance of western Europe.[9]

In this chapter the term 'type' is used for the large number of broad categories of dance that exist. In the general dance literature many different terms serve this purpose, some, such as 'dance form', giving rise to confusion because, in this instance, it can also refer to the structure of a dance. Of course the criticisms emanating from post-modern theory concerning categorizing by type need to be heeded although it is argued here that dance history is at the stage where such clarifications are beneficial rather than counter-productive. Another example of inexact terminology is in the use of words to describe performances such as 'reconstructions', 'reinterpretations', 'restagings', 'revivals' etc. Often these terms are used synonymously but at other times crucial distinctions are made.

Even the term 'research' is generally misused in dance history. Currently it has two distinct meanings. The first is allied to academic enquiry where the aim is to generate ideas, concepts and theories and to produce work that is new to the subject and, therefore, original. In the second sense it is used to denote any enquiry undertaken. What is discovered in this may be new to the enquirer but it is unlikely to be new to the body of knowledge. It is clearly important to distinguish between these two activities.

Although it is well beyond the scope of this text to tackle the problem of dance history terminology it is, nevertheless, useful to raise it here as just one example of an area in which all dance historians have responsibilities and can begin to rectify matters.[10]

The drive towards articulating a new dance history can, it is proposed, be carried out at many levels. It is of overriding importance that this is undertaken on the basis of what has been achieved and in the light of the vast potential to be realized.

1.6 SUMMARY

In this chapter the scope, rationale and defining characteristics of dance history as an academic discipline are presented together with its relation to general history and, especially, the wider field of dance study. Dance history is seen to be centrally concerned with past manifestations of dance situated within their diverse contemporary contexts and displaying various changes through time. The traditional core of dance history is examined in terms of its characteristics as a subject of study and with reference to some relevant late twentieth century theoretical positions. An agenda is proposed for the redefinition of dance history and some possibilities of a new dance history outlined.

It is axiomatic that those who work in the field of dance history have the responsibility to ensure that the subject enters the second millennium in a robust state. A new dance history should be in a position to embrace innovative ideas and developing technologies on the basis of its clearly articulated mission to further the understanding of dance of the past and, in so doing, to inform perspectives of the dance of the present.

NOTES

1 Earlier published versions of this model served slightly different purposes. For example, see J. Layson (1990), 'Dance history methodology: dynamic models for teaching, learning and research', in *The Fifth Hong Kong International Dance Conference Papers*, II: 56–65. In the current text the discussion has been extended.

2 See Appendix A, 1 for examples of texts which follow this format.

3 For a discussion of this phenomenon see Carol Brown (Chapter 13 below).

4 For example, see Theresa Buckland (Chapter 4 below) and Georgiana Gore (Chapter 5 below) for discussions on the role and nature of oral sources. The same topic is also explored in Chapter 2 below.

5 For further discussion of this notion see Chapter 14 below.

6 For a full account of the development of historical studies in Europe see Marwick (1989).

7 See Carol Brown (Chapter 13 below) for a wide-ranging overview and discussion of this area.

8 Garafola's (1989) publication on Diaghilev's Ballets Russes is cited in Chapter 3 below as a notable exception.

9 Such criticism does not apply to the text by Wendy Hilton (1981), *Dance of Court and Theatre: The French Noble Style 1690–1725*, London: Dance Books. In this, both the title and the contents are explicit in their time parameters and vague, generalized terms are avoided.

10 A planned text by Valerie Preston-Dunlop, *Dance Words*, is due to be published by Gordon & Breach in 1994. It is concerned exclusively with dance terminology and should stimulate debate in this vital area.

REFERENCES

Adshead, J (ed.) (1988), *Dance Analysis: Theory and Practice*, London: Dance Books.

Foucault, M. (1972), *The Archeology of Knowledge*, London: Routledge.

Garafola, L. (1989), *Diaghilev's Ballets Russes*, New York and Oxford: Oxford University Press.

Marwick, A. (1989) *The Nature of History* (1970), London: Macmillan.

Chapter 2

Dance history source materials

June Layson

2.1   INTRODUCTION

In this chapter the remnants and accounts of the past are characterized, categorized and discussed. The early focus on sources in this text is significant and serves two functions. First, it underlines the importance of these materials in dance history. Second, it alerts the reader to the different kinds of source bases used in the dance history texts discussed in Chapter 3, and in the specialist area chapters which constitute Part II of this book.

To be able to work efficiently and effectively with sources is a required tool of the dance historian's trade. Even though the use of computers has revolutionized documentation of historical sources the basic necessity remains to start from the extant evidence of dance. It may well be that as more advanced computer programs are developed so dance historians will need to re-tool and to re-appraise well-established practices, but the starting point for study is essentially with source materials, the bedrock of dance history.

2.2   TYPES AND CATEGORIES OF SOURCE MATERIALS

In history generally a fundamental distinction is made between types of source materials, and it applies equally to dance sources. This is the separation of 'primary' from 'secondary' sources, which is crucial since it determines the nature and value of study in an area as well as any written outcomes.

Primary sources are those that came into existence during the period being studied: thus they are first-hand and contemporary, and provide the raw materials for dance study. Examples of primary source materials in dance are a dance performance, a choreographer's working score or log with all its amendments and annotations, actual costumes worn by dancers for known performances and eye-witness accounts of certain dance events. *Secondary sources*, as the term suggests, are second-hand, processed, after the event accounts, often using hindsight to trace developments in the dance over a span of time. All the standard dance histories, dance encyclopedias and dance reference books come into the secondary source category. Some of these texts are based on primary sources though the more 'popular' histories often use materials previously published in other dance history books.

Some sources can be regarded as both primary and secondary according to the purposes for which they are being used. An example of this is the Kinney and Kinney (1936) dance history book. This is now a primary source for early-twentieth-century European theatre dance but in its time and subsequently it has also been used as a secondary source since much of the text reviews the development of dance from ancient Egyptian origins by reference to other published works.

The relative importance of primary and secondary sources usually depends upon the kind of work being done and the person undertaking it. The beginner, faced with too many primary sources at once, may be confused by apparently conflicting evidence, but to use only secondary sources could engender the attitude that all the interesting work has been done and dance history is fixed, undisputed and boring. The exclusive use of primary sources is the mark of the experienced dance researcher who refers to good secondary sources to provide background, points of entry for further study, bases of comparison, and so on. On the other hand, concentrating solely on secondary source material by reading many dance history books can be rewarding, interesting and informative, but as such this means reading about dance history and neither getting involved in the methodologies of dance history nor actually contributing to it.

Generally then, a balance that is appropriate to the kind of study being undertaken has to be maintained between the use of primary and secondary source materials, and this must be based on the recognition that the former are of a particular period and the latter are about a particular period, that the former were produced during the period and the latter after the period.[1]

Given the crucial primary/secondary source divide, in dance history it is often useful to make further categories in order to group similar sources and to gain an overall impression of the kind of evidence they present. However, while the assigning of primary and secondary source status is a necessary first step, subsequent categorization depends largely upon the source base of the topic area selected. For example, the sources gathered for a study of an eminent dance or dance teacher might usefully be placed in separate public and private categories, the first consisting of published material such as reviews and journal articles, the second of unpublished diaries and letters. Similarly, a focus on a particular dance style might suggest the grouping of written sources, such as class notes, monographs and textbooks, and non-written sources, including sketches, photographs and video.

The categories proposed here, of written, visual and sound sources, are broad and may need further subdivision in specific cases but they have the merit of reflecting the classifications used in many dance archives and collections. Since the order in which these categories are presented is non-alphabetical it clearly signals some kind of hierarchy. In fact the order is based on current importance and frequency of use, it being the case that, in western dance history scholarship, written materials have traditionally taken precedence over visual while, overall, sound sources are only minimally used. This reflects the hegemony of the printed and written word prior to the introduction of new technologies to record visual images and sound.[2] However, as 'new' dance history methodology develops and traditional practices and the outcomes they inevitably give rise to are questioned, it is likely that in the future more emphasis will be given to the use of visual and sound sources than hitherto.

1 Written sources – advertisements, autobiographies, bills, cast lists, choreographers' log books, critics' reviews, dance notations, diaries, edicts, journals, letters, literature, magazines, music notations, newspapers, parish records, posters, school records, theatre programmes, receipts, tracts etc.
2 Visual sources – primarily the dance itself, also architecture, costumes, designs for sets, films, musical instruments, paintings, photographs, prints, properties, sculpture, videotapes, etc.
3 Sound sources:
   aural – music (live and recorded), sound accompaniment
   oral – interviews (formal and informal), reminiscences

These lists are by no means exhaustive, indeed it is unlikely that definitive lists could be drawn up since different kinds of materials may be of value to the dance historian in different circumstances. Some materials are such that they could be placed in more than one category depending upon their use. For example, a theatre programme is a written source but it may also be of value for its visual contents such as lay-out, photographs, typeface etc. Similarly, a drum might be grouped with visual or sound sources according to its significance in the study.

The dance as a visual source in its own right is often taken for granted yet certain dances, even in the here and now of performance, are 'living history'. It was the recognition of this fact that prompted Cecil Sharp at the beginning of the twentieth century to start collecting the traditional dances of England and then to pursue this work in the USA where he and his assistants found that many of the seventeenth-century Playford dances were still being performed by descendants of the early British settlers. Similarly, a current performance of a ballet such as *Swan Lake* is but the latest presentation of a work that originated in 1877. Even though the choreography has changed, perhaps almost totally, its survival today is a modern manifestation of a theatre dance genre of considerable historical significance as well as testimony to the manner in which the ballet tradition is 'handed on'. Thus a dance performance may itself contain the historical threads which can be traced back from the present through time to its inception or earliest records.

Although written sources, both primary and secondary, have traditionally dominated western dance history study and writing, the need to use them in conjunction with visual and sound sources is becoming increasingly recognized.[3] This is certainly the case in working with early dance notation scores. An attempt to reconstruct a particular gavotte performed at the beginning of the eighteenth century from the Feuillet notation would of necessity involve reference to other contemporary written, visual and sound sources in order to achieve some degree of accuracy in steps, style, manner and movement quality.

2.3   PROBLEMATIC SOURCE MATERIALS

Most of the items given in the proposed three categories could readily be labelled as primary or secondary sources but some materials present problems in this respect.

Probably the easiest to deal with is photocopied material. The original item, such as a theatre programme, may be a primary source but a photocopy of it is clearly not. Whether the original is a written document or a visual source the quality of the photocopy paper will certainly differ. In addition, there may well be differences in size, colour, texture and so on, all of which may be of significance in the original. Therefore, a photocopy is just that, a photocopy of a primary or secondary source and it does not take on the status of the original. However, in the future current photocopied material will assume primary source status of a kind for the period in which it was produced.

Descriptions of village dance festivals and society balls often occur in historical novels and other fiction and appear authentic. Nevertheless, such literature is solely a primary source for the period in which it was written and cannot be regarded as evidence for the period about which it was written. There are, for example, several references to dance in Thomas Hardy's (1872) *Under the Greenwood Tree*, a novel set in early-nineteenth-century southern England. In 1926 the then English Folk Dance Society asked Hardy about the accuracy of his dance descriptions. It transpired that in his novel Hardy had described dances that he himself had performed fifty or sixty years earlier. In this instance

Hardy is recalling a personal experience, a primary source, but re-creating and placing it in a fictional context.[4]

Drawings, paintings, prints, sculptures and sketches of dancers by contemporary artists may at first sight be considered good primary source material; however, there is a need to be aware of prevailing artistic conventions and style. In her book *The Dance in Ancient Greece*, Lawler (1964) points to the consequence of not recognizing such practices in art.

> The Greek vase painter often draws figures without a 'floor line' – a convention which has led some modern interpreters to insert an imaginary 'floor line' of their own in a given scene, and then to deduce from its position all sorts of untenable conclusions, e.g. that the ancient Greeks engaged in something like ballet and even toe-dancing.
>
> (Lawler 1964: 21)

Lawler gives several further examples which show how necessary it is to treat such material with caution and, more especially, the dangers of using it as an exact record upon which to base a dance reconstruction. Even when it is known that a dancer co-operated with or posed for an artist, as in Isadora Duncan's case, it is necessary to realize that what is presented is seen through the artist's eyes. Sketches by Rodin and Bourdelle of Duncan dancing are very different in the impression they give of dynamism in Duncan's movement. The former are more static and robust, the latter more fluid and delicate. Therefore, although such material is primary, by virtue of its origins, it needs to be used with considerable care and understanding. Knowledge of artists' personal styles and the art movements or schools with which they identified is required. It may also be revealing to view them as witting or unwitting testimony (see section 2.4).

In the light of the difficulties that may arise in the use of visual works of art it might be assumed that photographs of dancers would be accurate and, consequently, impeccable primary source material. Yet this would not allow for the fact that many of the technical problems encountered in the early days of photography, such as exposure time and capturing movement accurately, remained unsolved until well into the twentieth century. Thus photographs (*c.* 1855) of Fanny Cerrito, one of the famous ballerinas of the Romantic period, were of necessity posed, as were most of those of Denishawn dancers taken between 1915 and 1931. Therefore, in using photographs as historical evidence it is important to distinguish between posed and action photographs and to establish location. Posed portraits are usually taken in the photographer's studio, although occasionally outdoor[5] and theatre locations are used, and the pose may or may not be from an actual dance. Action photographs, a comparatively recent development, may evoke a performance mood or quality, but even when captioned with the title of a dance it does not necessarily follow that such photographs were taken during an actual performance.[6]

Film and video may also seem to be easily classified as either primary or secondary source material and, generally, this is the case but here, too, caution is needed.

Much of the early dance film available presents difficulties in establishing date, place of origin and subject matter simply because such details, even if recorded at the time, can readily become separated from the film itself. Laboratory analysis may establish approximate dating; nevertheless, dance film shot in the first decade or so of the twentieth century is invariably unstable and also difficult to use. The apparent jerkiness of the movement can be rectified in the transfer to video format but it needs to be appreciated that since the filmed event is seen through the eyes of the cameraperson it is inevitably a selected presentation.

Video recordings are easy to use and amenable to various analytical techniques. Even so, whether the video is a primary source, as in the recording of a dance event (where occasionally it is necessary to distinguish between actual performance and rehearsal), or secondary, as in a documentary television programme (although these often include primary source inserts), here, too, the element of selectivity has to be taken into account. It is rare, for example, for the whole performance area to be in frame throughout a video recording of theatre dance and, similarly, a processional carnival with dance elements is unlikely to be recorded in its entirety.[7] Other matters which need to be allowed for when using dance video as a historical source are that the movement tends to be 'flattened', the space and dynamic can be distorted and the small dancing image depersonalized.

Sound sources may also be problematic in use. In this text 'sound sources' is the preferred category title although in general history texts 'oral sources' is used as the global term. This choice of terminology is deliberate here because it allows a distinction to be made between aural sources, such as music, and oral sources, which can then be reserved for the spoken word.

If the provenance of a music recording or disc can be established and the instruments being played identified then few problems will arise in the use of such materials, which are likely to be primary in origin. Nevertheless, if the current recording of a music work is being employed as a source for studying a dance choreographed to that music decades or even centuries ago it needs to be appreciated that such matters as tempi and other aspects of performance may well have changed during the intervening years. This is a further example of a secondary source which, although of value, cannot be used as if it had primary source status.

Oral sources are gaining importance as their unique significance in dance history is becoming increasingly recognized. Generally these sources are of two types. First, there is the oral tradition of a subgroup or culture which is passed on from one generation to the next and is liable to both embellishment or erosion but appears to retain essential features. Reference is made earlier in this chapter to the handing-on of roles in ballet. This is accomplished by means of a combined movement and oral tradition which is also an important element in social and traditional dance.[8] Second, there are the oral histories which are concerned with first-hand accounts of events and experiences lived through. These are primary sources of potentially great importance to the dance historian since they offer material not readily accessed elsewhere or even unavailable by any other means. Consequently, oral history sources need to be used with a clear understanding of what they can yield rather than with an undue emphasis on their perceived shortcomings.

Whether live or recorded, oral testimony may range from reminiscences given as a monologue to highly structured interviews. When dancers and other witnesses speak freely of the past and their involvement in it as recollections this resembles a sound autobiography. Typically, it is likely to be multilayered and possibly anachronistic but its value lies, for example, in the accuracy of remembered details of choreography, particular interpretations and performances and perceptions of events. Such testimony is 'lived experience' and is properly regarded as phenomenological. While former choreographers, critics and dancers may have reliable movement memories (although this is not necessarily so) it is likely that, as in a written autobiography, events recalled and retold may be subject to selection and re-ordering. Facts and other evidence can be cross-checked with reliable contemporary accounts but primarily these personal accounts need to be valued for what they offer in terms of insights, impressions, feelings and the overall ambience of a period rather than for factual matters.

Oral testimony of recent dance history has the merit of immediacy although long-term trends and developments may not be appreciated. Conversely a dancer reminiscing about events that occurred more than half a century ago may well be able to describe key events and personalities but the detail may be missing. Although all such sources are primary, as a general rule the greater the period of time that has elapsed between the event and the recall the more the necessity to augment with supporting and contextual material. Yet this need not detract from the inestimable value of such personal glimpses into the dance past.

Since the monologue style may not always yield the specific material sought, an interview format is often adopted. In this the recollection and narrative process can be given a degree of structure and kept 'on track' and this may lead then and there or subsequently to a memory being triggered.[9] Here again, though, there are pitfalls to be avoided and the interviewer needs to be aware that a potentially interventionist role may prejudice the gaining of unique insights.[10]

As the potential value of oral tradition and oral testimony in dance history is recognized it is likely that, along with video, the current generating of such material for dance archives and collections will gain momentum. If this proves to be the case then dance historians will need to acquire the techniques to use such material with a far greater degree of sophistication than hitherto in order to realize the potential of such unique primary sources.

2.4   EVALUATION OF SOURCE MATERIALS

With problematic source materials the need is to establish primary or secondary status and to understand the particular ways in which they can then best be used. In contrast some source materials can easily be categorized but they have to be judged by various criteria in order to determine their value to dance history study. Three examples illustrate the point.

Historical studies of dance that cross language divides necessitate using translations if texts cannot be read in their original form.[11] Translations made by non-dance specialists may place the dance essence of an account in jeopardy. Even when bilingual dance authors, such as Horst Koegler and Walter Sorrell, undertake a translation caution has to be exercised because some dance terms and nuances do not translate readily.[12] In such circumstances the dance historian has to attempt to evaluate the translations to hand in order to determine, for example, how much credence should be given to one translated text in relation to another.

Autobiographies, the written counterparts of oral histories, are often seized upon as being central primary sources especially when emanating from a choreographer or dancer. Yet these, too, require evaluation. Occasionally authorship is contested (this is discussed later in this section under authenticity) and some recent autobiographies have been acknowledged as partially 'ghost-written'. Other factors which need to be taken into account are the time-gap between when the events occurred and their written description, and whether the text is based on diaries kept and notes made at the time or largely consists of memories retained over the intervening years. Some autobiographies are written in a narrative style with the intention of adding a personal viewpoint to well-known events, others are motivated by the desire to 'set the record straight' and to challenge existing interpretations of cause and effect, although such underlying reasons are rarely made explicit. In this respect autobiographies tend to be more deliberate and less immediate than oral histories simply because the written word is perceived as the more permanent testimony and, thereby, to offer the opportunity to refashion and even recast past events. Autobiographies are valuable primary source material for what is revealed about authors, their personal relationships, their perceptions and views about the particular events in which they were involved and the prevailing climates of opinion within which they worked. But, as chronicles of facts, autobiographies can be downright misleading and understandably so. Therefore, in order to extract the full value of an autobiography in dance history terms it is necessary to evaluate it as a primary source of a particular kind and to use it in the full understanding of its various attributes.

Biographies may be classified as primary sources when written during their subjects' lifetime, or immediately afterwards, and secondary sources when written much later. Nevertheless, in some respects a more crucial distinction is by reference to the materials upon which the biography is based. In this case judgements have to be made as to the value and merit of the primary and secondary sources used as well as the balance between them. Other factors which can inform such evaluations are, for example, whether the subject of the biography is still alive[13] and if access to personal papers has been gained. Most biographies are of the chronological-narrative type, some are more thematic in structure and a few are written in the vein of other disciplines such as psycho-analytical studies.[14] It is important, too, in arriving at judgements about the value of a biography to include a consideration of its author in terms of interest in, links with and knowledge of the subject matter.

While translations, autobiographies and biographies are just three examples of source materials where prior evaluation promotes effective use, there are four further guidelines which can aid this process. These are to do with testimony, authenticity, reliability and value.

In general history Marwick (1989) makes a distinction between 'witting' and 'unwitting' testimony which is also relevant to the evaluation of dance history source materials. The term 'witting' testimony is used to describe those primary sources in which the originator of the source sets out intentionally to convey the information that the source contains. Examples of witting testimony abound in dance history. Macdonald (1975), in her study of Diaghilev, focuses the entire text on the writings of contemporary dance critics, an instance where witting testimony is used with considerable effect. Sachs (1933, trans. 1937) bases his classification of dance themes and types on the reports of

European travellers who, from the seventeenth century onwards, saw various kinds of tribal dancing in the then remote areas of Africa, Asia and other parts of the world. Sometimes these eye-witnesses to the event give information over and above what they intended and this is then termed 'unwitting' testimony. In many of the accounts included by Sachs the use of words such as 'obscene' and 'hideous' convey far more about the attitudes of the European onlookers than the quality of the dance being described.[15] Indeed, it is often this very failure to realize the culture-bound stance of observers and to ignore the unwitting nature of their testimony that makes the early dance history texts both suspect and difficult to use. An example of an author who uses statements about dance for both their witting and unwitting testimony is Rust (1969), much of whose work is derived from British teenagers' views on types of social dance current in the 1960s.

As well as eye-witness and participant accounts the official documents of national, regional and local arts organizations and dance companies offer particular examples of witting testimony and this is especially so when they include annual statements and financial accounts. In contrast, many of the photographs of women dancers taken during the first quarter of the twentieth century provide unwitting evidence which the dance historian can use to gain insight into the then prevailing attitudes both to the body and to women.

A second useful test in evaluating dance source materials is that of authenticity. This is to do with whether a source is what it purports to be in terms of its subject matter, date and provenance. Examples of this are Nijinsky's (1937) diaries and Duncan's (1927) autobiography, since both publications have been questioned on the grounds of authenticity. It has been suggested that the original writings of these dancers have been amended and altered and, in some instances, passages written by others inserted. However, unless the historical study is based on only one source, and this would be rare, questions of authenticity can usually be resolved or at least allowed for by reference to other primary sources.

The reliability or the degree to which a particular source can be trusted is a third important factor in making judgements about dance sources. A dance theatre programme listing choreographers and giving credits for the design of sets and costumes, sound accompaniment and lighting can normally be relied upon to give accurate information. Nevertheless, when dancers are injured, last-minute alterations in casting and even in the dances presented may have to be made and therefore what is printed regarding certain dances and performers in a theatre programme may not always be accurate.[16] This point is recognized by Bland (1981) in the notes to the 'Statistics' section of the fiftieth anniversary text on the Royal Ballet: 'sources for castings are the nightly programmes corrected, as far as possible, from Stage Management records or eye-witness accounts' (Bland 1981: 264).[17] In fact eye-witness accounts may also need to be assessed in relation to their reliability. It is often vital to know whether such a witness was an interested, although peripheral, observer or a key participant. But from this it cannot necessarily be assumed that the latter is likely to be more reliable than the former. Corroboration with other sources may confirm the reverse to be the case.

The value of a single item and the comparative value of several source materials is a fourth important factor in judging worth and usefulness. Shawn's (1954) book on Delsarte, the nineteenth-century movement theorist, is itself a secondary source but, since Delsarte did not publish his own work and the publications of his various pupils are largely unavailable, Shawn's text is often used in the initial study of Delsartean theory. It is important therefore to establish the value of Shawn's book as a means of gaining access to Delsarte's work. In this case, as in many others, the matter may be resolved to a certain degree by examining the bibliography and the references cited. Mere length in either case does not guarantee worth, but in Shawn's thirty-six-page bibliography 'with commentary' the Delsarte literature itemized consists almost entirely of primary sources and the annotations are particularly detailed. This is an indication of the book's value as good secondary source material to the dance historian studying Delsarte even though more recent studies have advanced knowledge in this area considerably.

The value of other sources may reside in their status. For example, the British *Dancing Times* (published monthly from 1910)[18] and the American *Dancemagazine* (published monthly from 1926) are the leading 'traditional' publications of their kind in their respective countries. They derive much of their authoritative status from their longevity, continuous publication and the resulting vast written source which has accumulated. This does not, of course, confer special status on any single item published in one magazine: rather it is the whole runs that cover many decades of dance history which are significant.

With some written material the value of the evidence it contains can be determined by relevant knowledge of the author and this is particularly so in using the work of the dance critics. Dance criticism at its best is objective and informative with the judgements made being supported explicitly by reasons and by references to the choreography, the performance and so on. Although dance critics may well enthuse and inspire, it is important in the study of dance history to be able to recognize the difference between matters of fact and matters of personal opinion in their writings. Beaumont's perplexed remark on first seeing Martha Graham dance in *Appalachian Spring* in London in 1954 – 'but why does she roll about on the floor . . .? It breaks the line'

(Beaumont in Roose-Evans 1970: 110) is understandable only in the light of the knowledge that Beaumont was an expert on ballet with scant knowledge of American modern dance. His remark as such is of little value to the dance historian trying to identify trends in Graham's choreography over time but it could be of considerable value to a dance historian interested in, for example, the development of different modes of dance criticism and the prevailing use of particular canons of judgement in theatre dance.

2.5 SUMMARY

The importance of source materials in dance history study cannot be overstated. All academic disciplines have their essential features, and in dance history one of these is its source base. Source materials in themselves do not constitute dance history but as the remnants of and commentaries upon the past they provide the basic starting point for study. It is, therefore, essential that students of dance history, at whatever level, understand the crucial importance of source materials and take steps to acquire proficiency in their use.

NOTES

1 It is important to note that, although the primary and secondary source distinction described here is that which prevails in the discipline of history, in anthropological studies a much more permeable boundary is adopted. For details of this see Georgiana Gore below, section 5.2.1.
2 This is another instance where historical and anthropological practices differ. As Georgiana Gore explains in section 5.2.3, sound sources, particularly the oral, often assume primacy and frequently are the only sources available in the study of traditional dance in West Africa. See also Theresa Buckland's discussion of the importance of audio and video recordings in collecting material on English traditional dances (section 4.4.2). In addition Carol Brown (Chapter 13 below) clearly signals the need for otherwise 'mute' voices to be heard in a feminist approach to dance history. This, in turn, challenges the notion of dance history based on the predominance of written sources.
3 See, for example, Kenneth Archer and Millicent Hodson (Chapter 7 below). The detailed reconstruction process described provides a vivid paradigm of the interrelated use of written, visual and sound source materials.
4 Theresa Buckland (Chapter 4 below) also refers to Hardy and another author who comes into this special category. Patricia Mitchinson (Chapter 6 below) cites a similar case.
5 Michael Huxley points to the dangers of making assumptions about studio and outdoor photographs (section 10.2).
6 Jane Pritchard (Chapter 9) discusses the different kinds of photographs and their value within a dance company archival collection.
7 This has implications for the use of video as a witting record of dance for archival purposes. It seems that several cameras would need to be used

simultaneously to record the dance overall and in its full setting as well as capturing close-ups of important segments.

8 Georgiana Gore (Chapter 5 below) discusses oral sources and oral tradition and the complex considerations entailed in their use.

9 In Chapter 7 below Kenneth Archer and Millicent Hodson recount the particular instance of Irina Nijinska's memory being jogged at the reconstruction première of Nijinsky's *Le Sacre du printemps* in 1987.

10 In Chapter 4 below Theresa Buckland warns of the possible bias and distortion which may result from the too-active intervention of the interviewer.

11 It is generally accepted that academic dance historians should be able to read texts in those languages relevant to their study areas. However this does not preclude the use of good translations, where these exist, and for dance students these are regarded as legitimate working materials. A translation cannot assume the primary or secondary source status of the original text but remains a translation of it. Even so, the implication of using a translation contemporary with the original as distinct from a current translation needs to be appreciated.

12 Michael Huxley (Chapter 10 below) discusses the particular difficulties which arise with the translation of certain German dance and movement terms into English.

13 See, for example, the different critical stances adopted by Kathrine Sorley Walker (1987) in her biography of Ninette de Valois and the spate of biographical writings published immediately following Martha Graham's death in 1991, such as that by Agnes de Mille (1992).

14 Donna Perlmutter's (1991) biography of Antony Tudor is written in a mode which both parallels and reflects Tudor's innovation of the 'psychological ballet'.

15 Georgiana Gore (Chapter 5 below) gives further and more detailed examples of different types of unwitting testimony in the early written sources which describe West African traditional dance.

16 Jane Pritchard (Chapter 9 below) describes the various ways in which programmes in the Rambert Dance Company Archives have been amended in response to last-minute cast and other changes.

17 Even an author's name may warrant further investigation. In this case Alexander Bland is the pseudonym of Nigel Gosling, author and critic, and his wife Maude Lloyd, the Rambert dancer who created many key roles in Tudor's ballets.

18 See Appendix C for notes on its pre-1910 origins.

REFERENCES

Bland, A. (1981), *The Royal Ballet: The First Fifty Years*, London: Threshold.

de Mille, A. (1992), *Martha: The Life and Work of Martha Graham*, London: Hutchinson.

Duncan, I. (1927), *My Life*, New York: Boni & Liveright.

Hardy, T. (1974), *Under the Greenwood Tree; or, the Mellstock Quire* (1872), London: Macmillan.

Kinney, T. & Kinney, M. W. (1914, 1936), *The Dance: Its place in Art and Life*, New York: Tudor.

Lawler, L. (1964), *The Dance in Ancient Greece*, London and Middletown, Conn.: A. & C. Black and Wesleyan University Press.

Macdonald, N. (1975), *Diaghilev Observed by Critics in England and the United States, 1911–1929*, London: Dance Books.

Marwick, A. (1989), *The Nature of History* (1970), London: Macmillan.

Nijinsky, V. (1937), *The Diary of Vaslav Nijinsky*, edited by R. Nijinsky, London: Gollancz.

Perlmutter, D. (1991), *Shadowplay: The Life of Antony Tudor*, London: Viking Penguin.

Roose-Evans, J. (1970), *Experimental Theatre*, London: Studio Vista.

Rust, F. (1969), *Dance in Society*, London: Routledge & Kegan Paul.

Sachs, C. (1933), translated by B. Schönberg (1937), *World History of the Dance*, New York: W. W. Norton.

Shawn, T. (1954, 1963), *Every Little Movement: A Book about François Delsarte*, New York: Dance Horizons.

Sorley Walker, K. (1987), *Ninette de Valois: Idealist Without Illusions*, London: Hamish Hamilton.

Chapter 3

The dance history literature

A reader's guide

Janet Adshead-Lansdale

Texts selected for discussion here are examples of dance writing in which the approaches outlined in Chapter 1 are particularly well defined. Similarly, the types of sources and the procedures of the historian described in Chapter 2 can be seen in practical use and the outcomes reviewed. The appropriateness of these different lines of investigation for the topic being pursued becomes clear. Certain limitations consequent upon the choice of topic and the manner of dealing with it also become obvious.

To attempt comprehensive coverage of dance history texts would be an enormous undertaking and one which is unrealistic in this context. The selection of a limited number of sources is necessary, therefore, if inevitably problematic. Only book-length texts are considered here and journal articles are not included although much of the literature of greatest value to historians may be contained in such sources. Indeed, the most recent writings of dance historians are likely to be found there. The books selected for comment are well known works which are generally available through bookshops and libraries. Appendix A (p. 252) is designed to complement Chapter 3 in summarizing and offering a brief evaluation of the contents of selected texts. Appendices B and C (pp. 274, 284) give longer and more comprehensive lists of books, journals, bibliographic sources, dictionaries, encyclopedias etc. with shorter annotations which are descriptive rather than evaluative in kind.

Most of the selected texts are explicitly historical in character but some are not. In the latter category sources which might be of great use to the historian, but which are not written specifically as histories, are included: for example the collected writings of choreographers, performers and dance critics. Some categories of historical writing are thinly represented in the overall selection, for example straightforward biographies and autobiographies, although these sources exist and are of value to the historian. The biographies included here are examples of those which place emphasis on the work of the person rather than on their private lives. Anthologies, which draw together the writings of important individuals in dance, e.g. by Brown (1980) and Cohen (1974), not only provide invaluable primary sources but also reveal the editor's perspective on what is and is not important in the history of dance. However, most anthologies are omitted from this chapter since they are not constructed primarily as historical accounts although they are listed in Appendix B.

The emphasis in this book is on the western European and North American heritage. There are two main reasons for this: there is little historical dance scholarship of substance on any dance forms and even less on the dance of African and Asian countries that is neither superficial nor patronizing.[1] The predominant emphasis within the study of dance history is on western theatrical forms and, while not condoning this, this book reflects the writings that are used to support it. Any aspect of dance has its history, an appropriate methodology for its study and a value and this is reflected to a greater extent than in the 1983 first edition in the inclusion of Chapter 5 on traditional dance in West Africa. The chapters on social and traditional dance forms in the UK are also updated. The literature in dance anthropology on the dance of non-western cultures is extensive, although mainly in journal form, but this demonstrates rather different methodologies and addresses different questions. It is worthy of separate debate.

The texts described in Appendix A are presented in tables and divided into a number of categories. The time-span and geographical range of each text is noted so that its coverage is clear. The overall scope of the work and its major aims, purposes and concerns is identified. The sources on which it is based are characterized and its structure and content described. Finally, an evaluation of the book, based on criteria for good historical communication and the usefulness of the text for the dance history student, is offered.

Table 1 General histories of dance spread widely over time and place
Table 2 General histories of an era and/or a type of dance
Table 3 Dance histories which cover a limited period
Table 4 Accounts of the emergence of new forms of dance
Table 5 Accounts of the life and work of notable figures in dance history
Table 6 Collected writings of choreographers, performers and theorists
Table 7 Collected writings of dance critics

3.1 GENERAL HISTORIES OF DANCE SPREAD WIDELY OVER TIME AND PLACE

The main feature of a general history of dance is its long time-span, often starting with speculation on the function of dance in 'pre-history' or 'antiquity'. Myths about the importance of dance in ancient societies are rehearsed in support of both dance and the writing of its history. It is perhaps significant that few recent dance scholars have attempted such ambitious projects, knowing from modern historical methods and social anthropological research how problematic enterprises of this kind are. Sachs (1933) originated a genre that might be called anthropological history, basing his work on travellers' tales. This world-wide span invites global statements of the 'origin' and 'function' of dance which have little credibility now. His, and many other historians', assumptions of an evolutionary progression from black, primitive, social or religious forms of dance to white, western, theatre forms is now seen in terms of pervasive ethnocentric bias. Vital reading to counteract this literature is Kealiinohomoku's well-known article on ballet as a form of ethnic dance.[2] General histories are also likely to range widely across North American and western European cultures and to give more attention to theatre dance than to other forms. Where a text limits its scope to one century or to a particular kind or function of dance, for example social dance, greater depth is possible. This might produce a more detailed account of the function of dance in that period, while still retaining the width of a general historical account. Where authors have first-hand knowledge the text becomes immediately more convincing and has greater validity, for example Kirstein's history (1935) of the ballet in the early part of the twentieth century.

3.2   GENERAL HISTORIES OF AN ERA AND/OR A TYPE OF DANCE

The incoherence that tends to result from a very wide area of study can be countered in different ways: by limiting the time-span, by considering the function of the dance (e.g. as a social form), by focusing on one genre (e.g. jazz dance) or by addressing certain political and ethnic concerns (e.g. in the rise of black dance).

Rust's (1969) investigation of 1960s dance practices in the UK provides an example of sociological analysis of dances performed for social reasons. In this text it is the social context of the dances that is important and these practices are situated in a history that is described over a long time-span from the thirteenth century to 1969. Richardson (1960) limits his time-span to the nineteenth century and his dancers to those from the upper strata of society; he remains within England. He can then afford to describe the dances in greater detail and discuss the manner of performance, that is, to focus on who danced and what they danced, and on stylistic elements. He also relates these factors to the physical performance space. The Stearns (1964) limit their study to a continent and a genre, that of jazz in the development of an American vernacular style. Emery's (1972) account of black dance limits the enquiry by ethnic concerns and to the USA.

It may be that, as understanding of history and historical processes is refined, the validity of such texts will be increasingly questioned. The possibility of doing justice to such vast time-spans in a single volume is remote. While they have value as introductory source texts and in many cases are carefully based on the scholarship available at the time to the authors, limitations are inevitable. Generalization, resulting from the broad sweep approach, has its compensations, however, in the sense of offering a delineation of an entire genre or period.

3.3 DANCE HISTORIES WHICH COVER A LIMITED PERIOD

These studies of a specific type of dance within a clearly defined era in dance history are also usually related to smaller geographical areas than the overview texts of Table 1 and to a shorter time-span than those in Table 2. In common with the books cited in Table 2, however, the parameters of time and location are governed by significant events.

It may be obvious only with hindsight that the character of the dance was changing or dramatically new forms emerging. Lawler's time-span is determined by the existence of ancient Greece and she considers all the types of dance that occurred during that era (Lawler 1964). In contrast Hilton's approach is to examine a distinctive style of dance, the French Noble style between 1690 and 1725, and the techniques required for its performance (Hilton 1981). Her time-span is only thirty-five years and the geographical span likewise limited to the area in which that style existed, i.e. in France, and by the people who danced, who were of a certain social class. Guest (1966) and Gautier (trans. 1932) both document the establishment of a new style of ballet, the Romantic ballet. Guest demonstrates very clearly the methods of the working historian in his account of the twenty-seven years of the emergence and establishment of this genre while Gautier's stance is that of the practising critic in the crucial years between 1837 and 1848. The two taken together provide first-hand accounts placed fully in historical perspective and demonstrate the reciprocal relationship between primary and secondary sources.

Garafola's recent study (1989) of Diaghilev's Ballets Russes brings new history methodologies to familiar material. She interprets the evidence in the light of political and economic factors, giving equal weight to the administration of the company, the reception it received and the making of the works. This approach is similar to that advocated by Marxist-derived theories of history in which the materialist inter-pretation is held to be of central importance and notions such as the mode of production and economic interests are crucial. Although new to dance history, this kind of interpretation is well established in history generally.

3.4   ACCOUNTS OF THE EMERGENCE OF NEW FORMS OF DANCE

These texts have in common the desire to document and explain the beginnings of new dance styles and genres. The time-span is typically fairly short, the focus is on one emerging form of dance. The texts described in Table 4 document the birth of modern dance and, more recently, postmodern dance. They cover the time-span from the middle of the eighteenth century, in searching for their roots, to the establishment of modern dance in the 1940s and postmodern dance in the 1960s. They attempt to explain the emergence of these forms and to identify crucial moments, people and works.

Ruyter (1979) bases her argument about the increasing respectability of modern dance on analysis of sources on Delsarte and refers not only to dance in the theatre but also to dance in education. In contrast, Kendall (1979), who writes on the same period, from the mid-nineteenth to the mid-twentieth century, focuses primarily on two major figures, Ruth St Denis and Martha Graham. Magriel (1948) brings together a varied group of readings and research articles, thus providing sources for further historical analysis of the emergence of modern dance. This text extends its field by reference to popular and musical theatre forms of dance as well as religious origins. They are all well-researched accounts and together provide a reasonably comprehensive account of the period.

Banes's two editions of *Terpsichore in Sneakers* (1980, 1987) illustrate the importance of hindsight. The first edition allowed the choreographers of the Judson Dance Theatre (New York) to speak for themselves. It brought together the writings of postmodern dance figures in the USA with explanatory commentary by Banes which served to interpret and contexualize works performed over a very short period of time, 1962–4. The second edition contains an introduction which proposes a number of styles of postmodern dance. It identifies several clearly distinct styles in this twenty-year period, thus revealing the evolution of the style, as well as giving an account of its emergence.

Two recent texts, by Jordan (1992) and Mackrell (1992), pick up the story of new dance, ostensibly in England but in fact almost exclusively in London. Jordan's text is based on primary interview material as well as critical practice and Mackrell's on the author's work as a practising critic. As a pair of texts they offer contrasting possibilities for the historian in the method of collecting and using information and bear comparison for their differences in the way they are written (see Chapter 15 on historical communication).

3.5 ACCOUNTS OF THE LIFE AND WORK OF NOTABLE FIGURES IN DANCE HISTORY

The texts described in Table 5 are typical of a substantial body of literature which focuses on the life and contribution of centrally important choreographers, dancers and, less frequently, critics and theorists. They have been essentially adulatory and anecdotal until recent years, rarely critical. They continue to multiply in number and to take many different forms.

Lynham (1972) and Shelton (1981), writing on Noverre and St Denis respectively, present life stories in a chronological manner combining theories of the dance with choreographic and performance details in a narrative of the individual's personal and social life. Buckle (1979), on Diaghilev, is perhaps the most detailed account of this type, providing an almost daily record. In contrast, Macdonald (1975) and Vaughan (1977), on Diaghilev and Ashton respectively, detach themselves from the intimate life of the person and discuss the works using critics' reviews as the major source. Vaughan's text is a much more elaborated account which uses quotations selectively while Macdonald produces verbatim the records of the time. Both are invaluable as scholarly examples of an investigation into the works of a theatrical impresario and a choreographer respectively and of the use of primary sources to illuminate and contextualize the subject.

Sorell's translation and editing of *The Mary Wigman Book* (1973) combines a personal tribute to her work with her own writings on dance giving a different approach to recording the life of a major figure. New texts in this genre since *Dance History* (1983) are numerous and selection is not easy. It would be hard to discount the first major studies of de Valois (Sorley Walker 1987) and Tudor (Perlmutter 1991) although they are quite dissimilar in form and style. They share a chronological structure and both attempt to identify themes. Sorley Walker, however, is writing about a living historic figure and reveals the choreographer, teacher and artistic director, while Perlmutter attempts a form of psychoanalysis, speculating on Tudor's beliefs and motivations, with questionable validity.

Siegel's text (1987) on Doris Humphrey's life and work is based primarily on an analysis of her choreographic output. She writes thematically in an impressive demonstration of the critic/historian at work. Substantial studies of major figures in modern dance have been slow to emerge. Since Graham's death, however, several biographical accounts have been published alongside her own autobiography *Blood*

Memory.[3] De Mille's account (1992) is that of a sometime friend, rival and contemporary practitioner. Not surprisingly it offers a personal insight rather than detailed historical documentation and it is valuable for exactly that reason, drawing on seventy years of private conversation and correspondence.

Kostelanetz's collection (ed. 1992) of thirty articles from previously published sources serves the purpose of bringing together relatively obscure material on Merce Cunningham but there is little coherence in the collection and no rationale offered for the selection. In contrast, Servos's and Weigelt's (1984) account of Bausch's life and work is held together by a philosophical introduction on the nature of her works and presented with ample photographic material. It is critical in character rather than historical and provides material which is of great value in any study of Bausch, given the few texts currently available in English.

3.6 COLLECTED WRITINGS OF CHOREOGRAPHERS, PERFORMERS AND THEORISTS

Some of the texts presented in Table 6 are limited to the writing of choreographers and/or dancers while others embrace theoretical writings on dance. There is some overlap with the following section which deals exclusively with the collected writings of critics, since an extract of a critic's writing may be included in a more broadly based collection. Both the Cohen (1974) and Steinberg (1980) collections contain articles by performers and choreographers. Steinberg's selection ranges from the mid-sixteenth century to the 1970s and includes contributions on the role and place of dance. Brown (1980) limits the scope of her text by the form of dance, that of modern dance, and hence, by definition, to the last years of the nineteenth century and to the twentieth century. The writings she presents are those of major choreographers. These sources, selected here to illustrate a range of dance styles and of writing styles, in combination with those described in section 3.4, begin to offer a wide and rich range of material for the historian.

The scope of Livet's text (1978) is also determined by the form of dance that it covers. The limit of the time-span is twenty years and the form is that of postmodern dance, overlapping to some extent with Brown but giving more detailed attention to the later period. This allows comment not only from choreographers but also from critics, theorists and other observers of the dance scene.

A text destined to become a classic in this field is the record of conversations with Merce Cunningham (Cunningham/Lesschaeve 1985). It is informal in style, revealing Cunningham's responses to open-

ended questions in fascinating detail from which emerges the philosophy and working methods of this crucial figure in twentieth-century
dance. For the historian the working method of using loosely structured
questions to obtain material is of substantial interest.

3.7 COLLECTED WRITINGS OF DANCE CRITICS

The collections listed in Table 7 constitute a rather special collection of
sources, namely eye-witness accounts of dances, often recorded immediately after their first performances. They are all of recent origin
illustrating, in their totality, the development of a new style of dance
history literature.

The collected writings of dance critics might be characterized as
representing the immediate response of a critic to a dance, whether it is
a new work or a different or later interpretation of an existing one. That
moment of response is historically important. Later reaction by the same
critic or reference to the reactions of other observers often demonstrates change in critical response. These differing responses accrue
over a period of time and, with the critics' opportunity to see a work on
many successive occasions, offer a rich seam of historical evidence.

Covering the earlier part of the twentieth century, Buckle (1980),
Coton (1975) and Denby (1949) document and interpret the new
ballets and modern dances of the period. Croce (1978) and Jowitt
(1977) cover almost the same time in New York, the mid-1960s to mid-
1970s and provide very valuable and complementary sources on the
dance of that time. These texts bear comparison for the changes in
writing style and focus of the content of reviews during this period and
for the contrast between British and American concerns.

The number of texts of this kind has increased markedly in recent
years. Some make vital sources from earlier periods much more easily
accessible than hitherto, for example, Guest's translated and edited
version (1986) of the reviews that Gautier wrote between 1836 and 1871
and Acocella and Garafola's edited version (1991) of Levinson's writings
from Paris in the 1920s. Further collections from Croce (1987), Jowitt
(1985) and Siegel (1991), which cover dance in New York between 1974
and 1987, contribute first-hand records and highly personal accounts.
These have value as eye-witness accounts of recent events for present
scholars and will also shed light for historians in the future.

Looking at dance history texts in this way is a starting-point in an
important process in moving away from accepting the words written on
a printed page as representing some kind of truth or reality. Becoming
critically aware that dance history consists of balancing available evidence and piecing together an interpretation of the sources encourages

an explanation of dance events that can be supported by evidence. It is in the nature of the historical study of dance that it is never fixed and undisputed. The appearance of new evidence, the development of techniques of analysis and further study of possible interpretations will always allow for increasingly refined evaluations of events in the history of dance.

Ideally, the professional dance historian develops an interpretation based on original source material which no other person has used in the same way. The texts described in this chapter are examples of some of the better works from that literature. However, a comparison of these with other texts should make it abundantly clear that much dance history writing is superficial and unverified, and that there is work to be done to raise the standard of historical writing about dance.

Several new texts which do not fit the categories established here give cause for optimism about dance history writing. Foster's *Reading Dancing*[4] attempts to extract choreographic conventions from the history of dance to decipher the codes operating in specific dances. Her work is allied to contemporary literary criticism and cultural theory thus employing modern theoretical approaches to illuminate the modern and postmodern dance forms which she describes.

Texts such as Novack's account of the development of contact improvization[5] and Jowitt's thematic concerns[6] in the history of dance share some of Sachs's early intentions but they are distinguished by far greater sophistication of cultural analysis and awareness of political issues. The effect of political and social upheavals and the interaction of art with life are richly revealed.

In a different sense a recent text by Berg, *Le Sacre du printemps: Seven Productions from Nijinsky to Martha Graham*, forges new methodologies and explores new ground.[7] Although it does not include the 1987 reconstruction of Nijinsky's original version by Kenneth Archer and Millicent Hodson for the Joffrey Ballet (see Chapter 7 below) its strength and interest lies in tracing the history of works to Stravinsky's score by choreographers such as Massine, Béjart, Alston and Graham.

The detail of the dance that it is now possible to record, reconstruct, video and notate heralds a new era of possibility for dance history scholarship; instead of describing everything except the dance it is now much more realistic to hope that the historian may evoke the dance itself.

NOTES

1   There are a few notable exceptions to the first point: one of these is Ranger's text (1975) *Dance and Society in East Africa*, London: Heinemann, which is set within a socio-historical perspective.

2 See J. Kealiinohomoku, 'An anthropologist looks at ballet as a form of ethnic dance', in R. Copeland and M. Cohen (1983) *What is Dance?*, Oxford: Oxford University Press: 533–49.
3 M. Graham (1991), *Blood Memory*, New York: Doubleday.
4 S. Foster (1986), *Reading Dancing: Bodies and Subjects in Contemporary American Dance*, Los Angeles: University of California Press.
5 C. Novack (1990), *Sharing the Dance: Contact Improvisation and American Culture*, Madison, Wis.: University of Wisconsin Press.
6 D. Jowitt (1988), *Time and the Dancing Image*, New York: William Morrow & Company.
7 S. Berg (1988), *Le Sacre du printemps: Seven Productions from Nijinsky to Martha Graham*, Ann Arbor, Michigan: UMI.

BIBLIOGRAPHY

The full bibliography for all the texts referred to in this chapter can be found in Appendix A.

Part II

Historical studies of dance in its traditional, social and theatrical contexts

Chapter 4

Traditional dance

English ceremonial and social forms

Theresa Buckland

4.1 INTRODUCTION

What constitutes traditional dance, or folk dance as it is frequently termed, has been the subject of recent debate in the United Kingdom (see Buckland 1983). Yet whatever the specific historical, cultural and socio-economic factors which have contributed towards its construction, a repertoire of English traditional dance has been recognized and practised as such since the early 1900s.

This canon of English traditional dance was primarily defined by Cecil Sharp (1859–1924) and consists of Morris, Sword and Country Dances. During the twentieth century, the repertoire has been extended, yet the criteria established by Sharp have been principally operative in the inclusion of any new dances.

A loose definition which might identify this repertoire is that its dances may be distinguished from other forms of dance by the fact that they have been handed down from generation to generation without close reference to national or international standards.

Traditional dances may begin their existence in the fashionable ballroom or, indeed, in the theatre. In many cases their origin cannot be discovered. However, the task of the student of the history of traditional dance is not to concentrate solely on origins but to extend present knowledge of the nature of the form, its context and transmission in the past.

Following Sharp's categorization, the traditional dances of England can be broadly classified into two major groups: those dances which are executed at particular times of the year in a performer/audience context, and those which are not tied to the calendar and are performed mainly for recreational purposes. The former group are referred to here as *ceremonial dances* and the latter as *social dances*.

Ceremonial dancing in England at the time of Sharp was traditionally most frequently performed by men, although there were notable exceptions, especially in the north-west region. Morris and Sword dancing (see Cawte *et al.* 1960) constitute the two most common forms of English ceremonial dancing. Social dancing in England usually involves simultaneous participation by both sexes. The majority of these types of dances, however, have their origin in the fashionable ballroom or, if derived from other sources, at least existed in this context at some time. The characteristics of the two groups described above are not totally distinct as there are several dances which at any one time may display both ceremonial and social features.

A late-twentieth-century addition to Sharp's canon of English traditional dance is step dancing. Known as clog dancing when performed in such footwear, it is open to men, women and children and, although more usually seen as a display, it can be danced as a social form.

4.2   PREVIOUS SCHOLARSHIP

Perhaps the most famous date in the history of English traditional dance scholarship is Boxing Day 1899. It was on this day that Cecil Sharp, then Principal of the Hampstead Conservatoire of Music, London, first witnessed the performance of a Morris team.

Although he noted down tunes which accompanied the dances, Sharp did not attempt to collect the choreography until 1905. In this year Mary Neal, who organized an association for underprivileged girls in East London known as the 'Esperance Working Girls' Club', approached Sharp with a request for traditional English dances for the girls to perform (see Judge 1989). Thus began the attempt to collect folk dances before, as was feared, urbanization and industrialization destroyed the rural setting where the traditional dance culture appeared to flourish.

Many dances were undoubtedly either in a dead or moribund state and it cannot be disputed that, had Sharp and his fellow collectors delayed in their task, knowledge of English traditional dancing in the second half of the nineteenth century would be infinitely poorer. In 1911 Sharp founded the English Folk Dance Society with the purpose of fostering the revival of English traditional dance. The collections of traditional dances published by Sharp and his associates form the main corpus of material employed in the national revival and set out the 'pagan origin' theory of traditional dance which, until recently, remained unchallenged in English publications.

In his theoretical writing on traditional dance Sharp concentrated on origins. This orientation he shared with nineteenth-century folklorists from whom, albeit indirectly at first, he drew his interpretation of folk custom.

The theory of cultural survival, formulated by the anthropologist E. B. Tyler and popularized by Sir James Frazer (1890) in *The Golden*

Bough, stated that all traditional customs had their origin in primitive rituals which still lingered in the countryside. Although there was no sound historical evidence to support this theory, it gained wide credence and remains today in many populist writings on traditional dance.

The effect of this theory was to channel the collecting activities of those interested in traditional dance into searching the countryside for any vestiges of a primitive dance culture. The towns and cities were ignored. Consequently, traditional dance types such as the Morris dancing of the north-west and the widespread traditions of solo step dancing often found in urban areas were not systematically collected.

An examination of the notes of early collectors such as Sharp, Maud Karpeles and Clive Carey reveal what today would be regarded as unmethodical collection, lack of social and historical data, insufficient detail on the context of documentation and a restricting belief that the purest form of traditional dance never alters its choreography except for the worse.

This latter point is again a feature of nineteenth-century folklorist theory: change and variation are thought to be indicative of degeneration from the primitive and pure archetype. Such an attitude demonstrates a misunderstanding of the practice of such dance forms.

However, with no historical records of the choreography available to the collectors, it was impossible for them to gain a historical perspective based on factual evidence. Furthermore social class differences between collector and informant supported the misleading notion of the uneducated, unreflective 'tradition-bearer' who had little of real significance to offer other than the dance itself. Instead of concentrating upon the obtainable facts from informants, the collector preferred to speculate upon the origins of dance in inaccessible antiquity.

The majority of past scholarship has tended to reflect the concerns of the national revival movement. Distinction between what might be designated as authentic tradition and as twentieth-century revival lies behind much of the literature. However, since the 1970s at least, these divisive categories of 'the tradition' and 'the revival' have been challenged (see, in particular, Sughrue 1988).

In general, the term 'traditional' or 'the tradition' has been used of dance forms and associated behaviour which have been practised largely outside influence from the national folk revival. This led to value judgements being made as to which dance activities were to be considered worthy of serious scholarly attention. Today, such distinctions cannot be supported as legitimate scholarly categories, although, as terms in common parlance within the folk scene, 'the tradition' and 'the revival' are still often employed to signify particular historical relationships and lineages.

Unless indicated otherwise, this chapter embraces both 'the tradition' and 'the revival' under the general heading of English traditional dance.

4.3   WRITTEN SOURCE MATERIALS

It must be stressed that, as a first port of call, the Vaughan Williams Memorial Library, housed at Cecil Sharp House, London, is essential to any student of the historical practice of traditional dancing in England.

There is in fact no general written introduction to English traditional dance to be recommended which does not suffer from inaccuracies or speculations. Hugh Rippon's (1993) *Discovering English Folk Dance* is perhaps the best and most concise introduction to date and is particularly illuminating on the interplay between 'the tradition' and 'the revival'.

Standard manuals on the performance of traditional dance are those produced in the early decades of this century chiefly by Sharp. Cawte (1983) has compiled a very useful index to Sharp's five volumes of *The Morris Book. A Handbook of Morris Dances* by Lionel Bacon (1974) is a more comprehensive 'aide-memoire' with regard to ceremonial dance, and an invaluable bibliographic tool is Heaney's (1985) listing of articles on Morris dancing which is obtainable from the Vaughan Williams Memorial Library. The *Community Dance Manuals* published by the English Folk Dance and Song Society (EFDSS) between 1947 and 1967 have made available in written form a larger repertoire of social dances than that published by Sharp. A helpful guide to writings on sword dancing is Corrsin (1990) and, for step dancing, Metherell's (1993) introductory bibliography brings together essential references concerning this new and expanding area of traditional dance research.

More specialized articles can be found in the *Folk Music Journal*, formerly known as the *Journal of the English Folk Dance and Song Society.* The magazine *English Dance and Song*, now published four times a year, contains relevant material and is also held in the Vaughan Williams Memorial Library. There is a published catalogue of the library's holding which is the largest collection of information on English traditional dance and includes archival film, photographs and sound recordings, in addition to manuscript and published material.

Other organizations in England which produce periodicals on traditional dance are the Morris Ring, an association of men's ceremonial dance teams founded by revival groups in 1934, and the Morris Federation, originally the female equivalent, established in 1975. Their respective publications are *The Morris Dancer* and *Morris Matters* (both currently twice a year), the latter published in association with Windsor Morris. These organizations can provide address lists of member teams and hold archives of film, video, books, photographs and manuscript material, access to which is possible for bona fide researchers.

A number of conference proceedings since the 1980s provide insight into the methodologies and interests of traditional dance scholars, many of whom have shifted focus on to more recent history, particularly that of ceremonial dance teams (see Buckland 1982–8, Sughrue 1987, The Morris Federation and The Morris Ring 1991).

With regard to indices of source materials, a preliminary checklist of traditional social dances as practised in England does not exist and reference has to be made to the footnotes and bibliographies, where given, in various publications. Researchers of ceremonial dance have a better resource in the indices of the geographical distribution of these dances compiled respectively by Needham (1936) and Cawte *et al.* (1960). The 1936 index lists all located references known at that time to ceremonial dance since 1800. The 1960 index extends its historical references to all known located records. There are inaccuracies and substantial omissions from this index (now in need of revision) but it does identify the chief characteristics of the regional forms and provides a ready checklist of sources. An exemplary listing is Heaney and Forrest's (1991) *Annals of Early Morris* which concentrates on sources for the three centuries prior to 1750 and refers to the whole of the British Isles. Such research aids should lead to more scholarly in-depth interpretations than hitherto.

4.4   SELECTION OF AN AREA OF STUDY

Detailed work on the history of traditional dancing in England has gathered pace (see, for example, the series of short monographs by various authors produced as *Morris Dancing in the South Midlands* (1983–7), but there remains a wide field for investigation. The student may select a particular geographical area, for example, and discover the various types of traditional dancing practised there within a given span of time. Alternatively, one type of traditional dance could be chosen and the various contexts in which this type appeared investigated (see, for example, Chandler 1993a for a definitive study of morris dancing in the south Midlands 1660–1900).

The study of the history of traditional dancing can be divided into: dances beyond living memory, and dances within living memory. Sources for the first group are to be found mainly in written form, whereas the second group may consist of both written and oral sources.

Some students may know of traditional dance forms either through their own active involvement or possibly through that of their family and friends. Such first-hand knowledge of an area presents an ideal starting point for study.

Clearly new traditions have arisen since the last century, particularly those prompted by the impact of the revival movement. These traditions of perhaps only two or three generations, or, indeed, years, present exciting new material to study. Since the early years of this century, new ceremonial dance teams, in particular, have sprung up all over the country, and numerous events take place at which revived traditional social dance can be seen. Teams and solo performers of step dancing would also repay close examination. These new developments need to be studied through both written and oral sources in addition to witnessing actual performances.

Revivals prior to those begun by the English Folk Dance and Song Society also require investigation. For example, the church and/or school within a community may have acted as patrons or even instigators of dancing. Very often introductions to ceremonial events such as May Day festivals or Jubilee celebrations were made which contained dance performances. Sometimes these introductions transformed already existing local customs into occasions for children who took on the main participants' role instead of adults.

It is clear that any attempt to account for the form of traditional dance must take social and historical contexts into account.

4.4.1 Dances beyond living memory

The primary sources which make reference to traditional dance are classified in chronological order in the following sections, although some types of material may occur in more than one historical period. Since the student is likely to be dealing with local history material, the guides by Rogers (1977), Richardson (1977) and Riden (1989) would be invaluable in understanding the techniques normally used in this area.

Churchwardens' accounts

These records were generally kept at the parish churches or the local and diocesan record offices, but copies are now often available at county record offices. They can be particularly valuable for details of costume and properties used in traditional ceremonial dances and for information on the payment of the performers, for example:

1521–2 Eight yerds of fustyan for the Mores-daunsars coats 0.16.0
(Kingston-upon-Thames Churchwardens' Accounts
quoted in Burton 1891: 106)

The church was responsible in varying degrees for organizing the celebrations of holy days. Some of the dancing activities watched over by the church were utilized to raise money for charitable purposes as at

Abbots Bromley, Staffordshire. Heaney and Forrest's (1991) *Annals of Early Morris* provides a useful starting point for examining such material.

Dance manuals

These exist in both manuscript and published form and are held chiefly in public and university libraries. In particular the collections at the Vaughan Williams Memorial Library should be consulted. Much of the published material does not deal with contemporary traditional dance but with popular and fashionable forms which may later become part of the traditional repertoire. There are no known British manuals of ceremonial dance predating the twentieth-century revival.

Diaries, journals, topographies, gazetteers

Many personal diaries such as that by Nicholas Blundell (1712), which contains a reference to an eighteenth-century performance of a Sword Dance near Liverpool, have been published. However, it is likely that many diaries and journals held in local libraries have not yet been consulted for references to traditional forms of dance. Most early diaries were written by people with leisure and education and thus tend to reflect upper- or middle-class attitudes towards traditional dancing. Therefore knowledge of the social status of the writer is vital to the interpretation of the record. Upper-class society is not always necessarily adverse to traditional customs, nor are those of more humble origins equally well disposed.

A type of publication which sometimes contains references to traditional dancing is the topography, a description of an area's natural and artificial features. Topographies were popular from the seventeenth to the early nineteenth centuries and, since they were often written on a county basis, are most useful for discovering references to local instances of ceremonial dancing. Thus Robert Plot's *Natural History of Staffordshire* of 1686 contains the earliest known description of the Abbots Bromley Horn Dance (p. 434). Similarly, gazetteers may also include details of dance customs performed at particular feast or market days in the year although they are generally not the best sources for reference to social forms of traditional dancing.

Newspapers and periodicals

From the second half of the nineteenth century (and earlier in cities and some large towns) the student's task is enormously eased by the growth in local newspapers. Most local libraries hold back copies or issues can be consulted at the newspaper section of the British Library.

Reports of ceremonial dance are again easier to locate than those of social dance. With the former's appearance at certain times of the year the potential field is clearly narrowed. However, it is necessary to be alert to changing patterns of ceremonial behaviour in the locality. For example, Morris Dances were performed at the traditional time of the local wakes (that is, the major annual holiday) in north-west England, some time between June and September. But reports of these occurrences became increasingly rare at the turn of the century and searches through the newspaper are more rewarding thereafter if references to May festivals, rose queen fêtes and carnivals held in the spring and summer months are found. Advance notices of ceremonial dancing were by no means uncommon in the local press of that area. In addition to advertisements there are occasional accounts of Morris dancers practising in the streets before the commencement of the wakes holiday. Sometimes newspaper references to Morris dancers after their performance date can be found when their names and activities are recorded in the list of court appearances together with charges of drunkenness or trespassing.

Accounts of social dancing in traditional contexts tend to be rare except in brief references to competitive step dancing in the advertisements placed by publicans to attract patrons to their houses during festive periods. It is also possible to find the occasional article of reminiscences about past local life which may include a description of the local social dance gatherings.

As with all dance material, the student must investigate the political, proprietary and religious sympathies, in this case, of the newspaper. In the northern county of Lancashire during the early 1860s, the Oldham press was extremely sympathetic towards local customs whereas, in the very same period, the Rochdale papers, anxious to advertise the town as being at the forefront of Victorian progress and rationalism, supported the campaign against traditional celebrations. In Oldham Morris dancing continued to flourish at the end of the nineteenth century but it appears to have died out during this period in Rochdale.

Folklore and local history collections

In the second half of the nineteenth century, references to ceremonial dancing increased with the development of local history and folklore studies. Where these contain eye-witness accounts of traditional dancing such sources can be classified as primary. A related source is the autobiography which may include information on traditional dancing either witnessed or practised in the author's youth.

Historical novels

Historical novels often contain references to traditional dances but these cannot be regarded as primary sources for the particular period in which the novel is placed unless the author is recalling a personal experience and setting it in the appropriate time-span. Examples of writers who use this device are Thomas Hardy (1872), referred to in this respect in Chapter 2, and the Lancashire author Ben Brierley (1844a, b) who described Morris dancing at the wakes. Nevertheless, such sources need to be checked against contemporary accounts since the novelist is not necessarily concerned to present a faithful record of remembered events.

Costume, regalia, photographs, film/video

Occasionally actual dance items such as dancing clogs are donated to museums. Unfortunately, the Cecil Sharp House collection of various artefacts of English traditional dancing was damaged by bombing in the 1939–45 war.

With the developing interest in the daily life of the past, many libraries are beginning to build up collections of old photographs depicting local life. These may include photographs of ceremonial dance teams. The North West Film Archive of Manchester Metropolitan University possesses two interesting films of Morris dancers at Whalley, Lancashire, in 1913 and 1919. Such rare visual records provide numerous starting points for study including, in this case, the possibility of analysing changes over a short period of time. More recently the Vaughan Williams Memorial Library has produced video-tapes of step dancers.

4.4.2   Dances within living memory

All the listings in the preceding section are also potential source material for the study of traditional dances within living memory. However, in the study of dances within living memory additional valuable information may be obtained from former participants.

Memories of former performers are best recorded on audio- or videotape to ensure accuracy and to communicate something of the character of the informant. Quotations from dancers help to illuminate the material from the human angle. Not only should students who are about to engage in collecting information from people familiarize themselves completely with operating their equipment, they should also practise interviewing techniques before starting fieldwork in order to achieve the maximum of freely-given information from their interviewees with the minimum number of questions. Of particular help in preparing to conduct interviews are Goldstein's (1964) publication and those of Ives (1980) and Agar (1980).

The performers

In the past very little emphasis was placed on the individuals who were involved in traditional dancing. Modern folklore study, however, insists that details such as the participants' age, sex, occupation and social status are collected in order to gain some understanding of the nature of traditional dancing.

Dancing styles are often transmitted through families, particularly in solo forms such as step dancing, although in the south Midlands kinship also played a vital role in the composition of Morris teams. Sometimes dance styles are the property of particular occupations such as the modified form of Lancashire step dancing performed by the lifeboat-men of Cromer, Norfolk.

It is important to ascertain how and why dancers become involved in their chosen style and also to discover how much or how little they had been exposed to it before participating. Dancers within revival groups may have joined after witnessing a public performance of a local team or through participation in some other aspect of the folk revival movement, such as being a member of a folk song club.

Distinctive modes of learning and rehearsing also need to be closely investigated. In Bampton, Oxfordshire, one traditional Morris team meets only a few weeks before their traditional day of Spring Bank Holiday Monday to practise whereas at Bacup, Lancashire, the 'coconut' dancers used to aim to rehearse once a week throughout the year. Practice nights are often social occasions as well as periods set aside to learn or maintain the performance of particular movements.

Occasions of performance

Most of the literature, following Sharp's example, has tended to refer to the annual traditional times of performance as if these were the only occasions on which ceremonial dance teams appeared. It is a partial assessment of the dancers' role in their society and fails to reflect adequately the response of dancers to their diverse and changing cultural contexts. Much information on the times of performance with regard to ceremonial dance can be gleaned from written records, particularly newspapers, and from former participants.

Informants should be questioned about all types of performance and about the existence and type of other activities taking place on the same occasion. Seemingly contradictory information on the performance routes undertaken by teams may be explained by changes introduced from year to year on the grounds of available time, personal choice and economics. The collection of money and hospitality shown by patrons to the dancers in the form of food and drink have a particular effect upon the choice of route. Ceremonial dancers in the past needed at least to cover their own expenditure and preferably earn some money from their exertions.

The dance

The chief rules in the collection of dance notations are to let the former participant provide the terminology and for the researcher to avoid any demonstration of steps since this might itself distort and bias the response.

   In the case of revival teams detailed enquiries should be made with regard to the source of the dance notation. If this is a written source, it should be checked carefully against the notations offered by former dancers and, where relevant, against the dance as it is currently performed. Variations may have occurred over the years and it is important to note them. It is also useful to realize that individual variations within a group dance may, in some instances, have been desirable. This may account for apparent discrepancies between nota-tions collected from different dancers. Such apparent discrepancies may also derive from differences in choreography and performance over time. The whole repertoire of dances should always be collected.

The music

Dancers and musicians have different perceptions of the performance and, accordingly, should be interviewed both separately and jointly if possible. This is especially valuable in determining timing and phrasing. All musicians with any connection to the dance should be recorded both playing and reminiscing. The provenance of music, how the musician came to be involved in the dance tradition, the process of learning the music, and her/his attitude towards it should all be investigated.

Costume and regalia

Queries regarding the dress for traditional dancing are as relevant to studies of social dancing as they are to considerations of the more obvious special attire of ceremonial dancers. Types of dress alter to suit the occasion, and footwear, in particular, has a marked effect upon the dance style.

Many of England's ceremonial dancers use properties such as sticks, swords and handkerchiefs, and the acquisition of those must be investigated. Information should also be acquired on the properties of the supernumeraries, such as hobbyhorses, fools and man/woman figures, which sometimes accompany traditional ceremonial dance teams.

4.5 CONCLUSION

Even if the student wishes to concentrate on one aspect of traditional dancing, for example the costume or the occasion of performance, the other components of the dance event must not be ignored. Characteristic relationships between particular types of dance and the environment, between costume and local industries, between the choice of musical instruments and the form of the dance, etc. may have existed and require discussion.

The number and quality of articles and monographs on English traditional dancing have significantly improved since the 1970s. Notable gaps remain in the history of social dancing, especially in the twentieth century, and opportunities for original research into dance practices at weddings, parties, barn dances, folk dance clubs and ceilidhs are abundant. Exploration of such practices will further illustrate the construct of 'folk' as the result of specific ideological and Eurocentric circumstances. There exists a wide range of primary sources, both written and oral, which, when explored, will not only deepen and broaden understanding of the form, transmission and context of traditional popular dancing in the past, but will also considerably illuminate the role of dance in society today.

REFERENCES

Agar, M. H. (1980), *The Professional Stranger: An Informal Introduction to Ethnography*, New York and London: Academic Press.
Bacon, L. (1974), *A Handbook of Morris Dances*, n.p., The Morris Ring.
Blundell, N. (1712), *The Great Diurnal of Nicholas Blundell of Little Crosby, Lancashire*, vol. 2 (1712–19), edited by J. J. Bagley (1970), Chester: n.p., The Record Society of Lancashire and Cheshire. See entries for 3, 7, 8, 9 July, pp. 25–6.
Brierley, B. (1884a), 'Trevor Hall', in *Tales and Sketches of Lancashire Life: The Chronicles of Waverlow*, Manchester: Abel Heywood & Son; London: Simpkin, Marshall. See esp. pp. 126–32.
—— (1884b) 'Christmas at Ringwood Hall', in *Tales and Sketches of Lancashire Life: Marlocks of Merriton. Red Windows Hall*, Manchester: Abel Heywood & Son; London: Simpkin, Marshall. See esp. pp. 148–9.
Buckland, T. (ed.) (1982–8), *Traditional Dance*, 1–6, Proceedings of the Traditional Dance Conferences held at Crewe and Alsager College of Higher Education, Alsager: Crewe and Alsager College of Higher Education.

—— (1983), 'Definitions of folk dance: some explorations', *Folk Music Journal*, 4, 4: 315–32.

—— (1991), 'Institutions and ideology in the dissemination of Morris Dances in the northwest of England', *1991 Yearbook for Traditional Music*, 23: 53–67.

Burton, A. (1891), *Rush Bearing*, Manchester: Brook & Chrystal.

Cawte, E. C. (1983), *An Index to Cecil J. Sharp The Morris Book 5 volumes 1911–1924*, Sheffield: The Morris Ring and The Centre for English Cultural Tradition and Language, University of Sheffield.

Cawte, E. C., Helm, A., Marriot, R. J., Peacock, N. (1960), 'A geographical index of the ceremonial dance in Great Britain', *Journal of the English Folk Dance and Song Society*, 9, 1: 1–41; 'Addenda and Corrigenda', (1961) *JEFDSS*, 9, 2: 93–5.

Chandler, K. (1993a), *Ribbons, Bells and Squeaking Fiddles: The Social History of Morris Dancing in the English South Midlands, 1660–1900*, Publication of The Folklore Society, Tradition I, Enfield Lock, Middlesex: Hisarlik Press.

—— (1993b) *Morris Dancing in the English South Midlands 1660–1900; A Chronological Gazeteer*, Publication of The Folklore Society, Tradition II, Enfield Lock, Middlesex: Hisarlik Press.

Corrsin, S. D. (1990), *Sword Dancing in Central and Northern Europe: An Annotated Bibliography*, n.p., distributed by Country Dance and Song Society of America, Northampton, Mass.

English Folk Dance and Song Society (1947–67), *The Community Dance Manuals*, 1–7, London: English Folk Dance and Song Society.

Frazer, J. G. (1890, 1900) *The Golden Bough: A Study in Comparative Religion*, 2 vols, 2nd edn, 3 vols, London: Macmillan.

—— (1907–15) *The Golden Bough: A Study in Comparative Religion*, 3rd edn, 12 vols (paperback 1957, reprinted 1976), London: Macmillan.

Goldstein, K. S. (1964), *A Guide for Fieldworkers in Folklore*, Hatboro, Pa.: Folklore Associates; London: Herbert Jenkins.

Hardy, T. (1974), *Under the Greenwood Tree; or, The Mellstock Quire* (1872), London: Macmillan. See esp. pp. 52–9.

Heaney, M. (1985), *An Introductory Bibliography on Morris Dancing*, Vaughan Williams Memorial Library Leaflet no. 19, Addenda (1990), London: English Folk Dance and Song Society.

Heaney, M. and Forrest, J. (1991), *Annals of Early Morris*, Sheffield: Centre for English Cultural Tradition and Language, University of Sheffield, in association with The Morris Ring.

Ives, E. D. (1980), *The Tape-recorded Interview: A Manual for Field Workers in Folklore and Oral History*, Knoxville, Tenn.: University of Tennessee Press.

Judge, R. (1989), 'Mary Neal and the Esperance Morris', *Folk Music Journal*, 5, 5: pp. 545–91.

Metherell, C. (1993), *An Introductory Bibliography on Clog and Step Dance*, Vaughan Williams Memorial Library leaflet no. 22, London: English Folk Dance and Song Society.

Morris Dancing in the South Midlands (1983–7), Eynsham, Oxfordshire: Chandler Publications.

The Morris Federation and The Morris Ring (1991), *The Evolving Morris: Proceedings of a One-Day Conference, Crewe and Alsager College of Higher Education 1990*, n.p., The Morris Ring and The Morris Federation.

The Morris Federation, The Morris Ring, and Open Morris (1992), *Influences on The Morris: Proceedings of a One-Day Conference, Cecil Sharp House, London, 1992*, n.p., The Morris Ring, The Morris Federation and Open Morris.

Needham, J. (1936), 'The geographical distribution of the English ceremonial dance traditions', *JEFDSS*, 3, 1: 1–45.

Plot, R. (1686, 1973), *The Natural History of Staffordshire*, Oxford: printed at the Theater; facsimile, Didsbury: E. J. Morten.

Richardson, J. (1974, 1975, 1977), *The Local Historian's Encyclopedia*, New Barnet, Herts: Historical Publications.

Riden, P. (1983, 1988, 1989), *Local History: A Handbook for Beginners*, London: B. T. Batsford.

Rippon, H. (1975, 1981, 1993), *Discovering English Folk Dance*, Aylesbury, Bucks: Shire Publications.

Rogers, A. (1972, 1977), *Approaches to Local History*, London and New York: Longman.

Sharp, C. J. (1907–14), *The Morris Book*, London: Novello (5 parts). Part 1 with H. C. MacIlwaine (1907, 2nd edn 1919) (reprinted 1974), Wakefield: E. P. Publishing. Part 2 with H.C. MacIlwaine (1909, 2nd edn 1919) (reprinted 1974), Wakefield: E. P. Publishing. Part 3 with H. C. MacIlwaine (1910, 2nd edn 1924) (reprinted 1974), Wakefield: E. P. Publishing. Part 4 (1911) (reprinted 1975), Wakefield: E. P. Publishing. Part 5 with G. Butterworth (1913) (reprinted 1975), Wakefield: E. P. Publishing.

—— (1909–22), *The Country Dance Books* (6 parts). Part 1 (1909, 2nd edn 1934): revised and edited by M. Karpeles (reprinted 1972), Wakefield: E. P. Publishing. Part 2 (1911, 2nd edn 1913, 3rd edn 1927) (reprinted 1972), Wakefield: E. P. Publishing. Part 3 with G. Butterworth (1912, 2nd edn 1927) (reprinted 1975), Wakefield: E. P. Publishing. Part 4 with G. Butterworth (1916, 2nd edn 1918, 3rd edn 1927) (reprinted 1975), Wakefield: E. P. Publishing. Part 5 with M. Karpeles (1918) (reprinted 1976), Wakefield: E. P. Publishing. Part 6 (1922, 2nd edn 1927) (reprinted 1976), Wakefield: E. P. Publishing.

—— (1911–13), *The Sword Dances of Northern England* (3 parts). Part 1 (1911, 2nd edn 1950) edited by M. Karpeles (reprinted 1977), Wakefield: E. P. Publishing. Part 2 (1913, 2nd edn 1951), edited by M. Karpeles (reprinted 1977), Wakefield: E. P. Publishing. Part 3 (1913, 2nd edn 1951), edited by M. Karpeles (reprinted 1977), Wakefield: E. P. Publishing.

Sughrue, C. M. (1987), *Proceedings of the Contemporary Morris and Sword Dancing Conference, University of Sheffield 1988, Lore and Language*, 6, 2.

—— (1988) 'Some thoughts on the "tradition" versus "revival" debate', *Traditional Dance* 5/6: 184–90.

Chapter 5

Traditional dance in West Africa

Georgiana Gore

5.1 INTRODUCTION

In most of this chapter I am concerned with historical methodology as applied to traditional dance in West Africa but the perspective from which it is written is anthropological. The use of the personal pronoun 'I' is an acknowledgement that the cornerstones of anthropology, fieldwork and ethnographic writing, are reflexive practices and, in some senses, autobiographical.[1] By 'traditional' dance I am referring to local forms which are said to belong to the cultural fabric of the people in question.[2] Moreover, while what I write is based mainly on my knowledge and experience of dance in the Nigerian context, much of it is relevant to other areas of West Africa that have comparable colonial pasts and where the local cultures are also largely constituted through discourses and practices which bypass the written word (though today not the radio and electronic media).

To speak of West African dance is in fact a misnomer. As has been well documented (Blacking 1983: 89; Grau 1983: 32; Kaeppler 1985: 92–4; Middleton 1985: 168; Spencer 1985: 140; Williams 1991: 5, 59), the ethnocentrically European term 'dance' is not applicable to systems of structured human body movement of non-European peoples, who have their own terms of reference for conceiving of such activities. For example, in southern Nigeria most ethnic groups have a generic term which includes dance among other activities which are construed as intrinsically sociable and usually rhythmic. The Bini word *iku* refers to 'play', 'dance', 'games' and the Igbo *egwu* to 'play', games, 'dance', 'music', song. In Bini the word for 'to dance' is *gbe*, which also denotes 'to beat', while in the related Isoko language *igbe* means 'dance'. The specific meaning of each of these expressions is context-dependent. Individual dances do, however, have their own names. The generic term may provide the basis for these names as in the Igbo compound *egwu-ugegbe* ('mirror-dance'), dances may be named after the accompanying drum as in the Bini *emaba* or *esakpaede* or may have emerged for other culturally-specific reasons. While acknowledging these complexities, the word 'dance' is used throughout the chapter; the indissoluble connections to music and play which exist in the word 'dance' for many if not all West Africans should not, however, be forgotten.

Moreover, it is not only that dance is conceptualized in culture-specific terms, but also that conditions and relations for its production and performance are different. Although the creation of a dance, for example, may be attributable to one person, it is unlikely that the dance will be either named after this person or recollected in those terms (see Begho 1986: 115). In religious cult dances, individual performers may introduce new 'unrehearsed' steps, but the acknowledged creator or choreographer is the god in question since this is the one who guides the performer's actions. This implies that, along with European notions of dance, those of 'choreography', 'performance' and 'appreciation' may need to be reconceptualized in the process of researching the dances of West Africa.

There are further reasons why the expression 'West African dance' should be used with caution. While West Africa may be considered as a geographical entity comprising some sixteen nation states[3] stretching from the Atlantic in the west and the Gulf of Guinea in the south to the Sahara in the north and Lake Chad and the Cameroon mountains in the east, it is not a homogeneous unit. Geographically it may be further defined by its north/south divide: a large but diminishing savannah belt in the north is squeezed between the desert and the tropical rainforest which occupies the southern coastal zone. A fundamental religious split between Muslim and Christian, a reflection of West Africa's colonial history, more or less mirrors this north/south divide; in addition, there are numerous indigenous religions, which still flourish especially in the rainforest belt. Muslim Arab and Christian European colonization have thus created a fundamental political and cultural rift within West Africa even if, simultaneously, they created forms of unification which cut across ethnic differences.

Colonization of black West Africa[4] began in the eleventh century with the Muslim Almoravid conquest of the then kingdom of Ghana and continued until the nineteenth century with the European 'scramble for' and subsequent 'carve-up' of Africa at the Berlin Conference in 1884. Kingdoms, such as that mentioned, are known to have existed since the eighth century and managed to survive, despite colonialism, in less accessible areas until its culmination at the end of the nineteenth century. With the consolidation of West African colonialism between 1900 and 1914, those kingdoms which had maintained their independence were brought under either French or British dominion. A period of 'stable' colonization lasted until Independence was granted in the

1950s and 1960s to all but two countries under Portuguese rule. Each contemporary West African nation state has, moreover, its individual history of colonization. None the less, certain common infrastructural features have been established at the level of social, economic and political organization, as well as a dependency on the west for all forms of commodity including cultural elements. It is important to note that the first Arab and European contacts, established through the gold trade and made before the eighth century with the Berbers and in the fifteenth century with the Portuguese, had already begun to influence the local cultures.

With the exception of Liberia,[5] the current national boundaries, which have been endorsed by the Organization of African Unity (OAU), were constructed by Europeans. To suit their own purposes, they constituted indigenous groupings of peoples into modern political units with little or no regard for ethnic differences. The contemporary West African nation state, the fragile product of colonialism, thus encapsulates a rich socio-cultural tapestry as well as containing enormous political and cultural tensions because of this arbitrary division of peoples.[6]

Finally, the most striking feature of West Africa is the tremendous diversity of its peoples and of distinct cultural traditions. For example, Nigeria alone, the largest African nation with a population in the region of 88.5 million (1990 census), has over four hundred distinct languages, a quarter of the languages of sub-Saharan Africa (Hansford *et al.* 1976); and while an ethnic group is not usually defined only by the language that it speaks, linguistic differences are a good indicator of cultural diversity. Each of these socio-cultural groupings, with their own forms of traditional political organization which operate substructurally within the nation state, has its own dance traditions. These are not usually enshrined within special dance institutions but operate in diverse contexts. Traditionally these include cultural groups, religious cults, guild systems, age-grade organizations, secret societies and associations with a variety of functions. There are, however, a number of contemporary special dance institutions. Local dance groups are run by individuals and usually perform only the dances of one cultural tradition; and, in Nigeria for example, the companies of the state (i.e. regional) arts councils perform the traditional dances of all the peoples of that state.

Membership of the local dance groups is largely a matter of either automatic affiliation, as with age-grade organizations, or voluntary adherence as with the cultural groups which alone choose performers specifically for their dance skills. In many instances, the choice of performers for a specific dance will depend on skill in relation to local ideas of what constitutes correct performance, and those groups with open membership will attempt to lure those who are known in the community as 'good' dancers to join them.[7]

From this brief discussion of the heterogeneity of West African culture it is possible to make a number of further generalizations about dance practice and production. For reasons of dogma and morality Islam and Christianity have outlawed dance at various points in time. Because of the longer-term and more deep-rooted Muslim colonization of the northern sahel and savannah belts, there is less visible dance activity there today than in the more densely populated Christian-dominated southern regions. Here, during the colonial era, much dance activity was banished and went 'underground' or rather into the 'bush', only to return after Independence to the larger villages and urban areas for revival and public performance, at least in the former British colonies. This rich dance culture of the south has in fact been sustained by the adherence to traditional religions, which continue to hold sway and flourish alongside various forms of Christian worship, and to a traditional *modus vivendi* in which the profane and the sacred are contiguous and overlapping fields and the mundane is, therefore, imbued with the numinous (Mbiti 1970; Uchendu 1965: 11–21). Thus, most traditional dance, whatever its context of production or performance, and although not specifically religious, has religious associations (Gore 1986: 54–5; Hanna 1987: 101–27), the significance of which is often difficult to grasp fully for those brought up in secular societies.

Finally, the importance of dance in societies which are traditionally based on oral and performance modes of communication and forms of knowledge requires highlighting.[8] Because of its polysemy, that is its capacity to bear many meanings, and its economy as a means of communication, and because the body is its 'instrument', dance can thus serve as a most effective mnemonic system (Connerton 1989: 102–4). It can store all kinds of embodied information for transmission through performance. These include occupational activities, historical narratives, moral precepts and a host of other symbolic, emotional and social codes.

The effect of common ecological niches, of intercultural exchanges or of parallel historical conditions has been to produce dances which may be said to display stylistic similarities.[9] No traditional dance, however, may be described as characteristically West African, for to isolate one as representative of the whole region would be to violate the richness and diversity of dance in West Africa.

5.2 SOURCE MATERIALS

A number of major problems emerge when researching the history of traditional dances in West Africa. Foremost there is a lack of written materials (including scholarship in the field), the conventional resource for the historian. This can be explained not only by the 'orality' of the societies in question but also by the fact that dance has generally been overlooked by those who have written about West African traditional cultures. This applies equally to indigenous and foreign writers, since written discourses in West Africa tend to be Eurocentric.[10] With the exception of Gorer's (1983) *Africa Dances*, a travel book first published in 1935, there are no texts which deal with dance in West Africa in general. Gorer documents a journey which he undertook with the Senegalese Wolof dancer Feral Benga through part of the French West African interior and the Gold Coast, to study traditional dances. The bulk of his observations concern all aspects of the socio-cultural context, including an indictment of the French colonial administration and its effects on traditional culture. None the less, descriptions of dances do pepper the book and one chapter is devoted to a description of the general characteristics of dance in West Africa together with a number of more detailed examples. Gorer (1983: 201) makes no claim to expertise in dance analysis, and his descriptions suffer from lack of precision as well as from the linguistic and ideological bias, if not prejudice of that era. They also lack anthropological rigour, as Gorer had not, by then, studied anthropology. They should, therefore, be approached with caution. Despite these reservations and the fact that any generalizations about West African dance are difficult if not impossible, his observations may be used as a historical source as regards, for example, the performance of certain dances in the 1930s.

There is no introductory general history of West African dances, nor indeed any published detailed histories of specific dances or dance traditions. The focus of texts written in English has been on the dances of East Africa (see Mitchell's (1956) *The Kalela Dance* and Ranger's (1975) *Dance and Society in Eastern Africa*).

Therefore, for each study of the history of a specific dance (or set of dances) a resource base of accessible primary and secondary materials, written and otherwise, needs to be constituted. Also, if at all possible, new primary materials need to be generated through contact with those who have first-hand knowledge of the dances in question. Ideally an extensive period of fieldwork (historical and ethnographic) in the 'indigenous' locale of the dance would be of most benefit; but fieldwork in Europe, for example, in the local West African communities with members born 'at home' would also produce valid and valuable source material.

5.2.1   Primary and secondary sources

The distinction between primary and secondary sources is not only a shifting one depending upon disciplinary perspective or the research in question: it is also a matter of strategy, that is a means of evaluating and validating sources by organizing them into a hierarchy of difference which accords them their relative significance and authenticity. So what is conventionally valued in both historical and anthropological methodology is the presence of the author (whether known, as is usually the case with ethnographic field notes on dance, or anonymous, as with publicity advertising a dance festival) at the scene of the dance event. This authenticates and confers authority on the document in question, considered as 'raw material' observed and recorded, and thus confers the title of primary source. However, since history usually deals with the inscription of the past and anthropology with the inscription of the present, the source which in history is considered primary (for example, P. A. Talbot's account of Nigerian Efik dances at a funeral ceremony (1923: 163–4)) would be generally considered secondary in anthropology. Field notes, and other documentary sources such as photographs generated by the researcher from first-hand experience, are the anthropologist's primary materials *per se*. The historian is almost always working with materials produced by someone else. Given the mobility of the boundary between primary and secondary sources, historical material on traditional dance in West Africa is described here according to its medium of communication, that is whether written, oral, visual or performed. It is important to note that my choice of categorization privileges the written over the oral (and relegates the performed to the last), and by implication foreign accounts over indigenous. It has the benefit, however, of enabling a preliminary overview and critique to be undertaken of the mostly foreign written secondary sources.

5.2.2 Written sources

Although written histories are sparse, there are a number of other texts from which dance historical information can be culled. Accounts from travellers, traders and missionaries who penetrated West Africa before the establishment of the colonial structures date back to the Middle Ages. One of the earliest descriptions of dance is the brief observations of Ibn Battuta, the African from Tangier and probably the greatest traveller of the medieval period (McEvedy 1980: 62), who, during his journey to the then West African Sudan in 1352–3, apparently witnessed a ceremonial dance procession at the court of a sultan in Mali (Thompson 1974: 29).

Descriptions such as Battuta's continue until the seventeenth century, when they become more detailed observations not only of general context, costuming and musicianship but also of the movements themselves. Many of such accounts, like those more natural scientific ones of the eighteenth century, demonstrate a genuine enthusiasm, lively interest and positive appreciation for West African dance. They construct a representation which affirms the cultural sophistication of the people and which is very much in keeping with the eighteenth-century image of the 'noble savage'. Like most accounts of the 'other', the practices observed are implicitly judged against those of the writer's own cultural expectations.

> They dress quite elegantly, especially the women when they wish to go dancing, which they execute with great presumption.
>
> (de Marees (1604) in Thompson 1974: 30)

> The Negroes do not dance a step, but every member of their body, every joint, and even the head itself, expresseth a different motion, always keeping time, let it be never so quick.
>
> (Adanson (1759) in Thompson 1974: 37)

In the nineteenth century, with the increase in colonization and eventual establishment of colonial administrative structures, accounts of West African, especially Gold Coast, cultures, including its dances, increase dramatically. It appears to be during this period (not surprisingly, when European 'Victorian' culture is being imposed upon or adopted by the local populations) that certain descriptions of the dances adopt the moral, prudish and prejudiced tone of the era, which represents them as non-aesthetic, sexually lewd and animalistic practices. A precursor of this form of description is Mungo Park's cursory reference to the dances of the people of the Galam region: 'The dances, however, consisted more in wanton gestures than in muscular exertion or graceful attitudes' (Park 1983: 49).

Simultaneously, a new source of written documentation emerges in the form of the newspaper. For example, in 1863 an enterprising Jamaican of mixed blood, named Campbell, founded in Lagos, Nigeria, the first locally published newspaper, the *Anglo-African*. This was the only local paper until the 1880s, when some five other publications in English were established. While these newspapers 'were specifically concerned with Lagos affairs' (Echeruo 1977: 6), traditional (Yoruba) dance and music practices, in so far as they impinged on Lagosian social mores (for example, burial ceremonies) and European-influenced culture (for example, concerts and plays), drew comment (Echeruo 1977: 67–79). Exceptionally, the *Record* of 2 January 1904 published a report on a meeting of Lagos chiefs with the Governor, Commissioner of Police and Lagos Executive Council to discuss 'the question of the prohibition of drumming in the town' (Echeruo 1977: 68), which would also imply a cessation of accompanying song and dance activities. This reached the press as drumming was a daily (or rather nightly) feature of Lagos life and, therefore, affected all Lagos citizens. From the report, which extensively quotes all those who participated actively at the meeting, can be gleaned the importance of drumming and dance in

Yoruba culture. It is likely that references to dance in West Africa also appeared in European newspapers, which would certainly constitute a valuable and as yet untapped source.

With the establishment of local colonial administrations the publication began, in the early twentieth century, of lengthy ethnographic reports (both official and unofficial) from government administrators, such as district officers and commissioners, or from government anthropologists. By this time the indigenous populations had become 'malleable inferiors to be subjugated and controlled as a labour resource' (Fothergill 1992: 48) by the expanding imperial interests and, in order to do this effectively, knowledge of local socio-cultural practices was invaluable. The degree to which dance was considered worthy of comment apparently depended on the author in question. For example, the government anthropologist Northcote Thomas (1910) produced an *Anthropological Report on the Edo-Speaking Peoples of Nigeria* in which dance is referred to but never described:

> These preparations finished, the Egwaibo was opened, and men and women danced; offerings of kola were made, and the images were painted. In the evening dancing began in the Egwaibo, preceded by a sacrifice in the ogwedion or shrine of the ancestors of the village.
>
> (Thomas 1910: 30)

Such passing reference to dance, without detailed description, seems to have set the tone for later ethnographic writings by professional social anthropologists. Like Thomas, they focus on the details of social organization and of cultural practices and their meanings to the exclusion of dance, 'an obscure rather than a challenging phenomenon, unwanted and dispersed as fragments in the anthropological literature' (Spencer 1985: ix). This can partly be explained by the lack of an available language and analytic framework as well by the textual precedents of omission or deliberate silence such as Thomas's. Bradbury (1973), for example, who has written extensively on the Benin kingdom of southern Nigeria, makes at least thirteen references to dance or dancing throughout the text and yet only in one instance does he engage in any detailed description of performers, costuming, overall structure, meanings etc. with the rider: 'There would be no point in describing the movements of the dance here' (Bradbury 1973: 194). Horton's (1960) monograph, *The Gods as Guests*, on Kalabari religious festivals similarly refers to dancing without detailed description.

On the other hand, there were those such as P. Amaury Talbot, a colonial official, whose extensive records of southern Nigerian peoples (1923, 1926, 1927), some of which were written in the style of travel books rather than 'scientific' texts, contain detailed accounts of dance including movements, costumes and properties, settings and, sometimes, meanings. Indeed his work on *The Peoples of Southern Nigeria* (P. A. Talbot 1926) includes a lengthy section on dance with a general introduction, followed by details of the practices of each peoples (802ff.). Along with a general characterization of southern Nigerian dance movement, Talbot attempts a classification of dances into 'styles'.

> The dances may be roughly divided into: mimetic, under which would be included those that portray the sexual emotions and the movements of birds, beasts and fishes, of men swimming, fighting, etc.; the more formal, symbolic, religious and conventional measures, in which the feelings are kept under restraint; and the ordinary social performances carried out purely for amusement. However they may be regarded from the aesthetic standpoint, the anthropological interest of many is very great.
>
> (P. A. Talbot 1926: 803–4)

Here Talbot's stance in relation to the aesthetic value of the dances is unclear, a characteristic, even today, of much writing on 'African dances', which invariably highlights their functions and thereby implicitly represents them as non- or un-aesthetic (Begho 1986). In general, his writing indicates a genuine appreciation derived from prolonged contact and familiarity with the dances, and, at the same time, it acknowledges the difficulties which his fellow Europeans might have in recognizing their 'variety and detail' (P. A. Talbot 1926: 803). The representation of southern Nigerian dances which Talbot constructs is very much the forerunner to many contemporary texts on 'African' or 'black' dance (for example Gore 1986, Thorpe 1989), which continue to use the discourse of evolutionism and otherness characteristic of the late nineteenth and early twentieth centuries.

Two trends in twentieth-century writings on the traditional dances of West Africa are discernible: the 'scientific' ethnographic texts of professional anthropologists with their conspiracy of silence (which even the publication of Spencer's (1985) *Society and the Dance* has not broken) and the 'non-scientific' Eurocentric writings of others. Both of these, it is proposed, belong to the same 'discursive formation' which Thomas and Talbot, as colonial government officials, were both subject to and in the process of constructing. Thomas's silence about the details of dance may have been a function of the more or less official ban on dance activity. This meant that it could not be witnessed 'save in the depths of the bush, where many of the old ceremonies [were] carried out whenever there [seemed] a chance of eluding the vigilance of "Government"' (D. A. Talbot 1915: 194). Thomas, a government anthropologist, could not therefore write about dance in an official government document, whereas P. A. Talbot could write openly since his texts were apparently private studies. This discursive formation enabled traditional dances to be evoked by those who had no voice in the growing world of academic anthropology and to be glossed over by those who belonged to it.

Less accessible than twentieth-century ethnographic and colonial government texts, but perhaps more useful because they constitute 'primary' sources, are the unpublished field notes of anthropologists and the unpublished government reports, which provide a more random and usually less purposefully constructed version of events. A degree of 'detective work' may be required to obtain these although they are often lodged in specialist libraries in Europe as well as in the locale of the dances.

Journals and magazines also constitute a further source of written documentation. Some useful ones date back to the nineteenth century,[11] others like *West Africa* are more recent, and those produced locally in West Africa largely began publication in this century. *Nigeria Magazine*, one of the best sources of information about traditional dances in Nigeria, has been published by its government since the 1920s. Included are reports on the many national arts or dance festivals and numerous contemporary descriptions of traditional festivals of which dance constitutes an intrinsic element. The former are interesting in that they provide an overview of dance traditions in Nigeria and sometimes critical appraisals of the dances, which give the reader a notion of aesthetic criteria. Especially valuable are the festival articles as they are mostly insiders' accounts in that they are written by people who come from the locality and culture in question. While these may in one sense be treated as historical primary sources, they should not be treated as 'raw data' since, in the process of describing the dances, of textual construction and of writing in English (the magazine's medium), the field experience of the dances has undergone a process both of transformation and of translation.[12]

The various institutions established to collect, document and preserve West African culture should not be forgotten as sources of information on dance. These include not only museums (for example, the Museum of Mankind in London, the Musée de L'Homme in Paris, the National Museum in Lagos as well as local museums) but also research centres such as the Institute of African Studies at the University of Ibadan, the Centre for Social, Cultural and Environmental Research at the University of Benin, and the Centre for Cultural Studies at the Ahmadu Bello University (all in Nigeria). In addition, the arts councils, both national and regional, often have small research units and effectively constitute living museums of cultural traditions. All these institutions usually house collections of a variety of documentary sources (oral, visual and written) and often produce occasional or regular publications; for example, the Institute of African Studies has, since 1964, been publishing a twice-yearly journal, *African Notes*, with regular articles on or including dance. All of these, and especially the arts councils, may also be a source of unpublished records relating to local dance practices. For example, documents relating to the organization of the state and national arts festivals in Nigeria, the first of which was held in 1965 as a forerunner to the Commonwealth Arts Festival of that year, may be useful sources on national or local distribution of specific dance traditions.

5.2.3   Oral sources and oral histories

It has already been stated that West African communities have traditionally depended upon discourses and practices which bypass the written word for the transmission of information including that of a historical mode. Such societies had in the past been characterized as having '"no history", that is in the "normal" sense of documentary records' (Finnegan 1992: 46). This in part provided the impetus for the emergence of oral history as a methodology which explicitly challenged such an assumption and which established oral traditions as alternative sources to the written and, later, the oral as a field of study in its own right. Oral sources constitute a privileged means of access to constructing dance histories, especially as the music, in particular drumming, and songs which accompany the dances usually refer in some way to the meaning, history or context of the dances. Moreover, the narrative of the dances, when recounted orally, is often historical and refers to events in the past which gave rise to the dance and which the dance therefore celebrates. The histories of the dances are commonly recounted in terms of myths of origin which refer to non-human worlds and often benevolent animal hosts. All those materials which are constituted from verbal interactions or performances, including the more obvious oral traditions such as myths, stories, folktales, epics, legends, etc. as well as music and song, are therefore relevant, as are the dialogic products of interviews.

Research has been undertaken since the 1950s on oral sources in West African communities.[13] None, it appears, has focused exclusively on constructing dance histories through oral sources. This research should, however, be consulted as a source of contextual material on the oral in specific cultures and of methodologies applied in the field. The constitution, through fieldwork 'at home or abroad', of oral sources on dance history in West Africa therefore becomes an essential task.

Collecting oral sources

Assembling oral sources (and indeed all cultural materials and practices) is not, as was once thought, simply a matter of collecting already existing artefacts or data. Rather, it is a question of production, with the implication that this is a socially constructed process subject to the rules and strategies of a particular discursive arrangement, 'the art-culture authenticity system' (Clifford 1988: 215–51). 'Every appropriation of culture, whether by insiders or outsiders, implies a specific temporal position and form of historical narration' (Clifford 1988: 232).

This growing awareness of the historical specificity of the collection and recording of oral sources, and of their politics, has led to a questioning of the conditions of production of oral texts. Thus, the 'collection' of sources which once depended predominantly on audio-recording has, with the recent interest in orality as performance, required photography and video-recording as further tools. Debates about the best methods for conducting and transcribing interviews (the most cited 'textbook' being Ives 1980) and also on the contexts and strategies for recording oral materials, whether in the 'natural' performance setting or in specifically contrived situations, whether overtly or covertly etc., continue. More recent discussions focus on the ethics of research and of its purposes, particularly on those of fieldwork, because this necessitates direct engagement with people in the research process, field assistants or collaborators, informants, performers etc.

Another key issue related to fieldwork is that of reflexivity, that is the notion that subjectivity, including the 'cultural baggage' of the researcher, is a crucial tool in the construction of materials and is always implicated in the process of research; 'reflexivity . . . can be seen as opening the way to a more radical consciousness of self in facing the political dimensions of fieldwork and constructing knowledge' (Callaway 1992: 32). Moreover, while a main tool for researching performance and context is participant observation, which implies some distancing between researcher and participants, emphasis has recently been placed on the research process itself as interactive, dialogic and intersubjective.[14]

Transcription, translation and the construction of oral texts

Requiring as much thought as other aspects of research is the transcription of oral materials and their construction into oral texts or other fixed forms for repeated study and circulation. Although there is a mechanical element in these tasks, the effects of the researcher's choices are important in determining the kinds of knowledge produced.

Decisions are required regarding the medium, mode and style of presentation. The use of print is conventional, but other media such as audiotape and videotape are increasingly common, as they more readily capture all elements of performance including setting, music and movement. In the case of textual construction, music and movement notation may be used as adjuncts to the verbal; recent experiments have been conducted using verse and special typographical representation to describe, for example, individual and choral performances which occur simultaneously.

There are even more preliminary issues to confront concerning transcription and translation. Key questions need to be addressed as to 'what is being transcribed [and translated], for whom, why, and the theory of language or communication that lies behind it' (Finnegan 1992: 196). Is it the factual content of an interview about changes in dance pattern since the inception of a new chief priest (leader of the cult and dances) or is it the speaker's views on those changes which are sought? Is the drum music being transcribed for comparative analysis with other performances of the 'same' dance and music, or for the translation of the tonal messages sent by the drummers to the dancers? Is it the expressiveness of the song's narrative which is of interest in conveying the mood of the dance or the onomatopoeic words (ideo-phones) for their percussive qualities? Literal translations which include everything (if these are ever feasible) may be useful as a first step, but are usually inadequate for analytical purposes and for publication. Selection is inevitable and should be a conscious process.

Moreover, given that transcription and translation are both culture-bound processes and that there is no equivalence or correspondence either between the oral and the written or between one language and another, understanding of context is essential. Knowledge of the specific and general socio-cultural contexts of the oral material, includ-ing local conventions for transcribing and translating (few languages today remain unwritten and untranslated), and of the socio-cultural contexts of the target language is essential. For example, the Ufe Yoruba ideophone *winni winni*, which usually describes broad patterns made up of smaller units on woven materials, is used in different ways in a number of songs. Not only is there no literal translation into English but the meanings differ in each case and can be translated only through the various contexts (Bamikunle 1984: 85–6).

Accuracy and faithfulness to the original, or at least lack of unfaithful-ness, are usually cited as the crucial factors in transcription and translation (Finnegan 1992: 190, 196). If, however, the process of textual construction is conceived as creation rather than re-creation or as a process of intertextuality (see Clifford in Clifford and Marcus 1986: 115ff.), reference to any 'original', however obtusely, is inappropriate. Furthermore, insiders' accounts of dance events are today constructed not only from lived or embodied traditions or *habitus*[15] and from consciously transmitted oral sources, but also from interactions with books, newspapers, radio and especially television, as well as with the researcher in the field.

Methods and problems of analysis of oral sources

Written sources are largely Eurocentric and logocentric, even when produced by insiders, and represent the dances from a position of otherness, the captivated observer's perspective. The oral narratives are often highly encoded ethnopoetic discourses, which are intelligible only to the insider. Considered as texts rather than performances, these are examined using methods of textual analysis for their style, structure and content. Methods popular until the 1970s included studies of narrative originals, of their variants and of their historical diffusion, classifications of narratives and indexes of motifs and tale types, and analyses of structure using Propp's morphological approach or Lévi-Straussian structuralism. Recent narratological methods have been derived from the last two approaches, although investigations of genre and style and conventional literary analyses continue to be undertaken. The latter use any number of perspectives from formalist and hermeneutic approaches to studies of symbolism, of authorial intentions, of the relations of text to context etc. Interest has recently been shown in quantitative and other analyses using computer technology.[16] As with the other stages of the research, choice of method will be determined both by the material in question and by the aim of the analysis as well as by implicit or explicit theoretical positions.

In the construction of dance histories from oral sources a number of analytical considerations are important. Whatever methodological approach is used, it is not feasible to construct, for dances beyond living memory, any history of their origins; it is also highly unlikely that changes to the dances over time can be accurately mapped. Equally contentious are attempts to chart the history of diffusion of a given dance for this would presuppose that its origins were established. Attention to the content of the narratives is, however, important and can assist in establishing the socio-cultural and political histories of the dance. Questions concerning the relationship of the oral narrative to other forms of historical statement, such as chronologies of established events, are relevant, as are those concerning the relationship between competing versions of the same narrative or between different narratives. When presented with material which conflicts, as with competing narratives or disjunctures between the 'fiction' of the oral source and 'fact' of the event, it is important to represent all the materials without authenticating any given one and to contextualize them. 'One of the lessons of new historiography is that different versions of historical events (or tales) are possible according to whose voices are heard' (Schechner 1990: 55). The socio-political position of the narrator may, for example, have produced a specific version of narrative events. The relationship of text to context, or rather the intertextual relationships, are therefore crucial in the process of historical construction.

Worthy of consideration are structural features of the oral narrative, especially in the analysis of oral histories about dances. For example, it would appear, from a superficial reading, that many of the myths of origin about southern Nigerian dances have comparable narrative structures with stock characters. A dance is often said to have been a gift to the community from a god, spirit (often a water spirit) or animal through the medium of one of its members who has strayed beyond the confines of the village into the bush. There spirits are encountered, initiation in the dance occurs, and on return home the dance is disseminated through rehearsals and performance. The narrative structure is characteristic of rites of passage, which invariably entail initiation and performance, and also echoes the oral accounts of individuals who acquire artistic skills in dreams from the gods. This seems to be a culturally acceptable explanatory mechanism for individual artistic creation in a context in which the collective and communal are prized above the individual, and in which creation and its products, including the artistic, are in a sense religious matters. Formal structural analyses of an adequate sample of myths of origins (assuming that they demonstrate certain features of regularity) could, therefore, assist in understanding indigenous notions of 'choreography', for example, as well as revealing indigenous historical methods.

5.2.4   Visual sources

While representations of dance in West Africa through the visual are legion, little has been done to assemble these for the purposes of dance research, historical or otherwise. Included as visual representations are both those 'visual accompaniments' to the dances, such as costumes, masks and properties, as well as the products of a variety of 'media', which range from the three-dimensional such as wood and ivory carvings to the two-dimensional such as illustrations, photography, film and video. The former represent the dance in a metonymic relationship, that is from masks as fragments of the dance the 'characters' and their movement styles may be reconstructed. The latter also represent the dance, but in metaphoric relations which re-frame and re-contextualize the dances into scenarios afforded by the era and by the conventions of the medium in question. An example of this is de Marees's early-seventeenth-century illustrations of an Akan funeral procession (in Thompson 1974: 31), in which the physiognomy of the dancers is not only European, but, apparently, classical Greek. As with the other sources, it is imperative to situate them contextually in order to obtain an appropriate reading.

A list of these sources in Nigeria would include such media as the Benin ivory carvings, which are predominantly in tusk form, the 'bronzes' of Ife and Benin (the most graphic of which are plaques), woodcarvings, including the rich variety of masks, costumes and textiles, newspaper and other photographs and illustrations, and most especially the made-for-television documentary videos of traditional dances. As regards the traditional sources, it is difficult to date many of them with any accuracy as the style and content of the representations follow time-honoured conventions. This does not negate their value as sources since the representations may, none the less, depict historically locatable events, as with the Benin tusk carvings which usually make reference to one of its kings.

Foreign sources include illustrations and engravings by traders, scientists and others, which in the late nineteenth century were largely superseded by photography. The history of foreign visual material parallels the 'colonial' history of written sources. This has culminated in the documentary and ethnographic film genres, both of which are engaged in forms of constructing the 'other', and which have now been constituted into the recent field of visual anthropology.[17] Many of such films do not directly address dance but contain copious dance material. Collections of visual material are usually housed with the ethnographic collections of national museums or in specialist collections such as the ethnographic film collection held by the Royal Anthropological Institute (RAI) in London.

5.2.5   Performance as a source

Given that much research will entail fieldwork with existing dances, performance constitutes a major source of information. One of the main features of this kind of research is the opportunity afforded to study 'living traditions' and, therefore, the ways in which 'traditions' are transformed or rather constructed in the process of performance. For example, in repeated performances of the same dance, the pattern of movements may change with the apparent introduction of new steps. While it may be possible to identify certain features of the dance (its 'structure', for example), what may be of greater interest are the creative processes and how these determine changes in the dance over time. Access to local aesthetic criteria, to decision-making and other aspects of the production process is thus granted. Also of special interest are audience–performer relations which can be documented only in the live context. Attention to these may assist in understanding local performance dynamics and local concepts of 'dance'.

As regards methodological approaches, much of what concerns the collection of oral sources is relevant. There is, moreover, one tool of special use in this context which Bovin has termed 'provocation anthropology' (1988: 21). This uses personal engagement to provoke interaction with the participants in the field (by for example offering a performance from the researcher's culture) and thereby creates the conditions for the exchange of new information for all the participants including the researcher. Blacking (1984) has urged similar participation in the field with an emphasis on research as a process of interactive construction, in which documentation and textual formulation, i.e. ethnographic writing, should both be done in the field. Most recently, Grau has proposed the expression 'dialectical anthropology' to describe 'a process in which there is an exchange between analysts and informants which brings into play two kinds of technical knowledge and experience, and in which informants share the intellectual process of analysis' (Grau 1992: 5–6). The term 'dialogic anthropology' would equally well describe this process, which emphasizes 'dialogue on an equal footing' (Grau 1992: 9). In all these approaches to fieldwork, the researcher's own subjectivity and 'cultural baggage' become consciously used tools.

Brief mention should be made of a further tool of use in the field and with certain visual sources, that is movement notation. Although this is an ethnocentric tool and may provide representations of the dances which are unfaithful to local conceptions, it can be useful as an *aide-mémoire* in producing field notes of the dance movements. The ephemerality of performance makes lengthy note-taking difficult, and notation, with photography and video, is often a more efficient means of documenting live performance. Notation may also serve as an economic means of communicating research findings regarding movement and as the basis for structural analyses.

5.3 EVALUATION OF SOURCES

That all source material is the product of specific social, historical and political conditions has been already established. A critical approach to the material is therefore essential and it is necessary to situate it especially in relation to the question as to 'who is speaking'. This not only applies to textual and visual material, much of which can be situated within already elaborated 'western' discourses, but also to oral and performance sources which are constituted in the field. Local discourses are equally formative in determining the range of positions from which people may speak or move and narratives are normally constructed from a particular perspective. Especially important are local socio-political hierarchies, which constitute an intricate network of overlapping and often shifting power relations, in which people struggle to assert themselves; a 'big' person in one context is a 'small' one in another. Moreover, people are stratified not only in relation to each other but also in relation to the gods who occupy a separate, more all-embracing and therefore powerful realm. This might explain why dances, which assist in organizing the human social world, are usually conceived as some form of gift from the gods. It is, therefore, often the case that different versions of the 'same' myth represent or articulate the interests of particular social groups, rather than those of individuals. A related issue, which requires attention, is that of attitudes embodied in the narrative. These may well be representative not of the local culture, conceived as some homogeneous whole, but of a section of the community, with specific vested interests, for whom the narrative is a weapon in the negotiation of personal and cultural identity (Clifford 1988: 273–4).

A further question relates to the status of sources and to their characterization as 'fact' or 'fiction'. Of particular interest in considering alternative and competing versions, this is also important when comparing the narrative fiction to the established so-called 'real' event, which, as earlier mentioned, merely belongs to a different category of historical statement. As with the division into primary and secondary sources, the categorization into 'fact' or 'fiction' carries with it an implicit notion of validation and authentication: one source is authorized as authentic, and therefore real, while the other is consigned to the margins of history as unauthentic. It is thus that a 'regime of truth' is constructed. This process of conferring historical validity occurs as much, *in situ*, with local narratives, be they oral, performed, visual or written, of which there is often an official 'true' version and then subordinate alternatives, as with Eurocentric ones. If, however, all sources are viewed in some sense as 'fictional', that is, fabricated, then they must all be treated as equally valid and given equal weight in the process of historical construction.

5.4   WRITING THE DANCE HISTORY OF WEST AFRICA

Given the lack of conventional, that is, written historical sources, one of the most important tasks is to generate materials through the construction of contemporary dance histories. This, therefore, requires using not only historical but also anthropological methodology, and it is this perspective which has informed much of what has been written.

There is, however, a fundamental tension between history and anthropology, which is of special relevance in this context. Much contemporary anthropology, in an attempt to dislodge or short-circuit its colonial history in which the 'other' is always framed within a Eurocentric discourse, conceives of fieldwork as an intersubjective process (thus jettisoning any mask of objectivity) and of ethnographic writing as a form of textual construction, verging on the fictional, which deploys all the literary devices available. This kind of anthropology is incompatible with a history which amasses and sifts evidence in the production of some true version of events. If, however, its aim is the construction of local histories, in which it is the participants' cultural perspectives and notions about 'dance' in interrelationship with the researcher that form the focus, then an interface with anthropology emerges.

Writing the dance history of West Africa may also be conceived as a process of intertextuality, and one of the most creative strategies, in what is effectively an emerging field, would be to encourage the production of local oral dance histories as texts both in the host and in the target languages.

Also useful are monocultural studies either of one dance performed in different social contexts and by different groups of people, for example, or of a number of dances viewed comparatively. Such studies would provide contemporary materials to serve a number of purposes including the provision of educational resources for the multicultural markets at home and abroad.

A final approach, although one which might offend cultural purists, is to undertake comparative studies of diverse dance traditions in West Africa. This in effect would be to construct 'West African dance' as an innovative and hybrid form, an undertaking already well under way in Europe and America in the theatre dance world.

NOTES

1 For further details on these and related issues, the text which emerged from the Association of Social Anthropologists' 1989 Annual Conference on Anthropology and Autobiography (Okely and Callaway 1992) should be consulted, in particular Hastrup's contribution, 'Writing ethnography' (1992: 116–33).

2 For a discussion of the term 'tradition' and its pitfalls, as well as other problematic terms such as 'oral', 'popular', 'discourse' etc., see Finnegan (1992: 5–17).

3 These include Benin (previously Dahomey), Burkina Faso (until 1984 Upper Volta), Cape Verde Islands, Gambia, Ghana, Guinea, Guinea-Bissau, Ivory Coast, Liberia, Mali, Mauritania, Niger, Nigeria, Senegal, Sierra Leone and Togo.

4 The first 'settlers' in West Africa were the Sanhaja Berbers, who, by the eighth century, had discovered how to survive in the Sahara. Until then little contact had been made with sub-Saharan black West Africa.

5 Liberia was created by an American charity between 1821 and 1847, as a haven for freed slaves, and constituted as an independent republic in 1847. It was, therefore, never colonized by Europeans.

6 This sketch of West African history has been produced mainly from McEvedy's graphic historical atlas (1980). For a more detailed history Ajayi and Crowder (1985 and 1987) remain a most reliable source.

7 For further elaboration on the contextual framework for dance production

Nketia's discussion of the 'social and cultural background' of musical production in Africa (1979: 364ff.) is most relevant.

8 The Muslim cultures of West Africa are included here since, despite Islamization and the impact of the written through koranic teachings, traditional *modus vivendi* are based on the transmission of the socio-cultural through oral and performance, and not written, methods.

9 The concept of style is problematic and is used here to refer only to visually comparable features of the dance with no reference to local or other meanings.

10 A number of West African authors (Acogny 1984 and Tiérou 1992, for example) have used dances from West Africa to represent African dance. While this practice may be a conscious strategy to place 'African dance' on the world map, as is the case with Acogny (1984), it does not always produce sound historical source material. Such writing can, however, produce useful contextual information.

11 For example, the *Journal of the Anthropological Institute*, which became *Man* in 1960, was first published in 1871. It had previously been the *Anthropological Review and Journal of the Anthropological Society of London*, which was established in 1863.

12 For an elaboration on the problems and politics of the notion of cultural and linguistic translation in anthropology see especially Asad (141–64), Crapanzano (51–2) and Tyler (139–40) in Clifford and Marcus (1986).

13 For further details see Finnegan (1970 and 1992).

14 Finnegan's comprehensive 'guide', *Oral Traditions and the Verbal Arts* (1992), should be consulted for further details on these issues and other research practices.

15 For a discussion of the term '*habitus*' see Bourdieu (1977); Connerton (1989); Gore (1982); and Mauss (1973).

16 See Finnegan (1992: 158–85) for a more extensive summary.

17 For an overview of issues in the field, see Crawford and Turton (1992).

REFERENCES

Acogny, G. (1984), *African Dance*, Abidjan and Dakar: Les Nouvelles Editions Africaines.

African Notes (1964–), Ibadan: Journal of the Institute of African Studies, University of Ibadan.

Ajayi, J. and Crowder, M. (eds) (1985), *History of West Africa, vol. I*, 3rd ed., Harlow: Longmans.

—— (1987), *History of West Africa, vol. II*, 2nd ed., Harlow: Longmans.

Anglo-African (1863–?), Lagos, Nigeria.

Bamikunle, A. (1984), 'Cross-cultural problems in the teaching of literature: the case of African oral literature', *Nigeria Magazine*, 151: 80–7.

Begho, F. O. (1986), 'Function and aesthetics in traditional African dance', *Journal for the Anthropological Study of Human Movement*, 4, 2: 114–22.

Blacking, J. (1983), 'Movement and meaning: dance in social anthropological perspective', *Dance Research*, 1, 1: 89–99.

—— (1984), '"Dance" as a cultural system and human capability: an anthropological perspective', in J. Adshead (ed.), *Dance – A Multicultural Perspective*, University of Surrey: National Resource Centre for Dance: 4–21.

Bourdieu, P. (1977), *Outline of a Theory of Practice*, Cambridge: Cambridge University Press.

Bovin, M. (1988), 'Provocation anthropology: bartering performance in Africa', *The Drama Review*, 32, 1 (T117): 21–41.

Bradbury, R. E. (1973), *Benin Studies*, edited by Peter Morton-Williams, London: Oxford University Press.

Callaway, H. (1992), 'Ethnography and experience: gender implications in fieldwork and texts', in J. Okely and H. Callaway (eds) (1992).

Clifford, J. (1988), *The Predicament of Culture*, Cambridge, Mass.: Harvard University Press.

Clifford, J. and Marcus, G. E. (1986), *Writing Culture: The Poetics and Politics of Ethnography*, Berkeley and Los Angeles: University of California Press.

Connerton, P. (1989), *How Society Remembers*, Cambridge: Cambridge University Press.

Crawford, P. I. and Turton, D. (1992), *Film as Ethnography*, Manchester: Manchester University Press.

Echeruo, M. J. C. (1977), *Victorian Lagos: Aspects of Nineteenth Century Lagos Life*, London: Macmillan.

Finnegan, R. (1970), *Oral Literature in Africa*, Oxford: Clarendon Press.

—— (1992), *Oral Traditions and the Verbal Arts*, London: Routledge.

Fothergill, A. (1992), 'Of Conrad, cannibals, and kin', in M. Gidley (ed.), *Representing Others*, Exeter: University of Exeter Press.

Gore, G. (1982), *The Social Topography of the Human Body*, unpublished Ph.D. thesis, University of Keele.

—— (1986), 'Dance in Nigeria: the case for a national company', *Dance Research* 4, 2: 54–64.

Gorer, G. (1983), *Africa Dances* (1935), Harmondsworth: Penguin.

Grau, A. (1983), 'Sing a dance – dance a song', *Dance Research*, 1, 2: 32–44.

—— (1992), 'Intercultural research in the performing arts', *Dance Research*, 10, 2: 3–29.

Hanna, J. L. (1987), *To Dance is Human* (1979), Chicago and London: University of Chicago Press.

Hansford, K., Bendor-Samuel, J. and Stanford, R. (1976), 'A provisional language map of Nigeria', *Savanna*, 5, 2: 115–24.

Hastrup, K. (1992), 'Writing ethnography', in J. Okely and H. Callaway (eds) (1992).

Horton, R. (1960), *The Gods as Guests*, Lagos: Nigeria Magazine.

Ives, E. D. (1980), *The Tape-Recorded Interview: A Manual for Field Workers in Folklore and Oral History*, revised edition, Knoxville, Tenn.: University of Tennessee Press.

Kaeppler, A. (1985), 'Structured movement systems in Tonga', in P. Spencer (1985).

McEvedy, C. (1980), *The Penguin Atlas of African History*, Harmondsworth: Penguin.

Man (1960–), London: Journal of the Royal Anthropological Institute; previously *Journal of the Anthropological Institute*, 1871; previously *Anthropological Review and Journal of the Anthropological Society of London*, 1863.

Mauss, M. (1973), 'Techniques of the Body', *Economy and Society*, 2, 1: 70–88.

Mbiti, J. S. (1970), *African Religions and Philosophy*, Garden City, N.Y.: Anchor Books, Doubleday.

Middleton, J. (1985), 'The dance among the Lugbara of Uganda', in P. Spencer (1985).

Mitchell, J. C. (1956), *The Kalela Dance*, Rhodes–Livingstone Institute Papers no.27, Manchester: Manchester University Press.

Nigeria Magazine (1928–), Lagos: Department of Culture, Federal Ministry of Social Development, Youth and Culture.

Nketia, J. H. K. (1979), *The Music of Africa*, London: Victor Gollancz.

Okely, J. and Callaway, H. (eds) (1992), *Anthropology and Autobiography*, London: Routledge.

Park, M. (1983), *Travels into the Interior of Africa* (1799), London: Eland Books.

Ranger, T. O. (1975), *Dance and Society in Eastern Africa*, London: Heinemann.

Record (1891–), Lagos, Nigeria.

Schechner, R. (1990), 'Wayang Kulit in the colonial margin', *The Drama Review*, 34, 2 (T126): 25–61.

Spencer, P. (1985), *Society and the Dance*, Cambridge: Cambridge University Press.

Talbot, D. A. (1968), *Woman's Mysteries of a Primitive People: The Ibibios of Southern Nigeria* (1915), London: Frank Cass.

Talbot, P. A. (1967), *Life in Southern Nigeria: The Magic, Beliefs and Customs of the Ibibio Tribe* (1923), London: Frank Cass.

—— (1926), *The Peoples of Southern Nigeria, vol. III*, London: Oxford University Press.

—— (1967), *Some Nigerian Fertility Cults* (1927), London: Frank Cass.

Thomas, N. W. (1910), *Anthropological Report on the Edo-Speaking Peoples of Nigeria, Part I: Law and Custom*, London: Harrison and Sons.

Thompson, R. F. (1974), *African Art in Motion*, Berkeley and Los Angeles: University of California Press.

Thorpe, E. (1989), *Black Dance*, London: Chatto & Windus.

Tiérou, A. (1992), *Dooplé: The Eternal Law of African Dance*, New York: Harwood Academic Publishers.

Uchendu, V. C. (1965), *The Igbo of Southeast Nigeria*, New York: Holt, Rinehart & Winston.

West Africa (1917–), London.

Williams, D. (1991), *Ten Lectures on Theories of the Dance*, Metuchen, N.J. and London: Scarecrow Press.

Chapter 6

Regional evidence for social dance with particular reference to a Yorkshire spa town, Harrogate, UK

Patricia Mitchinson

6.1 INTRODUCTION

The Yorkshire spa town of Harrogate was identified as the focal point for research in the knowledge that 'spas' or 'watering places' are historically reputed for their social activities of which dancing was an integral and important feature. The social life of the south of England spas such as Bath and Cheltenham is fairly well documented but, although the north of England spas are frequently referred to, little seems to be known of their dancing activities. The aim of the investigation was to discover whether this Yorkshire spa would prove to be characteristically similar to other better-known spas in terms of social dance trends. It is possible that the processes outlined here could be applied to historical studies in other regional cultures.

A regional locality can refer to any area or district delineated for the purposes of the study. It could, for example, encompass a whole or parts of a city, a town or village. A locality, might, therefore be identified for its urban or rural characteristics although inevitably there will be points of overlap.

There may be a number of possible reasons for identifying a specific locality for a dance history study. The distinctive character of a particular city, town or village could be a significant factor in determining the nature of the historical study. Special features may exist such as buildings of particular dance interest. The local city dance hall or palais de danse, the spa town assembly rooms, are landmarks in the history of dance and as such provide possible sources for investigation. The existence of other dancing places such as village maypoles or local 'dancing stones' may provide additional clues to the *context* in which the dance activity arose, for example, social or traditional, and the *type* of dance activity which took place there.

A significant example of a building providing a clue to an aspect of dance history exists in the city of Norwich, England, where a local cinema carries the name 'Noverre'. To anyone unfamiliar with the history of dance this name may well be meaningless, but to someone more knowledgeable it will be associated with the celebrated Jean-Georges Noverre (1727–1810). Further enquiries would reveal that this same Noverre was related to a well-known family of Norwich dancing masters and this could provide the basis for subsequent historical research (see Fawcett 1970).

Other approaches to identifying regional localities may lead to different kinds of dance history studies. It could be interesting, for example, to select a locality at random and by referring to the indigenous source material subsequently discover what, if any, dance activities currently exist. This could be described as a 'here and now' historical study based on present-day events. Similarly one might identify a locality in the knowledge that some form of dance activity does exist, a group of Morris or Sword Dancers based there, for example, and, by using this as a starting point, discover more about its historical background. Clearly, the level or standard to which the historical study is aimed will to a large extent determine both the viability of the project and the depth of the investigations.

The study of social dance in Harrogate was set against the background of the nineteenth century since it was evident that the town grew and developed as a fashionable spa during this period. The architecture of the town combined with the road and rail networks are indicative of Harrogate's emergence from two small villages in the Georgian period to a prosperous Victorian town by the end of the century. The vast common lying between the two villages, which Smollett (1771: 93) referred to 'as a wild common, bare and bleak, without a tree or shrub or the least signs of cultivation', was divided by the railway line built in 1862. The railway station provided a focus for the growth of the central area of Harrogate during the Victorian period and the street developments which followed are in the Victorian style. The picture is further enhanced by a statue of Queen Victoria erected at the time of her Golden Jubilee in 1887 which, even today, in spite of the recent redevelopment of the town centre, acts as a dominant reminder of that golden era.

6.2   LOCATING SOURCE MATERIAL

The locating of source material can be an unpredictable and frustrating task. The most relevant historical documentation is not always to be found in the most obvious places, as indicated by some of the examples given in this section. Nevertheless, the element of chance can be an important and exciting aspect of the search. The insights gained, for example, by an impromptu discussion with a local history enthusiast or the discovery of a hitherto unpublished manuscript on a musty library shelf often outweigh the disappointment of a predetermined lead which failed to provide evidence. This, of course, does not diminish the importance of a pre-structured line of enquiry based on identified regional sources. It does, however, endorse the value of a proactive approach to historical research which can result in fresh and previously undocumented evidence being revealed.

During the preliminary enquiries made in Harrogate for this study, references to source material not apparently available in Harrogate itself led to a wider search for evidence outside the immediate locality. To some extent this characterizes the nature of regional sources in that for practical reasons, such as the movement of material from one place to another, the search may extend beyond the physical boundaries initially selected. The increasing expansion of urban boundaries into rural districts, usually under the control of a centralized local government authority, can sometimes pose difficulties for the researcher in locating source material which may well have been moved from a library in one locality and relegated to the cellars of some other municipal building in another place.

6.3 HARROGATE SOURCES

Valuable sources of historical documentation were located in the reference section of the Harrogate Library which contained a considerable amount of primary and secondary source material. Other local sources proved less worthwhile and led to some initial setbacks in the research. The existing Assembly Rooms, for example, were built in 1897 and as such are unrepresentative of the social life in the earlier part of the century. However, from lithographs of local scenes, there was evidence of an earlier Assembly Room known as the Royal Promenade and Cheltenham Pump Room built by a private owner in 1835. This building was demolished to make way for a more modern concert hall now known as the Royal Hall. Today all that remains to be seen of the original building are some stone colonnades, resited in the Harlow Carr Gardens, and some lithographs and prints made at various stages during its brief history. Fortunately, a number of written descriptions of this grand 'salon' are extant and these provide a valuable source of information about the style of the building and the types of activities which took place there.

It became evident that the building changed hands, moving from private to municipal ownership by the end of the nineteenth century. It is possible that architectural records and conveyancing documents still exist which may be worthy of investigation.

The local newspaper offices similarly yielded little of value, since, although copies of nineteenth-century newspapers were held there, they were not easily accessible. To view the documents necessitated a newspaper employee laboriously carrying the bulky leather-bound folders of newspapers from a storage place in another building. This line of enquiry was eventually discontinued when it was found that back-dated copies, though not in complete sets, were held at the local library.

6.4   REGIONAL SOURCES

Owing to the lack of storage space at the Harrogate Library some documentation on Harrogate's past had been transferred to the Archives Department of the North Yorkshire County Records Office in the nearby town of Northallerton. Lack of storage space is a universal problem and it must be assumed that it is not uncommon for local source material to be moved from one archive to another. Normally, it is necessary to contact the archivist requesting permission to visit. This implies a prior knowledge of the existence of certain documentation if it is to be identified from amongst the vast amount of regional material often available.

In this case, a visit to the County Records Office proved disappointing as the particular diary requested, known as the 'Greeves Diary', written by a Harrogate surveyor around 1842 and thought to contain a reference to dance, was unavailable and, possibly, missing. Thus, even when primary source materials are known, it does not follow that these are easily retrievable, a factor which may determine the extent to which the investigation can be carried out.

Further difficulties were experienced in tracing Dr Augustus Granville's three-volume document, *Spas of England* (1841) which was cited by a number of authors as being a primary text on nineteenth-century spas. A damaged but original part-volume was eventually found in the University of Leeds Library, but the part which was relevant to north of England spas was missing. In the circumstances there was no alternative but to use a later edition of the work located in the same library.[1]

Despite initial setbacks due to the unavailability of some identified primary source material, a visit to the Leeds City Reference Library was more rewarding. City reference libraries frequently contain material on aspects of regional topographical interest and are always worth a visit. It is not unusual for private book collections to be bequeathed to local libraries and it is possible that valuable collections on specific subjects, such as local history, or even dance, may be available through a local reference library or other such facility. In this case a specially arranged visit to the Leeds Private Library, which has a membership by subscription, revealed a source of interesting though not rare eighteenth and nineteenth century dance books.

These regional resources were invaluable: not only did they prove the existence of social dance in Harrogate but they also served to highlight the individuality of Harrogate's social life when compared with other spas.

Research showed that whereas Harrogate was, to an extent, representative of the nineteenth-century social norms and fashions found elsewhere, its social life was influenced by a variety of factors linked to its growth and development as a regional spa. It was important to recognize, for example, that the increased growth and expansion which took place in the Victorian period in Harrogate was just one aspect of the increasing prosperity and greater social mobility. This was reflected within the wider macrocosm of society. Understanding was aided by background reading on nineteenth-century history, though no detailed study of any one particular source was undertaken. Spa histories, too, were useful in offering comparative accounts of the various geographical positions and amenities afforded by the better-known English resorts.

6.5   SOURCE CATEGORIES

Faced with a wide variety of source material, I found two factors important in identifying and evaluating suitable material for this historical study: to identify material which would confirm or disprove the proposal that social dance at Harrogate was compatible with popular social dance trends in other places; and to discover material which characterized the social life of Harrogate as a spa. The examples of primary and secondary sources listed in Table 6.1 correspond with the written, visual, and aural categories already outlined in Chapter 2.

6.6   PRIMARY SOURCE MATERIAL

The primary sources given here are taken in a sequence designed to give the most coherent account and are not placed in any chronological order. Newspapers proved to be a valuable source of evidence and the research was further enhanced by additional material from diaries, lithographs, medical treatises and fictional accounts, all of which contributed to the breadth of the investigation.

Newspapers of the period proved significant in tracing the growth and development of the Harrogate Spa and, more importantly, provided valuable evidence for the existence of dance in the form of articles, advertisements and published prints.

The founding and development of the Harrogate newspapers is historically interesting. *The Pallisers List of Weekly Visitors* was first established in 1835 and was printed in May prior to the start of the season, which at that time was in July and August. It is evident from this source that social activities mainly centred on those two months in the

Table 6.1 Examples of regional source material

Primary	Secondary
Social dance	Social Dance
written sources: spa histories, medical treatises, street directories, diaries, fictional accounts, newspaper articles, advertisements	*written sources*: local histories, spa histories, dance histories
visual sources: ball cards, dance invitation cards, lithographs and prints	*visual sources*: prints
Harrogate Spa	Harrogate Spa
written sources: almanacs, local histories, newspapers, spa histories, street directories, topographies, visitors' guides	*written sources*: local histories, spa histories
visual sources: maps, prints	*visual sources*: buildings, maps, photographs, prints
	oral sources: people with local knowledge including descendants from known Harrogate residents, local history enthusiasts

year when visitors congregated at the Spa. By 1840 the paper became known as the *Harrogate Advertiser* and gradually began to report on events of both local and national interest. In 1847 a rival paper was set up known as the *Harrogate Herald*, but the *Advertiser* was the more informative on social events, especially those which took place at the main Assembly Rooms known as the Royal Promenade and Cheltenham Pump Room.

The following newspaper discovery provided the first clue to the existence of the nineteenth-century Assembly Rooms.

The style of this superb edifice, whether we regard its external or its internal structure is preeminently superior to any similar erection in the neighbourhood having been built at the expense of several thousand pounds and being capable of accommodating upwards of 500 persons.

The proprietor contemplates that every arrangement for its completion will be effected previous to 21st August next, his most gracious Majesty's birthday, on which occasion it is his intention to gratify the expectation of the public by giving a splendid public ball.

(*Pallisers List of Weekly Visitors*, 25 July 1835)

A few days prior to the official opening on 17 August, another advertisement appeared.

> In addition to the Band of the Scots Greys, the proprietor has engaged an eminent Quadrille Band. The surrounding gardens and pleasure ground will be elegantly illuminated with variegated lamps, after the style of Vauxhall Gardens, London.
>
> (*Pallisers List of Weekly Visitors*, 12 August 1835)

A contemporary account of the events which actually took place at the grand opening ball was not discovered, but certain conclusions were nevertheless drawn from the advertisements. For instance, although the building had been styled in the mode of its earlier eighteenth-century counterparts, the reference to Vauxhall Gardens in London suggests that it was being promoted along the same lines as other fashionable assembly rooms, notably in the capital city. Also, the fact that a quadrille band had been engaged suggests that the social dances were fashionable, quadrilles, for example, being at the peak of popularity at this time (see Richardson 1960).

Evidence from newspaper articles and other sources indicates that dancing took place at various other local venues in addition to the Royal Promenade and Cheltenham Pump Room. Prior to the opening of the 1835 Assembly Rooms, social dancing had been a feature of the hotels and inns, an inheritance from the eighteenth century. This social pattern continued throughout the nineteenth century when the custom was to rotate the dances between several hotels, an arrangement which no doubt suited the hoteliers for obvious commercial reasons.

During the mid part of the century fresh evidence for the existence of social dance at Harrogate began to appear in the form of newspapers advertisements.

> Fashionable Readers – Our readers – we are sure, will be pleased to know that Mr Nicholas Henderson of London, whose name, from the fact of Mr Henderson having introduced Cellarius and several other beautiful waltzes into the fashionable circles of the metropolis has recently become so popular, is now in Harrogate, and purposes remaining during the season. To those who desire to become acquainted with the latest exportations in this delightful art which not to know is to be excluded from the assemblies of the select – will, we doubt not, avail themselves of the abilities of a gentleman whose style is much appreciated by the elite in London and elsewhere.
>
> (*Harrogate Advertiser*, 15 July 1848)

Approximately two weeks later Mr Henderson duly presented himself as follows:

Mr Nicholas Henderson (from 19 Newman Street London) begs respectfully to inform the nobility and gentry of Harrogate that he has just arrived for a limited period, and purposes teaching all the new and fashionable dances, as danced by his pupils at Almacks, and the nobility balls in London.

The Polka, Schottische, Valse a Deux Temps,

Redowa, etc., in three lessons. One guinea.

Schools and families attended.

10 Waterloo Terrace, Low Harrogate.

(*Harrogate Advertiser*, 29 July 1848)

These particular advertisements provided certain hitherto missing clues. For example, no reference had been found prior to this date of the existence of a resident dancing master in Harrogate. The advertisements would appear to substantiate the proposal that perhaps no resident dancing master of any note did in fact exist in Harrogate at this time since it would seem improbable that Mr Henderson would have been in a position to offer his services had any substantial local competition been available.

Other explanations for the apparent paucity of Harrogate dancing masters are possible. It is known, for example, that three dancing academies existed in the nearby city of Leeds and it is reasonable to propose that local Harrogate residents were serviced by these. The fact that a London dancing master, apparently of good repute, considered it worthwhile setting up business in a northern spa town during the season is in itself indicative of the extent to which social dancing had taken serious purchase. His fee of one guinea for three lessons is also worth noting, as although no direct evidence of charges for dancing lessons in London in the same period was discovered, other regional evidence indicates that the price for lessons in Norwich in 1819 was 'two lessons a week for one guinea per quarter' (Fawcett 1970: 137). Even taking account of possible subsequent rises in fees, it would appear that Mr Henderson's prices were relatively high. Finally, if it can be assumed that Mr Henderson did actually teach the dances listed in the advertisement, then it is possible to conclude that social dancing at Harrogate was compatible with the popular social dance trends of the period.

Several Harrogate histories, written by nineteenth-century authors, offered useful comparative information on Harrogate's development as a spa town. Historical research is frequently dependent upon descriptions of historical events which have to be interpreted and, in the light of this, knowledge of the authors themselves, where this is available, is an important factor in assessing the reliability of their source material.

William Grainge, for example, was a well-known Harrogate resident in the nineteenth century and wrote extensively on local history. It can, therefore, be assumed that his local knowledge was sound. Similarly, Dr Augustus Granville was considered to be an influential authority on spas, having travelled extensively visiting the English and German resorts. Though he was mainly concerned with the medicinal aspects of the spas, he makes some significant comments on the social life of these resorts. On a visit to Harrogate in 1839 in preparation for his book *Spas of England*, Granville provides an interesting account of an 'impromptu ball' at the Royal Promenade and Cheltenham Pump Room.

> The Doric Temple showed off to great advantage by night, like many of the ladies who figured it; and with a superior company, such as we meet here at a more advanced period of the season, a ball in it must be a mighty fine thing for killing time in Harrogate. The place was not crowded; but a good sprinkling of people of almost every sort was scattered over the floor, or occupied the different ottomans in the recesses. Some were dressed as for an evening party, for there had been sufficient notice given in the afternoon of this impromptu. Others had not thought it worth while to go home and dress, and the ladies appeared 'sans façon', in morning bonnets, with their partners en frac. Amidst these heterogeneous groups, the six or eight stewards, with their white rosettes and smart coats, appeared like so many turkey-trots strutting among the motley inhabitants of la basse cour.[2]
>
> (Granville 1841, vol.1: 47–8)

The impression gained from Granville's description of the ball is that it was a fairly informal affair, held during the late part of the season and attended by an assortment of people. It is also possible that the proprietor of the Royal Promenade and Cheltenham Pump Room may have seized the opportunity of Granville's visit to profit by an 'impromptu ball' at a time of the year when the season was coming to a close. The proprietor would, no doubt, have been mindful of the promotional opportunity afforded by Granville's forthcoming publication. Certainly, Granville's comments on 'Harrogate's magnificent Assembly Rooms' were praiseworthy and he also observed that the only significant social attraction at Harrogate was dancing, of which he clearly approved.

Wheater (1890) also gives fascinating accounts of the social life provided at various northern spas and comments on the 'respectable reputation' which Harrogate had developed during the eighteenth century in contrast to other more fashionable resorts. He attributes Harrogate's soberness to the fact that 'Harrogate never had a Beau Nash or a Captain Webster to corrupt it', an arrangement of which he clearly approves as he goes on to explain.

> At no time are we able to trace in Harrogate the existence of a Long
> Room or Assembly Rooms separate and apart from an hotel. The
> value to decorum of such an arrangement is obvious to all who have
> studied the lives of the beaux. Scarborough and Bath placed society
> in the hands of Masters of Ceremonies, but no such creatures were
> ever known in Harrogate. Scarborough had her notorious beau,
> Tristram Fishe. The vagaries of this Long Room eclipsed even those
> of Bath when card swindling was added to their other foibles.
>
> (Wheater 1890: 165)

The Masters of Ceremonies to whom Wheater refers were notable
luminaries of spa assemblies in the eighteenth century, one of their
functions being to uphold the etiquette of the ballroom. It is evident
that the role of Master of Ceremonies continued well into the nineteenth century in other places. The absence of such a figurehead in
Harrogate not only distinguishes the spa town as being unique in this
respect but raises questions as to how these social events were conducted. Feltham provides a plausible explanation.

> The Master of Ceremonies is elected by the company, of whom he is
> always one; and he retains his rank during his stay, when another
> gentleman is chosen in his rooms. To this office, good manners and
> a suavity of disposition are the only pass-ports; no intrigues, no
> solicitations are used to procure this appointment: – it is offered as a
> voluntary compliment to him who appears to deserve it best, and it is
> discharged without fee or emolument: the only reward, and it is
> enough to every generous heart, is the reflection that this distinction
> has been merited to be allowed.
>
> (Feltham 1824: 210)

This implies that there must have been members of the 'company', that
is, spa visitors, who were sufficiently well versed in the etiquette of the
ballroom to take on the role of Master of Ceremonies. Presumably the
impermanence of the office would have prevented the scandals of the
beaux of Bath and other notorious watering places gaining a foohold in
Harrogate. Even the establishment of the Royal Promenade and Cheltenham Pump Room in 1835 did not give rise to the appointment of a
Master of Ceremonies.

In the light of Wheater's evidence, combined with other source
material, it is open to argument whether there was a deliberate attempt
by Harrogate's nineteenth-century speculators to avoid the social problems experienced in other spas by precluding the appointment of a
professional Master of Ceremonies. The fact that Harrogate developed
as a latter-day spa would, no doubt, have enabled lessons to be learned
from the mistakes of the past. A likely explanation is that by this time

the social pattern in Harrogate, which had grown out of existing resources such as the inns, hotels and local musicians, was by now too firmly established for any radical change to take place.

A number of interesting first-hand accounts on aspects of spa social life were provided by diaries, written by some of Harrogate's leading visitors and residents. Though fascinating, not all of the accounts were directly relevant to this study and the whereabouts of the 'Greeves Diary' (referred to in section 6.4) which might have proved more informative on dance remained a mystery.

The most significant diary items relating to the early Regency period was discovered in the Smith Manuscript (1816), so called because only part of the original diary has survived. Smith provides a detailed contemporary account of his impressions of the ball-nights at the Crown Hotel, Harrogate, and highlights some interesting features.

> On Ball nights the drawing room is lit up with flame lit candles – and the charge is 2/6 per head, which includes negus. There is one ball in each principal house every week and generally a private dance on some intervening evening day, when you only pay a shilling. Invitations are usually sent by card from one to the other, requesting the favour of each others company on the ball nights.
>
> The ball nights in August were Monday at the Dragon, Wednesday at the Crown, Thursday at the Queens Head, Friday at the Granby – The private dances at the Crown were on Saturdays. The master of the inn charges the waiter for the candles, from 2–4d. indeed the charge is as he pleases, for he obliges the waiter to tell the number of half crowns he gets, (for the purchase money is the waiters) and then he puts on accordingly for the candles, which generally lasts 3 nights, on one of which is a private dance for which the master charges one shilling per head. The waiter also pays about 7d. each to five musicians; one of whom is an excellent harpist.[3]

(Smith 1816: n.p.)

Much of Smith's attention centres on the cost of dances, a point which, though not pursued here, could prove to be of some relevance as a yardstick for assessing the relative importance of dance as a social activity compared with other types of social events and other spas.

Smith's reference to the custom of sending invitation cards from one 'principal' house to another is also worth noting. Smith differentiates between the 'ball nights' held at the 'principal hotels' and the 'private dances' which, it would seem, were held for the benefit of residents at the individual hotels. It can be assumed that the custom of presenting invitations was designed to exclude lodging houses of a lesser standing, thus keeping the company respectable and elite. It is possible that the cost of 2s 6d per head, in addition to candle charges, may also have been a prohibitively expensive factor to those less well off. This source material could prove useful in a differently focused study, for example to establish the relationship between social class and the types of dances performed. Its value to this particular study was in the contribution made to the whole since pertinent facts emerged which enabled certain conclusions to be drawn.

An interesting and unusual fictional account of a social season at Harrogate during the Regency period exists in the form of Barbara Hofland's book *A Season at Harrogate* (1812). The book takes the form of a series of verse letters written by the character Benjamin Blunderhead to his mother about his activities during a stay at Harrogate spa. Despite both the fictitious and satirical nature of the narrative the text is, nevertheless, worth noting in view of what is known about the author.

The *Harrogate Advertiser* indicates that Hofland came to Harrogate in 1809 as Mrs Hoole, a widow in her early thirties. Needing to support herself, she began teaching and took over a girls' boarding school at Grove House, where, for financial reasons, she also accommodated paying guests. She later married the artist T. C. Hofland. This newspaper article suggests that Hofland wanted her book to be profitable and therefore 'made it more palatable to the general reader by presenting it in the guise of a romantic love story' (*Harrogate Advertiser*, 16 April 1960). Hofland utilizes the narrative as a convenient framework into which she weaves her realistic images of life at Harrogate as a spa. It is probable that the social context of Hofland's account is authentic since it is based on her observations of the local residents and visitors to the town.

Hofland adds colour to her young, headstrong hero Blunderhead by making him a keen dancer. His obvious love of dancing thereby enables her to present vivid descriptions of some of the other characters present on these social occasions. The literary device employed here by Hofland affords her the opportunity of commenting on what was obviously an important social pastime during this period.

Obviously this source material does not, in isolation, constitute evidence for the existence of dance at Harrogate because its fictional basis must be taken into account. Nevertheless, in the light of what has already been outlined it does represent an added dimension which, combined with other source material, offers fresh insights into the level of socialization which might have taken place during this period.

Street directories, like parish registers, can provide useful sources of information. Before the advent of telephone directories and Yellow Pages, street directories frequently acted as professional registers listing names, addresses and the professional occupations of private individuals as well as commercial and business enterprises.

It is likely that 'dancing masters' would also have used this outlet as a means of advertising their professional role. However, an examination of the nineteenth-century street directories revealed only one name of any relevance:

> Coverdale, J. 7 Gladstone Street, Commercial teacher and professor of dancing.
>
> (*Harrogate Directory* 1877, p. 19)

No further reference to Coverdale was discovered in earlier or subsequent directories. The information was, nevertheless, of value in that, combined with evidence from other sources, it served to underline the point made previously that no celebrated Harrogate-based dancing master was in residence for any length of time.

Medical treatises were not consulted in the initial stages of the study as they were thought to be purely of scientific interest. However later on in the research, and partly as a result of a conversation with a Harrogate doctor, this unexpected source of evidence for social dance was discovered. This points to the importance of scanning *all* potential primary source material and not prejudging the worth of any source at the preliminary stage.

An examination of the medical treatises revealed some fascinating hints on the practice and benefits derived from 'spawing', that is participating in spa life, of which physical exercise was referred to as an important aspect. The following extract from one of these documents shows the esteem a Victorian medical practitioner attached to the pastime of dancing as a means of achieving good health in body and mind.

> Than dancing, there is no species of exercise which can be taken within doors more cheering to the mind, and renovating to the body; and though usually considered a fatiguing recreation, it seldom produces any bad consequences. The music alone has remarkable power over many individuals in soothing the mind and equalizing the passions; and a placid state of mind becomes in turn a powerful auxilary in the treatment and cure of no small number of the most inveterate diseases. The weak and delicate ought not to exert themselves like the strong and vigorous and in no instance should the body when over-heated be suddenly exposed to the cold air. The warm bath, though from the usages of society rarely compatible with dancing hours, is a real luxury after this exercise, and will frequently induce sound and tranquil sleep.
>
> (Hunter 1846: 174)

This evidence is significant in that it reflects one of the popular justifications for social dancing made during the nineteenth century, namely that dancing should be not only regarded as a social pastime but also valued for its beneficial effect on the physical well-being.

The view put forward by established dance historians such as Richardson (1960) and Rust (1969) suggests that in contrast to the eighteenth century, dancing became less popular towards the end of the nineteenth century in that it was no longer considered a necessary social accomplishment. It is, therefore, not surprising to find the emphasis on physical well-being used again in these medical treatises as a justification for dancing at a nineteenth-century spa.[4]

The somewhat sober approach to spa social life reflected in much of the written evidence may have been influenced by other prevailing attitudes in society at that time. For example, the Evangelical Movement had a fairly strong influence in the mid part of the nineteenth century and it is known that a group was actively at work in Harrogate in 1841 (see Haythornthwaite 1954, 1960 and Sheppard 1971). A detailed investigation which focused on the shifts in attitudes towards social dance at a time of changing religious beliefs and new patterns of social behaviour could provide the starting point for a related study.

6.7   SECONDARY SOURCE MATERIAL

The secondary sources used were valuable for several reasons. Some of the written sources, such as local histories, drew their material from existing primary sources and, therefore, provided a variety of references from which to make further research. Jennings's edited *History* (1970) is a good example as it consists of material compiled by a number of local history enthusiasts. Such sources are normally well documented and it may be assumed that the evidence is a reliable starting point. Even so, a researcher always needs to check the accuracy and validity of any material consulted.

From visual sources, such as buildings, prints and photographs, it was possible to piece together a picture of the development of the town from the early Georgian period to the end of the century. Prints taken from original lithographs provided evidence of the architectural features of the 1835 Royal Promenade and Cheltenham Pump Room which, combined with written descriptions, made it possible to gain an appreciation of the style of this unique social centre.

People, too, provided interesting oral accounts of Harrogate's past. The local Harrogate doctor who suggested medical treatises as a possible source also gave a lively and enthusiastic description of the 'practices' of the Victorian spa doctors. The custom was for the visitor to select a doctor from among the many portraits which hung in the local chemists' shops. Following this somewhat random choice the visitor would then consult the doctor at his rooms as to the most appropriate 'cure'.[5] Disappointingly, no one was discovered whose own memories of family 'folklore' extended to a well-known dancing master or a celebratory ball. The fact that such people were not located, however, does not preclude the possibility of their existence.

6.8   CONCLUSION

The regional evidence used in the Harrogate study showed that the social dance activities were, to some extent, idiosyncratic when compared with other documented spa assemblies of the same period. Harrogate was characteristically different from other prototype spa towns such as Bath and Cheltenham in that it did not have Assembly Rooms until 1835. The late coming of the Assembly Rooms undoubtedly contributed to the absence of any known professional Master of Ceremonies, a feature which further distinguished Harrogate from its contemporaries.

It would seem that while Harrogate emulated the social dance trends of the period, following in the wake of the popular dances of London and elsewhere, it did so within the context of its own resources and social development.

By the early nineteenth century, social dancing at Harrogate was already established in the inns. This trend continued to develop in the new hotels as these emerged, a pattern which carried on throughout the nineteenth century. The Royal Promenade and Cheltenham Pump Room provided an additional social venue for dancing on a larger, grander and more fashionable scale, and undeniably added a new dimension in terms of the balls and social occasions which took place there.

Evidence suggests, however, that, by the mid part of the nineteenth century, social attitudes were changing, and that these Assembly Rooms, modelled on their eighteenth-century counterparts, and referred to locally as Spa Rooms, were out-dated. This would explain why the buildings were demolished in the early part of the twentieth century to make way for more modern facilities suited to the social tastes and fashions of a new age.

The Harrogate study underlines the regional individuality evident in the patterns for social dancing at this particular spa in the nineteenth century. Such a conclusion could only be stated on the basis of a study in which a thorough search and analysis of regional sources had been undertaken and the regional evidence then studied within the national context. Parallel work based elsewhere would no doubt similarly high-light the distinctiveness which foregrounding a regional location in the study of dance history can engender.

NOTES

1 It is possible that conflicting evidence may occur when more than one
   edition of an author's work has been published over a period of time. A

second or subsequent edition may change in detail such that an examination of the first and later editions of a publication can in itself be of value in historical research.

2 'Sans façon' was used to denote simple, unpretentious dress, literally meaning without fuss or style. 'En frac' means wearing tails, a tail coat, a dress or frock coat. 'La basse cour' is a reference to the farmyard.

3 'Negus' was the term given to a hot drink of port with lemon juice, often spiced and sweetened, and named after its eighteenth-century English inventor.

4 These documents provide unique and valuable material for the study of Harrogate as a spa town. Subject to similar texts being available at other spa locations it is likely that they would constitute a largely untapped source for use in future dance history studies.

5 This became the generic term to describe the medicinal effects of drinking spa water and participating in the various spa activities, such as promenading and dancing, deemed to be health-giving.

REFERENCES

Addison, W. (1951), *English Spas*, London: B. T. Batsford.

Fawcett, T. (1970), 'Provincial dancing masters', *Norfolk Archeology*, XXXV, 1.

Feltham, J. (1824) *A Guide to all Watering and Sea-bathing Places*, London: Richard Phillips.

Fletcher, J. S. (1920), *Harrogate and Knaresborough*, New York: Macmillan.

Franks, A. H. (1963) *Social Dance: A Short History*, London: Routledge & Kegan Paul.

Grainge, W. (1871), *The History and Topography of Harrogate and the Forest of Knaresborough*, London: Smith.

—— (1875), *A Guide to Harrogate and Visitors' Handbook*, Pateley Bridge: Thomas Thorpe.

Granville, A. B. (1841), *Spas of England and Principal Sea-bathing places*, Vols 1–2, London: Henry Colburn.

Grove, L. (ed.) (1895), *Dancing*, London: Longmans & Green.

Harrogate Advertiser (1839–79), Harrogate: Robert Ackrill.

Harrogate Directory (1877), Harrogate: J. L. Armstrong.

Haythornthwaite, W. (1954), *Harrogate Story: From Georgian Village to Victorian Town*, Yorkshire: The Dalesman Publishing Company.

—— (1960), 'Victorian Harrogate', nos 8, 9, *Harrogate Advertiser*, August.

Hofland, B. (1812), *A Season at Harrogate in a Series of Poetical Epistles*, Harrogate: R. Wilson.

Hunter, A. (1846), *A Treatise on the Waters of Harrogate and its Vicinity*, London: Longman.

Jennings, B. (ed.) (1970), *A History of Harrogate and Knaresborough*, Huddersfield: Advertiser Press.

Lennard, R. (ed.) (1931), *An Englishman at Rest and Play: Some Phases of English Leisure, 1558–1714*, Oxford: Clarendon Press.

Luke, T. D. (1919), *Spas and Health Resorts of the British Isles*, London: A. & C. Black.

Pallisers List of Weekly Visitors (1835–9), Harrogate: Pickersgill Palliser.

Patmore, J. A. (1963), *An Atlas of Harrogate*, Oxford: Alden Press.

Piggot, G. W. R. (1865), *The Harrogate Spas*, Harrogate: Thomas Hollins.

Pimlott, J. A. R. (1947) *An Englishman's Holiday*, London: Faber.

Richardson, P. J. S. (1960), *The Social Dances of the Nineteenth Century in England*, London: Herbert Jenkins.
Rust, F. (1969), *Dance in Society*, London: Routledge & Kegan Paul.
Scott, E. (1892), *Dancing as an Art and Pastime*, London: Bell.
Sheppard (1971), *London 1808–1870: The Infernal Wen*, London: Secker & Warburg.
Smith, D. W. & daughters (1816), Notes of visits to Harrogate in 1816, Harrogate Reference Library.
Smollett, T. (1771), *The Expedition of Humphrey Clinker*, Oxford: Oxford University Press.
Wheater, W. (1890), *A Guide to and History of Harrogate: Its Story Grave and Gay*, Leeds: Goodall & Suddick.

Chapter 7

Ballets lost and found

Restoring the twentieth-century repertoire

Kenneth Archer and Millicent Hodson

Partly by chance and partly by intention we have worked on the reconstruction of three ballets each by Vaslav Nijinsky (1888/9–1950), George Balanchine (1904–1983) and Jean Börlin (1893–1930). The first two choreographers, launched by Sergei Diaghilev's Ballets Russes, are now regarded as master builders of the modern repertoire. Börlin, whose career was even shorter than Nijinsky's, has remained an unknown quantity since his sudden death at the age of 37 in 1930. His large output for Rolf de Maré's Ballets Suédois was characterized by extremes of innovation and conventionality. For that reason his oeuvre may never demand full restoration. But the more radical of his ballets did alter the course of avant-garde dance. Thus we feel they deserve the same detailed attention we give to the lost works of Nijinsky and Balanchine.

Until recently Nijinsky's choreographic reputation rested on the legends surrounding his few ballets, except for several contradictory versions of *L'Après-midi d'un faune* (1912). Our reconstruction of his *Le Sacre du printemps* (1913), which we staged in 1987 for the Joffrey Ballet in the United States, enabled audiences to look at a documented production on which to base their views on his choreography.[1] The decoding of Nijinsky's *Faune* score by Ann Hutchinson Guest and Claudia Jeschke in 1989 led to their authenticated staging of this more familiar Nijinsky ballet.[2] Currently we are reconstructing his other two works. *Jeux* (1913) is being planned with a European company.[3] *Till Eulenspiegel* (1916) is in preparation for the Paris Opéra in 1994.[4] So by the middle of the 1990s serious students of choreography will be able to study the complete reconstructed works of Nijinsky. His contribution is the smallest in number by any renowned choreographer in ballet history, yet each work is distinct, marking a path of exploration for the future. Notorious in their own time, his ballets and their historical impact were partially eclipsed by his tragic withdrawal from the theatre.

Balanchine's career, long and full, was quite the opposite of both Nijinsky's and Börlin's. His works attracted ever greater acclaim during his lifetime, although the early ballets had met with hostile criticism as well as guarded admiration. It was this period of his burgeoning creativity that we felt needed to be seen in order to be appraised. Also, because Balanchine continually borrowed from himself, it seemed crucial to establish a concrete notion of the ballets he created in Europe prior to his epoch-making achievements in America. *La Chatte* (1927), which we reconstructed for Les Grands Ballets Canadiens in 1991, was his first acclaimed success.[5] It was the synthesis of his initial experiments in the Soviet Union and those made during his first encounter with the west.

Unlike Nijinsky and Börlin, whose choreography developed through the support and control of a single dominating director, Balanchine lost such a figure when Diaghilev died in 1929. Colonel Vassili de Basil and René Blum then formed a successor company in 1932, the Ballets Russes de Monte Carlo, and Balanchine served as choreographer, but only for one year. His *Cotillon* (1932), which we restored for the Joffrey Ballet in 1988, opened de Basil's first season.[6] It was presented with *La Concurrence* (1932), which Balanchine made as its companion piece, and which we may mount with a ballet company for its 1995 season.[7] After 1932 Balanchine worked almost exclusively as an independent artist, freelancing or forming companies himself.

Börlin's *Relâche* (1924), which was his last major ballet, was also the final production of the short-lived Ballets Suédois. This work, now in the process of reconstruction, was more a Dada event than a formally choreographed piece.[8] But the audacity of this non-dance still has repercussions in contemporary performance. In contrast, his *Skating Rink* (1922) was a highly formalistic ballet based on the minimal moves of roller skating.[9] Börlin took yet another tack for his ballet, *Within the Quota* (1923), which juxtaposed the movement styles of silent movie types and an archetypal immigrant. We are researching this choreographic cartoon and hope at the time of writing to stage all three Börlin ballets within a couple of years.[10]

7.1   RELATIVITY

Before discussing our reconstruction methods, it is necessary to raise certain questions for consideration by anyone who wishes to put the pieces of a ballet back together again. The reconstructor's task hinges on how the terms 'lost' and 'found' are understood. Both concepts are relative. How much of a ballet has to be missing for it to be considered lost? And how much has to be recovered for it to qualify as found? Just because a ballet is no longer being performed, is it lost? If it is recorded on film or video, can the ballet be said to exist? Or, if it has been notated, does the score stand as the complete work? Ballet masters and *répétiteurs* often regard film and video as insufficient means for restaging a ballet. No camera record indicates all the stage action simultaneously. On the other hand notation, as even those who write scores concede, does not usually reveal the elements of style and performance quality that make a work unique.

Prior to the widespread preservation of dance through modern recording methods, it was a maxim that ballets passed from one generation to the next via performers themselves. This kind of apostolic succession has prevailed throughout the history of dance despite periodic advances in notation. The systems of Raoul-Auger Feuillet and Pierre Beauchamp in the eighteenth century, or Arthur Saint-Léon, Friedrich Zorn and Vladimir Stepanov in the nineteenth, developed ever more precise ways of notating body movement, patterns in space, and time values in relation to music. These efforts culminated in the system of Rudolf Laban and that of Rudolf and Joan Benesh in the twentieth century, coinciding with the emergence of film and video technology. All the same, the presence of a ballet's original dancers, or their successors, is still taken by many as the guarantee of authenticity, notwithstanding progress in recording dance by camera or notation score.

As yet there is no substitute for what Martha Graham called 'motor memory', the knowledge of a dance from the habit of doing it. But then, who knows what some holographic-laser-writing-device may display on the unimagined screens of the future? For the time being, ballet masters and *répétiteurs* maintain that the testimony of a performer is the *sine qua non* of restaging choreography. And notators, setting movement from scores, still value the corroboration of such a material witness. The problem is, of course, that rarely can any one performer remember everything about a particular work, especially an evening-length ballet. So a variety of testimonies provides a more accurate picture. However, in the event of conflicting recollections, which is almost inevitable, who is to arbitrate? The answer to that question may vary in different situations, but, for our part, as reconstructors, we consider ourselves responsible for the final decision.

However, as regards the relativity of 'lost' and 'found', what happens in a case such as the following: a ballet has disappeared from repertory; none of the original performers or their successors survives; and neither a notation score nor a continuous visual record exists? Need the ballet be gone for good, even though a wealth of other documentation may be retrievable? Some Renaissance and Baroque dances are reconstructed under these circumstances; yet, for modern ballets, the given sources may strike us all as inadequate. Does this conclusion make sense? Or is it simply a response to the fact that recent works were created in the context of this century's high-tech computer notation and instant video replay? In other words, if 'lost' and 'found' are relative, then there are no anachronisms in dance reconstruction.

Contemporary accounts, hand-drawn sketches and, perhaps, notes on a music score should suffice as sources for a ballet from the 1950s if they are enough for one from the 1750s. Just because Kenneth MacMillan's career as a choreographer paralleled the phenomenon of dance on video, it does not follow that all his works were recorded by camera. Should reconstructors not allow him the same advantages they extend to Jean-Georges Noverre?

If conventional wisdom states that a ballet is lost, we query how lost it actually is. In answer to the question, how can it be found, our experience indicates that every 'lost' ballet generates its own method of rediscovery, according to the nature of the extant information and, equally important, according to the unique style of the work itself. Our reconstruction methods have evolved from the consideration of such questions and from the solution of problems which arise from one ballet to another. These methods are not laws graven in stone but working principles. In this chapter some of the problems that have presented themselves in the course of our work on the nine ballets named above are discussed. The reconstructions we have done thus far date from the two vibrant decades of dance between 1912 and 1932. However, the methods we use should serve for the restoration of ballets from any period.

7.2   LAST MINUTE LINKS AND CLUES

Our reconstructions go through three orderly and arduous phases. The first is the research phase, gathering all the available information about the ballet and its historical context. The second phase is the preparation of this material which is presented in dossiers documenting the decors and costumes and in notebooks logging the choreography measure by measure. Although it may be impossible to recover every last detail of the stage designs or dance steps, the aim throughout is to be scrupulously exact and comprehensive. The third phase is the rehearsal and production period, during which we take our dossiers and notebooks to the ballet company, where we supervise the making of the decors and costumes and set the choreography on the dancers.

These phases sound precise, deliberate, procedural, and indeed they are. But neither life nor theatre is ever so neat. The phases often overlap or run simultaneously. No matter how systematic the research, who can predict when a long-anticipated link or an unexpected clue will emerge? Each of our reconstructions is a matrix. The closer we get to the première date, the more it stimulates attention, and sometimes even information, which can be awkward to receive at the eleventh hour or even later. So we make it our policy if something of substance turns up just before or after the opening to incorporate it immediately into the production. Last-minute links and clues, attracted as they are by the prolonged efforts of everyone involved in the project, constitute a reconstruction problem of the very best sort.

La Chatte provided a case in point. The final scene of this ballet is a *cortège* in which six men each carry two large Constructivist shields. All the shields are made up in various geometrical forms, black on one side and white on the other. The men turn the shields back and forth, exploiting the many permutations of line and curve and light and dark. For the dancers, every move with the cumbersome shields is a strain. But for the audience, the spectacle is fascinating, a surprising, futuristic ritual. The designer for *La Chatte*, Naum Gabo, worked with Balanchine to set the movement for this scene. After close analysis of verbal accounts and microscopic study of surviving photographs, we established the exact line-up and sequence of movement for the squares, rhomboids, ellipses, circles and so forth.

At the party after the première the administrative director of Les Grands Ballets Canadiens, Colin McIntyre, who had invited us to reconstruct a Diaghilev ballet from the 1920s, gave us a large envelope tied with a ribbon. Inside was a press cutting dated 1927 with another *cortège* photograph, one we had never seen. As it happened, two days before, one of McIntyre's research assistants, who was compiling a Ballets Russes tour itinerary, had come across the cutting in a university library. The photograph verified our line-up but indicated yet another movement, which we added for the second performance. The card with McIntyre's gift read, 'Reconstructing a ballet is like eating sardines directly from the can – there is always a little bit in the corner you can't quite get out.'

Similarly, the morning after the reconstruction première of *Le Sacre du printemps*, we learned precisely how the Maidens push the Chosen One into the centre of the ceremonial circle. The previous night's performance had jogged the memory of Irina Nijinska, daughter of Nijinsky's sister, Bronislava. Irina had suddenly remembered the draft of a letter by her mother, which described the Maidens' forceful push. Although she had told us earlier about the actual letter, which we then saw in Leningrad, Irina had not realized that the draft contained an additional clue, indicating the vehemence of the action. Irina telephoned us straight away, and at the next rehearsal we used this clue, which intensified the harshness of the scene. Another instance occurred during the last week of rehearsals for *Cotillon*, when a packet was delivered from a relative of de Basil's former *régisseur*. Months before we had inquired whether any rehearsal notes for this ballet had been preserved. A sheaf of papers suddenly arrived which showed the ground pattern for the finale, the sequence we were staging that very day. So we included these details, enriching what we had already culled from film fragments of the ballet.

Figure 7.1 Composite of *Le Sacre du printemps* sketches. The one on the left is by Valentine Gross-Hugo, drawn in the dark during a performance at the Théâtre des Champs Elysées in 1913. The sketch on the right is by Millicent Hodson, deciphered for the reconstruction, as the Old Woman leaping behind a group of Youths and Young People. Act I, scene i, 'Augurs of Spring' (1913 drawing courtesy of Jean Hugo).

7.3   WHICH ORIGINAL IS WHICH?

At the beginning of a reconstruction we immerse ourselves in the personal memoirs of the artists who worked on the ballet. It is important in this initial period to experience vicariously the hopes and expectations of the collaborators and to understand their early intentions, even though the project may have become something quite different. In this way we observe the formation of the style unique to the ballet at hand. As material is gathered, we distinguish as rigorously as possible between what was conceived and what was realized. Our aim is to reconstruct the original ballet, as it was performed on the opening night. We agreed this principle with Robert Joffrey during work on *Le Sacre*, and ever since it has helped us clear up ambiguities in other reconstructions.

If, after its first season, a now lost ballet was kept in repertoire for a long time, it will probably have undergone some alteration, most likely in steps or costumes, owing to cast changes. In such circumstances, we may have to use details dating from what could be called the second 'original', that is, the same version by the same collaborators, but as it evolved and became best known. So it is still the original work albeit in vintage condition. Circumstances like these we explain to the company and press because it is important that all concerned understand what they are doing or watching. Part of our task as reconstructors is to make our methods known, and, of course, the way the original version of a ballet developed is fundamental to its history.

Cotillon exemplifies this situation. It had, so to speak, three 'original' versions. It was continuously in repertoire over the fifteen-year period between 1932 and 1946, and performed in Europe, Australia, North and South America. Not surprisingly, since it toured throughout the Great Depression and the Second World War, it changed. The three versions of *Cotillon* correspond with the three generations of dancers who performed it. For example, the mysterious character, the Hand of Fate, was danced primarily in the ballet's early period (1932–4) by Lubov Rostova, in the middle period (1935–8) by Vera Zorina and Sono Osato, and in the late period (1939–46) by Tamara Grigorieva.

Documentation of Balanchine's Hand of Fate pas de deux is rich; there are films, photographs, prose descriptions and demonstrations by surviving dancers. All these sources evinced differences from one performer to the next, some subtle and some not. In the absence of the complete duet from 1932, we used as a base the late version recalled by Grigorieva, who set it for us to study on dancers at the Teatro Colón in Buenos Aires. We adjusted details in it according to photos and reports of Rostova from the première. Then, having acquired from the Australian Ballet a film excerpt of Osato in the middle version, we discussed it with her and incorporated elements that adhered to accounts of the original. Thus the reconstruction presented a synthesis of what the company performed. However, our version did not draw upon later stagings of this pas de deux by de Basil dancers because of the time lapse between the revivals and the period when the ballet was consistently in repertoire.[11]

In *La Chatte* there was a comparable occurrence. Alicia Markova danced the 'third' original version of the solo for the Cat. Balanchine had created it on Olga Spessivtseva, who resisted its modernity and who, despite her success at the Monte Carlo première, had a convenient injury the day the ballet opened in Paris. Diaghilev overruled Balanchine's request to substitute Alexandra Danilova, who knew the part. So the choreographer refused to teach the solo to Alicia Nikitina, who instead learned it from the ballet's male lead, Serge Lifar. Several months later, however, Balanchine delighted in setting it, and elaborating the steps, on Markova, the acrobatic baby ballerina. Spessivtseva's version (the 'first' original) and Nikitina's (the 'second' original) were not available to us. But it is safe to say, in this instance, that Markova's (the 'third') was the most authoritative, in so far as Balanchine preferred it and created it so close in time to the première.

The reverse was true, however, for the costume of the Cat. Even though photos of Markova in the role had become well known, her costume deviated significantly from the original. Considering her arms too slender, Diaghilev had outlined them with fur, robbing the costume of its chic flapper line. More importantly, to facilitate her sliding exit, he dispensed with the innovative vinyl skirt which Gabo had hung over the Cat's white tutu. This see-through garment, like the vinyl accessories of other characters, was crucial to the ballet's glass-and-steel aesthetic. We felt compelled to opt for the 'first' original costume, which was reconstructed from the many pictures and accounts.

7.4   LESS IS MORE

Early in the work on a reconstruction, it becomes clear which elements of the ballet are relatively simple to trace, which ones may require vigorous research and which ones are apparently lost. For the latter category our method is to start collecting auxiliary information immediately. Often, by building up this support system, we come across data that can approximate to the lost elements. We have also learned that, the more distinct and even exaggerated the style of a ballet, the more possible it is to predict the nature of missing detail. This tendency applies across the board, whether such detail relates to scenario, music, dance or design. Also, anything we can discover about the habitual working practice of the artists involved can be turned to good account. Sometimes, by imitating their creative process, we can generate the material that connects one known part to another.

The costumes and decors for *Till Eulenspiegel*, for instance, were evidently left in storage at the Metropolitan Opera in New York, when Diaghilev's dancers rejoined him in Europe at the end of the 1916–17 tour. All traces of the actual curtain, backdrop, ground cover, stage props, garments and accessories have been lost, probably in one of the fires at the Met. Nevertheless, this production designed by Robert Edmond Jones is among the best documented of any for the Ballets Russes. Our task was to gather and collate all the disparate and widely dispersed proof about each item of the costumes and decors. Because the ballet was toured throughout the United States, there was a wealth of information in newspapers wherever the company performed. Particularly in provincial cities, where the Ballets Russes was such a novelty, writers devoted many column inches to description of this 'grotesque' ballet.

LA CHATTE DANCE SCORE: Scene 4/"Danse de la Chatte"
Reconstruction of Balanchine Choreography by Millicent Hodson & Kenneth Archer

ILLUSTRATIONS: Scene 4 [23] 2-6 and [24] 1

Costume Sketch for ›La Chatte‹, 1926
Pencil and pastel, 27.3 × 21.5
Inscribed, lower right (in Russian):
Design for Spesisova [sic]/›La
Chatte‹ of Diaghilev/Gabo-
Family Collection

Figure 7.2 La Chatte, dance score, scene iv, 'Danse de la Chatte'. Page from
a reconstruction notebook.

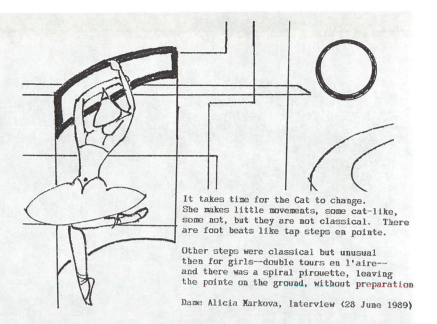

It takes time for the Cat to change.
She makes little movements, some cat-like,
some not, but they are not classical. There
are foot beats like tap steps en pointe.

Other steps were classical but unusual
then for girls--double tours en l'aire--
and there was a spiral pirouette, leaving
the pointe on the ground, without preparation

Dame Alicia Markova, Interview (28 June 1989)

The young man prays Aphrodite, an implacable divinity of isinglass and white, to
suffer his beloved, a cat, to come to life. His prayer is granted and thence,
Nikitina, her _tutu_ covered with a layer of isinglass, floats on to the scene in
an entrance of exquisite and indescribable delicacy, gravity and precision. The
dances are of the older sort, combinations of attitude, entrechat, rond de
jambe, pas de basque, etc., of the strict regime.

Lincoln Kirstein, "The Diaghilev Period" (1930), reprinted in Ballet:
Bias and Belief (1983), p. 21.

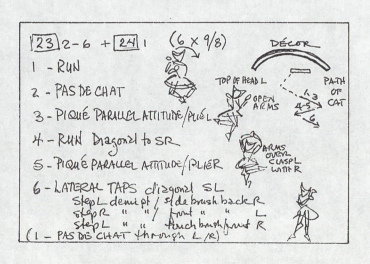

23 2-6 + 24 1   (6 x 9/8)   DÉCOR

1 - RUN

2 - PAS DE CHAT

3 - PIQUÉ PARALLEL ATTITUDE/PLIÉ L

4 - RUN Diagonal to SR

5 - PIQUÉ PARALLEL ATTITUDE/PLIÉ R

6 - LATERAL TAPS diagonal SL
   Step L demi pt / side brush back R
   Step R "   " / front   "   L
   Step L "   " touch brush/front R
(1 - PAS DE CHAT through L/R)

TOP OF HEAD L
OPEN ARMS
PATH OF CAT
ARMS OVER CLASP L UNDER R

The fact that Jones was the only American artist associated with the company drew extra attention to the visual aspects of *Till*.

In addition to the many press clippings, we tracked down the original costume design for almost every character in this densely populated ballet. Likewise, we located the decor designs and stage photographs showing the relationship of all the visual elements. The restricted palette Jones used for his backdrop of the medieval market place was described in contemporary accounts and indicated on the maquette. His reductive attitude toward scenic colours limited our choices, helping us identify his typical greens, blues and oranges. Similarly, although the costumes involved a more extensive palette, Jones kept to a few swathes of complementary colour for each character. He divided the body horizontally: head, shoulders, torso, waist, hips, legs, feet, keeping the colour zones solid and distinct.

Nijinsky's radical stylization of movement provided just such a predictive principle for the recovery of *Le Sacre du printemps*. He reversed the turned-out position of the feet in classical ballet, forcing Imperial dancers to experience awkwardness. The inverted posture put them through an ordeal something like that of the primitive Slavic ritual the ballet portrayed. Each movement was performed in this 'straitjacket', as his assistant, Marie Rambert, called it. The turned-in basis of the choreography provided a formula for the restoration of lost steps. By extension, in *Till Eulenspiegel*, Nijinsky used turned-in positions for the poor, socially deprived members of his medieval community, turned-out for the rich and propertied, and parallel positions for the serving class who mediated between the two extremes. Thus he created a demography of the dancing body, and his stringent economy of means made possible our rediscovery of *Till*.

Skating Rink was as far from an archaic rite as any up-to-date ballet of the early 1920s could be. Yet critics of the time labelled it the *Sacre* of the Ballets Suédois, comparing the repetitive push and glide of Börlin's skaters to the trampling and bobbing of Nijinsky's Slavs. These ballets had the same obsessive quality, which arose from the dancing of massed figures in rounds of ritualized movement. Once again, the rigid stylistic principle of the choreography aided the process of recovery.

Furthermore, we knew something about how the ballet's creators had developed its style. Hanging out at dance halls, they studied the body language and glad rags of *déclassé* Parisians doing the Apache, the violent precursor to the Lindy Hop. In the ballet Börlin accentuated the dangers of this daring style, making the dancers do the precarious lifts and throws of the Apache while sustaining the perpetual motion of skaters. As they raced around the illusory rink, the bold colours and patterns of their Cubist costumes, designed by Fernand Léger, became kinetic forms of the future.

7.5   CONTRADICTIONS

When reconstructing a ballet, we are grateful for every bit of information found. And, as the pieces fall into place, we experience the pleasure of compulsive puzzle-solvers. But there are moments when conflicting evidence presents itself. Our method on these occasions is to re-evaluate the sources and place them in hierarchical order. We ask which document or documentor has the greatest authority and use the information accordingly.

In *Le Sacre du printemps* we confronted highly particularized examples of contradictory evidence. Notes about Nijinsky's choreography had been written on two piano rehearsal scores of the ballet. They were not always easy to reconcile. One score was annotated by Stravinsky, who sometimes played at rehearsals, and the other by Rambert, who was the only person besides Nijinsky who knew every step for every dancer. In the case of musical cues for entrances and exits, if the indications varied, we tended to give Stravinsky priority. But Rambert got the first say in any allocation of movement to bars of music. Effectively, they ruled in their own realms of expertise.

Often, however, the effort to resolve such contradictions in *Le Sacre* ended up as a kind of Zen exercise in multiple truths, and we would discover how to use both sources at once. In the above case of entrance cues, disagreement sometimes arose because a handwritten note by Stravinsky, for instance, referred to only one group coming on stage, whereas the movement for a different group altogether was described by Rambert in her handwritten note for the same bar of music. If it could be proved from other data that the movement of both groups occurred simultaneously, then we have verified that both documentors were right and the contradiction was resolved to advantage.

In a more general way, *Skating Rink* presented another example of proofs which seemed to cancel each other out. Research yielded evidence of two contrary performing styles for this ballet. Some contemporary accounts likened the skaters to mechanical puppets. This stylization accords with Léger's painting at the time. The metallic robot figures on his canvases resembled the Swedish dancers, particularly in Léger's mask-like make-up, with large eyes for all, lips or moustaches for a few and a strange Cubist eye patch for the principal male, the Madman. Léger and Börlin clearly wanted to show massed forms in motion, fragmented by bold colour and pattern. What they put on stage invited critical clichés about mechanization in modern life.

Conversely, other contemporary accounts made much of the ballet's passionate style of performance, not just for the Madman and the lead couple, the lovers, but also for the skating crowd. The more we learned about the Apache dancing which influenced the ballet, the more we

Figure 7.3 Le Sacre du printemps page from piano score marked with Marie Rambert's notes from the 1913 rehearsals, showing musical cues for the repetitive falls. Act II, scene iii, 'Evocation of the ancestors'. (Courtesy of the Rambert Dance Company Archives.)

realized that the debate about puppets versus impassioned performers posed only an apparent contradiction; it matched exactly the persona of those addicted to this dance craze. Apache dance halls in the poor *arrondissements* of Paris were infamous for anonymous encounters, full of attraction, aggression and loss. Contemporary critics had trouble embracing the paradox of this ballet's performing style. Their reviews fixated on one aspect or the other, mechanical or near pathological. Both critical reactions were defensible but incomplete in themselves.

Relâche provided the most complex example of contradictory data. Its defiance of convention turned contradiction into a principle of aesthetics. The ballet's title is itself a contradiction in terms. The French word *relâche* means 'closed, no performance'. The creators of the ballet chose a title which said 'the theatre is shut', but they really meant the opposite: the theatre is opening up, starting anew. To this end they acted by the law of contraries. Instead of letting cinema threaten the theatre, they incorporated the virgin art of film into their ballet; rather than idealizing the dancers with footlights, they made a decor of glittering headlights so that the audience was in the performers' spot, facing the glare; but the real tour de force was that they passed off a meticulously rehearsed spectacle as improvisation. Spontaneity, glamour, the exhilarating momentum of life in the 1920s: they made room in the theatre for these qualities by dismantling tradition through mockery. Instead of a plot they had what seemed like impromptu events: a flapper pushing a wheelbarrow, a fire drill, and a curtain call with the composer and designer driving a miniature Citroën.

In *Relâche* the collaborators struggled to defeat predictability. But their success magnified our standard problem of predicting lost material. And since their principle of creation was to say one thing and do another, they complicated our normal procedure of building up proof through measuring statements of intention against results. We had to question all the pronouncements they made, before, during and after the première.

Asked to describe *Relâche*, Francis Picabia, its scenarist and designer, said: 'you will see in it a very lovely woman, a handsome man, many handsome men in fact', adding that it moved like 'a 300 HP engine on the best road, lined with trees slanting in the illusion created by speed' (De Maré 1932: 74; Häger (1989/1990: 252). The slanting road and trees were a special effect in René Clair's film *Entr'acte*, which was made for projection between the two acts of the ballet. The throng of handsome men derived from Picabia's draft scenario: thirty men in tuxedos were to rise from their seats at the Théâtre des Champs-Elysées and mount the stage in single file. It sounds like a Busby Berkeley film, and indeed Hollywood tuxedo movies of the 1930s owed something to this ballet, which launched the ironic use of modern evening dress on stage and screen. In the event, *Relâche* had only ten men in tuxedos, one of many changes made in the course of the work. As reconstructors, we have had to distinguish between the Dada pose of contrariness adopted by Picabia, Clair, Börlin and composer, Erik Satie, and the usual contradictions of evidence that result from the fact that the ballet became lost.

7.6   CONTEXT IS ALL, ALMOST

Every reconstruction benefits from the effort of building up layers of contextual information. This exercise is as effective for ballets of the twentieth century as it is for those of the Renaissance. However, the passage of time helps period style to gel. The very proximity of the ballets of our century, and the masses of documentation about the life surrounding them, make it necessary to identify sharply the context of each work. For example, when we researched for *La Chatte*, we tried to specify what made the year 1927 unique. In the newspapers and magazines where we found reviews of the ballet, we studied popular news items, fashion pages, advertisements for new gadgets and so forth. We discovered that the vinyl headgear Gabo had designed for the male corps was not only based on the helmets of Greek warriors but also resembled haute couture hats for Parisian women that season, cloche-shaped with vinyl visors, imitating the aviator's kit worn by hero of the hour, Charles Lindbergh. Specificity is what makes the twentieth century, and its ballets, fascinating to the people still living in it.

The study of context has proven to be especially important for those ballets that make modern life their subject. For audiences now it can be hard to imagine a world in which ballet never treated life in the present. The ballet of Imperial Russia, under Marius Petipa, had dealt obliquely with contemporary events, but always as a springboard out of real time. Well-known photographs show Petipa in the sole of Lord Wilson in his *Daughter of the Pharaoh* (1862), dressed in the desert wear of a British Egyptologist. Exploration of the pyramids was a modish adventure of the mid-nineteenth century, but Petipa's contemporaneity began and ended with that costume. His ballet was not about Victorian exploits but an opium fantasy in an Egyptian tomb, based on *The Romance of the Mummy* by Théophile Gautier.

Nijinsky's *Jeux* was the first ballet to show the twentieth century to itself. To reconstruct it we immersed ourselves in contextual research. Nijinsky had decided, while watching tennis at the seaside resort of Deauville, that dance should make use of actual movement from modern life (Buckle 1971: 290). He explored this conviction in *Jeux*. The ballet's subject, a love triangle, was not unusual but that it took the form of a contemporary game was. 'It is said that M. Nijinsky's intention was to provide, in this ballet, an apologia in plastic terms for the man of 1913', reported *Le Figaro* after the première (Buckle 1971: 289). We traced books and articles from the years before the First World War that dealt with tennis and other sports Nijinsky admired, and we compared the images with the drawings and photographs that survive of *Jeux*, looking closely at distribution of weight, muscular tension and posture. In 1913 critics and spectators joked about the idosyncrasies of 'Russian tennis', but, of course, Nijinsky was doing much more than demonstrating athletic moves. He was sculpting them into emotional statements by the three players. The novelty of *Jeux* derived, above all, from how the choreographer exposed the psychological awkwardness of the triangular affair through fragmented movement.

Critical reviews and commentaries on the ballet all made an issue of this fragmentation, which contrasted so with the fluidity of Claude Debussy's score. *Jeux* had the disjunctive unity of film. It looked to the audience like a 'cinematographic ballet in which movements are broken down into their component parts and which are not normally visible to the eye' (Krasovskaya 1974/1979: 253). As another reconstruction method, we sought out newsreels of the period, analysing the reportage of sports, searching for sources to the stop-and-start rhythm of the steps which troubled Nijinsky's contemporaries. Even though there was no film of *Jeux* itself, the medium was already so vital to the context of daily life that film became an aid in reconstruction.

A decade later the choreography of Börlin for *Within the Quota* literally had cinematic roots. He danced the role of the Swedish immigrant who has just arrived in Cole Porter's Manhattan. As Gilbert Seldes wrote in *Paris Journal* in 1923, 'The figures passing before the immigrant's eyes are the mythical heroes of modern American life, in part as the average European imagines them from the cinema, in part as they really are' (Häger 1989/1990: 212). As a reconstruction method, we studied movies featuring the ballet's archetypes: multimillionairess, cowboy, jazzbaby, observing not only their body language but also how the camera presented them to the spectator. The ballet includes among its characters a cinematographer who directs the others in their poses.

Another decade later, Balanchine's *La Concurrence* drew upon contemporary fashion photography and illustration. Boris Kochno, who oversaw this ballet about a competition between tailors, was a confidant of Coco Chanel. Even though the ballet was set in provincial France of the late 1890s, it really reflected urbane fashion feuds of the early 1930s, calling to mind the battles we now witness between designers like Giorgio Armani and Gianni Versace. The tip-off from Kochno about such feuds as influences on *La Concurrence* sent us to archives *de la mode* to compare fashion plates with photographs of the ballet. In the absence of other documentation, contextual sources like these often provide crucial clues which can transform a ballet from lost to found.

NOTES

1 The select bibliography lists recommended reading about the original ballets and reconstructions discussed in this essay. We have restricted the recommended books to general texts about the companies and choreographers. Articles about reconstructions are limited to those which primarily deal with working methods. In the notes that follow, production details of each work are given to correspond with the first reference in the text. All reconstructions, except *L'Après-midi d'un faune*, are by the authors.

   Le Sacre du printemps: scenario, Nicholas Roerich and Igor Stravinsky; music, Stravinsky; decor and costumes, Roerich; choreography, Vaslav Nijinsky. Première: 29 May 1913, by Sergei Diaghilev's Ballets Russes, Théâtre des Champs-Elysées, Paris.

   Reconstruction première: 30 September 1987, by Joffrey Ballet, the Dorothy Chandler Pavilion, Los Angeles. Second staging: 3 April 1991, by Paris Opéra Ballet, Palais Garnier, Paris. Third staging: 11 March 1994, Finnish Ballet, Finnish National Opera, Helsinki.

   Video of Joffrey production: *The Search for Nijinsky's Rite of Spring*, WNET/THIRTEEN with BBC2 and La Sept; première: 24 November 1989, New York.

2 *L'Après-midi d'un faune*: scenario and choreography, Vaslav Nijinsky; music, Claude Debussy; decor and costumes, Léon Bakst. Première: 29 May 1912, by Sergei Diaghilev's Ballets Russes, Théâtre du Châtelet, Paris.

   Reconstruction première: 11 April 1989, Beppe Menegatti and Carla Fracci production with Teatro di San Carlo, Naples. Second staging: 27 October 1989, Les Grands Ballets Canadiens, Salle Wilfrid-Pelletier, Montreal. Third staging: 8 December 1989, Julliard School, New York.

   Video of Julliard production: *A Revival of Nijinsky's Original L'Après-midi d'un faune*, Harwood Academic Publishers, London and New York.

3 *Jeux*: scenario and choreography, Vaslav Nijinsky; music, Claude Debussy; decor and costumes, Léon Bakst. Première: 15 May 1913, Théâtre des Champs-Elysées, Paris.

4 *Till Eulenspiegel*: scenario, Richard Strauss and Vaslav Nijinsky; music, Richard Strauss; decor and costumes, Robert Edmond Jones; choreography, Nijinsky. Première: 23 October 1916, by Sergei Diaghilev's Ballets Russes, Manhattan Opera House, New York.

   Reconstruction première: 9 February 1994, by Paris Opéra Ballet, Palais Garnier, Paris.

5 *La Chatte*: scenario, Boris Kochno (Sobeka); music, Henri Sauguet; decor and costumes, Naum Gabo and Antoine Pevsner; choreography, George Balanchine. Première, 30 April 1927, by Sergei Diaghilev's Ballets Russes, Théâtre de Monte-Carlo, Monte-Carlo.

   Reconstruction première: 3 May 1991, by Les Grands Ballets Canadiens, Salle Wilfrid-Pelletier, Montreal.

6 *Cotillon*: scenario, Boris Kochno; music, Emmanuel Chabrier, orchestrated by Chabrier, Felix Mottl and Vittorio Rieti; decor and costumes, Christian Bérard; choreography, George Balanchine. Première: 17 January 1932, by Colonel Vassili de Basil's Ballets Russes, Théâtre de Monte-Carlo, Monte-Carlo.

   Reconstruction première: 26 October 1988, by Joffrey Ballet, City Center Theater, New York.

7 *La Concurrence*: scenario, decor and costumes, André Derain; music, Georges Auric; choreography, George Balanchine. Première: 17 January 1932, by

Colonel Vassili de Basil's Ballets Russes, Théâtre de Monte-Carlo, Monte-Carlo.

8 *Relâche*: scenario, decor and costumes, Francis Picabia; music, Erik Satie; cinematic entr'acte, René Clair; choreography, Jean Börlin. Première: 4 December 1924, by Rolf de Maré's Ballet Suédois, Théâtre des Champs-Elysées, Paris.

9 *Skating Rink*: scenario, Riciotto Canudo; music, Arthur Honegger; decor and costumes, Fernand Léger; choreography, Jean Börlin. Première: 20 January 1922, by Rolf de Maré's Ballet Suédois, Théâtre des Champs-Elysées, Paris.

10 *Within the Quota*: scenario, decor and costumes, Gerald Murphy; music, Cole Porter, orchestrated by Charles Koechlin; choreography, Jean Börlin. Première: 25 October 1923, by Rolf de Maré's Ballet Suédois, Théâtre des Champs-Elysées, Paris.

11 At the time we reconstructed *Cotillon* in 1988, the Hand of Fate pas de deux was known from a 1983 Brooklyn College programme by the Tulsa Ballet. Its directors, Roman Jasinski and Moscelyne Larkin, knew it from their tours with Alexandra Danilova in the 1950s as well as from their days with de Basil's Ballets Russes. As we had access to early performers of this pas de deux, we decided not to consult the video of the Tulsa version, although Jasinski and Larkin very kindly advised us on other roles from *Cotillon* which they had danced.

SELECT BIBLIOGRAPHY

A single asterisk (*) indicates a text on the Ballets Russes of Sergei Diaghilev, 1909–29; a double asterisk (**), the Ballets Suédois of Rolf de Maré, 1920–4; and a triple asterisk (***), the Ballets Russes of Colonel Vassili de Basil, 1932–52.

*Archer, K. (1986–7), 'Nicholas Roerich and his theatrical designs: a research survey', *Dance Research Journal*, 18, 2: 3–6.

*—— (1987), 'Roerich's *Sacre* rediscovered: the Lincoln Center exhibition', *Ballet Review*, 15, 2: 75–82.

*—— (1990), 'Nicholas Roerich' and 'Un Festin visuel d'une violence absolue', in E. Sourian *et al.*, *Le Sacre du printemps de Nijinsky*, Paris: Cicero: 75–96 and 97–103.

***Archer, K. and Hodson, M. (1988), 'The Quest for Cotillon', *Ballet Review*, 16, 2: 31–46.

*—— (1991), 'Hot purrrsuit: in search of Balanchine's La Chatte', *Dance*, 65, 5: 42–7.

*—— (1992), 'Nijinsky for the 90s – Till Eulenspiegel is coming back', *Dance Now*, 1, 1: 10–20.

**Banes, S. (1978–9), 'An introduction to the Ballets Suédois', *Ballet Review*, 7, 2–3: 28–59.

*Beck, J. (ed.) (1991), 'A revival of Nijinsky's original L'Après-midi d'un Faune', *Choreography and Dance*, vol. 1, part 3 (with video) London and New York: Harwood Academic Publishers.

*Buckle, R. (1971), *Nijinsky*, London: Weidenfeld & Nicolson.

*—— (1979), *Diaghilev*, London: Weidenfeld & Nicolson.

***—— (1988), *George Balanchine, Ballet Master*, London: Hamish Hamilton.

**De Maré, R. (1932), *Les Ballets Suédois*, Paris: Trianon.

***Detaille, G. (1954), *Les Ballets de Monte-Carlo, 1911–44*, Paris: Arc-en-Ciel.

*Everett-Green, R. (1991), 'Dance notation: ballet's missing link', *Globe and*

Mail, Toronto, 4 May, section C3: 1.

*Garafola, L. (1989), *Diaghilev's Ballets Russes*, New York and Oxford: Oxford University Press.

***García-Márquez, V. (1990), *The Ballets Russes*, New York: Alfred A. Knopf.

*Guest, A. (ed.) (1991), *Nijinsky's Faune Restored*, Philadelphia and Reading: Gordon & Breach.

**Häger, B. (1989), *Ballet Suédois*, Paris: Jacques Damase Editeur and Editions Denöel; English ed. 1990, trans. R. Sharman, London: Thames & Hudson.

*Hodson, M. (1985–6), 'Ritual design in the new dance', *Dance Research*, 3, 2 and 4, 1: 35–45 and 63–77.

*—— (1987), '*Sacre*: searching for Nijinsky's Chosen One', *Ballet Review*, 15, 3: 53–66.

*—— (1990), 'Puzzles chorégraphiques', in E. Souriau *et al.*, *Le Sacre du printemps de Nijinsky*, Paris: Cicero, pp. 45–74.

*Jowitt, D. (1987), 'The shock of the old: restoring Nijinsky's "Sacre"', *Village Voice*, New York, 3 November: 22, 24, 27–8.

*Krasovskaya, V. (1974), *Nijinsky*, Leningrad; English ed. 1979, trans. John E. Bowlt, New York: Schirmer Books.

*Macdonald, N. (1975), *Diaghilev Observed by Critics in England and the United States, 1911–1929*, London: Dance Books.

**Näslund, E. (ed.) (1990), *Fernand Léger & Svenska Baletten*, exhibition catalogue, Stockholm: Dansmuseet & Bukowskis.

*Segal, L. (1987), 'The re-Rite of Spring', *Los Angeles Times*, 5 July, calendar section: 54–5, 58.

***Solway, D. (1988), 'How "Cotillon" was reborn', *New York Times*, 23 October, arts and leisure section.

***Sorley Walker, K. (1982), *De Basil's Ballets Russes*, London: Hutchinson.

***Taper, B. (1963), *Balanchine: A Biography*, 3rd rev. ed., New York: Times Books.

***Victorica, V. (1948), *El Original Ballet Russe en America Latina*, Buenos Aires: Arturo Jacinto Alvarez.

Chapter 8

Enrico Cecchetti

The influence of tradition

Giannandrea Poesio

8.1 INTRODUCTION

Among the great pedagogues and theorists who have made a substantial contribution to the development of ballet technique, Enrico Cecchetti (1850–1928) is one of the most prominent figures. Cecchetti, in the same way as Thoinot Arbeau, Pierre Rameau and Carlo Blasis, owes his fame mainly to the written codification of his teachings and to the creation of a 'method' through which his doctrines have been passed on to posterity.

This Italian dancer, choreographer and ballet-master is generally regarded as the man who perpetuated the principles of a tradition which otherwise might have been lost. According to documented biographical sources, Cecchetti received the fundamentals of his art from Giovanni Lepri, a former pupil of Carlo Blasis who is considered 'the first pedagogue of the classical ballet' (Beaumont 1959). In consequence dance historians have considered the 'Cecchetti Method', codified and published in 1922, to be directly derived from Blasis's precepts. This assumption can, however, be questioned, for it is based on a superficial equation which omits significant elements. Moreover, the attention paid to the analysis of both the Method and its vocabulary has diverted dance research from other and no less important aspects of Cecchetti as an artist.

For example, with the exception of some biographical accounts, a study of the milieu in which the young Cecchetti began his career has not been written. Similarly, the years he worked in Russia as a performer, a teacher and a choreographer have largely been ignored, the only element of interest being his influence on the evolution of the Russian ballet technique, regardless of his other activities. Finally, there are no written works providing a comparative analysis of Cecchetti's career.

It is significant that Cecchetti operated within three different areas of theatrical dancing: that is, the Italian *ballo grande*, the Russian Imperial Ballet and Diaghilev's Ballets Russes, passing from one to the other with remarkable eclecticism. What is surprising is that his artistic principles, formulated during the first years in Italy, suited all these different contexts. This is particularly evident in relation to the work Cecchetti did while with Diaghilev's Ballets Russes. Within this context, the Italian 'Maestro', as the dancers of the company referred to him, could have easily appeared to be the living symbol of both the balletic tradition and the theatrical conventions which they were expressly leaving behind. None the less the 'Maestro' was invited to teach the company and to coach some of its most important stars, including Nijinsky and Lifar. Furthermore, his artistic skills, mainly as a mime dancer, were used in several ballets belonging to the new genre such as *Le Carnaval* (Fokine, 1910), *Shehérazade* (Fokine, 1910), *Firebird* (Fokine, 1910), *Petrushka* (Fokine, 1911) and *The Good Humoured Ladies* (Massine, 1917).

8.1.1   The sources

Although a comprehensive collection of the sources directly related to Cecchetti does not exist, the Dance Collection of the New York Public Library (NYPL) is particularly important, for it holds some of the most significant Cecchetti items. This material was formerly part of the private collection of Cia Fornaroli, an Italian ballerina and one of the last pupils of Cecchetti at La Scala, who became the principal of La Scala ballet school after the death of the Maestro. Among these items are the manuscript of the daily classes Cecchetti taught in St Petersburg together with a considerable number of ballet scenarios and programmes, photographs and clippings recording the artistic activity of each member of the Cecchetti family. This material, however, illustrates only certain sections of the Maestro's life, and needs to be integrated with other more detailed documentation.

The NYPL dance collection also contains most of the written works about Cecchetti, and the updated listing of these publications in the catalogue provides a useful instrument for reference. Under the heading 'Enrico Cecchetti, works about', there are fifty-one items. With the exception of eleven ballet scenarios, a miscellany of clippings and photographs and two articles in Italian, the works are all in English. There are two reasons for this. On the one hand, dance history literature has developed more in English-speaking countries than elsewhere. On the other, since the Method was codified and published in England, where the foundation of the Cecchetti Society took place, Cecchetti has come to be regarded as belonging to the English theatre culture. This is also demonstrated by the scarcity of sources written in other languages, none of which are included in the NYPL collection, a rare example being a biographical study in Italian by Rossi (1978).

Among the fifty-one works listed in the NYPL catalogue are thirty-seven articles or brief essays. The remainder includes a technique book in which the Cecchetti Method is compared with the teachings of Auguste Bournonville (Bruhn and Moore 1961); a reference book where Cecchetti is discussed in relation to Diaghilev's Ballets Russes (Beaumont 1940); and two biographies, one in the form of collected memoirs (Racster 1922) and the other a short monograph (Beaumont 1929). The articles are not homogeneous in their range: 2 per cent discuss some aspects of the Maestro's discipline; 18 per cent contain personal recollections of eye-witnesses; 35 per cent are brief biographical accounts, and 45 per cent are of mixed content, technical and biographical.

This heterogeneous secondary source material has contributed, through the years, to the creation of a well-established image of the Maestro. However, analysis reveals changes in attitudes to Cecchetti; it shows how some features have been highlighted and others neglected and, in some instances, it may provide the reasons for these choices. At the same time, an evaluation reveals several different approaches to the subject: biographical, anecdotal and critical. Finally, the investigation of these components enables the historical dimension of the topic to be delineated. The challenge then is to verify, to test and to reassess the posthumous image of Enrico Cecchetti, thereby to create a new framework for subsequent research.

The early years of Cecchetti are particularly problematic to the historian. Immediately after 1861, the offices and the archives of the newly unified Italian kingdom were more concerned with the problems of the nascent political establishment than with the recording of theatrical matters. Hence, the only reliable sources are the private archives of the theatres of that period, together with ballet programmes, play-bills and the reviews published in various newspapers. The press material is certainly the most abundant and the most interesting, for these accounts reveal the taste and the trends of the period. Moreover, despite the absence of 'dance critics', the reviewers were competent ballet-goers, and left a quantity of invaluable detailed technical description. In this respect, a useful publication is the monthly newspaper *L'Italia artistica*, published in Florence between 1860 and 1889. This newspaper dealt only with theatre news, providing extensive reviews of the main events, constantly updating reports of the theatres' seasons, as well as descriptions of the artists' engagements both in Italy and abroad, and general biographical information about the artists, including their schools. This source of information is particularly relevant to research on Cecchetti, for it covers the years he spent in Italy. Moreover *L'Italia artistica* provides a basis for the contextualization of the subject. The newspaper was published during the years Florence was 'capital' of the new kingdom, namely from 1865 to 1870; therefore it aimed to cover theatre facts on a national scale. In consequence, articles related to dance give an almost complete description of that epoch of Italian theatrical dancing.

Theatre archives and private collections are a more complex field of research. With the exception of the museum annexed to La Scala, Italian theatres seldom house archives with comprehensive records going back to the Cecchetti period. Some of the theatre collections are kept in public libraries or in institutions related to the theatre arts such as the Conservatoire of St Cecilia in Rome, which includes a rich collection of ballet programmes from the last century. Private collections are the most difficult to deal with, for some of them are generally unknown or inaccessible. Fortunately a number of these collections have been donated to public archives. For example, the Historical Communal Archives in Florence include large portions of the collection of the Accademia degli Immobili, which administered La Pergola Theatre in the same town for three centuries.

In contrast, the source material related to the years Cecchetti spent abroad does not present particular problems. The Theatre Museum in St Petersburg provides a unique point of reference as it houses vast documentation about the era of the Imperial Russian ballet, hence providing relevant contextualization to the subject. In addition, the works of Slominsky (1937), Krasovskaja (1963) and Roslaveva (1966), although not directly related to Cecchetti, supply an important source of analysis of the period from different historical perspectives.

Similarly, the years Cecchetti spent with Diaghilev's Ballets Russes are very well documented. Archives and collections have been acknowledged in the abundant publications related to the Ballets Russes and there is no need to reproduce those listings in this context. The same applies to the English part of Cecchetti's life which is accurately documented by the Cecchetti Society and, more particularly, by Cyril Beaumont's various texts. The early appearances of Cecchetti in England can be traced either through reference to recent works, as in Guest (1959 and 1992), or by consulting public or private collections. Finally, the last years of the Maestro's activity in England and in Italy can be documented through the recollections of many witnesses who are still alive.

8.2   THE ITALIAN YEARS: CECCHETTI AND THE *BALLO GRANDE*

Within the context of nineteenth-century European dance history, Italian theatrical dancing is unique in failing to respond to foreign influence, not even being susceptible to the widespread appeal of the French Romantic ballet. This is evident from sources such as the chronicles of the performances at La Scala theatre in Milan (Cambiasi 1906) or the annals of La Pergola Theatre in Florence (Morini 1926). Dancers, choreographers and works in the Romantic style were generally welcomed, but they never monopolized the Italian ballet, which remained linked to the modes of a well-defined national form of choreography. Ballet scenarios or programmes of that period show the tendency to use the word 'ballet', and its Italian equivalent *balletto*, in connection with productions imported from abroad. The term *ballo* indicated the Italian genre. Although it would be too hazardous to state that the use of different terms corresponded to a straight classification of two genres of theatrical dancing, there are no doubts that the *ballo* was based on principles stemming from a well-rooted tradition which found its forerunner in Salvatore Viganò, and was not related to the canons of the French 'ballet'.

In the first decade of the century, Viganò had given new vital impulses to the renewal of the choreographic art, by creating the *coreodramma*, where a rhythmic use of mime gestures had more prominence than pure dancing. The *coreodramma* required large-scale productions, and although Viganò's successors were not able to reproduce his artistic formulae, they preserved the colossal dimensions of the performances. Hence the name *ballo grande*, or 'great *ballo*', which, in the second half of the nineteenth century, came to refer to a form of theatrical dancing based on a mixture of different techniques and different theatrical elements. This mixture mirrored the various stages that Italian choreography had passed through in the first fifty years of the century.

In 1837 the French–Italian dancer and ballet master Carlo Blasis was appointed Director of the Academy of Dance attached to La Scala theatre in Milan. Blasis is said to have codified the principles of the classical ballet technique still practised today. It can be argued that his contribution was to revise and to adapt the formulae of the French school where he had been trained (Blasis 1820, for discussion of this see Poesio 1993). With the advent of Blasis, pure dancing, previously rejected by Viganò, returned to fashion. Choreographers of Blasis's period (1837–50) had to face the problem of an artistic compromise between the classical 'French' dancing and the rhythmic 'Italian' mime action. The result established the definitive structure of the Italian *ballo grande*: a vast, spectacular production, generally in four, five or even six acts, in which the action was mainly mimed, interspersed with incidental dances. The difference from the canonic French ballets, where the mime action and the dancing were integrated in a different proportion, is evident.

In the first decade of the second half of the nineteenth century the *ballo grande* reflected the superficial optimism which followed the unification of the Italian kingdom. This attitude was the product of a blind faith in both politics and progress combined with an aura of bourgeois prosperity, either real or imagined. It was in this context that Enrico Cecchetti, born in 1850, learned the rudiments of his art, because his father, Cesare Cecchetti, in whose creations Enrico made his first professional appearances (Poesio 1992), was an exponent of that choreographic school. One of the prerequisites of the *ballo grande* was a specific 'spectacular' technique, based on 'tours de force' and on an endless outpouring of virtuoso feats. The young Cecchetti proved to be particularly suitable for this genre. According to *L'Italia artistica* (Anon. 1866: 8) he had reached the status of *primo ballerino assoluto* at the age of sixteen, despite the fact that he was short and had rather strong features and, therefore, lacked the necessary 'elegance' pre-scribed as one of the essential elements in order to be a principal or 'serious dancer' (Blasis 1830: 88–92).

It would be a mistake, however, to consider Enrico Cecchetti as the first Italian male dancer to gain popularity for his technical skills. His was not a unique case, since he belonged to a well-affirmed tradition of Italian male dancers (Pesci 1886: 155; Tani 1983: 490–1). This is a factor which deserves particular attention. In dance history manuals it is generally reported that in nineteenth-century Europe, with the ex-ception of Russia and Denmark, the figure of the male dancer played no significant role in ballet. An example of this historical generalization can be found in Jean-Pierre Pastori's comprehensive study (1980: 65–6) on the evolution of the male dancer throughout different epochs. The assertion is disputable for it does not take into consideration either the Italian tradition or several other elements. In Italy the male dancer, as an artist with a well-defined identity, and not just as a human support for the ballerina, had reached independent status since Carlo Blasis's appearances on several stages (Anon. 1854; Tani 1983: 474–6; Poesio 1993). Later, it was Blasis who, as director of the Milanese Academy, formed and trained several generations of 'primi ballerini' as indicated in a brief account of the Academy which registers the name of Blasis's most important pupils (Blasis 1847: 75–7).

By the end of the century the *ballo grande* tended towards the imitation of the formulae of the French *féerie*, namely a spectacular performance where the plot was a pretext to produce theatrical effects. The most characteristic examplars of this artistic influence were the three *balli* performed at La Scala theatre in Milan and created by Luigi Manzotti, a mime dancer and choreographer who had worked with Cesare Cecchetti. *Excelsior* (Manzotti, 1881) celebrated scientific pro-gress and discoveries such as electricity and steam-engines, with a finale in which, once Light had defeated Obscurantism, the various nations, led by Civilization, joined together in an optimistic and lighthearted gallop. *Amor* (Manzotti, 1886), in which Enrico Cecchetti created the role of a satyr, was a more ambitious project. It summed up the history of love through the ages, with a large deployment of animals, acrobats and machinery (Poesio 1990: 28–35). Finally, *Sport* (Manzotti, 1897) was a fantasy on the various sports of the world. The style of this *ballo* was very close to that of the French *grande revue* as still practised today at the Moulin Rouge; the choreography, with the exception of the solos and the pas de deux, which were very demanding, resembled the creations of Hollywood's Busby Berkeley in the 1930s. None the less Manzotti's works were greatly acclaimed and became the symbols of the era. *Excelsior* in particular, with its message of international brotherhood, became so popular that it was performed outside Italy. In 1885 the *ballo* received its London première, with Enrico Cecchetti as principal dancer.

8.3   THE YEARS ABROAD

8.3.1   Cecchetti and the Imperial Russian Ballet: from principal dancer to ballet-master

A recurring factor in the history of Italian theatrical dancing is that, since the Renaissance, Italian dancers and ballet-masters have left the country to pursue their careers abroad. This innate artistic nomadism, the analysis of which would make a separate study, characterized the life of several dynasties of dancers, the Cecchetti family among them. In 1857, the Cecchettis, including 7-year-old Enrico, travelled to the United States and toured in Philadelphia, Louisville and Baltimore (Racster 1922: 11–14). In 1874, as a young professional dancer he performed in Denmark, in Norway and, together with his sister Pia and his younger brother Giuseppe, at the Orpheum Theatre in Berlin, where, in 1878, he married Giuseppina de Maria, destined to become a celebrated mime of the Imperial Russian Ballet and of the Diaghilev Company. In 1887 Cecchetti appeared in St Petersburg, as both the principal dancer and the manager of a small group of Italian dancers, which included his wife Giuseppina and the ballerina Giovannina Limido. Cecchetti had already made his debut in Russia, dancing for the first time in 1874 in St Petersburg and then in 1881 at the Bolshoi Theatre in Moscow. However, it was the 1887 engagement that changed his life and that of Russian ballet.

The Arcadia Theatre, where the company performed, was a theatre of 'varieties' and not a stage of cultural reputation (Legat 1932: 15). This is particularly interesting, for it indicates the Russian attitude towards Italian dancing at this time. Prior to the arrival of Cecchetti, Virginia Zucchi, another great Italian dancer who had a notable influence on the Russian ballet, made her debut at a 'cabaret' and only afterwards was invited to appear on the stage of the Imperial Theatres (Roslaveva 1966: 113). The dazzling feats and the Italian taste in choreography, which favoured spectacular elements to the detriment of artistic qualities, appealed to the Russian audiences only as an entertainment or as a 'theatrical' phenomenon, very close to the circus. Witnesses of the time report that the Italian technique was based mainly on 'tour de force' and possessed neither grace nor elegance (Legat 1932: 16), while dance scholars affirm that Marius Petipa, the French choreographer and ballet-master who directed the Petersburg ballet for fifty years, 'denied any artistic value in *Excelsior* and its like' (Roslaveva 1966: 113). The repertoire of Cecchetti's company at the Arcadia Theatre was, in fact, a compendium of Italian taste. The brief season included *Excelsior*, in a reduced version, *Sieba* (1878), a work also by Manzotti, based on a mixture of Saxon legends, and *Le Pouvoir de l'amour* (1887), a ballet choreographed by Cecchetti himself. The three works were an excellent device to show the skills of the two Italian dancers at their best. In summarizing the enthusiastic comments written in the journalistic style of the period, Lifar reports that Limido 'sung with her pirouettes' (Lifar 1954: 145) and that Cecchetti's 'batterie' made him 'look like a cyclone' (Lifar 1954: 146).

The sensation caused by Cecchetti's technique was one of the main causes for his engagement as a principal dancer of the Imperial Ballet on 4 November 1887, although it should be remembered that it was fashionable during this period to 'import' foreign dancers. The earlier cult of Virginia Zucchi had induced people to believe in a supposed superiority of the Italian school over the Russian. Although the Russian schools prepared male dancers in the 1880s, people lamented the lack of a 'real artist', as revealed in the memoirs of the Russian mime dancer Timofej Stukolkin (in Wiley 1990: 109). Therefore it is not surprising that the engagement of Cecchetti, regarded as another exotic phenomenon of the dance, was so prompt.

However, Marius Petipa was well aware of the limitations of the Italian dancer. Cecchetti never had access to those 'noble' roles usually related to the rank of principal dancer. With remarkable intuition, Petipa knew how to employ Cecchetti's talent, using it for a selected range of interpretations, an aspect rarely emphasized sufficiently in previous research. The Italian dancer was usually employed either as a mime or as a particular kind of dancer, which could not be properly classified. In *Kalkabrino* (Petipa, 1891) he was a smuggler, a 'grotesque' character, and in *The Caprices of a Butterfly* (1889), a minor ballet by Petipa, he appeared as a grasshopper with a little violin. Even the most celebrated role he created, that of the Blue Bird in the third act of *The Sleeping Beauty* (Petipa, 1890) is hybrid, half way between a 'character' role, as revealed by the nature of the part, and a 'noble' role, as determined by the range of steps employed.

Cecchetti maintained the rank of principal dancer until 1902, even though he had ceased to dance long before that date. In the meantime he was appointed second ballet-master in 1887 and in 1892 he became a teacher of the Imperial School of Dancing. About this appointment, Nicolas Legat wrote the desire to exploit Italian technique to the utmost was exemplified by the invitation to Enrico Cecchetti to form a class at the Imperial Theatre School. It was referred to as the 'parallel' class, and was for girls only. Cecchetti was as brilliant a teacher as he was dancer, exceedingly thorough and painstaking, through terribly hot-tempered. But he taught the Italian style only.

(Legat 1932: 22)

To be second ballet-master meant also to stage and to choreograph ballets, but Cecchetti's choreographic activity in Russia was unsuccessful. It had started with the ballet *Le Pouvoir de l'amour* at the Arcadia in 1887, which had had a cold reception. Later, in 1889, in collaboration with the composer Riccardo Drigo, the 39-year-old Enrico restaged an old Romantic ballet, *Cattarina, la fille du bandit,* originally choreographed by Perrot in 1846. In 1893 he contributed a few sections to the creation of *Cendrillon,* by Petipa and Lev Ivanov and, finally, at the request of Petipa in 1894, he staged a new version of the ballet *Coppelia* for the Italian ballerina Pierina Legnani. Guest reports that 'although the ballet was generally well received, Cecchetti's choreography was criticised for its lack of taste' (1970: 37).

The Italian taste, in fact, did not match the French–Russian choreographic canons formulated and developed by Petipa, while the formulae of the *ballo grande* in the Manzotti style did not appeal to audiences accustomed to the refined geometrical patterns which characterized ballets such as *Sleeping Beauty.* In consequence, following his appointment as teacher of the ballet school, Cecchetti directed his choreographic efforts only to the creation of ballets for his pupils. Interestingly, however, despite the fact that Cecchetti was not directly involved in the creation of *The Sleeping Beauty* or of *Raymonda* (Petipa, 1898), in both ballets there are some choreographic elements which might have been 'suggested' to Petipa by the technical combinations from the Italian artistic tradition. In particular, as acknowledged by Luigi Rossi (1978: 66), the male variation and the coda of the Blue Bird pas de deux (*The Sleeping Beauty*) are structured on an intricate aerial *batterie* which was characteristic of the Italian school. In various instances this factor has led dance historians to conclude that part of the choreography of the pas de deux must be credited to Cecchetti (Koegler 1977: 63). More cautiously, Natalia Roslaveva affirmed that

the delicate, elegant pattern of the Princess Florine's dancing, and the soaring leaps and batterie of the Blue Bird, were conceived by Petipa (as in the case of all the characters from Perrault's fairy-tales) with the special talents of the two performers in view.

(Roslaveva 1966: 105–6)

Similarly, the variation for four principal male dancers in the grand pas in the last act of *Raymonda* can be considered as another derivation from the Italian school. Lifar has suggested that 'this was Cecchetti's idea' (Lifar 1954: 156). Although there is no documentation to support Lifar's theory, it is interesting to note that in Cesare Cecchetti's ballet *La donna di marmo* (1872), premièred at La Pergola theatre in Florence, the same choreographic feature occurred, one of the four men being Enrico, Cesare's son (Anon. 1872: 7).

8.3.2 Cecchetti and Diaghilev's Ballets Russes: tradition and new formulae

In 1902 Cecchetti left the Imperial Ballet. The reasons for his resignation are uncertain and there is no clear evidence since the facts of the case are unavailable. On the one hand, it is reported that

> after some time he was told that at the end of twenty-five years' service to the Tsar he would be entitled to a comfortable monthly pension of 900 roubles besides his salary, should he continue teaching. However, for this a small formality was necessary: he must become a Russian citizen, as had his predecessor Marius Petipa (who became Marius Ivanovitch) and the Dane Johannsen. Cecchetti, hearing this, frowned, and asked 'How does one write personally to the Tsar?' His letter follows: 'I, Enrico Cecchetti, desiring to keep my Italian citizenship, as an Italian should, have the honor of resigning as teacher at the Imperial Academy of Ballet.'
>
> (Celli 1946: 162)

On the other hand, other sources (Crisp 1990: 37) suggest that Captain Telyakowsky, appointed Director of the Imperial Theatres in 1901, was responsible for the dismissal of Cecchetti. Telyakowsky formulated a policy to renew the Imperial Theatres. This policy, which led to the subsequent dismissal of Marius Petipa in 1903, 'prepared the ground for the exodus of talent that eventually drained the Imperial Ballet of its younger generation' (Garafola 1989: 5); as a consequence, many of those artists were ready to join Diaghilev's company in 1909.

Enrico Cecchetti, however, did not belong to that group of dancers. In 1902 he accepted a post as ballet-master at the Imperial Dance School in Warsaw which he maintained for three years before going back to St Petersburg, where he opened a private school. The period in Warsaw is generally overlooked by dance historians, although its importance was considerable. Through Cecchetti the Russian ballerinas Olga Preobrajenska, Mathilde Kscehssinska, Vera Trefilova and Anna Pavlova performed in Warsaw, giving a significant impetus to the development of Polish ballet. Moreover, two of Cecchetti's Polish pupils, Stanislas

Idzikowsky, who later helped Cyril Beaumont in the codification of the Cecchetti Method, and Léon Woizikowsky, became principal dancers in Diaghilev's Ballets Russes.

The majority of the dancers who followed Diaghilev in his twenty-year-long enterprise had been trained under Cecchetti at the Imperial Ballet School. Therefore

> it was for this reason that Diaghilev's next move was to approach the eminent Italian professor of ballet Enrico Cecchetti who was at that time a member of the Mariinsky company and renowned as a master not only for dancing, but also for mime.
>
> Cecchetti, to his delight, agreed to join him; and Diaghilev announced the news to the assembled committee in high glee.
>
> (Grigoriev 1953: 45)

With the exception of the year 1913, which was spent accompanying Pavlova on her American tour, Cecchetti remained active with the Ballets Russes until 1918 when, for reasons of age and health, he decided to settle in London and to open a school. The ten years with the Diaghilev company confirmed Cecchetti's international reputation as his teachings answered the demands of different choreographers, such as Fokine, Nijinsky and Massine equally well. The Maestro knew how to adapt the rigid vocabulary of classical ballet to new modes and new styles without altering or misinterpreting the fundamentals of that vocabulary.

There is no evidence that Cecchetti shared the enthusiastic opinion of other dancers, choreographers and critics about the Ballets Russes or that he fully understood the artistic value of the whole enterprise. None the less, he appeared as a mime dancer in works which were far from the artistic canons to which he was accustomed. However, it is significant that he remained particularly attached to those parts which reflected the old traditions, such as that of Pantaloon in Fokine's *Le Carnaval* (1910). His appearances as a mime dancer lent a new shape to the art of ballet mime. Although he had matured artistically in full respect of the conventional gestures which could convey either sentences or single words, Cecchetti did not have any difficulty in combining the old rules to the new formulae of a more natural and freer range of movement, as demanded in works such as Fokine's *Petrushka* (1911).

8.4   THE METHOD

As I watched these classes, I would often ask myself this question. Maestro is nearly seventy. If anything should happen to him, what would become of this wonderful system of training. I decided that it must be recorded. In the same way that one is suddenly moved by an

uncontrollable impulse rashly to embark on a cherished scheme, I
became obsessed with the notion that I must attempt this task. I had
no special technical qualifications for the work, but I thought that I
could learn. I first appealed to an old friend, Stanislas Idzikowsky, a
premier danseur of the Diaghilev Ballet, and one of Maestro's
favourite pupils.

(Beaumont 1954: 2)

In this way Beaumont recalled what prompted the codification of
Cecchetti's teaching. Beaumont, with the initial help of Idzikowsky,
approached Cecchetti, who was by then living and teaching in London,
to propose the idea of writing the 'Cecchetti Method'. Since its
publication the book has been considered as the definitive written
compendium of Cecchetti's teaching and it is used today as the only
reference for analysing his particular kind of technique (Beaumont
1922). However, it is a rather limiting source of guidance, for this
codified Method represents only one version of Cecchetti's teachings,
that used in England. A comparison with the manuscript of the daily
classes in Russia immediately highlights several differences, especially
in the structure and the combination of the daily exercises, the use of
the arms, or *port de bras*, and, in some respects, the naming of the steps.
Similarly a comparison with the handwritten notes of some of Cecchetti's last pupils at La Scala, taken during the last four years of his
life (Radice n.d.) indicates significant variations from the Beaumont
text (1922).

From a historical point of view, the exercises contained in the *Manual*
are regarded as directly linked to the elements of dance practice
contained in the first of Blasis's treatises (Blasis 1820). What is generally
overlooked is the fact that some eighteen or nineteen years elapsed
between Lepri completing his dance training with Blasis at La Scala,
about 1845–6, and the opening of Lepri's celebrated school in Florence
in 1864, where Enrico Cecchetti studied. During these years Italian
ballet technique evolved towards forms and modes which were substantially different from those codified by Blasis. In 1851 Blasis resigned
from La Scala and his post was taken by Augusto Huss, a French–Italian
dancer, whose theories about theatrical dancing were opposed to those
of his predecessor. Huss embodied the new spectacular or 'virtuoso'
style and, being at La Scala – always considered as the most important
institution in the field of theatrical arts – provided the Italian ballet with
a constant reference for style and fashion. Although a specific study on
the subject has not yet been undertaken, there is evidence that Lepri's
dancing reflected the new trends. The abundant journalistic descriptions of his technical skills are, in this respect, a useful source.
Lepri's solos and 'variations' were structured on technical patterns

which were unknown to Blasis, as a comparison with the latter's manuals demonstrate (Poesio, 1993). Certainly Lepri passed on to Cecchetti the essential elements of this type of technique. It is clear, however, that some of the older principles formulated by Blasis were retained, especially in relation to the carriage of the arms. A forthcoming study on the evolution of Italian ballet technique in the nineteenth century will provide more evidence about these facts and a more detailed technical contextualization of Cecchetti, in order to allow a better evaluation of the Maestro (Pappacena forthcoming).

8.5   CONCLUSION

The death of Enrico Cecchetti, on 13 November 1928, coincided with the decline of Italian ballet. The advent of fascism, which considered ballet as an effeminate and lesser form of art, and the inputs of German Expressionist dance which found a fertile ground in Italy in consequence of the new political regime, were two of the main causes of this decline. Both as a dancer and a teacher Cecchetti was the last representative of a celebrated class of artists who did not have any *raison d'être* within the new cultural context.

None the less, thanks to several generations of dancers who had been trained with the Maestro, his teachings were perpetuated outside Italy. In the same way as Marius Petipa's formulae influenced the canons of many twentieth-century choreographers, particularly those of George Balanchine, Cecchetti's principles characterized the works and the careers of many artists of the dance. This influence is evident mainly in England, where the Cecchetti training was at the base of the works by Ninette de Valois, Marie Rambert, Frederick Ashton and Antony Tudor and still forms part of the study of dance for many professionals, choreographers and dance students.

In Russia the method formulated by Agrippina Jacovlevna Vaganova in 1934 and taught at the St Petersburg School, generally considered as one of the most complete set of ballet rules of this century, contains several elements derived from Cecchetti's principles. Vaganova was in fact a pupil of Olga Preobrajenska, one of Cecchetti's students in Russia. In France, both Preobrajenska and Mathilde Kschessinska taught until their deaths in Paris, respectively in 1962 and 1971, thus passing Cecchetti's doctrines on to many contemporary dancers. Finally, in the United States the influence of Cecchetti arrived through George Balanchine and Adolph Bolm, both dancers of Diaghilev's Ballets Russes, and also through the various Italian pupils of Cecchetti who pursued their careers in America. Among these pupils were Luigi Albertieri, a prominent teacher in New York till 1930, Cia Fornaroli, who taught at the School of American Ballet and at her own private school in New York from 1943 to 1950 and Gisella Caccialanza (1971), who published the *Letters from the Maestro*, which record the last days of Cecchetti.

BIBLIOGRAPHY

Anon. (1854), *Delle composizioni coreografiche e delle opere di Carlo Blasis*, Milan: Oliva.
Anon. (1866), 'Il ballo I Due Rivali', *L'Italia artistica*, Florence, 7, 6.
Anon. (1872), 'La Donna di marmo', *L'Italia artistica*, Florence, 14, 1.
Beaumont, C. W. (1929), *Enrico Cecchetti, a Memoir*, London: Beaumont.
—— (1940), *The Diaghilev Ballet in London*, London: Putnam.
—— (1954), 'Address from Mr. Beaumont', *Tribute to Maestro Cav. Enrico Cecchetti 1850–1929*, collected papers of a programme presented on Sunday 17 January 1954 at the Rudolf Steiner Hall, London.
—— (1959), 'The Cecchetti Society: a Dancing Times supplement', *Dancing Times*.
Beaumont, C. W. and Idzikowsky, S. (1922), *A Manual of the Theory and Practice of Classical Theatrical Dancing (Méthode Cecchetti)*, London: Beaumont.
Blasis, C. (1820), *Traité Elementaire, théorique et pratique de l'art de la danse*, Milan: Beati et Tenenti.
—— (1830) *The Code of Teprsichore*, London: Bulcock.
—— (1847), *Notes upon Dancing*, London: Delaporte.
Bruhn, E. and Moore, L. (1961), *Bournonville and Ballet Technique*, London: Putnam.
Caccialanza, G. (1971), *Letters from the Maestro: Enrico Cecchetti to Gisella Caccialanza*, New York: Dance Perspectives, 45.
Cambiasi, P. (1906), *La Scala 1778–1906*, Milan: La Scala.
Celli, V. (1946), 'Enrico Cecchetti', *Dance Index*, New York, 5, 7.
Crisp, C. (1990), Introduction to V. A. Telyakowsky, 'Memoirs', *Dance Research*, London, 8, 1: 37–46.
Garafola, L. (1989) *Diaghilev's Ballets Russes*, New York and Oxford: Oxford University Press
Grigoriev, S. (1953), *The Diaghilev Ballet, 1909–1929*, London: Constable.
Guest, I. (1959), 'The Alhambra Ballet', *Dance Perspectives*, New York, 4: 5–72.
—— (1970), *Two Coppelias*, London: Friends of Covent Garden.
—— (1992), *Ballet in Leicester Square*, London: Dance Books.
Koegler, H. (1977, 1982), *The Concise Oxford Dictionary of Ballet*, London and New York: Oxford University Press.
Krasovskaja, V. (1963), *Russian Ballet Theatre: Second half of the XIXth century*, Moscow and Leningrad.
Legat, N. (1932), *The Story of the Russian School*, London: British-Continental Press.
Lifar, S. (1954), *History of Russian Ballet*, London: Hutchinson.
Morini, U. (1926), *La R. Accademia degli Immobili ed il suo Teatro 'La Pergola'*, Pisa: Simoncini.
Pappacena, F. (forthcoming) *Italian Ballet Technique*, Rome.
Pastori, J. (1980), *L'Homme et la danse*, Paris: Vilo.
Pesci, U. (1886), 'Amor', *L'illustrazione italiana*, Milan, 14, 8.
Poesio, G. (1990), The story of the fighting dancers', *Dance Research*, 8, 1.
—— (1992), 'Maestro's early years', *Dancing Times*, 82: 984.

—— (1993), *The Language of Gesture in Italian Dance from Commedia dell'Arte to Blasis* (unpublished Ph.D. thesis, University of Surrey).

Racster, O. (1922), *The Master of Russian Ballet*, London: Hutchinson.

Radice, A. (n.d.), Ballet notes, manuscript, private collection.

Roslaveva, N. (1966) *Era of the Russian Ballet*, London: Gollancz.

Rossi, L. (1978), *Enrico Cecchetti, Maestro dei Maestri*, Milan: Edizioni della Danza.

Slominsky, Y. (1937), *Masters of the Ballet in the Nineteenth Century*, Leningrad.

Tani, G. (1983), *Storia della danza*, Florence: Olschky.

Vanelli, F. M. (1986), *An Examination of the London Career of Enrico Cecchetti (1885–1921)* (unpublished dissertation, Roehampton Institute of Higher Education, London).

Wiley, R. J. (1990), *A Century of Russian Ballet*, Oxford: Oxford University Press.

Chapter 9

Rambert Dance Company Archive, London, UK

Jane Pritchard

Worldwide it is quite usual for major opera houses and some national theatres to set up their own archives. These usually include information on the building and running of the theatres as well as the full range of events performed within their auditoria. Such important collections can be found at the Paris Opéra,[1] La Scala, Milan[2] and the Royal Theatres of Stockholm and Copenhagen.[3] In London the Royal Opera House, in Covent Garden, established its own archive in the 1950s. This preserves archival material on the Royal Ballet, particularly since 1946 when it became resident there.[4] It is less usual to find archives in dance companies which lack a permanent theatre-base. Those that have established archives include the Merce Cunningham Dance Company in the United States;[5] the National Ballet of Canada;[6] and the Australian Ballet.

In the past decade British theatre dance companies have taken a new interest in their individual heritage and developed a concern for record-keeping in a way hitherto neglected. Indeed any survey of the main resources for dance in Britain now has to take note of company archives as well as collections in libraries, museums and other centres. These very specific archives usually complement national collections although in Britain their establishment was certainly accelerated by the delay in the full opening of the Theatre Museum, the National Museum of the Performing Arts, which is part of the Victoria and Albert Museum, London.[7]

A company archive is generally more comprehensive in terms of that particular company's work than any national, university or private collection could hope to be, simply because it gathers material at source as it is generated. It does, however, depend on an active archivist to keep its records up to date. The usually precarious existence of any dance company dictates that concern for the future rather than the past tends to take priority and, where no one is responsible for keeping the records, much material is of necessity dispersed. As companies move from one base to another, accumulated papers which are perceived to be of no immediate value are often discarded, the last poster, programme or photograph for a production is given away simply in response to demand. It was because these problems were recognized that two leading British companies, English National Ballet and Rambert Dance Company, established their archives in 1975 and 1982 respectively.

The range of materials found in any dance company archive is likely to be similar although each will have its own collection policy which clearly defines its focus and selection procedures. The Rambert Dance Company Archive[8] documents the organization's existence from 1926 to the present day. The Company, founded by Marie Rambert (1888–1982), a Polish-born dancer and teacher, emerged from her school (established in 1920) and developed through performances at London's Ballet Club[9] in the 1930s into a medium-scale classical touring company in the 1940s. In 1966 it was reformed as a smaller, more innovative, ensemble with an increasingly modern repertory. Throughout the Company's existence it has been noted for discovering new talent, encouraging dancers and designers, commissioning new scores and, above all, for giving opportunities to new choreographic talent. Among Rambert's own protégés were the choreographers Frederick Ashton, Antony Tudor, Andrée Howard, Walter Gore, Norman Morrice and Christopher Bruce. The Rambert Dance Company, under the direction of Richard Alston, continued this commitment to new work.[10] The Archive, therefore, includes material on the large number of works created for the Company and on their creators. There is also a wealth of material on the life and career of Dame Marie Rambert[11] and some on other organizations which have directly affected the Company or grown out of it. These include the Camargo Ballet Society (1930–3),[12] Dance Theatre (1937),[13] London Ballet (1938–40),[14] and Ballet Workshop (1951–5),[15] as well as other productions[16] that took place at the Mercury Theatre,[17] Ladbroke Road, the home of the Ballet Club and Rambert's School[18] from 1928 to 1979.

The programme collection is a frequent starting point for researchers. This has become increasingly complete (in part thanks to donations from supporters) although a number of gaps are evident in respect of early performances. There are very few programmes for Marie Rambert's personal recitals in France between 1905 and 1914 (in all probability programmes were printed only for her performances in theatres and not at private engagements) and for her appearances in British productions. The main collection begins in 1926 with the revue *Riverside Nights* at the Lyric Theatre, Hammersmith, for which Frederick Ashton created his first ballet *A Tragedy of Fashion*, and continues up to the most recent performances presented by Rambert Dance Company on its current tour.

Commencing June 23rd, for Two Weeks only

A SEASON *of* BALLET
KARSAVINA
and the MARIE RAMBERT DANCERS

Monday Evening, June 23rd, at 8.30

Subsequently at 8.45   Matinees Wed. & Sat. at 2.45

KARSAVINA.

LYRIC THEATRE, HAMMERSMITH
Lessee and Manager   -   Sir Nigel Playfair

Figure 9.1 Publicity material for Ballet Rambert's first season at the Lyric Hammersmith in 1930. (Courtesy of the Rambert Dance Company Archives.)

Printed programmes, of course, only reveal the intention to perform particular works and the expected cast. Some programmes, however, contain corrections which indicate changes of cast and ballets performed. These may be in the form of alternatives pasted over the original copy, slips loosely inserted into the programme or annotations by a member of the Company or the audience. Hand-written changes are often of value as they are usually jotted down in response to official front-of-house announcements or as a result of a Company supporter recognizing who is dancing. However, it is always useful to know the source of the change in order to check the validity of any amendments. Unfortunately Rambert Dance Company has not established the practice (which proves invaluable at English National Ballet) whereby a member of the ballet staff amends a cast list at each performance to record who actually went on, right down to the last corps-de-ballet dancer. Stage management reports (sometimes known as show reports), which are completed by the stage manager at the conclusion of each programme as a record of what happened, indicate major cast changes or those that occur because of accidents during a performance.

Kept together with the programmes is a collection of printed ephemera advertising performances. This includes occasional beer-mats (coasters) and paper bags, printed with the Company's logo and advertising performances at specific theatres, together with announcements on post-cards from the 1930s and, in more recent times, leaflets sometimes appropriately referred to as 'throwaways', an indication of their usual fate. There are also illustrated booklets for festivals at which the Company performed and announcements for special events. The latter include references to lectures by Marie Rambert as well as various educational projects.

The material for a week of performances 4–8 February 1986, at the Royal Northern College of Music, Manchester, exemplifies the conflicting information that may be found in these sources. The original publicity and press releases announce that for the season the productions would be: Programme 1, *Light and Shade* (North, 1985),[19] *Soda Lake* (Alston, 1886), *Dangerous Liaisons* (Alston, 1985) and *Death and the Maiden* (North, 1984); and Programme 2, *Java* (Alston, 1985), *Pierrot Lunaire* (Tetley, 1967) and the world première of Robert North's *Fabrications*. The printed programme shows Programme 1 unaltered but, because of North's departure as Artistic Director after the publicity leaflets were printed, *Fabrications* was cancelled and replaced by *It's a Raggy Waltz* (Bethune, 1986) and *Songs of the Ghetto* (Carty, 1986). To complicate matters further an undated insert announces that, owing to the indisposition of certain dancers, *Death and the Maiden* (on Programme 1) would be replaced by *Wildlife* (Alston, 1984). As well as the programme changes it is worth noting that neither the publicity leaflet nor the programme itself records that this is the Company première of *Soda Lake*. Furthermore, the dates in the programme do not include the year. This is a surprising omission but, nevertheless, an all too common one in dance programmes which still persists today. Observant researchers might pick up the reference to 'Industrial Year 1986' or a Universal Calendar could be used in conjunction with the incomplete dates in the programme to identify the year. Older programmes often include actual dates in the printer's coded reference at the back. In a properly-constituted company archive the indices list the full sequence of changes but, without such a record, facts about performances are sometimes difficult to document.

As with the programme and general publicity collections the poster collection is stronger since the Company's 1966 reformation than before it. The few early posters announce, for example, Ballet Rambert's visit to the Birmingham Repertory Theatre from 'Monday June 13 to Saturday June 28, 1938'; or to the Théâtre Sarah Bernhardt, Paris, in May 1950. These simply identify the principal dancers and list the repertory to be performed. Rambert's posters from the late 1960s, in common with those of other dance companies, become more pictorial. While many recent poster images are drawn from colour photographs, others have been created by the artists who designed productions. These include Howard Hodgkin for *Night Music* (Alston, 1981) and *Pulcinella* (Alston, 1987) and Bruce McLean for *Soldat* (Page, 1988). Most of the posters of the 1970s were the work of graphic artist Michael Carney, among whose designs was the powerfully striking image for *Cruel Garden* (Bruce/Kemp 1977), a production which concerned the life and work of the Spanish poet, playwright and artist Federico García Lorca (1898–1936). Not only did this poster suggest the dynamism of the dance but the image itself was inspired by those reproduced in the well-known Parisian art periodical of the 1930s, *Minotaure*,[20] with its own links to surrealism, Spain and bullfighting.

The earliest poster in the Archive highlights some of the problems researchers face with such documents. It is a double-crown sheet, printed in green ink on white paper and reads:

PALLADIUM
OPERA HOUSE
Sole Proprietor J. L. Crown
EVERY EVENING DURING THE WEEK AT 8.45
ENORMOUS SUCCESS
OF
MDLLE.
RAMBERT
THE GREAT RUSSIAN CLASSICAL DANCER

There is no indication of date or town but the inclusion of the name of the theatre and its proprietor narrows the field. After fruitless searches through theatrical newspapers such as *The Era* and *The Stage*, both of which include details of regional venues, the chance location of a programme in a private collection in connection with unrelated research into performances by Stanislas Idzikovsky showed that in December 1914 he had danced at the Palladium Opera House, Brighton, and that the proprietor there was a Mr Crown. Having established the venue, a letter to Brighton Reference Library revealed that no information on the long-demolished theatre under that name was held. Nevertheless, a trawl through the local paper, the *Argus*, from mid-1914, when Marie Rambert settled in Britain, led to the establishment of the fact that this poster announces performances that took place during the week 6–11 September 1915 when Marie Rambert was an additional attraction, performing as yet unidentified solos, in a programme otherwise made up of films including the latest Keystone comedy.[21]

Press cuttings, including announcements, reviews and interviews, cover the years 1937 to 1949 and 1958 onwards in depth. At present, coverage for other years is less complete although former Company members have been generous in presenting personal scrap-books to the Archive. Marie Rambert kept scrap-books recording some of her work with the Stage Society[22] and Andrée Howard collected material relating to her work as a dancer, designer and choreographer up to 1943.[23] Other personal volumes were compiled by dancers including Patricia Clogstoun (who performed at the Ballet Club and danced in the 1937 première of Tudor's *Dark Elegies*), Charles Boyd (an Australian dancer who created Mr Tebrick in Howard's 1939 *Lady into Fox* in London and re-joined the Company during its 1947–9 tour of Australia), Beryl Goldwyn, Company ballerina in the 1950s, and Thelma Lister who documented the Company's 1957 visit to China. Press cuttings for the period until 1966 are mounted in books[24] but more recent ones are now on single loose sheets to allow easy chronological filing under venue, production or individual.

Photographs, the majority of which are black and white prints, provide a visual record of the dances, individual performers and designs. In addition to production shots (either showing the full stage with settings or close-ups of individuals or groups) there are dancers' headshots for publicity, posed studio images that may not necessarily record poses or complete costumes from specific productions, as well as informal photographs and snapshots showing Company members at receptions, during overseas tours, in class and at rehearsals. The Archive includes photographs that document Marie Rambert's family and personal career, including the famous carte de visite showing her when she first went to school in her 'severe brown uniform' holding her 'big and splendid' Florentine straw hat 'with a red taffeta frill all round it'.[25] Among the earliest photographs is a unique collection of stereoscopic slides on glass showing dancers from Emile Jaques-Dalcroze's School in Geneva (c. 1909) at which Marie Rambert studied for three years.[26] Although the early photographs are in a number of formats those produced since the Second World War are generally standard 10 by 8 inch black and white original and copy prints. However, from the 1980s the emphasis has been increasingly on colour transparencies, some of which have been subsequently reproduced in the Company's souvenir brochures. *La Sylphide* (Rosen after Bournonville, 1960) is the earliest production which is documented in colour although a few earlier individual colour transparencies exist and there is one damaged autochrome of Marie Rambert at the outset of her performing career.

Identifying photographs in the Archive can present some problems. Recent shots (of which master prints are deposited in the Archive immediately on acquisition) are indexed by the archivist with complete details of photographer, date and place of photograph as well as what is recorded in the picture. Some of the earlier photographs were not identified at all, let alone in this manner, and attributions on the reverse of others are quite wrong. Nevertheless, the majority of production photographs can be identified completely although some rehearsal and offstage prints have proved more difficult as one rehearsal in the studio can look much like another by the same choreographer and how many people in a group photograph of a dancer's wedding that took place forty years ago can the Archivist be expected to recognize? The Archive rarely holds full copyright on photographs although some photographers have been generous in this respect and have even donated the original negatives and copyright in those photographs to the Archive. Under current British law copyright expires fifty years after the death of the photographer.[27]

Photographs have certainly helped to record the changes within productions when they have been adapted for different stages. It was fascinating to receive prints from the Australian photographers Jean Stewart and Walter Stringer showing that for performances in 1947 of Ashton's *Capriol Suite* at the large Princess Theatre, Melbourne, a setting of wrought-iron gates and a maypole had been devised.

Within the Archive there are some original designs for costumes, sets and a few set models. Most of the models, including those for *Gala Performance* (Tudor, 1940), *Giselle* (Coralli/Perrot, 1945–6) and *Winter Night* (Gore, 1948), are in pieces for flat storage, although a few, notably Ralph Koltai's blood-spattered bullring for *Cruel Garden* (Bruce/Kemp, 1977), are made up. The Archive includes the model theatre made for Bridget Riley to demonstrate the effects her cloths and the moving figures in front of them would have in *Colour Moves* (North, 1983) and the small sample canvases copied by scenic artists.

Restrictions on space prevent actual settings for works from being kept. The cloths for *Façade* (Ashton, 1931), *Jardin aux lilas* (Tudor, 1936), *Gala Performance* (Tudor, 1940) and *Colour Moves* (North, 1983) were offered to the Theatre Museum but *Jardin aux lilas* was not accepted as it was in a state of partial disintegration. The 'stable doors' from the *Façade* set on which the figure of the Polka dancer is painted remained with the Company and now decorate the wall of the staircase leading to the reception area at the Company's headquarters. The Archive also holds floor and lighting plans for some productions, as well as the actual slide projections used for the purpose of decor in *Conflicts* (Morrice, 1962), *Ziggurat* (Tetley, 1967) and the original version of *Swamp* (Clark, 1986).

Marie Rambert's personal collection of designs was bequeathed to the Theatre Museum in 1982 but the Archive holds photographic records of that collection. These include Sophie Fedorovitch's designs for *A Tragedy of Fashion* (Ashton, 1926) and *Mephisto Valse* (Ashton, 1933) as revised for the Australian tour, set designs by Nadia Benois for *The Descent of Hebe* (Tudor, 1934) and by William Chappell for *Atalanta of the East* (Tudor, 1933) as well as the lively costume designs by Edward Burra for *Canterbury Prologue* (Paltenghi, 1951). The Archive has also acquired some early designs such as the alternative versions of the costume for the eponymous heroine in *The Descent of Hebe* worn by Pearl Argyle, who created the role, and her successor Elisabeth Schooling, versions of four costume designs for *Lady into Fox* (Howard, 1939) which Nadia Benois re-drew several times, and William Chappell's 1983 version of the *Capriol Suite* costumes for the ballet's revival at the Marie Rambert Memorial Gala. Chappell donated these designs, as did Richard Smith his for *Wildlife* and *Dangerous Liaisons*. Other costume documentation includes a colour chart of fabric samples that Mark Lancaster supplied for the costumes for *Fielding Sixes* (Cunningham) in 1983, and diagrams and colour charts from the Merce Cunningham Dance Company's wardrobe department for Rambert's 1987 production of *Septet* (Cunningham). In addition the Archive holds some designs, such as those by Harry Cordwell for Walter Gore's dramatic ballet *Antonia* (1949), on permanent loan.

Costumes in the Archive are no longer worn in performance. The oldest garment in the collection is a length of beige and blue fabric woven for Marie Rambert. This is not a stage costume, as a note in Rambert's hand explains: 'Raymond Duncan[28] wove this dress for me in 1906 in Paris. I wore it as evening dress.' The earliest stage costumes also came to the Archive from Marie Rambert and include her two costumes for Fiammetta in *La Pomme d'or* (Donnet, 1917). One, in white silk with a floral motif in blue and green, was worn in the Botticelli-inspired scene 'Beato's Vision', while the other, a long crimson dress with gold-painted decoration at the neck, was created for the scene 'In the Chapel' which evoked the paintings of Fra Angelico. This costume was reused for Rambert's appearances in 1930 as the Madonna, a role she created in both Susan Salaman's *Our Lady's Juggler* (1930) and Ashton's *A Florentine Picture* (1930). Other costumes dating back to the Ballet Club era include Tamara Karsavina's blue and purple tunic worn as Venus in Ashton's *Mercury* (1931) for which no pictorial records are extant. The Chief Nymph's short gold shift for *L'Après-midi d'un faune* (Nijinsky, 1931), which is extremely fragile having been worn in performances from the 1930s until 1971 and copied for the 1983 revival of the ballet, and Sally Gilmour's Fox costume from *Lady into Fox*, are also held. There are costumes made in the early 1960s to John Armstrong's original designs for *Façade* (only those for the Valse have been redesigned since the first Camargo Society performances), to Hugh Stevenson's designs for *Jardin aux lilas*, to Peter Farmer's designs (also in the Archive) for *Running Figures* (North, 1975), and to Nadine Baylis's instructions for *The Tempest* (Tetley, 1979). By including the original 1960s and re-made 1970s costumes the change in the choice of fabrics for costumes worn in *Ricercare* (Tetley, 1967) is documented. Similarly, the change in colour preference from the deliberate day-glo pinks, yellows and oranges of the 1960s to more subtle tones and shading of the 1980s costumes for *Embrace Tiger and Return to Mountain* (Tetley, 1967) is evident. The selection of costumes represents not only those worn by famous dancers or created by eminent designers or costumiers but also examples of more usual stage attire.

Notes and notation for specific productions are also preserved in the Archive. There is Ninette de Valois's personal transcription of her only creation for Rambert *Bar aux Folies-Bergère* (1934) and there are also individual roles or sections of ballets from the 1930s written out in note form. These include Pierrot's role in Fokine's *Le Carnaval* (1930), Mr Tebrick in *Lady into Fox*, the corps de ballet's movements for Mars in Tudor's *The Planets* (1934), and the Two Young Ladies for Ashton's *Les Masques* (1933). This last appears to have been recorded shortly after the ballet's creation since the description is given in terms of the two women who created the parts, Betty Cuff and Elisabeth Schooling, and linked to the gramophone records the dancers rehearsed to. For example the note begins:

the following poses are those that come between the various dances, and are written up (unless otherwise stated) from Schooling's point of view. All Cuff's movements are opposite.

Figure 9.2 L'Après-midi d'un faune: 1931 at the Ballet Club. William Chappell as the Faun and Diana Gould as the Chief Nymph. Choreography: Vaslav Nijinsky; music: Claude Debussy; design: Léon Bakst. (Courtesy of the Rambert Dance Company Archives.)

A little further on the notes continue:

> *Second Record:* Unwind Alicia's dress and reach column by end of phrase; stand in arabesque, L. arm curved over head, R. arm on column, R. leg behind. Developé [sic] into arabesque slowly, R. arm with R. forefinger stuck in R. eye.

At the Ballet Club and even later gramophone records were used both for rehearsal and performance as in the film *The Red Shoes*.[29] Therefore, the collection of records, including some that play at 78 revolutions per minute, has helped considerably with the reconstruction of works by indicating contemporary tempi. Such recordings can also provide an explanation for a specific choreographic detail as a student working on Gore's 1948 *Winter Night* discovered when she noticed that a particular pose was sustained because it coincided with the change from one side of a record to the other.[30]

For a few early productions written notes are extant for all roles. *L'Après-midi d'un faune* (for which there is also a piano score annotated in Tudor's hand from the time Léon Woizikovsky was teaching the work to Rambert's dancers)[31] and *Dark Elegies*, both revived on numerous occasions, are the ballets to survive in the most complete form. Since 1967, when the Company appointed its first notator, the repertory has been recorded in Benesh Movement Notation although works choreographed by guest choreographers tend to have been more completely notated than those by in-house choreographers. Masters of the scores are deposited at the Benesh Institute in London (a practice begun before the Company Archive was established)[32] but the Company retains copies and working materials.

The documentation of productions has also been undertaken on film and video. Some of the works from the 1930s were recorded by the amateur film-makers Walter and Pearl Duff, including the Woizikovsky/ Sokolova staging of Nijinsky's *L'Après-midi d'un faune*, Ashton's *Mars and Venus* (1929), *Foyer de danse* (1932) and *Les Masques*, Howard's first creation *La Belle Ecuyère* (1931) and a rehearsal for her *Cinderella* (1935). At the end of that decade *Lady into Fox* was filmed and in the early 1960s Edmée Wood recorded Tudor's *Dark Elegies* and *Judgment of Paris* (1940) and Kenneth MacMillan's *Laiderette* (1955) on an undecorated stage so that the actual choreography would be clearly documented.[33] Since the mid-1970s all the Company's productions have been recorded on video but, owing to poor original stock, many have suffered from oxydization and are no longer viewable. The master copies of all the films are deposited at the National Film Archive.[34] Brighton Polytechnic (now Brighton University) and the National Film Archive have carried out considerable work on the conservation of the films and early videos. It should be noted that, as is the policy with most dance companies, video recordings of works are made strictly for internal viewing and available only to members of the Company.

The Archive holds copies of many of the musical scores for productions, including some original manuscript material of scores commissioned by the Company. There are also sound recordings on tape, made both for use in rehearsal and to accompany performances, as well as tapes of the spoken word. The latter range from Marie Rambert's talk on Serge Diaghilev given at the Jeannetta Cochrane Theatre, London, on 30 September 1972 and interviews with Company members by Margaret Dale in 1976 for her BBC television documentary *50 Years of Rambert* (1976) to Richard Alston talking to Trisha Brown at the Institute of Contemporary Arts, London, on 15 November 1991. Administrative records cover a wide range of primary materials including minutes of meetings, financial records, reports and correspondence. There is little extant documentation of the early years of the Company but an increasing volume since the Company returned from Australia and began to employ its own administrative staff. Inevitably a greater amount survives since 1971 when the Company moved into its current permanent base in Chiswick and this has grown as the number of administrative staff has risen from five in 1971 to eleven in 1992.

Minutes exist from the first meeting on 14 July 1950 of the Mercury Theatre Trust, Rambert's parent body, which was known until November 1951 as Mercury Players (Ballet) Limited. It is in these minutes that the decision to reform the Company in 1966 is recorded. There are also the Arts Council of Great Britain's papers relating to Ballet Rambert from 1947 to 1955 which were presented to Marie Rambert, as a note on the file records, 'to celebrate the occasion of her 90th birthday'. The subsequent papers relating to the Company are housed in the Arts Council's Dance Archive at the National Resource Centre for Dance, University of Surrey. Also in the Rambert Archive are papers and minutes relating to the Two Ballets Trust which considered the possibility of merging Ballet Rambert with London Festival Ballet. The Trust formally existed between 1965 and 1966 but negotiations leading to its establishment began in 1963.

In addition to the accounts, the Company's financial records include details of wages (a useful source for double-checking periods of employment) and royalty books which, in the absence of stage management reports, confirm the precise details of when ballets were actually performed. There are, however, some productions that carry no royalties; for example Alston's *Soda Lake*, without music or sound accompaniment but with a setting (a copy of a sculpture by Nigel Hall) which was paid for outright. There is little practical need to keep a precise record of these works so details are not included in such books. Other documentation relating to day-to-day activities include call-sheets and schedules which are sometimes annotated with changes and corrections.

The Archive does not include original contracts for artists and productions before 1969 although a few dancers who have retained their own have donated copies.

Correspondence includes both administrative records, such as negotiations for tours, as well as personal correspondence between individuals. Some letters contain information about plans which never came to fruition, ballets proposed but unrealized, choreographers who were invited to work with the Company but who for various reasons were unable or unwilling to accept the invitation, proposals for collaborations that radically changed during the creative period, and advice on why it would be inappropriate to visit certain countries at certain times.

Among the correspondence are some letters sent to Marie Rambert and preserved by her which include fascinating and valuable documents such as the letter from Frederick Ashton (undated but from its contents clearly written in the late summer of 1928) in which he minutely describes working with Bronislava Nijinska, particularly in her creations for Ida Rubinstein's Company.

Users of the Archive can be divided into three distinct groups: internal users, that is Company members who need access to information in connection with their work, and two groups of external users, professionals and students. The consideration of the needs of Company members is outside the scope of this chapter but suffice to say that the Archive is constantly referred to and used for a wide range of Company activities, including reviving and reconstructing productions from the Company's past repertory, checking up on activities at specific venues, guidance with programme planning and providing information for publicity, sponsorship activities, programme notes, commemorative publications and educational resource-packs.

Professional users come to the Archive for equally varied reasons. They may be authors working on biographies, journalists compiling profiles or obituaries, or researchers involved in television programmes. The Archive has contributed to, for example, the 1988 BBC *Omnibus* feature on Frederick Ashton, the documentary section of *Dance in America*'s 1990 presentation of Tudor's *Jardin aux lilas* and *Dark Elegies*,[35] and a French television survey of twentieth-century dance (yet to be transmitted). A certain amount of administrative material is of a confidential nature and permission for researchers from outside the Company to be allowed access to it has to be granted by the Administrator or Chairman of the Company.

The Archive is used by numerous picture-researchers who may know precisely which productions, performers or poses they are looking for or may simply want to see the most interesting dance photographs held.[36] Not all professionals using the Archive are scholars since occasionally a picture-researcher's brief is no more than to find an energetic dance-image. Now that the photographic collection is organized under headings such as productions, individuals, photographers and dates, most requests can be met quickly. Prints are supplied only on a commercial basis and then subject to copyright clearance where necessary.

Other professionals who use the Archive are active in the theatre. A designer, for example, wanted to familiarize himself with a choreographer's work before embarking on a collaboration. Ralph Koltai asked to see copies of his design material for *Cruel Garden* in 1992 when re-creating the work for Deutsche Oper Ballett, Berlin, and the translation into German of the scenario for the section 'The Afternoon Stroll of Buster Keaton' (made for Rambert's 1980 tour to Germany) was referred to for that revival. Reconstructors of other ballets have used the Archive to contribute to their work. Millicent Hodson studied Marie Rambert's note on *Le Sacre du printemps*[37] and Ann Hutchinson Guest the material on *L'Après-midi d'un faune*[38] during research for their respective recreations of Nijinsky's ballets.

However, the largest group of users each year comprises students whose projects and dissertations regularly include topics such as the Company's 1966 reformation, the contribution of painters, sculptors and fashion designers to stage productions, and the choreography of Tudor, Bruce and Alston. The Archive serves not only dance students but also art students working in the areas of graphics, fashion, fabrics and paintings.

At all levels of research the most convenient approach to the Archive is by letter or fax giving a brief outline of the research project and indicating what the researcher hopes to locate in the Archive and any other sources being used. This enables the Archivist to advise on how much and what material in the collection is relevant for the researcher to study and it also avoids duplication. In the absence of a published catalogue it is necessary to ascertain from the Archivist what is available. A range of leads is useful in attempting full coverage of any topic.

With a specialist repository, such as the Rambert Archive where facilities for research are restricted, it is essential to be well informed before using it. The Archive's small collection of books may be consulted in conjunction with primary material but it is not intended for introductory reading. Appointments are essential as the Rambert Archive, like many other dance-company archives, is staffed only on a part-time basis and pressure on the limited space is, at times, very considerable. If researchers are visiting from abroad appointments need to be made on that basis.

Photocopies of some material may be made available (subject to copyright laws and other restrictions) but neither manuscript material nor fragile items may be copied. Sometimes material will be unavailable until conservation work has been undertaken and if researchers want access to items that are awkward to handle, such as costumes, then these should be requested in advance. Some costumes from recent repertory, not yet officially part of the Archive, may be made available. Rambert's reconstruction of costumes to Léon Bakst's designs for *L'Après-midi d'un faune* are frequently requested and the current wardrobe includes a few costumes, for example those worn by the bedraggled prostitutes of Tudor's *Judgment of Paris*, that date back to the 1950s. Indeed that worn by Minerva is a replacement costume originally made for the short-lived production *The Life and Death of Lola Montez* (Carter, 1954). Telephone enquiries, putting straightforward questions, about the date a particular television programme on the Company was transmitted or the designer for a certain production or whether a specific dancer worked for Rambert, normally receive an immediate answer.

School students working on projects are best advised to contact the Company's Education Department which is used to dealing with routine enquiries and has information-packs available on general aspects of the Company, its history and the current repertory. More unusual and specific requests will automatically be passed on to the Archivist. It is rare for such students to be invited to use the Archive in person although an enterprising and well-worded initial enquiry may lead to their being accommodated. Teachers need to discuss the content of any letter a school student writes to avoid such irritating requests as 'Tell me all about dance by Friday' or even 'I'm doing a project on your company, please send me some information'. Even at college and university level tutorial guidance is valuable so that, instead of a letter asking for information in connection with a study of Ashton's 1961 ballet *The Two Pigeons* (which would simply elicit the response that Rambert has never performed the work, advising the writer to contact the Royal Ballet), the student explained that although the study area was *The Two Pigeons* the Rambert Archive was a potentially valuable source for information on Ashton's 1932 choreography for *Foyer de danse*, in some respects a precursor of the later work. Any student using a company archive should take the trouble to be clear about basic facts and questions before turning to a specialist repository. The Archivist's responsibilities include selecting, preserving and arranging the material as well as making it available to those who need it and there is no time to deal with those who have omitted to prepare themselves adequately prior to visiting. Occasionally a researcher is able to add to the knowledge about materials in the Archive by applying information gained elsewhere to specific items.

The Rambert Archive was officially established in 1982 although some material had been gathered in the years following the Company's fiftieth anniversary in 1976 which, in itself, highlighted the need to keep detailed records of its work. Subsequently it has developed into a significant research resource catering for a wide range of users. Although there is always an awareness of the need for balance between use and conservation it is an excellent example of what can be achieved when a small company takes the documentation of its own heritage seriously.

NOTES

1 For further details see I. Guest (1980), 'Archives of the dance (3): the library and archives of the Paris Opéra: the Opéra preserve', *Dance Research*, 2, 2 (summer): 68–76 and M. Kahane (trans. M. M. McGowan) (1984), 'Archives of the dance (4): the library and archives of the Paris Opéra: part 2', *Dance Research*, 3, 1, (autumn): 67–71.

2 For further details see *La Scala Theatrical Museum Guide*, Milan: Museo Teatrale alla Scala (1975).

3 For further details see M. Hallar (1989), 'The Royal Theatre library and archives', *Nordic Theatre Studies*, University of Copenhagen, 2/3: 188–93.

4 For further details see F. Franchi (1988), 'Archives of the dance (8): dance material in the archives of the Royal Opera House, Covent Garden', *Dance Research*, 6, 2 (autumn): 78–82.

5 For further details see D. Vaughan (1984), 'Archives of the dance (2): building an archive: Merce Cunningham Dance Company', *Dance Research*, 2, 1 (spring): 61–7.

6 For further details see D. W. Ladell (ed.) (1988), *Putting it Back Together: Preserving the Performing Arts Heritage*, n.p., Association of Canadian Performing Arts Archivists.

7 For further details see J. Fowler (1989), 'Archives of the dance (9): early dance holdings of the Theatre Museum, London', *Dance Research*, 7, 2 (autumn): 81–8, and S. C. Woodcock (1990), 'Archives of the dance (10): later dance holdings of the Theatre Museum, London', *Dance Research*, 8, 1 (spring): 62–77 The founding collection of the Theatre Museum was the impressive and wide-ranging archive relating to the British stage which Mrs Gabrielle Enthoven gave to the Victoria and Albert Museum (V & A) in 1924. By 1974 the Theatre Museum was sufficiently large to become a separate department within the V & A. In 1987 it moved from the V & A's South Kensington site to its own premises in Covent Garden, London, and now holds one of the most important collections in the world. For further reading see J. Scott Rogers (1985), *Stage by Stage: The Making of the Theatre Museum, London*, London: Her Majesty's Stationery Office.

8 The Archive is housed at the Company's base 94 Chiswick High Road, London.

9 The Ballet Club was established 'to serve the twin purposes of tradition and experiment. We shall preserve old ballets, the movement of which is now handed down from artist to artist by word of mouth alone; and we shall create new works that will bear transference to a larger scene as occasion offers' (programme for opening season of the Ballet Club 1931, p. 2). It was a club initially as the building at Ladbroke Road was not licensed for public performance. Even after it had a performance licence it continued as a club

to allow performances on Sundays. It was not until the Sundays Theatre Act of 1972 that theatres in Britain were permitted to give public performances on Sunday.

10 The development of the Company is documented in J. Adshead and J. Pritchard (1985), *Dance Company Resource Pack 2: Ballet Rambert 1965–1975*, National Resource Centre for Dance, University of Surrey; L. Bradley (1946), *Sixteen Years of Ballet Rambert*, London: Hinrichsen; M. Clarke (1962), *Dancers of Mercury: The Story of Ballet Rambert*, London: Black; C. Crisp, A. Sainsbury and P. Williams (eds) (1981), *Ballet Rambert 50 Years and On*, London: Rambert; and S. Rubidge (ed.) (1990), *Rambert Dance Company: An Illustrated History through its Choreographers*, London: Rambert.

11 Marie Rambert was awarded the DBE in the 1962 New Year Honours List.

12 The Camargo Society was established in London after the death of Serge Diaghilev to 'provide original and classic ballets before a subscription audience' at West End theatres four times a year: these were to involve 'the collaboration of eminent composers, painters and choreographers' and 'the best dancing talent' (Prospectus for the Camargo Society 1930). Although the foundation of the Camargo Society coincided with that of the Ballet Club, Marie Rambert's dancers contributed a substantial element to performances in 1931 and 1932.

13 Dance Theatre was established by Antony Tudor, Hugh Laing and Agnes de Mille. It performed for one week, 14–19 June 1937, at the Playhouse, Oxford.

14 London Ballet, a company under the direction of Antony Tudor, was established in 1938 to give regular performances at the newly opened Toynbee Hall Theatre in the East End of London. After Tudor left for America in September 1939 it was reformed at the Arts Theatre in the West End under deputy directors Peggy van Praagh and Maude Lloyd. In June 1940 it amalgamated with Ballet Rambert and the two performed as the Rambert–London Ballet until 13 September 1941.

15 Ballet Workshop was an enterprise directed by Angela and David Ellis at the Mercury Theatre to give choreographers, composers and designers the opportunity to experiment. Established as a club, it performed on Sunday evenings.

16 From June 1933, when the theatre had been granted a licence for public performance, plays were presented at the Mercury Theatre. In the 1930s and 1940s it became the home of poetic drama. There were also music recitals, performances by Intimate Opera and the Lanchester Marionettes and by Agnes de Mille, Angna Enters, Paul Draper and Beth Dean.

17 The Mercury Theatre had been built as a church hall for the nearby Revivalist Temple in 1848. It was purchased by Ashley Dukes, Marie Rambert's husband, with royalties from his successful play *A Man with a Load of Mischief* (1924) and was initially used as studios for Rambert's school. The studio opened with a reception and performance on 10 March 1928. From 1931 it became the Ballet Club. In 1987 the building was sold and converted into a private residence; see L. Bolton (1990), 'Period Production', *House and Garden* (June): 132–5.

18 In 1920 the Rambert School was based at 9 Bedford Gardens, Kensington and then at the Mercury Theatre until 1979. In 1983 the Ballet Rambert School was established at the West London Institute, Twickenham, Middlesex. There is little material relating to the school in the Rambert Archive.

19 Dates after productions denote *first performance by Rambert* and not necessarily the date of the work's première, which is the normal convention. *Soda

Lake, for example, was premièred at Riverside Studios, London on 15 April 1981, but was not performed by a Rambert dancer until 1986.

20 *Minotaure*, edited by Albert Skira, was issued in Paris between 1933 and 1939. It featured the work of Picasso, Chirico, Dalí, Tanguy, Ernst, Ray, Brassai and many others.

21 Films shown on 6, 7 and 8 September 1915 included *Brother Officers* by Leo Trevor and the latest Keystone Comedy *His Taking Ways*, and on 9, 10 and 11 September 1915 *Who's Your Lady Friend?* and *A Tale of Florence*. At the time, when live music accompanied films, it was quite usual for dancers to appear on programmes which included short films.

22 The Incorporated Stage Society was founded in 1899 to produce plays of artistic merit that were unlikely to be acceptable to commercial managements. It remained active until the outbreak of the Second World War in 1939, performing on Sunday evenings and Monday matinées. Only two ballets were presented by the Society, both arranged by Vera Donnet and featuring Marie Rambert.

23 Later press cuttings from Andrée Howard's collection are in the Benesh Institute's Archive, London.

24 Conservation matters are outside the scope of this chapter but it is worth noting that the glues and adhesive tape used comparatively recently caused more damage than earlier materials had done. The press cuttings from the period 1966 to 1979 needed extensive treatment before they could be made available to researchers.

25 M. Rambert (1972), *Quicksilver*, London: Macmillan: 15.

26 Emile Jaques-Dalcroze (1865–1950) created a system of musical education based on movement, known as Eurhythmics. Marie Rambert worked with him as pupil, teacher and demonstrator between 1910 and 1912 in Geneva and Hellerau.

27 Copyright, Designs and Patents Act 1988.

28 Raymond Duncan (1878–1966), the brother of Isadora, adopted a lifestyle inspired by classical Greece. After establishing a self-supporting community outside Athens he settled in Paris where in 1911 he founded a school for Greek arts and crafts and a colony in the suburb of Neuilly. Marie Rambert met him at a party in 1905 and he encouraged her to become a dancer. She participated in Nathalie Barney's play about Sappho in which Raymond Duncan arranged the dances.

29 *The Red Shoes* (1948) by Emeric Pressburger and Michael Powell, starring Moira Shearer, includes a guest appearance by Marie Rambert recreating a scene in the Mercury Theatre where *Swan Lake*, Act II is being performed to gramophone records.

30 Sergei Rachmaninov's Concerto no. 2 in C minor op. 18 played by Benno Moiseiwitsch and the London Philharmonic Orchestra conducted by Walter Goehr, released by His Master's Voice C7501 as a four-record set.

31 Tudor's handwriting is easily identified and there is a note by Marie Rambert with the manuscript that reads, '*Faune* annotated by Tudor when Woysikovsky [*sic*] was teaching us'. Léon Woizikovsky (1899–1975) performed the title role with Serge Diaghilev's Ballets Russes for the 1924 revival of the ballet. Rambert's Nymphs learnt their roles from Lydia Sokolova (1896–1974) who had performed in the ballet with Nijinsky.

32 See I. E. Berry (1986), *Benesh Movement Notation Score Catalogue: An International Listing of Benesh Movement Notation Scores of Professional Dance Works Recorded 1955–1985*, London: The Benesh Institute of Choreology.

33 Edmée Wood, née Wessweiler, photographer and film-maker, was the wife of

Michael Wood (former Public Relations Officer and General Manager of the Royal Ballet and second Director of the Royal Ballet School). She performed a similar documentary service for the Royal Ballet.

34 These can be viewed by appointment at the British Film Institute, 21 Stephen Street, London.

35 Shown in Britain by BBC2 as *Dancemakers: Antony Tudor*, 22 August 1992.

36 For example William Ewing (1987) in the compiling of his *The Fugitive Gesture: Masterpieces of Dance Photography*, London: Thames & Hudson.

37 *Le Sacre du printemps*, choreographed by Vaslav Nijinsky to music by Igor Stravinsky and designed by Nicholas Roerich, was premièred by Serge Diaghilev's Ballets Russes on 29 May 1913 at the Théâtre des Champs-Elysées, Paris. The ballet was reconstructed and staged by Millicent Hodson, with designs reconstructed by Kenneth Archer, for the Joffrey Ballet who first performed it on 30 September 1987 at the Dorothy Chandler Pavilion, Los Angeles. It was filmed for television by Dance in America and entered the repertory of the Paris Opéra Ballet in 1991. The reconstruction is documented in E. Souriau *et al.* (1990), *Le Sacre du printemps de Nijinsky*, Paris: Cicero. See also Chapter 7 above.

38 The professional première of the reconstruction of Nijinsky's 1912 *L'Après-midi d'un faune* by Ann Hutchinson Guest and Claudia Jeschke was presented by Les Grands Ballets Canadiens on 27 October 1989. It was also performed and a video made of the production by the Julliard Dance Ensemble, New York, in December 1989. The Julliard production is documented in J. Beck (ed.) (1991), *Choreography and Dance: A revival of Nijinsky's original L'Après-midi d'un faune*, Reading: Harwood Academic.

Chapter 10

European early modern dance

Michael Huxley

This chapter outlines aspects of the historical study of a dance genre through examination of some of the particular problems encountered with European early modern dance during the period 1910–39.[1] The subject is examined in terms of: the nature of the topic itself; methodological problems brought to light by the study of the subject; suggested areas and approaches for historical study.

10.1 EUROPEAN EARLY MODERN DANCE: THE CHANGING VIEWPOINT

The German dance critic Hans Brandenburg compiled various editions of one of the earliest surveys of modern dance in Europe. His 1921 edition of *Der Moderne Tanz* catalogued and reviewed the production of dance in Germany during the preceding decade. He included German dancers such as Mary Wigman, German-based dancers including Rudolf Laban, American artists working in Europe such as Isadora Duncan, dancers from Russia ranging from Nijinsky to Pavlova, the work of many other dancers and of dance schools of various styles. 'Modern dance' appears to have been taken to refer to 'dance of the time' without great regard for artistic distinctions and, in the descriptions of the work of the dance schools, the making of an art product as such.

By the late 1920s, the German definition changed to one which, whilst acknowledging the early influence of Duncan and Pavlova, concentrated exclusively on central European artists. A good example of this is Lämmel's survey, *Der Moderne Tanz* (1928), where he classifies the 'present' as the 'second flowering of modern dance',[2] referring only to German and Austrian artists. After 1933 the German consensus becomes explicitly nationalistic in its renaming and redefinition of modern dance as *Deutsche Tanz*, German dance.[3]

In the next decade, following Martha Graham's first performances in America, John Martin attempted to characterize what was, from his critic's standpoint, the modern dance. He made it quite clear that in considering dance as a 'fine art' the major distinction was between modern dance on the one hand and classical or romantic ballet on the other, each having 'distinguishing features' (1933: 3–5). However, his stated differences between the work of German modern dancers and their American counterparts were given as a matter of emphasis rather than category. Maynard (1965) took a similar view some thirty years later after the 'burgeoning' of modern dance in America. Her genealogical account, using a family tree of influence, attempted to locate common origins for American and European modern dance prior to 1910 by reference to François Delsarte and his theories. The genealogical approach was used again by McDonagh (1976) to establish categories of generations of modern dancers. This approach, which was adhered to for the next decade, took for its content dancers who were almost exclusively American. This American-dominated consensus was further compounded by writers such as Murray (1979).[4]

McDonagh's revisionist view began to be redressed both by American dance historians such as Cohen (1977) and Brown (1980) and by the increasing literature on European early modern dancers made available during the 1980s. Cohen and Brown compiled primary source collections according to generations of modern dancers: they reaffirm the place of Mary Wigman, for instance, and Cohen includes Wigman's seminal essay from 1933, 'The Philosophy of Modern Dance'. By the late 1980s the change is largely acknowledged in historical overviews,[5] Au's account (1988) being particularly accurate in acknowledging the transatlantic origins.

The redefining of the area continues, however, as further information comes to light. If European early modern dance is placed within the European art context of the period, serious consideration must be given to including the Russian and Soviet experiments between 1913 and 1935,[6] which none of the aforementioned accounts do.

The problem for the dance historian is one of determining when a consensus existed, the reasons for it and how these are located in the dance itself, in its components, relationships and meanings. Subsequent accounts may help to identify a period within the genre as a whole but often, as shown in McDonagh's case, they may conspire to confuse the reader. This is of particular importance because the topic is usually approached from the standpoint of a current consensus.

Three ways of describing a genre of dance have been illustrated in this example through looking at one of its styles. The term 'modern dance' has named different types of dances at different times. The consensus during the period 1920–33 appears to have changed from one that included ballet to one that excluded it but considered 'modern dance' to be a transatlantic phenomenon. The view of modern dance as a whole, and during this period specifically, has given greater or lesser emphasis to this consensus according to the author. Authors of both primary and secondary sources have identified distinctive concepts, particularly Martin (1933) and Maynard (1965).

10.2 STUDYING EUROPEAN EARLY MODERN DANCE 1910–1933/39

The following points assume a chosen subject area and, in this case, indicate some examples of sources and their usage.

10.2.1 Availability of source material

The quantity and type of the more common sources change noticeably from 1910 to 1939. At the start of the period most published material is in the form of reviews and articles in non-dance periodicals. The number of books relevant to dance in general and modern dance in particular increases markedly throughout this time. The first German specialist dance journal, *Der Tanz*, was published as late as 1927.[7] A similar situation obtains in the case of film but for different, technical, reasons. Comparatively little theatre dance was filmed prior to 1920: some German dance was recorded during the 1920s but more film was made in America in the 1930s of American modern dance. Compared with later periods of modern dance, film is a rare source and reliance must be placed upon written materials to a considerable extent. None the less many photographs were taken during this period and books were well illustrated. Technical limitations required that most dance was posed in the studio rather than captured in performance. Action photographs were often obtained using daylight conditions out of doors but it would be inaccurate to assume from photographic evidence alone that dance was not performed in the theatre. In addition, some dances from the period were notated in a rudimentary form of what was to develop into Kinetography Laban (Labanotation). Reading these sources requires a historical reinterpretation of the notation system itself from a starting point such as Knust (1979) in comparison with Laban (1930).

There is an imbalance between American and European material.[8] Whereas much of the American material of this period is readily available, a great deal of its European equivalent is not. Four main reasons may serve to highlight the problem. First, American material is well collected and documented in archives such as the New York Public Library: no compilation of comparable size and scope exists yet in Europe for the period. Second, some material has had limited accessibility: for instance archives in what was East Germany were not always open to western dance researchers although this situation has now changed. Third, much of the German and some of the English material in existence during the period was destroyed or dispersed during the Second World War. Fourth, film stock of the period was nitrate-based and this type of film deteriorated drastically with time: some film has been retrieved and copied but much has been lost for ever.

The main lesson to be learnt here is that the limited amount of source material readily available obscures the extent of sources that were extant. The increasing interest in this area by Eastern European scholars may well lead to further rediscoveries.

10.2.2   Problems associated with translation and cultural differences

Studies of dance forms which derive from more than one country often involve the use of translation. Although translations into English are most valuable, scholars, ultimately, need a working knowledge of the original language of their sources.

When it comes to translation, two writers and dance historians are particularly well known in the field of European early modern dance, Horst Koegler and Walter Sorell. The following example illustrates how writers such as these have gained a reputation for accuracy. Koegler has written two monographs on dance in Germany during the Weimar period. His first study was written from mainly German sources, in German, for a German publication. When asked to write an English version, he chose to write it in English from the same German sources rather than to translate it. Being bilingual he was able to write directly about the dance and its meaning rather than merely transposing words from one language to another. Whilst it is not anticipated that everyone studying in this area has that facility it would be expected that the reliability of a translated source would be tested in a similar manner.

The quantity of translated material may impose limitations on the type of study attempted. For instance, Laban wrote prolifically from 1920 to 1933 but only one of his six books from the period was published in English (1930). However, there is doubt as to its authorship and it is not widely available. His only other book in translation is a biography (1935) and as such is not representative. The main body of his writing for German periodicals is to be found in the years 1920–30: of forty articles, there are three instances in translation. Of course, subsequent to his arrival in England in 1938 a number of books appeared in English, but these were written in England some twenty-five years after his first German publication. The case of Laban is typical of other dancers and writers of the period. Wigman (e.g. 1975) follows a slightly different pattern, having been extensively translated into English. Dance historians and critics, of whom Brandenburg is an important example, remain largely untranslated.

There are further considerations, however, in addition to the translating of the written word, and these relate to its accuracy and its availability. The structure and use of language is inextricable from its meaning. What is described in Germany as *Tanz* does not necessarily correspond to its direct English translation 'dance'. Cultural differences must also be considered. The following example illustrates how dance is culture-bound, that is to say, that the meaning of a particular manifestation of dance may be specific to its place of origin as well as to its historical location. In Germany during the 1920s many terms were associated with what the Germans described as *moderne Tanz*. Two of these terms cause particular difficulty: *Ausdruckstanz* and *Bewegungskunst*. Koegler makes it clear that *Ausdruckstanz* should be taken to mean 'dance of expression, not expressionist dance' (1974: 4). Many English writers from the 1920s onwards have, however, used the latter term loosely in making a witting comparison between modern dance and the artistic genre of Expressionism or, more unfortunately, in making an unwitting comparison. Such an inaccurate account based on the naming of dance should not be confused with considered comparisons between modern dance and Expressionism by writers such as Patterson (1981), where distinctive conceptual similarities are identified. A further common misinterpretation is to use 'expressive' as a literal translation of *ausdrucks*, a fault made by writers familiar with the related but distinctly different method of teaching 'expressive dance' in English schools. The reasons for this difficulty can be traced to the German language itself. Its structure allows the use of complex nouns to make subtle distinctions between different styles of dance whereas in English there is a tendency to make use of transferable adjectives. There is nothing surprising in the use, particularly during this period, of combined German nouns. Words like *Tanzkunst* (dance art) and *Bewegungskunst* (movement art) were appropriate for the era and were related to each other in a manner similar to *Tanzschrift* (dance writing) and *Bewegungschrift* (movement writing) which were subtly different but often interchangeable. When Laban came to England in 1938 the terms accompanied him. The translation of a word from that earlier period in a different culture was chosen to describe his work: *Bewegungskunst* became 'art of movement'. However in England, unlike Germany, this usage was largely in isolation from the similar, earlier terms. At the same time in the early 1940s, a new term was coined: 'modern educational dance'. The continuing confusion caused by this choice of a translated German term and the concurrent coining of a new English expression is well illustrated by the many discussions about the differences between 'art of movement' and 'modern educational dance'. The complexities of the assumed distinctions between the two are well shown in Hamby's analysis forty years later (1978). Problems of translation and cross-cultural differences provide, in themselves, one of the most interesting and challenging fields of dance history.

10.2.3   Interpretation of source material

Bias can be found in the work of writers used as primary sources and that of translators. It may be necessary to place the source in question within the context of its author's other writings in order to establish her/his world view of dance and the place of modern dance within that world view. A major topic in this area is the antipathy towards European early modern dance shown in the bias of British ballet critics of the time. Such a bias should be suspected but not taken for granted. For instance, Fernau Hall, writing in 1950 on modern English ballet, appears at first reading to be both knowledgeable about and sympathetic toward what he describes as 'the free dance'. His observations go well beyond the brief appreciation of Jooss typical of contemporary ballet critics such as Haskell. Indeed, Hall goes so far as to detail one European expatriate's work extensively: his book contains one of the most appreciative accounts of the work of Ernest Berk. However, Hall's work is put in perspective when it is understood that his training included not only ballet under Sokolova but also 'modern' with Berk and that he performed with both ballet and modern companies.

Scrutiny of sources in this way not only makes the student aware of bias inherent in critics' writing but also acknowledges the role played by such critics in defining the descriptive and evaluative features of a dance genre.

When considering interpretation according to historical location, it is worth re-stating that the first concern of dance history is dance and not history in general. However, the question does arise as to what level of knowledge outside dance is necessary to give an accurate historical account. The following example is given to illustrate the ways in which historical location of source material is necessary.

In this chapter European early modern dance has been placed within the period 1910–33/9. The choice of 1933 to mark a hiatus within this period is not arbitrary, nor does the date refer to a specific dance event: 1933 marks both the end of the Weimar Republic and the seizure of complete political power by the Nazi party in Germany with the establishment of the Third Reich. Of course the dance makers of this period continued to work, often in a recognizably similar way, for some years after 1933, but the change is so profound as to need a delineation. Other writers use a similar dating criterion but choose a period appropriate to the particular art under discussion, ending with the Nazi seizure of power: thus Willett (1978) selects 1917–33; Patterson (1981),

Figure 10.1 Mary Wigman in *Hexentanz* (Witch Dance), 1914.

in discussing German theatre, considers 1900–33. An exception is
Koegler (1974), his monograph 'In the shadow of the swastika: dance in
Germany, 1927–1936' being specifically concerned with chronicling
dance in the light of the rise of Nazism. Political events from 1933
onwards directly impinged on the arts in general and dance in particular, and the period 1933–9 takes on a particular importance in the
light of this knowledge and needs recognizing as such.[9]

A close examination of dance in Germany during the 1920s and 1930s
emphasizes the direct connection between dance and political change.
Two of many manifestations illustrate this point. First, in 1933 and
during the subsequent years many artists and dancers fled from
Germany: in dance the most prominent example was the emigration of
Kurt Jooss, Sigurd Leeder and their entire company and school. Many
of these artists and a number of the members of Ballets Jooss, such as
Jooss's composer Fritz Cohen, were Jewish. Second, at a more subtle
level there appears to be a change in terminology associated with dance
in Germany evidenced in increasing concern for 'Deutsche Tanz'
(German dance) both by journalists such as Böhme (1933) and by
artists such as Laban (1934) and Wigman (1935). Both these observations require direct reference to specific political changes. In 1935 the
Nuremberg Laws and the National Law of Citizenship decreed who was
to be excluded from German citizenship, thereby formalizing the
persecution of Jews in particular. Of the many political changes in the
arts the most often quoted is the attempted exclusion of modernism
from public life which culminated in the Munich 'Exhibition of
Degenerate Art' in 1937. The vilification of the artists of the modern
school throughout Europe, including Dix, Kokoschka, Kandinsky and
Mondrian, was contrasted with the adulation of ideologically pure work
in the accompanying First Exhibition of German Art.

The Nazi search for racial purity included not only the artist but also
the art work itself. The change in naming, from 'modern' to 'German'
dance, is consistent with the changes in the other arts. Having identified this change the task for the student of the period is to distinguish
between those authors and dancers who adopted the adjective 'German'
to signify their commitment to Nazi ideology, those who used it out of
expediency and those who adopted it to secure their safety against a
hostile regime. For instance, on the basis of recently published evidence by Müller (1986, 1987), it is reasonable to conclude that
Wigman's book of the period *Deutsche Tanzkunst* (1935) might be
considered in the last category. The contrary position is well illustrated
in Koegler's (1974) survey of articles from *Der Tanz*. He draws attention
to Böhme's seminal article 'Is ballet German?' (1933) in which the
author concludes that it cannot be because it is unsuited to the German
national character.

The point to be taken from these examples is that there are times when substantial research outside the immediate area of dance is necessary to give an accurate interpretation of source material within. The 1930s in Germany was an era when political events impinged directly on dance and the topic itself demands such examination.

10.2.4   Selection of material

In looking at the early stages of any new style, in this case European early modern dance, it is first necessary to retrace the steps of its formation through accounts of known practitioners or significant events. In the beginning these may well be secondary sources which lead to primary sources as they become available. It is only when the full extent of the dance of the period has been ascertained that the work of artists which has endured can be located and evaluated within the genre as a whole. An excellent example of this process can be found in re-evaluations of the art of the Weimar period that had been ignored, lost or forgotten since the Second World War.[10]

Assuming that most of the relevant sources have been located and that these sources have been scrutinized and evaluated, it is necessary to define the limits of the study and the criteria for the selection of material to be used. The central concern should be dance and the criteria dependent on the three central features identified by Adshead (1988): choreography, performance and appreciation. However, when considering modern dance as a genre, and European early modern dance in particular, it is insufficient to assume the existence of a 'genre' and to select material accordingly. Rather, the converse is true. The historical task is to seek those features in the dance and the work of dancers that allows a 'genre' or 'style' to be established. This task is easier at certain times that at others.

The following example considers just one aspect of selection: the direct relevance of certain dance activities to an understanding of modern dance as a distinct theatre dance genre. In most historical studies of twentieth-century dance theatre consideration is paid almost exclusively to professional dancers. However, in Germany, particularly during the 1920s, there were numerous dance groups which consisted of amateurs and students. These lay dancers, *Laientanzer*, often performed together in movement choirs, *Bewegungschöre*. Taken separately, the lay dancers' activities, essentially massed dancing for the appreciation of the participants, differed markedly from those of the professionals in the theatre or on the concert stage. However, Laban, in particular, choreographed on these lay dancers for public performances. Equally, both he and Wigman used the formal aspects of movement choir choreography in their theatre presentations. More significantly a number of Laban's choreographies for his theatre company required the participation of large groups of dancers, and these were recruited from the lay movement choirs. During the mid-1930s it was this type of dancing which gained a great deal of support and funding from the new government, culminating in the ill fated mass choreography, *Die Tauwind und die neue Freude*,[11] for the Lay Dancer Festival planned as part of the cultural activities of the 1936 Olympic Games. The accompanying programme *Wir Tanzen* clearly shows the flirtation between what had now become called 'community dance' and aspects of Nazi ideology. Yet it was the very dress rehearsal that caused Goebbels to cancel the performance and withdraw support because the work was not in line with party thinking.

The implication is that aspects of the choreography and training of the dancers had features held in common by both types of practitioner despite the fact that the purpose of the dance and its appreciation differed markedly: in the case of the lay dancer the appreciation was primarily for the dancer rather than for an audience. With these features in mind it becomes necessary to include lay dancers in any study of dance of the 1910–33/9 period.

The significant question is whether such features of a dance style are contributory factors to the genre as a whole or whether they are significant only in characterizing a particular period. It is most important to be aware of, and to make explicit, the distinction.

10.3   THE STUDY OF EARLY MODERN DANCE AS A DISTINCTIVE STYLE: APPROACHES AND TOPICS

This section draws on the methodologies described earlier to suggest various types of approach and subject matter. In choosing a topic it is best to err on the side of a narrowly-defined subject either in time or through time. The following examples, drawn from European early modern dance, illustrate the ways in which this approach may be employed without limiting the scope of a study.

10.3.1   In-depth study of a concise historical period in modern dance

Such a study may involve the selection of a period of interest that arises from an extensive survey of the genre in secondary sources, for example 'A comparison of American and European modern dance in America following the arrival of Hanya Holm in New York (1931–9)'.

The delineation of geographical scope should also be precisely stated: whether in one country, two countries or internationally. As a general rule the geographical scope should be balanced by the length of the historical period in order that a coherent subject area is retained.

A wide geographical area limits the historical area, for example 'Early modern dance in Germany, Austria, the Soviet Union and America at the time of the German Dancers' Congresses (1927–30)', and conversely, for example 'European early modern dance in London during the period 1926–39 with reference to visiting and expatriate German and Austrian dancers'.

The emphasis in this type of study is on what went on. Periodicals and books provide a most useful source, backed up, where possible, by company or dance school archives. A good example of the study of a concisely stated historical period is Koegler's review of dance in Germany 1927–36 (1974). One consideration for this type of study is the difficulty of isolating the period in question. This involves deciding whether knowledge of what happened before and afterwards should be taken into account and, if so, how this can best be summarized without distorting the main focus.

10.3.2   Genealogical study of modern dance

There are many possibilities for the further study of 'family trees' in modern dance as in other dance theatre genres. Whilst there is some value in the drawing of a genealogical tree in itself, the main purpose of such a quest should be to use the structure to lead into a historical study through time. A basic structure of who worked with whom and when may be purely descriptive but the purpose should be to try to identify features of choreography and performance that have resulted from choreographer/dancer or teacher/pupil relationships, for example 'Hanya Holm as a teacher: Surviving features of European style in American modern dance'.

Dance school or company records and programmes may prove to be particularly fruitful sources with which to begin the detailing of such a study. Biographical accounts may indicate areas of influence that may be pursued. The writing of dance critics who are particularly aware of a dance genre's lineage is similarly useful.

It should be recognized that the type of influence may differ according to the historical context. Three typical kinds of influence attributed to people are most commonly found. First, as in American early modern dance, a straight genealogical development is readily discernible among those dancers who served a long and close apprenticeship with Graham, Humphrey or Holm. Second, there is the increasingly common case of a dancer working for short periods with numerous choreographers in various types of performance. Third, there is the kind of connection that is often most difficult to establish where a dancer attributes 'influence' to a brief acquaintance. The last of these is particularly important for European early modern dance where many of Laban's pupils opened schools in his name after a short apprenticeship and without his approval. These examples should illustrate why a family tree is only a starting point.

10.3.3   Longitudinal study to show changes within a dance theatre genre through time in choreography, performance and appreciation

In the historical study of dance theatre genres, and of modern dance in particular, the genre may change through time, internationally or culturally, but the common features of choreography, performance and appreciation remain recognizable. They can be used to anchor facts and values in a seemingly wide-ranging topic. Although these three concepts cannot be regarded as independent of one another they can, either in themselves or in their sub-categories, act as a focus in the approaches illustrated. Because these studies are followed through time, it is particularly important that the chosen concept is established in terms of the genre as a whole and, when using examples, within the genre at a particular time.

The following examples concentrate on topics that attempt to identify features of choreography, performance and appreciation of particular importance to the identification of modern dance as a recognizable genre.

Choreography

Example: 'Expressionist narrative: a distinctive feature of European modern dance from Laban to Bausch (1920–80)'. Such a study would attempt to distinguish characteristic features of modern dance choreography, such as the use of a particular type of narrative through time. The emphasis here is in identifying choreography that shows a direct relationship between emotional experience in the real world and a heightened state as expounded on stage. European works that could be cited would include, in the early years, Laban's *Die Gaukelei* (1923) and Wigman's *Schwingende Landschaft* (1929) cycle to Bausch's *1980 – A Piece by Pina Bausch* (1980) and *Kontakthof* (1978). Cross-reference could first be made to the early years of American modern dance to demonstrate the way narrative changed. It could then be followed up with a consideration of how, in postmodern dance, narrative disappeared and then became deconstructed, whilst European modern dance retained it as a distinctive feature, albeit with different vocabularies.

Performance

Example: '*The Green Table* in performance: Interpretations by Ballets Jooss and other companies from 1932 to the present'. This has been

Figure 10.2 Wigman in *Schwingende Landschaft* (Shifting Landscape), 1929.

chosen to illustrate how performance itself is historically located. Such a subject should be considered initially in terms of how the work has been reconstructed for companies other than Ballets Jooss. The wealth of material available arises from the fact that at least twenty-eight companies have taken the dance into their repertoire (Markaard 1985). A sub-topic might refer to the different interpretations given by ballet and modern dance companies (e.g. Birmingham Royal Ballet and Batsheva Dance Company respectively). Such interpretations need to be located within the period in which they were performed, for instance, those performances given before the war that Jooss anticipated could be compared with those given after it.

Appreciation

Both choreography and performance require consideration of critical writing to illuminate them as topics. It is also possible to focus on appreciation itself using critical writing as a primary source. Example: 'The role of the critic in forming a view of early modern dance as a distinctive style'. Particular critics could be identified in different countries at different periods: Brandenburg in pre-war Germany, Coton in England, Martin in pre-war America and more recently Croce, Jowitt and Servos. The task would be to identify the features of modern dance upon which the critic bases an evaluation, to locate these within the relevant period and to identify what was modern within the changing nature of the genre as a whole. Critical writing would naturally be a major source but it would also be necessary to refer such writing back to the dance performance itself wherever possible and also to use recorded material if available.

10.3.4   The study of dancers and choreographers in modern dance

Much of dance history consists of straightforward accounts of the work of individual dancers as performers and/or choreographers. When the emphasis is on the study of a dance genre, there is no reason why a representative dancer cannot be chosen to act as a focus. However, it would be wrong to think that merely describing the work of one of the better-known dancers of a period of itself gives insight into the genre. It is preferable, when considering the work of individual dancers, to place them within a topic that acknowledges the concepts of period, choreography, performance and appreciation, hence: 'Women's dance groups in modern dance with particular reference to Mary Wigman's group 1920–36'.

Figure 10.3 Wigman in *Mütterlicher Tanz nach Frauentänze* (Maternal Dance from Women's Dance Cycle), 1934.

10.4   CONCLUSION

This chapter has examined some aspects of modern dance as a genre. In focusing upon European early modern dance style in particular, certain considerations have been highlighted. Naming and consensus views have been shown to cause difficulties if taken at face value and the need to identify distinctive concepts has been stressed. Problems of translation highlight the difficulties of using some source material. More importantly, emphasis has been placed on the need to locate a dance genre both historically and culturally. These considerations should be approached as challenges rather than stumbling blocks and the topic examples given show the diversity of approach suggested by European early modern dance as a subject and the value of structuring dance history in terms of choreography, performance and appreciation.

NOTES

1   In the first edition of this book the author wrote of early European modern dance 1910–33. The changes in both name and dating, though small, are significant. They came about through a continuing examination of the source material and owe a great deal to an ongoing discussion of the topic with June Layson.
2   In the original 'Zweite Blütezeit des Modernen Tanzes'.
3   See, particularly, Koegler (1974: 34) for a description of the process and Wigman (1935) for a major example of the naming change (cf. Wigman (1933)).
4   She dismisses European early modern dance in Germany as 'Continental excursions' (1979: 81).
5   Although there is room for a greater acknowledgement of Austrian artists: see MacTavish (1987), for instance, on Gertrud Bodenweiser.
6   Made possible by the recently published post-*glasnost* research of Souritz (1979/1990 and 1991) and Misler (1991). This leads to the further, interesting consideration of whether to include Italian Futurist dance within the style.
7   This compares with the development of regular journals in England and America, *Dancing Times* from 1910 and *Dancemagazine* from 1926 respectively.
8   This is despite recent publication of translated primary sources from the period, such as articles from the periodical *Schrifttanz* by Preston-Dunlop and Lahusen (1990) and the production of archive video footage of Mary Wigman (1991).
9   See, for instance, specific articles on dance and Nazism such as those by Müller (1987) and Preston-Dunlop (1988).
10   See, for example, Willett (1978 and 1984).
11   Literally meaning 'The warm wind and the new joy' (author's translation).

REFERENCES

Adshead, J. (ed.) (1988), *Dance Analysis: Theory and Practice*, London: Dance Books.

Armitage, M. and Stewart, V. (1935, 1970), *The Modern Dance*, New York: Dance Horizons.

Au, S. (1988), *Ballet and Modern Dance*, London: Thames & Hudson.

Baer, N. V. N. (1991), *Theatre in Revolution: Russian Avant-Garde Stage Design 1913–1935*, London: Thames & Hudson.

Böhme, F. (1933), 'Ist Ballett Deutsch?', *Deutsche Allgemeine Zeitung*, 25 April.

Brandenburg, H. (1921), *Der moderne Tanz*, 2nd edn, Munich: G. Muller.

Brown, J. M. (ed.) (1980), *The Vision of Modern Dance*, London: Dance Books.

Cohen, S. J. (ed.) (1991), *Dance as a Theatre Art: Source Readings in Dance History from 1581 to the Present* (1977), London: Dance Books.

Coton, A. V. (1946), *The New Ballet: Kurt Jooss and his Work*, London: Dobson.

Goldberg, R. L. (1979, 1988), *Performance Art*, London: Thames & Hudson.

Hall, F. (1950) *Modern English Ballet: An Interpretation*, London: Melrose.

Hamby, C. (1978) 'Dance in education – is it an adventure into the world of art? Part 1', *Laban Art of Movement Guild Magazine*, 60: 11–29.

Hodgson, J. and Preston-Dunlop, V. (1990), *Rudolf Laban: An Introduction to His Work and Influence*, Plymouth: Northcote House.

Jooss, K. and Huxley, M. (1982), 'The Green Table: a dance of death', *Ballet International*, 5, 8/9.

Knust, A. (1979), *Dictionary of Kinetography Laban*, vols 1 & 2, London: Macdonald & Evans.

Koegler, H. (1972), 'Tanz in die Dreissiger Jahre', *Ballet 1972*, Velber: Friedrich.

—— (1974), 'In the shadow of the swastika: dance in Germany, 1927–1936', *Dance Perspectives*, 57 (spring).

Laban, R. von (1928a), 'Basic principles of movement notation', *Schrifttanz*, 1, 1, translated and republished in Preston-Dunlop and Lahusen (1990): 32–4.

—— (1928b) 'Dance composition and written dance', *Schrifttanz*, 1, 2, translated and republished in Preston-Dunlop and Lahusen (1990): 38–9.

—— (1930), *Script dancing – La danse écrite*, Vienna: Universal Edition.

—— (1931), 'Anna Pavlova', *Schrifttanz*, 4, 1, translated and republished in Preston-Dunlop and Lahusen (1990).

—— (1934), 'Deutsche Tanz', *Singchor und Tanz*.

—— (1935), *Ein Leben für den Tanz: Erinnerungen*, Dresden: C Reissner.

—— (1975), *A Life for Dance: Reminiscences*, translated from 1935 edition and annotated by L. Ullmann, London: Macdonald & Evans.

Lämmel, R. (1928), *Der Moderne Tanz*, Berlin: P. Oestergaard.

McDonagh, D. (1976), *The Complete Guide to Modern Dance*, New York: Doubleday.

MacTavish, S. D. (1987), *An Ecstasy of Purpose*, Dunedin, N.Z.: MacTavish, Humphrey Associates.

Markaard, A. and H. (1985), *Jooss*, Cologne: Ballett Bühnen.

Martin, J. (1933, 1965), *The Modern Dance*, New York: Dance Horizons.

Maynard, O. (1965), *American Modern Dancers: The Pioneers*, Boston: Little, Brown.

Misler, N. (1991), 'Designing gestures in the laboratory of dance', in Baer (1991).

Müller, H. (1986), *Mary Wigman*, Cologne: Ballett Bühnen.

—— (1987), 'Wigman and National Socialism', *Ballet Review*, spring.

Murray, J. (1979), *Dance Now*, Harmondsworth: Penguin.

Odom, M. (1980), 'Mary Wigman: the early years 1913–1925', *The Drama Review*, 24, 4.

Patterson, M. (1981), *The Revolution in German Theatre 1900–1933*, London: Routledge & Kegan Paul.

Preston-Dunlop, V. (1988), 'Laban and the Nazis', *Dance Theatre Journal*, 6, 2.

Preston-Dunlop, V. and Lahusen, S. (1990), *Schrifttanz: A View of German Dance in the Weimar Republic*, London: Dance Books.

Scheyer, E. (1970), 'The shapes of space: the art of Mary Wigman and Oskar Schlemmer', *Dance Perspectives*, 41.

Servos, N. and Weigelt, G. (1984), *Pina Bausch: Wuppertal Dance Theater or the Art of Training a Goldfish*, Cologne: Ballet Bühnen.

Souritz, E. (1979, trans. 1990), *Soviet Choreographers in the 1920s*, edited by S. Banes, and translated by L. Visson, London: Dance Books.

—— (1991), 'Constructivism and dance', in Baer (1991).

Wigman, M. (1933), 'The philosophy of modern dance', *Europa*, 1, 1 (May–July), reprinted in Cohen (1991).

—— (1935), *Deutsche Tanzkunst*, Dresden: Reisner.

—— (1966), *The Language of Dance*, translated by W. Sorell, London: Macdonald & Evans.

—— (1975), *The Mary Wigman Book* (1973), edited and translated by W. Sorrell, Middletown, Conn.: Wesleyan University Press.

—— (1991), *Mary Wigman 1886–1973*, video produced and directed by A. F. Snyder, Pennington, N.J.: Princeton/Dance Horizons.

Willett, J. (1978), *The New Sobriety 1917–1933: Art and Politics in the Weimar Period*, London: Thames & Hudson.

—— (1984), *The Weimar Years: A Culture Cut Short*, London: Thames & Hudson.

Chapter 11

Expression and expressionism in American modern dance

Deborah Jowitt

The visual arts and, even more so, music have the ability to express only the nature of the medium: the interplay of colour, surface, and shape, or of tone, rhythm, texture, and harmony. They do not, of course, always do so. When a vogue for figurative painting supersedes abstraction, or when thickly laid-on whorls and splatters of paint bespeak muscular application and suggest emotional states, the art critics can allude confidently to 'expression', and everyone understands what they are talking about. When the New York Philharmonic presented its 'Horizons '83' concerts, a catalogue and four symposia examined the issues implicit in the festival's subtitle: 'Since 1968, a New Romanticism?' To perceive the swing away from the intellectuality of twelve-tone music towards what the Philharmonic's then composer-in-residence Jacob Druckman called 'acoustic sensuality' (in the work of Luciano Berio, George Crumb and others) did not require highly trained ears.

As I hope this chapter will make clear, the human body, guided by its intellect and spirit, can never be a neutral artistic medium. It is never inexpressive. It is not, in fact, an 'it' but the physical manifestation of a gendered and unique person. When we speak of expression in dance, we are often speaking of fictions, of the dancer expressing emotions that she or he is not, at the moment, in the grip of; of the dancer assuming a character or role that is not her or his own in terms of the performance taking place; of a gesture being emphasized in such a way as to convey a specific meaning beyond its own expressive actuality: an arm raised, say, to point at a destination, rather than simply to lift (with all that that may communicate to the viewer).

In 1965, the *Village Voice*'s dance critic, Jill Johnston, chastised choreographer Kenneth King for 'applying vanguard tactics to a moribund expressionism' (Johnston 1965: 8). Johnston's 'expressionism' in this case referred to mainstream modern dance, the work of reigning monarchs Martha Graham and José Limón and their followers, which emphasized dramatic scenarios and movement rooted in emotional gesture. Also, like writers today who loosely apply 'expressionism' and, more frequently, 'expressionistic', to dance, Johnston may have meant that the work in question trafficked in those fictions and emotional colorations mentioned above.

Expression, as an issue to be defined and debated, predates the rise of modern dance in America during the late 1920s. Isadora Duncan railed at what she felt to be the innate inexpressiveness of the ballet vocabulary, or rather detested the fact that the pre-eminent image ballet expressed to her was one of discipline, arbitrary choices and aristocratic decorum. Neither was the ideal dancer one of those who 'by concentrating their minds, lead the body into the rhythm of a desired emotion, expressing a remembered feeling or experience' (Duncan 1928: 51). Instead, the dancer should come to understand that he is expressing something greater than self, that his body 'is simply the luminous manifestation of his soul' (Duncan 1928: 52).

From Duncan on, a theme that surfaces in writing and talking by American choreographers is a dread of dancing becoming merely (and 'merely' is often a part of the statement) self-expression. That this idea was reiterated indicates that self-expression was rampant, especially in the wake of Duncan. Her theories, as they were appropriated by educators, were often misunderstood.

In the years between 1927, when Martha Graham made her first 'modern' works and Doris Humphrey developed her ideas of group choreography, and 1992, choreographers' ideas about the role and nature of expression in dance have swung in several directions.

In the late 1920s and early 1930s, one could make a case for linking choreographers like Graham and Doris Humphrey with Expressionism, the early-twentieth-century art movement that involved a highly subjective use of colour, shape and rhythmic stress in painting and music, as well as experiments in non-naturalistic drama. Unlike German *Ausdruckstanz* pioneer Mary Wigman, who knew and admired German Expressionist painters Emil Nolde, Wassily Kandinsky and others, the Americans had no personal contact with those painters who banded together in Dresden in 1905 as Die Brücke or in Munich as Der Blaue Reiter (1911). However, in 1923, New York's Anderson Gallery mounted the first major exhibit of German Expressionistic painters in America, and Klee, Kandinsky and others had one-man shows during the 1920s and 1930s. It is known that Graham admired the sculpture of Ernst Barlach and the drawings of Käthe Kollwitz. Later, she became familiar with Paul Klee's writings. On the basis of similar ideas expressed by the American dancers and the German painters, as well as a certain kinship evident in their work, one can assume that the dancers absorbed what interested them, and only that, in the credos of German Expressionism.

To the American choreographers, as to the painters, freedom meant the discarding of old forms and the creation of forms born of necessity. In 1912 Kandinsky wrote: 'the form is the outer expression of the inner content' (in Chipp 1968: 157). Graham's wording was strikingly similar, if terser and more percussive as befitted her choreographic style: 'Out of emotion comes form' (Armitage 1978: 97). Humphrey, in a letter to her mother, called it 'moving from the inside out' (Humphrey 1927a). As Kandinsky explained in his 1911 essay 'Concerning the Spiritual in Art', the artist's emotion, projected on the subject and shaped into the art work, should awaken similar emotion in the viewer who apprehends the work (in Hall and Ulanov 1967: 168). It was to this end that he studied the physical and psychological effects of colour. In the final moments of Doris Humphrey's *Color Harmony* (1928), the dancers, the 'warm and capricious' yellows, the 'rich and sturdy' reds, and so on, are united by a figure in white, a 'silver arrow' that contains in its whiteness all colours (Humphrey 1927b). One suspects that Humphrey had been influenced not only by the physical properties of colour and light but also by Kandinsky's ideas, and especially by the reference in his 1912 essay 'On the Problems of Form' to '*the white fertilizing ray*' that 'leads to evolution, to elevation' (in Chipp 1968: 155).

Expressionist art's emphasis on subjectivity militated against realism and made distortion a key stylistic ingredient. According to the dictionary description, lower-case expressionism in art or music is also characterized by distortion. As art historian Wylie Sypher remarked in the course of distinguishing Monet from the Fauves and the Expressionists, 'Expressionist art is not *plein air*, but an exasperation of what is seen' (Sypher 1960: 180). And certainly an artist painting what Norwegian Symbolist painter Edvard Munch in 1907/8 called 'the images on the back sides of the eyes' (in Chipp 1968: 114) produces not an impression of reality but an expression of its impact on the soul.

One must be wary, however, of the 'Expressionist' label, especially if applying it to dance. In the first place, Graham, Humphrey, Charles Weidman and other American modern dancers were not, like Mary Wigman, mystical in their thinking about the body, nor could their fervent insistence on being American and dancing as Americans be equated with the German yearning for connection with a Fatherland hallowed by Teutonic myth. The Americans were plainer, more down-to-earth, more concerned with the individual *vis-à-vis* contemporary society. If they absorbed ideas from German Expressionists and choreographers involved with *Ausdruckstanz* (expression dance), they were also drawn to the pragmatic idealism of the architects associated with modernism like Le Corbusier, Walter Gropius and Mies van der Rohe. In eschewing decorative movement, much as the designers dispensed with ornament, they too wanted to reveal the essential nature of the material, the architecture of muscle, sinew and skeleton. Their focus inevitably involved the actuality of the human body, even though that body was moulded by personal vision.

As I have pointed out, the body, as a medium, automatically evokes human action and feeling, no matter how abstract the choreographer wishes to be. By the same token, the degree to which a subject can be distorted by emotion is limited by the body's capabilities, although in a terrifying solo as the Matriarch in *With My Red Fires* (1936), Humphrey did come close to becoming more than just a woman driven insane by rage and jealousy, as did Graham as Medea in *Cave of the Heart* (1946). Their very skeletons seemed melted out of shape by the heat of their passions.

Two early solos, Graham's *Lamentation* (1930) and Humphrey's *Two Ecstatic Themes* (1931) are emblematic of the American choreographers' approach to individual feeling. In *Lamentation*, Graham's body, encased in a taut tube of stretch jersey, is all jutting angles straining against the cloth or protruding from its open ends – knees, elbows, hands with fingers pressed together, clubbed feet. The few moments of symmetry stand out against moments when the seated body is rocked off balance, distorted by the externalization of inner pressure.

Humphrey's *Two Ecstatic Themes* is less severe and more 'natural'; however, her ideas, too, are cast on the body, turning emotion into action, rhythm and design. The first part, 'Circular Descent', is essentially one long fall. A powerful pressure to yield bends her body back in a long curve hinged at the knees. In her circling, in her temporary return to an upright position, one feels the precariousness of her equilibrium, the luxury and the peril of giving in to a pressure that is both outside and inside her. The quicker, more staccato 'Pointed Ascent' gradually returns her to standing, but to a new more resolute position. As her biographer, Marcia B. Siegel, writes, 'the dance is a perfectly fused meeting of passion and will' (Siegel 1987: 103).

In both of these groundbreaking solos the forms themselves embodied the feelings and, intense as the performances were, neither woman mimed emotion. Recent interpreters of *Lamentation* tend towards literal 'acting'. Graham and Humphrey kept their faces relatively calm, part of a gesture flung by the entire body against the surrounding space.

By the mid-1940s in Graham's dance-theatre works, the expression of feeling, however hotly enacted, was gradually becoming codified through the development of a Graham vocabulary of movement. She, along with Humphrey's pupil José Limón (by then one of the best known and most influential of American choreographers), shaped dramatic narrative into sequences of dreamlike intensity affected by their viewpoints as central performers in their own works. The role of 'she-who-remembers', which, increasingly in Graham's dances, offered some respite to her ageing body, also firmly anchored the dances in her eye and mind and presented almost every onstage act as personal recollection. In Limón's *Emperor Jones* (1956), based on Eugene O'Neill's play, the six men of the chorus transform themselves from subjects to trees to nameless shadowy fears, depending on the hero's crazed imagination. However he sees them, we see them.

Beginning in the 1950s, Anna Sokolow, a dancer who had left Graham's company in the 1930s to embark on an independent choreographic career, evolved an idiosyncratic, dark-souled form of expressionism. Concerned with political oppression and with the anomie that plagues modern society, Sokolow (by then no longer performing in her own compositions) would allow various soloists to emerge from her haunted crowds and then sink back into a futile but desperate, and desperately gloomy, existence. As her biographer, Larry Warren, remarks, 'The truth she seeks onstage has nothing to do with a narrative . . . but rather about how it feels to live in [the characters'] inner worlds' (Warren 1991: 153).

The people in the dances that Sokolow continues to choreograph often make gestures extreme in their emotionality, clapping both hands over their faces, crashing down, stretching out shivering fingers, arching back as if waiting for the sky to open and cool their thirst. When they touch one another, even in the most lyric of passages, their heads avert or lift, giving the impression that intimacy is perilous. Their rhythms are punctuated by silent outbursts, howls and gasps made with the entire body.

Some of the gestures, the groupings, have a painterly clarity. The extraordinary opening section of *Dreams* (1961), a piece inspired by the Holocaust, shows a woman groping her way forwards by walking on the shoulders of a group of dark-clothed men, whose faces the audience never sees and whom she seems not to see. As she steps, holding the men's impersonally lifted arms, the men at the back keep slipping to the front of the group, so the woman can never come to the end of this road, of this living nightmare.

Beginning in the 1930s then, American choreographers associated with modern dance developed an approach to emotion that did not rely on naturalistic acting, strict linear narrative, or the pantomime of ballet story-telling. The choreography involved a styling of both individual bodies and the ensemble into icons of feeling, abstract in the sense that Graham meant when she said that if designer Isamu Noguchi was an abstract artist, he was abstract in the way that orange juice was an abstraction of an orange (Schonberg 1968: 29). One became an abstractionist by pressing out the essence and abandoning everything else.

It would seem prudent at this point to abandon the term 'expressionism', both upper and lower case, because of its powerful associations either with a particular movement in art history or with stylistic elements such as distortion and dissonance, intensity of colour and strong outline. A more useful term might simply be 'expressive' dance, although this too can be misleading. Subtly in the 1950s and with bellicose zest in the 1960s, certain choreographers (Alwin Nikolais, Erick Hawkins, Merce Cunningham and the group gathered together in New York as Judson Dance Theater) began in diverse ways to query what it meant to be expressive and what was being expressed.

Merce Cunningham's influential ideas, often quoted, often misunderstood, can be seen as a counterstatement to the dominant emotionalism, narrative and role-playing that had developed in the work of Martha Graham, in whose company he danced from 1939 to 1945. The Cunningham credo as passed down by dancers' word-of-mouth and journalists' assessments is that movement is not supposed to be about anything, that it is just movement. (Balanchine lore is similar: 'Don't think, dear, just do' is his most often quoted advice to dancers.) But Cunningham's ideas about expression are subtle and deep. He told interviewer Jacqueline Lesschaeve, 'I don't think that what I do is non-expressive . . . I always feel that movement itself is expressive, regardless of intentions of expressivity, beyond intention' (Lesschaeve 1985: 106). Cunningham's concentration on movement and form, his use of chance procedures in composition, his refusal to direct his dancers do not, as he once put it, 'separate the human from the actions that he does' (Cunningham 1968, n.p.). One *can* see Cunningham dancers simply as particles moving in a pattern that is mysterious, even chaotic, yet which also has a logic and harmony that one can sense. However, one can also see images of human volition and passion. Remarkable duet passages, such as those that Cunningham in earlier days performed with Carolyn Brown, reveal through elegant, unusual movement ineffable truths about men and women together, truths more profound than emanate from many pas de deux intentionally cast as romances.

Cunningham presented his position eloquently in a 1955 essay:

In reference to the current idea that dance must be expressive of something and that it must be involved with the images deep within our conscious and unconscious, it is my impression that there is no need to push for them . . . if you really dance – your body, that is, and not the mind's enforcement – the manifestations of the spirit through your torso and limbs will inevitably take on the shape of life. We give ourselves away at every moment. We do not, therefore, have to *try* to do it.

(Cunningham 1955: 72–3)

Cunningham avoids movements with obvious emotional associations: no storms at the centre of the body, no gestures delivered with the force of anger. Graham's style was built on the essentially Dionysian technical base of contraction and release; Cunningham style is by nature Apollonian. The limbs are extended, almost balletic at times in their elegance; the stance is essentially upright, the gaze serene. This is in keeping with his generous intent not to impose *his* feelings on the steps, the dancers or the audience.

His long-time colleague, composer John Cage, wrote of the need to relinquish control of sounds and 'set about discovering means to let sounds be themselves, rather than vehicles for man-made theories or expressions of human sentiment' (Cage 1979: 10). For Cunningham, it is in allowing movements to 'be themselves' that some deeper 'expression' emerges.

That his ideas should be taken by some spectators, critics and Cunningham dancers to be advocating non-expression is unfortunate. Non-expression was, however, a hot political issue in the vanguard movement that developed in New York during the 1960s. The choreographers who participated in Judson Dance Theater took some of John Cage's ideas to an extreme position in dance, disavowing Cunningham's continuing interest in difficult and beautiful dancing. In their aesthetic of dailiness and rejection of elitism, expressivity became a taboo. Not only might it connect them with the mainstream modern dance that they were rejecting, it manipulated the audience, just as the prevailing political and social power structures, in their view, were manipulating thought and feeling in everyday American life. An integral part of the 1965 manifesto embedded in an article that Yvonne Rainer contributed to the *Tulane Drama Review* concluded, 'no to moving or being moved' (Rainer 1965: 178). Later, she wrote that 'the artifice of performance has been reevaluated in that action, or what one does, is more interesting and important than the exhibition of character and attitude, and that action can best be focused on through the submerging of the personality; so ideally one is not even oneself, one is a neutral "doer"' (Rainer 1974: 65).

The quest to present the performer as completely neutral is a somewhat quixotic one. In Rainer's case, no matter how much she averted her gaze from the audience in her famous *Trio A* (1966), no matter how much she flattened out phrasing (with its suspect emphasis on climax and hierarchy), she remained inherently expressive; her determined neutrality became in itself provocative and even dramatic.

As Noël Carroll pointed out in a paper delivered at one of a series of philosophical sessions on dance presented at the American Dance Festival in 1979, *Trio A* was also clearly expressive in another sense: 'it is discursive – it calls attention to hitherto unexplored, even suppressed, movement possibilities of the dance medium' (Carroll 1981: 101).

The 1960s work that Sally Banes has termed 'Breakaway Post-Modern

Dance' (Banes 1987: xv) not only raised questions about expressiveness, it, even, on occasion, made anti-expression its subject. In one section of Rainer's *Dialogues* (1964), a series of loaded sentences delivered by Rainer and Judith Dunn was undercut by their workmanlike simultaneous solos and their matter-of-fact delivery of the lines ('Help help.' 'I am angry.' 'No, I am ecstatic.' 'I am always anxious', etc., Rainer 1974: 296). 'Love', from Rainer's *Terrain* (1963), consisted of Rainer and a partner (William Davis) performing a series of poses drawn from an Indian erotic treatise. The performers manoeuvred into position as if working at a mundane job, and intermittent remarks like 'I love you' and 'Say you love me' clinically detached the gestures from any emotional context of motivation. The effect was to debunk emotional pas de deux that implied the sexual act, but disguised it by glamour and virtuosic dancing. That the duet also 'expressed' to some viewers a contemporary detachment of spirit and flesh was not, I think, any part of Rainer's intent.

Even among vanguard choreographers who began to show work in New York in the 1960s, there were exceptions both to Cunningham's the-movement-is-the-meaning aesthetic and to the deliberate avoidance of expressiveness on the part of some Judsonites. Meredith Monk and Kenneth King, who were not affiliated with the Judson group (although they presented work at the church where the latter regularly performed), created highly striking, often mysterious theatrical imagery without resorting to conventional 'expressive' performing. Instead they utilized for expressive purposes postmodern strategies such as neutral performing style, collage techniques and the juxtaposition of dissimilar elements. Their imagery and their props (for instance, in King's 1966 *Blow-Out*, a table that had legs of different lengths) recalled the spatial distortions of the Expressionists); but the performers remained objective 'doers'. At the climax of Monk's mixed-media piece *16 Millimeter Earrings* (1966), the choreographer stood erect and motionless in an open trunk while red streamers blew up around her and a film of fire burning a doll played over her body.

Monk was to develop techniques learned in the 1960s to striking effect in her great music-theatre works such as *Quarry* (1975) and *Education of the Girlchild* (1972–3). In these, emotion is generated at the intersection of voice, movement and image. Especially in recent years, Monk's wordless, feeling-laden songs invade the singers' bodies and colour their precise yet enigmatic gestures, so that body image seems to be generated by and fused with music.

There were other worthy exceptions to the predominantly contentless and increasingly analytical branch of early postmodern dance. William Dunas's ongoing series of related solos offered fragmented images of a Beckettian survivor in some bleak, claustrophobic limbo.

The mysterious agrarian ordeals presented by Kei Takei in her gradually accumulating epic, *Light* (1969 and ongoing), drew in part on Takei's background in Japanese modern dance (which had been influenced by Mary Wigman's teachings) as well as on more contemporary methods.

A renewed interest in meaning, emotion and narrative began to surface in postmodern dance at the end of the 1970s. As Sally Banes has suggested, the trend may be related to the vogue for French intellectual theories, structuralism and post-structuralism, that foreground meaning and interpretation (Banes 1987: xxviii). The visits of Pina Bausch, although no direct and obvious influence on American choreographers can be detected, somehow legitimized the investigation of human feelings and made them interesting again as a subject for dance. The rise of Mark Morris, who unselfconsciously made use of traditional approaches to music and expression, yet brought a fresh vision to dance, shows that the fervour for innovation in movement and form that had marked the 1930s and the 1960s was no longer paramount. Certainly the new emphasis on emotion coincided with the emergence in dance of elements that had for some time been integral to post-modernism in architecture and painting: eclecticism, quoting styles of the past, a taste for luxury and virtuosic display. The new emotional emphasis in dance may also have stemmed from unsettled times that saw an increase in urban violence and the rise of AIDS, as well as the ironic mating, set off during the Reagan presidency, of public and private greed with economic distress.

Twyla Tharp, a choreographer who had, from her earliest per-formance in 1965, been concerned primarily with the resonance of movement and form (and to a subtle degree with behaviour) began in 1980 with *When We Were Very Young* and the violent *Short Stories* to experiment with character, text, narrative and emotion. These works were followed the next year by *The Catherine Wheel* and by *Bad Smells*, an almost expressionistic, hallucinatory vision of terror and ferocity amplified by the simultaneous projection of distorted video images of the onstage action. Interviewed in 1984 Tharp remarked that although the form-for-form's-sake approach had once seemed enough, 'It's not enough now. We need that form to express something. Something in society won't buy abstract art at the moment. I know I won't' (Jowitt 1984: 83).

For young choreographers raised in the Cunningham aesthetic, grappling with meaning presented problems. They hadn't been bred to produce 'expressive' movement tailored to subject matter. Some had political and social concerns that they felt couldn't be articulated by movement alone. Jane Comfort, experimenting with sign language and then with text, remarked in 1988, 'I had things to say that I absolutely didn't know how to do with my body' (Jowitt 1988: 9). So many choreographers turned to text that festivals featuring dances with text were held two years running (1980 and 1981) at PS 1 (a former city school turned into alternative galleries). Comfort, Ishmael Houston-Jones, Stephanie Skura, David Rousseve and Amy Pivar are just a few of the 'young' choreographers who often go beyond embedding passages of text in a dance; instead they might be said to script plays shaped by a dance sensibility.

At Judson Church, the juxtaposition of movement and text had been a matter of suggesting structural analogies or referring to process. (In the 1970s, Judson choreographers Trisha Brown and David Gordon took word–movement analogies to new heights, he in many works, she in her *Primary Accumulation With Talking Plus Water Motor.*) In some of the works by the next generation of choreographers, text deliberately, if obliquely, reveals content. Here is Marcia Siegel's 1989 account of the 'car crash' section in San Franciscan Joe Goode's *The Disaster Series*: 'smoke wafts into the room and Goode croons terse reports from a police blotter into an upstage microphone' (Siegel 1989a: 15). Beginning in the late 1960s, Kenneth King had made works that featured non-stop dancing and feverishly intellectual theorizing spangled with provocative plays on words; colliding, the movement and linguistic systems offered structural insights into each other as well as tapping (one could feel it) into some kind of mystical network of cosmic correspondences. Thirty years later, the energetic dancing that some performers do as they speak does not so much illumine a text or its structure as provide some kind of motor to power speech and give it heat and conviction.

When Bill T. Jones and Arnie Zane showed their *Monkey Road Run* at the Kitchen in New York in 1979 and *Blauvelt Mountain* the following year, one could clearly identify compositional devices developed in the previous two decades, but these were being put to different uses. Jones and Zane delighted in such gambits as re-presenting material seen earlier in a work, pressing new meanings from the altered context. But, although the form was cool, the movement could be hot, explosive (in one of the often-repeated moves in the earlier piece, the two men crouched, clutched each other, and looked warily about). Dancing might be combined with text, often autobiographical; the juxtaposed discourses illumined one another without literally corresponding. And in *Blauvelt Mountain,* as in many subsequent works, Jones's voice dramatically escalated words in the style of a Baptist preacher exhorting the congregation to repent.

Like many choreographers of their generation, Jones and Zane had been exposed to Contact Improvisation. The 'art-sport' developed in the 1970s by Steve Paxton had been for many in dance's counterculture a kind of 'national social network' uniting like-minded people regard-less of skill (Novack 1990: 206). When the deliberate presentation of feeling became a desirable ingredient of dance, Contact Improvisation was one of the movement sources that nourished it. Even in their purest form, Contact duets tend to be inherently expressive, allowing the audience fleetingly to perceive the dancers as lovers, playful children, drunks and combatants, while the physical allure of the daring lifts, falls and catches arouses strong kinaesthetic responses.

It must be pointed out too that, in the 1960s, not all of the back-to-basics dance favoured the pointedly inexpressive, minimal-energy per-forming styles often utilized by Rainer, Deborah Hay and Paxton himself, among others. Programmes by vanguard choreographers also featured rambunctious game or task structures by, for instance, Trisha Brown, Simone Forti and Carolee Schneeman. The notion of task may have fed directly into the repetitive patterned works made by choreo-graphers like Lucinda Childs, but it also became a guiding principle of Contact Improvisation and for the imaginative movement tasks that Trisha Brown developed into her present rich dance style.

Contact Improvisation moves, the slippery complexity of Brown's dancing, and the shrugging, twisting elegance that Twyla Tharp drew from black vernacular dance and her own salty imagination in turn became the bases of expressive vocabularies for an age of uneasiness. By the late 1980s in New York, audiences were being treated to a spate of dances in which partners hurled themselves into each other's arms, sagged against one another with full body weight, shoved people to the floor and then hauled them up into an embrace. As pointed out in an article by Patrick Kelly and Otis Stuart entitled 'Neoromanticism, Men, and the Eighties', the subject of choice has become human relationships, and the duet the central image (Kelly and Stuart 1989: 34–8). These duets rarely stress the gender warfare or images of dominant–submissive relationships that inform works by Pina Bausch. Bebe Miller, Ralph Lemon, Doug Varone, David Dorfman, Susan Marshall are but some for whom the duet can become a desperate grappling in which supporter and supported constantly exchange roles. The encounters are not always uncomplicatedly loving, and many are terrifying. This may reflect the sad fact that AIDS galvanized the dance community into developing support systems and made tenderness and rage often hard to separate. In Susan Marshall's *Interior with Seven Figures* (1987), a dancer identified in the programme as Mother scrabbles to climb up one identified as Father. Before, she has run and leaped certain of being caught; she has received his diving body and gently lowered it down. Now she labours as if being in his arms were a right to be insisted on. At another point, the man, clutching her, slowly revolves in a crouch, repeatedly gluing his lips to hers until we feel that the kisses are draining both of them.

Reading contemporary dance criticism makes it clear how strongly the element of emotion figures. When Marcia Siegel can write of

Wildwood (1989) by Douglas Dunn, who once focused almost exclusively on movement, 'She seems to ingest this substance and then falls into a kind of trance. The others lift her, jerking and writhing, and try to control her' (Siegel 1989b: 12), we know that the picture has changed. As we do when Joan Acocella asserts in a review of Bebe Miller's remarkable 1989 solo: '*Rain* is a dance about the reunification of the earth and the human spirit' (Acocella 1989: 69). Doug Varone's extraordinary *Force Majeure* (1991) might even be considered as neo-expressionistic with its family, stiff and grotesque as cartoon figures, indulging in fierce, curious games and rites and eventually, I think, devouring a visionary misfit.

These postmodern forays into emotion are not stylistically similar to modern dance in its early days or at its height of emotionality and literariness in the 1950s (when Louis Horst's dance composition syllabus *Modern Forms*, with its solo assignment on 'Introspection', was still dogma). The impulsive body language, the edge of dailiness give the dances a different look. It is, however, interesting to think that a notion related to Martha Graham's 1935 statement 'the Dance is action, not attitude' (Armitage 1978: 103) seems to be guiding some young choreographers of today. One shows frustration by trying to climb a wall, not by crouching beside it and doing the gestural equivalent of moaning. This principle distinguishes expressiveness from self-expression. Emotion is released to the spectator as a by-product of tasks impelled from deep within: to keep telling a story even as someone tries to knock the wind out of one; to burrow under a pile of inert bodies, no matter how often one is dragged out; to keep one's body touching another at all times.

'The body shooting into space is not an idea of man's freedom', wrote Merce Cunningham, 'but is the body shooting into space. And that very action is all other actions and is man's freedom, and at the same instant his non-freedom' (Cunningham 1955: 72). The statement, ambiguous as it is, reinforces the notion of the dancing body as an inevitable bearer of significant ideas and feelings, even when a choreographer never traffics in those fictions that so many equate with expression. Surely, the subject for debate ought not to be whether a particular dance is 'expressive' or 'inexpressive'. We must instead ask what 'story' it is telling us and note well the manner of the telling.

REFERENCES

Acocella, J. (1989), 'Nice Green Pillow', *7 Days*, 13 December: 69.
Armitage, M. (ed.) (1978), *Martha Graham: The Early Years*, New York: Da Capo Press.
Banes, S. (1987), *Terpsichore in Sneakers* (1st edn 1980), Boston, Mass.: Houghton Mifflin, (2nd edn 1987), Middletown, Conn.: Wesleyan University Press.

Cage, J. (1979), *Silence: Lectures and Writings* (1961), Middletown, Conn.: Wesleyan University Press.

Carroll, N. (1981), 'Post-modern dance and expression', in G. Fancher and G. Myers (eds), *Philosophical Essays on Dance*, Brooklyn, N.Y.: Dance Horizons: 95–104.

Chipp, B. (ed) (1968), *Theories of Modern Art: A Source Book by Artists and Critics*, Berkeley: University of California Press.

Cunningham, M. (1955), 'The impermanent art', *7 Arts*, 3, edited by Fernando Puma, Indian Hills, Colo.: The Falcon Wing's Press: 69–77.

—— (1968), *Changes: Notes on Choreography*, edited by Frances Starr, New York: Something Else Press.

Duncan, I. (1928), *The Art of the Dance*, edited by Sheldon Cheney, New York: Theater Arts.

Hall, J. B. and Ulanov, B. (eds) (1967), *Modern Culture and the Arts*, New York: McGraw-Hill Book Company.

Humphrey, D. (1927a), letter to her parents, 8 July, Doris Humphrey Letters (New York Public Library).

—— (1927b), Doris Humphrey Collection, M–19 (New York Public Library).

Johnston, J. (1965), 'Horizontal baggage', *The Village Voice*, 29 July: 8, 12.

Jowitt, D. (1984), 'Twyla Tharp: the choreographer faces the world', *The Village Voice*, 24 April: 83

—— (1988), 'Talk to me', Dance Special, *The Village Voice*, 19 April: 9–10.

Kelly, P. and Stuart, O. (1989), 'Neoromanticism, men, and the eighties: dancing the difference', *Dance Magazine*, January: 34–8.

Lesschaeve, J. (1985), *Merce Cunningham: The Dancer and the Dance*, New York and London: Marion Boyars.

Novack, C. J. (1990), *Sharing the Dance: Contact Improvisation and American Culture*, Madison, Wis.: University of Wisconsin Press.

Rainer, Y. (1965), 'Some retrospective notes on a dance for 10 people and 12 mattresses called *Parts of Some Sextets*, performed at the Wadsworth Atheneum, Hartford, Connecticut, and Judson Memorial Church, New York, in March, 1965', *Tulane Drama Review* 10, 3: 168–78.

—— (1974), *Work 1961–73*, Halifax, Nova Scotia: The Press of the Nova Scotia College of Art and Design/New York: New York University Press.

Schonberg, H. (1968), 'Isamu Noguchi, a kind of throwback', *The New York Times Magazine*, 14 April: 26–34.

Siegel, M. B. (1987), *Days on Earth: The Dance of Doris Humphrey*, New Haven, Conn.: Yale University Press.

—— (1989a), 'Hazards of the self', *New York Press*, 13 October: 15.

—— (1989b), 'Faux Primitifism", *New York Press*, 29 December: 12.

Sypher, W. (1960), '*Rococco to Cubism in Art and Literature*, New York: Random House, Vintage Books.

Warren, L. (1991), *Sokolow, Anna: The Rebellious Spirit*, Princeton, N.J.: Princeton Book Company Publishers.

Chapter 12

Beyond expressionism

Merce Cunningham's critique of 'the natural'

Roger Copeland

METHODOLOGY

In their well-known book *Theory of Literature* (1949), René Wellek
and Austin Warren distinguish between 'intrinsic' and 'extrinsic' approaches to criticism. Intrinsic critics (most notably, the so-called 'New
Critics' who dominated literary scholarship in America during the
1940s and 1950s) sought to concentrate the critic's attention on the
formal properties of the art object itself rather than on the social or
historical context in which it was created. Merce Cunningham is widely
acknowledged to be one of the contemporary dance world's foremost
practitioners of a formalist aesthetic. Thus it seems entirely appropriate
that most of what has been written about Cunningham falls into the
category that Wellek and Warren refer to as 'intrinsic' criticism. This
body of writing is essentially descriptive in nature; and, at its best,
it performs an invaluable service by providing the reader with a closely
observed, physically palpable sense of the Cunningham body-in-motion.
Applied to the work of some formalist choreographers, a detailed
descriptive approach (or what the New Critics would have called a 'close
reading') is often more rewarding than other critical methods. But for
reasons that I intend to explore in this chapter, an 'intrinsic' response
to Cunningham's dances constitutes only the first, most tentative step
towards accounting for his significance. Dance writers are so eager
to credit Cunningham with having liberated choreography from the
burden imposed by various sorts of meaning (narrative, symbolism,
personal expression, etc.) that they often fail to consider properly the
meaning of this liberation. So rather than celebrating the 'autonomous'
nature of Cunningham's choreography, this chapter examines his movement style in a broader context, that is, not a social but an aesthetic
context. It argues that the fullest appreciation of Cunningham requires
us to examine the relationship between his movement and the work of
those composers and visual artists (Cage, Rauschenberg, Johns, etc.)
with whom he collaborated most often. An even richer understanding

of Cunningham's work emerges if we examine his innovations within the particular 'dance-historical' context of the 1950s. That was the decade in which Cunningham forged an aesthetic rejecting many expressionist elements in the modern dance tradition of Martha Graham. At the same time, his principal collaborators were rejecting another expressionist heritage: the ethos of abstract expressionism in the visual arts. This essay examines the similarities between Cunningham's repudiation of the Graham aesthetic and his collaborators' repudiation of the spirit of abstract expressionism.

THE CUNNINGHAM CIRCLE

During the late 1970s, when the Sony Walkman craze was still in full fashionable swing, it was not uncommon for members of the Cunningham/Cage audience to bring their battery-powered headsets along with them to the company's performances, in effect providing their own auditory accompaniment as the Cunningham dancers went through their cool, brainy, elegant paces. At the time, this struck me as a perfectly logical, perhaps even inevitable, extension of the Cunningham/Cage aesthetic in which movement, sound (and, for that matter, decor) are all conceived and executed independently of one another, steadfastly refusing to meld into a fixed, organic whole. The separate elements all exist simultaneously before us, inhabiting what Cunningham calls an 'open field'. The order and manner in which we combine those elements is up to us. And I thought to myself: if Cunningham refuses to control the way we look at and listen to his work, what is wrong with seizing the initiative and maximizing one's auditory options?

But a few years later I had the privilege of participating in a panel discussion with John Cage and I took the opportunity to ask him what he thought of this phenomenon. Cage's generosity was legendary and his tolerance for eccentricity seemingly boundless. So I fully expected him to nod his approval and say 'why not?', perhaps even issue a fully-fledged endorsement. But much to my surprise, he raised a series of objections, the most trenchant of which was: how do we know what the Walkman-wearers are listening to? What if the sound they supply has not been composed by chance operations? And if so, how can it possibly constitute an appropriate accompaniment for a dance by Merce Cunningham where chance operations routinely determine a number of variables such as spatial arrangement of the dancers and the order in which disparate choreographic phrases follow one another?

His comments struck me with the force of an epiphany, for they made me realize that, contrary to popular opinion, the relationship of sound, movement and decor in a Cunningham piece is not entirely arbitrary.

Granted, the sound and the movement do not provide a metrical support structure for one another; and the decor and costumes do not set out to embody a central concept that governs the entire enterprise. But there *is* a shared sensibility at work.

Chance may determine many aspects of the Cunningham experience, but Cunningham does not choose his collaborators by chance. They all belong, we might say, to the Cunningham circle. And what a circle it is! In addition to Cage, the 'founding members' included the composers Earle Brown, Morton Feldman, David Tutor and Christian Wolff. The circle also encompasses many of the visual artists who pioneered the transition from abstract expressionist painting to pop, hard-edge, colour-field and 'post-painterly' art: painters and sculptors such as Robert Rauschenberg, Jasper Johns, Andy Warhol, Robert Morris and Frank Stella.

Not since the Diaghilev era has so renowned a group of composers and visual artists been willing to design sound scores, costumes and decor for a dance company. That much at least, everyone seems to agree upon. Thus one would expect a large, flourishing scholarly industry to centre on the aesthetic sensibility that Cunningham shares with the other members of this illustrious circle.

But the plain, sad truth of the matter is that the dance community has always been a bit embarrassed by, impatient with and ultimately condescending towards the sorts of sound scores and decor that Cunningham commissions from advanced composers and visual artists. Examples of this prejudice are so numerous that to cite particular instances runs the risk of arbitrariness. But just for the record, consider what Marcia Siegel had to say about Cunningham's concert at The Brooklyn Academy of Music in 1972:

> Two of his three new works (*Landrover* and *TV Rerun*) involved a minimum of pop-art gadgetry, and they looked so bare and complete that I really got involved in them. Bizarre decors and sonic environments lend theatricality and sometimes fun to Cunningham's dances, but his unadorned works are as starkly satisfying to me as a tree against a February hillside.
>
> (Siegel 1977: 274)

After this audible sigh of relief, Siegel goes on to complain about the third work on the programme: '*Borst Park*, the last of the new works, seems of lesser importance, containing less dancing and more tricks than I care for' (Siegel 1977: 276). Even Arlene Croce, arguably the most perceptive and erudite of America's working dance critics, had this to say about Cunningham's *Exchange* which premièred in 1978: 'I wish I had been able to watch it more closely, but my concentration broke about halfway through under the battering of David Tudor's score ... How can you watch a dance with V2 Rockets whistling overhead?' (Croce 1982: 125). She concludes by criticizing the non-dance elements of Cunningham's work for often being so 'interfering and dictatorial'. Several weeks later, Croce elaborated on this complaint when she made a passing reference to an older Cunningham work in which John Cage reads aloud from his writings while Cunningham dances: 'When Merce Cunningham and John Cage combine forces in *How to Pass, Kick, Fall, and Run* . . . they kept the words and the dancing on separate planes, and the result was that Cage distracted us every time he opened his mouth' (Croce 1982: 130). More recently, in a 1987 *New Yorker* piece, Croce complained once again about 'the more intrusive sound scores devised for Merce Cunningham by John Cage and His school of intruders' (Croce 1987: 105).

Croce proceeds on the assumption that every production element exists in order to support or better illuminate the movement. Apparently, it never occurs to her that Cunningham's approach to collaboration might be *about* the nature of interference, static, white noise, audio/visual discontinuity, and about the habits of attention one needs to cultivate in an urban environment of unceasing sensory overload. Thus to complain about distraction and intrusion is, to paraphrase Brecht, reproaching the linden tree for not being an oak.

I suspect that Croce, and other dance writers as well, would like to believe that by ignoring or de-emphasizing those obstreperous visual and sonic environments they are simply saving Cunningham from himself, from his own cheerful brand of nihilism. So they wind up patronizing him, reluctantly tolerating his more eccentric whims, providing that he manages to deliver the goods (i.e. classically clean and legible movement, which is then written about as if it existed in a soundproof glass case).

Of course, there are a few dance critics who realize that Cunningham's choreography cannot be fully appreciated without reference to the world of the other arts. Unfortunately, the central analogy they almost invariably draw, between Cunningham and Jackson Pollock, simply confuses the issue. Far from constituting a painterly counterpart to Merce Cunningham's choreography, Pollock embodies almost everything that Cunningham set out to repudiate. And how could it be otherwise, given the fact that throughout the late 1950s and early 1960s the vast majority of Cunningham's costumes and settings were designed by Robert Rauschenberg and Jasper Johns, the painters who led the movement away from the hot, emotive, highly personal images of abstract expressionism towards the cooler, more impersonal, and 'ready-made' icons that would begin to dominate pop and minimal art?

But dance writers persist in pressing the analogy between Cunningham and Pollock. A few examples will suffice. Jill Johnston, in a 1976 essay called 'The New American Modern Dance', argues that it has often been remarked that Pollock's paintings suggest an infinite extension beyond the picture plane. Cunningham's dances suggest the same extension; and since he often juggles the order of the parts by chance, it is clear that he considers one beginning as good as another.

(Johnston 1976: 156)

Much more recently, in 1988, Anna Kisselgoff said of Cunningham's *Eleven*, 'This is one of Mr. Cunningham's decentralized dances, whose spatial arrangements have often been compared to the abstract expressionism of Jackson Pollock' (Kisselgoff 1988: C3). By far the most extensive exploration of the Cunningham/Pollock analogy comes in Deborah Jowitt's book *Time and the Dancing Image*. Therein she writes: 'that Pollock never actually touched the canvas with his brush slightly distances, almost undermines, the almighty power of the artist's hand, as chance mildly subverts Cunningham's choreographic taste' (Jowitt 1988: 291–2). Her assertion that Pollock's process of dripping paint undermines the 'almighty power of the artist's hand' could not be further from the truth. The principal characteristic of Pollock's paintings is the virtually calligraphic nature of his drip marks and spatterings; they are as distinct as his handwriting, as ineluctable as a finger print. (Like some legal test of identity, they could belong to no one else.) And that is because the process of 'action painting' engaged so much of Pollock's body and its unique way of moving, rather than somehow holding his 'imprint' in check and allowing paint to be applied to canvas in a more impersonal and distanced way. Pollock's bodily traces do indeed have a close choreographic counterpart; but it is not to be found in the work of Merce Cunningham. The choreographer with whom Pollack has the most in common is the choreographer with whom Cunningham has the least in common: Martha Graham.

PAINTING AS DANCING

In 1950, the film-maker Hans Namuth persuaded a reluctant Jackson Pollock to execute one of his famous 'action paintings' on a canvas of glass while the camera recorded Pollock's frenzied gyrations from below. Although neither of them realized it at the time, their collaboration had resulted in one of the world's most significant *dance* films. For it demonstrated (in a way the paintings alone rarely do) that a fundamental impulse behind action painting was the *desire to transform painting into dancing*.

Abstract expressionism, or, more accurately, the bodily and gestural phase of it that Harold Rosenberg called action painting, can be thought of as the culminating phase of modern art's love affair with 'the primitive'. Ecstatic dancing is, of course, a central element in many of those rituals we think of as 'primitive'. And Pollock's conception of painting-as-dancing evolves directly out of those works he executed in the 1940s, works which took their primary inspiration from images of primitive ritual and mythology.[1] But beginning in the late 1940s, rather than reproducing the iconography of primitive art, he attempted to work himself into an 'altered', virtually 'primitive' state of consciousness.

INTERIOR VOYAGES: POLLOCK AND GRAHAM

The action painter's metaphysical credo was much the same as Martha Graham's 'Movement does not lie'. Now, needless to say, no one watching Namuth's film has ever mistaken Pollock for a Graham dancer. But Graham's variety of modern dance has much in common with abstract expressionism: both were Jungian, gravity-ridden, and emotionally overwrought. Compare the titles of the major works that Pollock and Graham created in the 1940s. Pollock painted *She Wolf, Pasiphae, Guardians of the Secret* and *The Totem, Lesson I.* Graham danced works bearing equally incantatory titles: *Cave of the Heart* (1946), *Errand into the Maze* (1947) and *Night Journey* (1947).[2]

In Graham's masterwork of 1946, *Dark Meadow*, a central character is named She of the Ground. Her flatfooted, downward motion beckons and guides the character called The One Who Seeks. And what the protagonist (portrayed of course by Graham herself) seeks is 'the thing itself': The Instinctive, The Natural, The Archetypal, The Authentic, The Mythic, all of those ancient 'truths' that have presumably been repressed by an urbanized, industrialized and all too secularized civilization.

Graham and Pollock were exemplary modernists for whom the road to authenticity led in two principal directions, the unconscious and/or 'the primitive', both of which were presumed to be in some sense natural, pristine, unspoilt, uncolonized. Significantly, both Graham and Pollock underwent Jungian analysis in the 1940s; and both derived inspiration from the American Indian culture of the south-west. Pollock was deeply influenced by Native American sand painting. Animal figures and totems abound in his paintings of the late 1930s and early 1940s. And the hieratic gestures of Graham's *Primitive Mysteries* (1931) and *El Penitente* (1940) are deeply indebted to the mystical blend of Native American ritual and Mexican Catholicism that Graham associated with the American south-west.

Both Pollock and Graham believed that they knew where the treasure is buried: deep down under. The contractions in *Dark Meadow* (1946) are like excavations of the earth, an uncovering and dredging up of all that is normally repressed by polite society. For Graham (and presumably for Pollock as well) the unconscious was literally a *sub*conscious, a dark, subterranean realm located below consciousness and eternally associated with the earth. Graham and Pollock both embody what might be called the 'ethos' of abstract expressionism.

ERASING DEKOONING

In 1953 Robert Rauschenberg challenged this ethos by creating his *Erased DeKooning* (in which he painted over the surface of a work by the famed abstract expressionist). Rauschenberg's gesture was probably too playful to be considered a passionate declaration of war on abstract expressionism. But it is no coincidence that the work he chose to erase belonged to an action painter. In 1957 Rauschenberg created *Factum*, his notorious 'double painting', which was created 'spontaneously' in the manner of an action painting, the other a meticulously recreated duplicate. His point: the product is not necessarily dependent on the process. The same result can be achieved without any of the anguished, instinctual histrionics that the abstract expressionists considered synonymous with authenticity. Two years later, he created his most direct and stinging parody of Pollock, *Winter Pool*, which plays on the action painter's famous statements about being 'in' his own paintings. Rauschenberg's work includes a ladder which invites the viewer to climb in.

It is not surprising that Rauschenberg received very little encouragement from the art world in the early 1950s, immersed as it was in the abstract expressionist ethos. More surprising is the fact that one of his earliest admirers was a former Graham dancer with whom he became acquainted at Black Mountain College in 1953. The dancer's name was Merce Cunningham and the most significant thing about his association with Graham was the fact that it had ended. The dances Cunningham was now choreographing were much more balletic than Graham's; they were fast, light, ironic in tone and virtually devoid of 'expressive' or symbolic elements.

Even more unusual was Cunningham's determination to 'free' choreography from a dependence on music. In Cunningham's work, movement and sound existed independently of one another; choreography and music were both performed in the same space and time, but without affecting (or even acknowledging) one another. Not only do Cunningham's dancers not perform *to* music; they must concentrate in such a way as not to be affected by it. No doubt, this is part of what Carolyn Brown meant when she said that Cunningham technique is 'designed to develop flexibility in the mind as well as in the body' (Brown 1975: 22). James Klosty elaborates on her point:

> Traditional ballet is a far more Dionysian enterprise, for the dancer can ride the musical pulse, using it as a kind of surrogate heartbeat on

which bodily functions play without consciousness. Absence of metrical accompaniment only intensifies the mental effort needed to establish the strict order that supports each dancer's part.

(Klosty 1975: 12)

Furthermore, the typical Cunningham sound score is anything but 'propulsive'. One characteristic that much of the music of Cage, Brown, Wolff and Feldman has in common is a tendency toward stillness, an absence of progressions that drive inexorably toward climax or completion. The result is a spatial field of calm, free-floating sound, interrupted occasionally by an abrupt, disruptive change of pitch or volume.

Another significant innovation: the stage space in Cunningham's dances was 'de-centralized', so that someone standing upstage left was no less central to the visual focus than someone standing downstage centre. As Carolyn Brown once observed, everyone on stage in a Cunningham piece is always a *soloist*. Not only is everybody a 'soloist' in Cunningham's choreography, every section of every *body* can become a soloist as well; for Cunningham often sets the head, arms, torso, and legs moving in opposition to one another. As early as 1953, Cunningham had choreographed a piece, *Untitled Solo*, in which the movement for each of several subdivisions of the body was determined separately and by chance. Thus the atomized body became a microcosm of the company-at-large. Appropriately, Edwin Denby once described Cunningham's style as 'extreme elegance in isolation' (Denby 1968: 281). The 'isolation' (of one body from another, of one part of the body from another) is to Cunningham technique what the contraction (based on the more 'natural' and organic rhythm of breathing) is to Graham.

But by far the most eccentric of Cunningham's innovations was the use of chance procedures to 'dictate' his choreographic sequences. Beginning in 1951 with his *16 Dances for Soloist and Company of Three*, Cunningham decided to determine the arrangement of sequences by tossing coins, thereby invoking an 'impersonal' (and more objective) sense of order, rather than structuring the dance according to the subjective dictates of his own 'taste'. In all his subsequent works, numerous variables (the locations of the dancers, the speed with which phrases are performed, the order in which steps are combined, the number of dancers who might appear in a sequence) were arrived at not by intuition, instinct or even the faculty of 'taste' but by a wide variety of aleatoric methods (rolling dice, picking cards, tossing coins, consulting the *I Ching*, matching up imperfections on pieces of paper, etc.).

In 1953, Cunningham performed his *16 Dances* in New York in a programme that included May O'Donnell's *Dance Sonata* (1952), Nina Fonaroff's *Lazarus* (1953), Pauline Koner and José Limón in Humphrey's *Deep Rhythm* (1953), and Pearl Lang in Graham's *Canticle for*

Innocent Comedians (1952). Doris Hering, reviewing the concert for *Dance Magazine* wrote:

> although Merce Cunningham was also raised in the Graham cradle, he has completely severed himself from her sphere of influence. And on these programs, where so many of the choreographers were Graham bred, he seemed like a creature from another planet.
>
> (Hering 1953: 15)

THE POLITICS OF INSTINCT

Graham's self-professed goal was to 'make visible the interior land-scape' by choreographing dances so personal that 'they fit her as her skin fit her' (Graham 1974: 135). Harold Rosenberg said something similar about the action painting of Pollock: 'a painting that is an act is inseparable from the biography of the artist' (Rosenberg 1952: 39) By contrast, Cunningham, Rauschenberg, Johns and for that matter Cage as well, often use impersonal, 'found' materials that come from the world of outer rather than inner experience: Johns's Ballantine Ale cans, the readymades and found objects in the 'combines' of Rauschenberg, the non-musical, 'found' sounds in the compositions of Cage. (And Cunningham uses elements of pre-existing ballet vocabulary which might be referred to as 'found' movement.)

Thus Cunningham's repudiation of Graham and modern dance directly paralleled Rauschenberg's and Johns's repudiation of abstract expressionism. But a logical, indeed inevitable, question arises: why did Cunningham, Cage, Rauschenberg, Johns and the rest of their 'circle' reject instinct, the unconscious and the interior voyage as a principal 'wellspring' for the creative process? Why did they place so much emphasis on detachment and impersonality, on coolness, playfulness and irony? And why did they care so little for those privileged moments of inspiration, those 'spontaneous' bursts of creativity, those spurts of uninterrupted flow?

Listen to John Cage discussing the surrealist (and abstract expressionist) goal of automatism: 'Automatic art, in fact, has never interested me, because it is a way of falling back, resting on one's memories and feelings subconsciously, is it not? And I have done my utmost to free people from that' (Cage 1988: 173). Later in the same interview (conducted in 1966), Irving Sandler asked Cage to comment directly on Pollock and abstract expressionism. Cage expressed his general distaste for Pollock and then Sandler pressed him a bit harder: 'But what about the pitch of intensity, the excitement?' Cage's response was:

> Oh, none of those aspects interested me. They're precisely the things about abstract expressionism that *didn't* interest me. I wanted them to

change my way of seeing, not my way of feeling. I'm perfectly happy about my feelings . . . I don't want to spend my life being pushed around by a bunch of artists.

(Cage 1988: 177)

Again, it is necessary to compare Cunningham and Rauschenberg with Pollock and Graham. Both abstract expressionism and modern dance were animated by Freud's belief that below the culturally conditioned ego lies the 'natural' id (or in Jung's version, 'the collective unconscious'). According to this high modernist myth, one must suspend the control of rational consciousness (typically through drugs, alcohol or some mode of surrealist 'automatism') in order to re-establish contact with the instinctive, natural and uncorrupted regions of the psyche. As Pollock once put it, 'when I am *in* my painting, I'm not aware of what I'm doing' (Pollock 1987: 95).

But as Giorgio de Chirico was among the first to point out, even the unconscious is in danger of becoming fully 'acculturated' amidst the subliminally manipulative, sensory overload environments of twentieth-century consumer society. It is no coincidence that Cunningham's aesthetic was forged in the mid-1950s when the new medium of television was rapidly becoming an American institution. In an environment designed to stimulate desires that have little relation to instinctive 'need', we have no way of knowing that what *feels* natural is not largely the result of cultural conditioning (in effect, culture or 'second nature' masquerading as nature). The idea that the worldwide dissemination of western advertising and mass media have blurred the boundaries between 'nature' and 'culture' does not come as news to anyone, but it leads none the less to a radically revised view of both the unconscious and the natural world.

Fredric Jameson speaks of

a prodigious expansion of late capitalism, which now, in the form of what has variously been called the 'culture industry' or the 'consciousness industry', penetrates one of the two surviving pre-capitalist enclaves of Nature within the system – namely the Unconscious. (The other one is pre-capitalist agriculture and village culture of the Third World.)

(Jameson 1983: 3)

The moment one can no longer view the unconscious (and/or 'the primitive') as a source of inviolable purity, the ethos of action painting (and presumably of modern dance as well) is fatally compromised.

Suspicious of 'the instinctual', artists like Cunningham, Cage, Rauschenberg and Johns set out to examine critically that which 'feels natural' rather than simply surrendering to it. Their motivations may not be as overtly political as those of a Bertolt Brecht or a Jean-Luc Godard, but their attitude toward 'naturalness' is much the same.

Freedom for Cunningham is not to be found in 'nature' or instinct. This marks a decisive break with the tradition of modern dance. From Duncan through Graham, the pioneers of modern dance have always considered themselves apostles of freedom. To them, being free meant liberating oneself from the stuffy conventions of puritanical culture; it meant rediscovering the 'natural' body and the origin of all movement (the solar plexus for Duncan, the inhalation and exhalation of breath for Graham).

But for Cunningham, Rauschenberg and the extraordinary community of composers, painters and dancers with whom they collaborated, true freedom has more to do with seeing (and hearing) clearly than with the (often illusory) sensation of moving freely.

BALLET AND CHANCE

No aspect of the Cunningham legacy has been more misunderstood than his use of chance procedures for dictating choreographic sequence. In *Next Week, Swan Lake*, Selma Jeanne Cohen tells us that 'Cunningham relied on certain chance procedures to put his movement in touch with nature' (Cohen 1982: 34). But Cunningham's use of chance does just the opposite: it makes certain that his choreography is not animated by his 'natural' way of moving. Cohen falls victim to a common misperception, one that fails, fatally, to distinguish between Cunningham's use of chance and mere improvization.

The chance mechanisms in Cunningham's work do not attempt to break through the resistances of conscious control so as to unleash unconscious or 'natural' impulses. Quite the contrary: he utilizes utterly impersonal, chance-generating mechanisms (coins, dice, the *I Ching*, etc.) so as to avoid what might otherwise 'flow' in an organic way. This is why so many dancers complain that Cunningham's choreography is often excruciatingly difficult to perform: it does not *come naturally* to the human body. (In Cunningham's choreography, a body can move from whiplash fouette into penchée arabesque without apparent transition.)

And here lies another major distinction between Cunningham and the early modern dancers, from Duncan to Graham, who repudiated what they perceived to be the unnatural (and orthopedically unhealthy) vocabulary of ballet in favour of movements more in keeping with the natural inclinations of the body. Cunningham was one of the first modern dancers to cross the ideological picket lines in order to study at The School of American Ballet. When almost everyone else in the Graham-dominated world of modern dance was carrying the weight of the universe on her or his shoulders and affirming the elemental (i.e. natural) force of *gravity*, Cunningham was perfecting his lightness and speed.[3]

These are not the sort of qualities one associates with the typical Graham dancer (certainly not in the 1940s). But Cunningham's verticality, the emphasis his technique places on the back rather than the torso, the quickness and complexity of his footwork, these are more than just knee-jerk repudiations of the gravity-ridden expressionism that dominated modern dance in the 1940s. They are a renewed affirmation of balletic impersonality.

The modified attitudes and arabesques that figure so prominently in Cunningham's movement vocabulary function as a variety of 'ready-made': movement forms that pre-existed the choreographer, that weren't invented by him. (What the classic modern dance choreographers found most objectionable about ballet was that its vocabulary came, in a sense 'ready made', and therefore incapable of expressing their unique personal histories.)[4]

It may seem ironic that Cunningham could be simultaneously attracted to compositional strategies based on chance *and* to a movement vocabulary markedly more balletic than Martha Graham's. But for Cunningham, chance and the ballet vocabulary are two means towards the same end: they liberate the choreographer from the limitations of his instincts.[5]

SEPARATING THE ELEMENTS

Here is a quotation that tells us more about Cunningham than almost anything that has been written about him in the last thirty years.

> So long as the expression '*Gesamtkunstwerk*' (or 'integrated work of art') means that the integration is a muddle, so long as the arts are supposed to be 'fused' together, the various elements will all be equally degraded, and each will act as a mere 'feed' to the rest. The process of fusion extends to the spectator who gets thrown into the melting pot too and becomes a passive (suffering) part of the total work of art. Witchcraft of this sort must of course be fought against. Whatever is intended to produce hypnosis, is likely to induce sordid intoxication, or creates fog, has got to be given up. *Words, Music, and setting must become more independent of one another.*
>
> (Brecht 1964: 37)

The writer is none other than Bertolt Brecht; and his is perhaps the last name one would expect to arise in connection with Cunningham. Yet Brecht, in his 1930 essay 'The modern theatre is the epic theatre', had anticipated Cunningham's way of working. Brecht is here rejecting Wagner's theory of the *Gesamtkunstwerk* in which music, text and movement were seemlessly woven together. For Brecht it came as no coincidence that Wagner occupied such a privileged place in the cultural life of Nazi Germany. Brecht regarded Wagner's music as a massive 'wall of sound' which forcibly subdues the listener. To Brecht, the Nuremberg Rallies were one great Wagnerian opera: the masses mesmerized, the Führer unified with his followers.

Brecht's alternative is intentional disunity, a separation of the elements which ultimately serves to keep the audience at a respectful distance, and which prevents them from passively consuming (or being absorbed into) the spectacle around them.

No one, and that includes Brecht himself, has carried this principle of separation farther than Merce Cunningham. In Cunningham's work, every collaborative element maintains its autonomy. The choreography, the score, the settings are all created in isolation and often do not encounter one another until the very first performance.

In fact, the setting, lighting or even the score for a Cunningham work often serves to impede a more direct, 'uncomplicated' perception of the choreography. As early as 1954, in *Minutiae*, Rauschenberg designed an assemblage of flats that often concealed the dancers as they darted behind and around them. For Cunningham's *Tread* (1970), Bruce Nauman designed a row of standing industrial fans lined up downstage directly between the audience and the dance. In *Walkaround Time* (1968), Jasper Johns designed a series of movable plastic boxes which served a similar function. Ditto for Frank Stella's brilliantly bright rectangles of coloured cloth moved around on aluminium frames for Cunningham's *Scramble* (1967). In *Canfield* (1969), the stage space was repeatedly dissected by a mobile, burningly bright beam of light designed by Robert Morris. The end result, in each of these cases, is that we view the work more actively than we otherwise might.

Note that for Brecht, the ultimate goal of disunity is to preserve the spectator's perceptual freedom. (Recall what he said about the danger of the spectator 'getting thrown into the melting pot too'. We might also think back to Cage's distaste for being 'pushed around by a bunch of artists'.) Cunningham's motives are similar.

> We don't attempt to make the individual spectator think a certain way. I do think each spectator is individual, that it isn't *a public*. Each spectator as an individual can receive what we do in his own way and need not see the same thing, or hear the same thing, as the person next to him.
>
> (Cunningham 1985: 171–2)

AT HOME IN THE CITY

This Brechtian 'separation of the elements' undermines another key characteristic of 'the natural', its organicism. Goethe once observed: 'in nature we never see anything isolated, but everything in connection with something else which is before it, beside it, under it, and over it' (Goethe 1979: 101). The great modern dance choreographers almost always looked backwards (longingly) toward the wholeness of the natural world. Doris Humphrey said of the modern dancer: 'he is, in a sense, a throwback. He is aware of this but believes that his art is rooted so deeply in Man's fundamental instincts that he can read back into His unconscious remembrance before the atrophy of civilization set in' (Humphrey 1979: 58–9). Graham, in her Notebooks, wrote: 'what is the beginning? Perhaps when we seek wholeness – when we embark on the journey toward wholeness' (Graham 1973: 305).

But Cunningham, by contrast, doesn't hark back to some distant, agrarian, pre-industrial point of origin or totality, a womb-with-a-view. He wants us to 'keep our distance'. There is no invocation to 'oneness' in his work. No celebration of nature or 'the organic'. Cunningham is thus the first choreographer to embrace the basic conditions of city life (which Humphrey equated with 'the atrophy of civilization').

What Graham or Humphrey would have dismissed as urban blight becomes for Cunningham a potential source of delight. Rather than lamenting fragmentation and disunity, Cunningham encourages us to savour the peculiarly urban experience of 'non-relatedness'. Cunningham provides us with a do-it-yourself survival kit for maintaining our sanity, or at least perceptual clarity (which may amount to the same thing) in the contemporary city, where everything seems to clamour for attention. During a Cunningham performance, we may decide to 'background' or 'turn off' a sound so as to focus more intently on the movement. Or we may cultivate a skill John Cage calls 'polyattentiveness', the simultaneous apprehension of two or more unrelated phenomena. (David Tudor, who has composed many scores for Cunningham, often listens to several radios while he practises at the piano.) Above all, the relations we establish between diverse stimuli are flexible; we can radically alter our mode of perception several times in the course of a single performance; often we need to practise a variety of 'selective inattention'. It is entirely appropriate that one of Jasper Johns's 'target' paintings appears on the famous poster he designed for the Cunningham company. Johns asks us to distribute our visual attention evenly throughout each circular band of the image, despite the fact that we have been conditioned to zero in on the target's bullseye. Writing about Johns's painting *Target with Four Faces*, Leo Steinberg suggests that 'Johns puts two flinty things in a picture and makes them work against one another so hard that the mind is sparked. Seeing them becomes thinking' (Steinberg 1972: 14), a description that applies equally well to Cunningham's separation of the elements. When seeing and thinking are combined in this way, the result is perceptual freedom. Peter Brook put it best when he described Merce Cunningham's work as 'a continual preparation for the shock of freedom' (Brook 1968: 89).

NOTES

1 Pollock was deeply influenced by three exhibitions at the Museum of Modern Art in the late 1930s and 1940s: the 'African Negro Art' exhibition of 1935, 'Prehistoric Rock Pictures' in 1937 and 'Indian Art of the United States' in 1941.

2 Pollock's *Guardians of the Secret* from 1943 alludes abstractly to priests and priestesses who stand guard over a mysterious biomorphic web of pigment in the centre of the canvas. It is not unlike Graham's great duet of 1947, *Errand into the Maze*, in which the female protagonist journeys 'into the maze of the heart's darkness'.

3 Reviewing Cunningham's very first solo concert in New York in 1944, Edwin Denby noted that 'his instep and his knees are extraordinarily elastic and quick; his steps, runs, knee bends and leaps are brilliant in lightness and speed. His torso can turn on its vertical axis with great sensitivity; his shoulders are held lightly free and his head poises intelligently. The arms are light and long, they float' (Denby 1968: 280).

4 If any single statement can be said to have provided the theoretical foundation for Merce Cunningham's innovations, it is surely John Cage's short essay of 1944 'Grace and clarity', originally published in *Dance Observer*. Early in the essay, Cage writes, 'personality is such a flimsy thing on which to build an art. . . . And the ballet is obviously not built on such an ephemeron, for, if it were, it would not at present thrive as it does. . . . That the ballet *has* something seems reasonable to assume. That what it has is what the modern dance needs is here expressed as an opinion', (Cage 1961: 90). The problem with modern dance, notes Cage in same essay, is that it 'was not impersonal, but was intimately connected with and ultimately dependent on the personalities and even the actual physical bodies of the individuals who imparted it' (Cage 1961: 89). Thus 'Grace and clarity' functions not only as a broadside against the cult of personality in modern dance but also as a defence of (indeed a plea for) a rapproachment of sorts between ballet and modern dance (a new fusion of the two that Cunningham, along with Paul Taylor, would soon pioneer).

5 This is not to suggest that Cunningham's choreography is ever so 'objective' as to be anonymous. His unique and highly personal manner of moving is always apparent, both in his solos and in his group choreography. In his Buster Keatonish way, Cunningham is also one of America's great comic actors. Even after age and arthritis had begun to take a toll on his dancing, he remained a cunning ham. Still, he disciplines his 'natural' inclinations according to the dictates of chance-generated systems.

REFERENCES

Brecht, B. (1964), 'The modern theater is the epic theater', in *Brecht on Theatre*, translated and edited by J. Willett, New York: Hill & Wang.

Brook, P. (1968), *The Empty Space*, New York: Avon.

Brown, C. (1975) (untitled) in J. Klosty (ed.), *Merce Cunningham*, pp. 19–31, New York: Saturday Review Press/E. P. Dutton.

Cage, J. (1961), 'Grace and clarity', in *Silence*, Middletown, Conn.: Wesleyan University Press.

—— (1988), R. Kostelanetz (ed.), *Conversing with Cage*, New York: Limelight Editions.

Cohen, S. J. (1982), *Next Week, Swan Lake*, Middletown, Conn.: Wesleyan University Press.

Croce, A. (1982), 'Quintessence', in *Going to the Dance*, New York: Alfred A. Knopf.

—— (1987), *The New Yorker*, 21 November.

Cunningham, M. (1985), *The Dancer and the Dance*, in conversation with J. Lesschaeve, New York: Marion Boyars.

Denby, E. (1968), *Looking at the Dance* (1949), New York: Horizon.

Duncan, I. (1927), *My Life*, New York: Boni & Liveright.

Goethe, J. W. von (1979), quoted by Sergei Eisenstein, 'A dialectic approach to film form', in G. Mast and M. Cohen (eds), *Film Theory and Criticism*, 2nd edition, New York: Oxford University Press.

Graham, M. (1973), *The Notebooks of Martha Graham*, New York: Harcourt Brace Jovanovich.

—— (1974), 'A modern dancer's primer for action', in S. J. Cohen (ed.), *Dance as a Theatre Art*, New York: Dodd, Mead.

Hering, D. (1953), 'Modern dance – a ritual for today', *Dance Magazine*, June.

Humphrey, D. (1979), 'What a dancer thinks about', in Jean Morrison Brown (ed.), *The Vision of Modern Dance*, Princeton, N.J.: Princeton Book Company.

Jameson, F. (1983), 'Pleasure: a political issue', in *Formations of Pleasure*, London: Routledge & Kegan Paul.

Johnston, J. (1976), 'The new American modern dance', *Salmagundi*, 33–4 (spring/summer).

Jowitt, D. (1988), *Time and the Dancing Image*, New York: William Morrow & Company.

Kisselgoff, A. (1988), 'Cunningham spirit at heart of premiere', *The New York Times*, 11 March, C 3.

Klosty, J. (ed.) (1975), *Merce Cunningham*, New York: Saturday Review Press/ E. P. Dutton.

Newman, B. (1987), quoted in Shiff (1987).

Pollock, J. (1987), quoted in Shiff (1987).

Rosenberg, H. (1952), 'The American action: painters', *Art News*, September.

Shiff, R. (1987), 'Performing an appearance: on the surface of Abstract Expressionism', in M. Auping (ed.), *Abstract Expressionism: The Critical Developments*, New York: Harry N. Abrams.

Siegel, M. (1977), *Watching the Dance Go By*, Boston: Houghton Mifflin Company.

Steinberg, L. (1972), *Other Criteria*, New York: Oxford University Press.

Wellek, R. and Warren, A. (1949), *Theory of Literature*, New York: Harcourt, Brace.

Chapter 13

Re-tracing our steps

The possibilities for feminist dance histories

Carol Brown

Dance, as an academic discipline, is in a good position to accommodate feminist problematics in the writing of dance history. Feminism theorizes culture from woman's point of view, and it is women who constitute the majority of practitioners within western theatre dance. Both feminism, as a politics, and dance, as a cultural practice, share a concern with the body. For feminists the body is understood as the primary site of social production and inscription (Grosz 1987), whereas for dance it is its capacity for movement which is the central concern. As a feminist dance scholar I speak from the dance department at the University of Surrey, whose very existence has depended upon the committed endeavours of women, and it is women who in the main continue to develop the expanding field of dance research. Yet dance remains on the margins of feminist critical studies in the arts and feminist debates about culture have not yet been taken up in a comprehensive way within dance studies. This is despite the fact that it seems increasingly incongruous for dance and feminism to ignore each other given the possibilities which new analyses of ideology, representation and social relations bring to the study of the dancing body (Wolff in Adair 1992).

Christy Adair has laid the groundwork for the productive engagement of feminism and dance in *Women and Dance: Sylphs and Sirens* (1992). It is the first comprehensive British study of dance from a woman's point of view and as such it instigates new approaches to dance history which draw on cultural and feminist theories. Adair's discussion is wide-ranging, providing a sound introduction to many of the issues which feminist perspectives can bring to an understanding of dance. However, the kind of feminist position which Adair adopts is generally implicit within her text. There is no explicit encounter with the range of feminisms which can enrich understanding and which may be differentially adapted to suit the kinds of analyses being undertaken. For in taking up different positions within feminist debates it is possible to offer a range of readings of the meanings of the dancing body in any given time or place. Any attempt to establish a radical praxis for feminism and dance needs to account for the range and diversity of such positions whilst adapting these to the specific problematics for feminist dance scholarship.

Attention is directed in this chapter to several major strands of feminist thought, those which endorse subject-centred, materialist and post-structuralist approaches, and an attempt is made to knit these with the history of dance as encountered through the political lens of feminism. As 'stagings' of some of the possibilities for feminist dance history, they are of necessity schematic and provisional. Schematic in the sense that the constraints of a summary chapter limit representation of the full depth and complexity of the analysis, and provisional in that until feminist theories are comprehensively worked through, extended and refined by dance scholars we can but touch on the potentialities which such endeavours promise to unearth.

13.1   METHODOLOGICAL FRAMEWORKS FOR FEMINIST DANCE HISTORY

Feminists claim that traditional epistemologies exert an androcentric bias in their exclusion of women as agents of knowledge, arguing that history has in the past generally been written from only one point of view, that of the dominant white male. The main causes of this are rooted in the male-centredness of historical institutions; in the numerical dominance of men as historians; in the areas of interest their research reflects; and in the research methodologies which are employed. It follows from this that the history of western knowledge is formulated upon a dichotomy of subject/object relations which are gendered, in that masculine subjects act upon and observe feminine objects, obscuring and undermining their role as 'knowers' (Beauvoir 1949; Coltheart 1986; Thompson 1986). The history of dance writing in the west reinforces this hierarchical separation as it has been men who, up until the mid-twentieth century, provided most of the literature on dance and much of this in a style fixated with the dancer as an object of beauty and desire.

Much of what has been accredited as dance history in the past has relied upon platitudes, impressions and anecdotes which circulate around the ideal of the dancing body as an ahistorical entity. Scholarly texts on ballet for instance, are a relatively new phenomenon supplanting adulatory writing by men who identified themselves as 'balletomanes'. The Romantic period produced a number of such critics and commentators, many of whose writings continue to be recycled as authoritative accounts of ballet's 'golden age'. One of the most prominent of these is Théophile Gautier (1811–72), whose writings are distinguished by his obsessive idealization of feminine beauty (Guest

1986). Subsequent readings of his work have done little to dispel his impressions of the Romantic ballerina as a purified essence of femininity (see for example Beaumont 1930).

The close associations of dance with the body, and by inference with nature and femininity, have significance for dance historians who, as subjects, act upon and interpret the dance object. We need to ask what kind of relationship the feminist historian is to establish with her 'dance-text' if she is to avoid the colonization of its body in her own writing. How specific dance practices contribute to the construction of woman as 'other' needs to be considered in conjunction with the perpetuation of dichotomous thinking in the official histories of the subject.

As a corrective to the asymmetry of traditional historical accounts, feminists advocate women's increased participation both as subject of research and as object of analysis. The latter is coterminous with the appropriation of alternative theories of knowledge that legitimate women as 'knowers', situating them as agents and therefore subjects within history.

The methods, methodologies and epistemologies which delineate the field of feminist research are shaped by the need to articulate the experiences of women from a woman-centred perspective. In particular, feminists focus on sex, along with race and class, as a category of analysis. Fundamental to this approach is the understanding that the relation between the sexes is a social and not a natural one. Feminism has made clear that the fact of being a woman means having a particular kind of social and historical experience (Kelly-Gadol 1987). This is not, however, to elide the differences between women under a universal term, 'Woman'. Recent feminist scholarship acknowledges that there is no notion of 'woman' beyond that which is socially constructed and historically located. To talk of 'women's experience' is therefore to relate the specificity of a particular social constituency of women, within an identifiable period and geographical location, to a particular area of research. As Denise Riley (1988) explains, although the category of woman has been crystallized throughout modern western history it is important to acknowledge its indeterminacy.

In reinstating women as full historical subjects, feminists disclose a different framework for history, one which challenges its customary periodization according to progressive change. Using the status of women as an index of the general emancipation of the age we find that beliefs in periods of cultural advancement, such as the Renaissance, are challenged. For there was no 'Renaissance' for women, in fact the increasing restrictions on women's freedoms during the fifteenth and sixteenth centuries in Europe were a characteristic feature of the age (Kelly-Gadol 1987). The iniquitous distribution of the benefits of an age are often overlooked in accounts of dance history which are evolutionary in character.

The court ballets of Renaissance Europe are generally regarded as foundational to the development of theatre dance in the west. As elaborate ceremonial occasions, they functioned as affirmations of the monarch's power and the male status quo. Formalized through a succession of royal benefactors, the surviving treatises and notation scores of these early ballets were authorized by men, who also occupied the role of dance master and choreographer within the court. Though some women participated as dancers, male dominance prevailed within the hierarchical ordering of these spectacles. To consider the role of women within the court ballets is therefore to expose their lack of power. This leads Adair to conclude that it is 'a male constructed vision of dance which makes up the ballet heritage' (Adair 1992: 90). Contrast this with Copeland's (1982a, 1982b, 1990b) view of women's pre-eminence in modern and postmodern dance and it can legitimately be argued that for women their 'Renaissance', at least in dance, originated with the celebratory lyricism of the barefooted and uncorseted dancer at the turn of the century.

A feminist historiography disrupts accepted evaluations of the significance of historical periods. It challenges the notion that the history of women is the same as the history of men, and that the classification of periods within the arts has had the same impact for one sex as for the other. When women are excluded from certain cultural advances, such as participation in the production of a court ballet, we need to look at those advances to find the reasons for the separation of the sexes and their impact on the development of the genre (Kelly-Gadol 1987).

A feminist methodology is an analysis of how a particular strand of feminist theory might be applied in a defined research area. Whilst the methods of gathering research used by feminists may be the same as those of traditional approaches, it is the way in which these sources are operated on and how they are applied that distinguishes their analysis from that of their androcentric counterparts.

The methodological principles of value-free, detached scholarship and of a hierarchical, non-reciprocal relationship between the research subject and the object of research are challenged by feminist methodologies. Amongst other things, feminists advocate 'conscious partiality' in the gathering of evidence, so that for instance in interviewing women, the researcher engages and partially identifies with the informant (Mies 1983). This levelling of the traditional hierarchy makes for a more equitable relation in the documenting of evidence while, in placing the researcher within the same critical plane as the subject of research, the researcher's own bias and positioning within the terms of analysis is revealed, and becomes part of the research process. An example of this practice is found in Adair's introduction in which she describes her background in white, working-class English culture, her love of dance, and her commitment to political activism. This is useful because, as Harding states in stressing the importance of the individual woman's voice in testimony, '[she] appears to us not as an invisible, anonymous voice of authority, but as a real historical individual with concrete, specific desires and interests' (Harding 1987: 9). By avoiding the 'objectivist' stance, prized amongst androcentric methods of research, and entering her own subjectivity into the research equation, the feminist recognizes how her cultural beliefs shape the orientation and outcomes of her research and in this way some of the distortions within what has been accepted as the orthodox view of history may be avoided.

A feminist approach to dance history entails the politicizing of existing methodologies and epistemological structures. It makes explicit the politics of historical accounts whilst attempting to reconstitute dance knowledge through a variety of methods tailored to suit the particularities of dance practice from the point of view of women.

13.2   WITHOUT TRACE: THE FEMINIST CHALLENGE TO HISTORICAL EVIDENCE

At issue for feminism in relation to the discipline of history is the epistemological question of what counts as positive historical evidence. Dance historians claim that the foundation of historical writing is the 'establishing of facts' (Layson 1991: 4). But history, as the study of the 'present traces of the past' (Elton 1967: 20), is confined to the representation and interpretation of surviving discourses. This creates certain limitations for dance historians who deal with an art form whose primary artefact, the dance, is characterized by its non-permanence and 'constant evolution over time and through space' (Daly 1992: 245). For as Elton (1967: 20) states: 'If men [*sic*] have said, thought, done or suffered anything of which nothing any longer exists, those things are as if they had never been.' Elton's attitude is the product of historical thinking reliant on positive historical evidence such as letters, autobiographies, books, reviews, articles, dance scores, videos, film, designs and photographs. Ranking these as primary or secondary source material, and evaluating them according to notions of authenticity, reliability and value, they constitute what are generally regarded as the materials of the historian who interprets and analyses their significance to the research topic (Layson 1983).

Feminists problematize this traditional approach to historical writing, claiming that it stifles their endeavours to articulate the dance knowledge of women of the past for whom little or no literary or visual record remains be that as performers, producers or consumers of the dance. They critique the failure of History to account for the absences and silences in surviving discourses whilst dismissing evidence which is partial, accrued through inference or deduction, and which cannot necessarily be verified (Allen 1986). Given that it is women's voices and movements which are often left out of official records, feminist historians demand the scrutiny of extant evidence not just in terms of the context in which it was elicited but also in epistemological terms.

Appropriate modes of investigation for the feminist researcher start with the theoretical and political interrogation of available sources. Feminist researchers need to ask who is doing the 'speaking', and whose interests it represents? What do we expect the surviving record to account for and what is it likely to omit or misrepresent? But, given that not all kinds of dance activity are likely to have left a historical record, a feminist 'reading' of evidence allows for modes of inference and deduction to be made based on the analysis of related discourses and their bearing on the particular area of research. Such an undertaking is crucial for the dance historian because, as June Layson states, they 'normally have to base their work on fragments of information for it is only rarely that the dance itself is extant' (1991: 4).

To return to the image of the Romantic ballerina as perpetuated within traditional dance writing, we see how the construction of her sex as 'other' relied upon her not answering back. Here Gautier, in describing the libretto for *Le Lutin de la Vallée* (1853) by Saint-Leon, refers to the marriage of Katti, a 'poor, mute girl' danced by Mme Guy-Stéfan, to the rich and powerful Count Ulric: 'If this marriage seems unsuitable to you, remember that Katti is mute, which is better than a dowry, and besides, she speaks such pretty words with her feet' (Gautier 1977: 88). As the embodiment of the sylph the Romantic ballerina is silenced so as not to disrupt the safe fantasizing of her male voyeur. The Romantic ballerina is seen but not heard within the surviving records of the period, highlighting the need for feminist dance historians to recoup her autonomous subjectivity by working through the gaps and silences of what remains.

13.3   DANCE AND THE FEMALE BODY: THE ISSUE OF REPRESENTATION

Though women have been excluded from positions of power and agency, they have throughout history been involved in cultural production. Deprived of the means of making art, women have in the past turned their bodies into the medium or vehicle for the art process itself. As model, muse or dancer, women have been engaged as subject matter and source for the creative endeavours of mainly male, but also occasionally female, artists. Though the centrality of 'woman' as the great theme of art has been established as a major concern for feminist critics and historians (Bovenschen 1985), it is important to bear in mind that this applies to only certain kinds of women. Whereas white women have been over-exposed in western art, black women, still largely invisible in mainstream dance productions, have not figured prominently. Their invisibility needs to be countered by the active intervention of the feminist in both explaining this absence and positively reinscribing their *presence*.

Of crucial importance to the feminist politics of representation is the issue of how we choose to portray ourselves, and, in contrast, how women are depicted by men. Feminist analyses of images of women seek to disclose their hidden ideologies. For representation, as feminists view it, is not an innocent term. Far from functioning in a mimetic relation to reality, signification, or the construction of images, is the process through which meanings are produced (Pollock 1988). As signifying systems, representations carry with them sets of values and attributes which are embedded in particular ideologies and are, therefore, capable of creating, endorsing or subverting ideas about gender.

Dance history which addresses feminist concerns could do well to begin with the neglected field of the politics of signification because the primacy of the body in choreography is what distinguishes it from all other art forms (Brown 1993). Representation of the female body depends on the sets of rules, codes and conventions which are specific to a genre and period of dance, and in turn, are related to prevailing beliefs and ideologies within the wider context of society.

Historical research into gender and representation within different dance genres reveals how women have been depicted by men. Ann Daly (1987), writing on ballet, characterizes the genre as reliant upon an idealization of 'Woman' which rigidly enforces patterns of dominance and subjection. She sees patriarchal ideology as underpinning depictions of gender in ballet and as crystallizing dichotomies which are harmful to women.

> In ballet, the female form has long been inscribed as a representation of difference: as a spectacle, she is the bearer and object of male desire. The male on stage – the primary term against which the ballerina can only be compared – is not inscribed as a form, but rather as an active principle.
>
> (Daly 1987/8: 57)

In an earlier essay Daly decodes the image of 'the Balanchine Woman' to reveal its hidden ideology as an 'icon of femininity' (1987: 8). Her analysis systematically reveals the workings of patriarchal ideology within the choreography of George Balanchine and within ballet in general. Copeland, in his defence of formalism, refutes these claims by arguing that Balanchine's work, far from denigrating women, 'forces us to transcend our own "personal" experiences, thereby entering a shared and public realm' (Copeland 1990a: 38). Arguments such as these, reliant as they are on the transcendental powers of the 'Man of Reason', are inimical to the feminist project (Lloyd 1989). Such humanist conceptions are reductive in that they presume the essential 'sameness' of 'Mankind' in surpassing bodily existence through 'Enlightenment'. Copeland's politics of 'disinterestedness' is countered by feminists' bid to accommodate a theory of embodiment through a process of 'engaged vision', one which accounts for the material activity and specificity of concrete human beings (Hartstock 1983).

The difficulties ballet has to contend with in attempting to take on serious social issues were made powerfully evident in Kenneth MacMillan's *Judas Tree* (1992). Purporting to deal with the issue of 'betrayal as it affects human relationships' (Goodwin 1992: 16), MacMillan's ballet hinges on the figure of a woman who is gang-raped by a group of men in a wrecker's yard. If we are to believe that the woman is a woman at all, and Jann Parry (1992) sees her as a series of mythological impersonations of woman, as Magdalene, Salome, Madonna and Giselle, then we cannot fail to see how badly MacMillan's ballet, in glorifying in the virtuosity of the male dancers, fails to perceive the issue of rape from a woman's point of view.

The history of western theatre dance is characterized by ruptures instigated by women who sought to present alternative representations to those which were dominantly inscribed. Isadora Duncan is frequently acclaimed as a 'feminist' for her times because she sought to reappropriate the dancing body *for* women. As she states: 'the dancer of the future . . . will dance not in the form of nymph, nor fairy, nor coquette, but in the form of woman in her greatest and purest expression. She will realize the mission of woman's body and the holiness of all its parts' (Duncan 1928: 62–3). But as feminist critics of essentialism have revealed, there is a precarious balance between subversion and reappropriation. Much of what Duncan writes comes uncomfortably close to reinforcing the harmful assumptions of femininity which feminists of the 1990s seek to distance themselves from. Duncan was radical for her time but, like all women, she needs to be viewed as historically and socially positioned, and therefore caught in conflicting webs of identifications. Whilst she did radicalize ideas about dance and transgress the limiting conventions of femininity for her time, Duncan was still a product of her age and its ideologies. Feminists contend that it is impossible for women to create an alternative imagery or code of representation outside its dominant forms (Moi 1985). In order to create, women artists have often strategically allied themselves with the very sources of their identification as 'other', with nature, motherhood and feminine values. An analysis of Duncan's radicalism needs to consider how she was able to position herself as a great artist through her manipulation of society's representations of her sex. Such an approach would make explicit how her positioning as a woman not only enabled her to pursue her passionate interest in dance but also circumscribed the kinds of artistic production she engaged in and the conditions of its reception by her audiences.

Approaches to history which rely on the documentation and inter-pretation of 'images of women' aim to decode dominant representa-tions of femininity and revalue women's representations of women for women. The former has tended to characterize these images as 'good' or 'bad', whereas the latter strategy is concerned to reinstate women's creativity through the appropriation of its female imagery for feminist purposes. Applied to dance, the limitations of such an approach become apparent in analyses which attempt to decode images of woman in a bid to reveal their underlying sexism. For this tends towards a measuring of men's (false) representations of femininity against what are presumed to be women's (authentic) experiences of their gender. The former is exemplified by historians' denigration of the Romantic/ classical ballerina en pointe being manipulated by her male partner and the latter by invocations of the liberatory spirit of the uncorseted, nature-loving Isadora. But such approaches to the writing of feminist dance history are of limited value. As measures of the degree to which representations of women reinforce or subvert the conventions of the male status quo, such analyses force historians into a 'no-win situation' as their thinking remains contained within the walls of patriarchal thought. This is because, as Ann Daly (1992) explains, theories of the 'male gaze' (the structuring of desire in the representation of images of women and their reception) are reliant on a universal sex opposition which is impervious to changes in time and place. Daly also claims that in privileging vision over the other senses, feminist re-presentations of images of women fail to account for the multi-sensory appeal of dance as a kinesthetic art form. She circumvents these problematics by applying the insights of Julia Kristeva's theory of the 'semiotic chora' to a reading of Isadora Duncan's dance practice (Kristeva 1974). Her reading proves the productiveness of approaches to dance which account for the mutuality of linguistic and psychic processes in the production of meaning. Kristeva's theory of language and the radical deconstruction of the identity of the subject allow for anti-essentialist approaches to the study of women's artistic production. However, valuable as these insights are in accounting for the 'revolutionary' subject, they tend to gloss over the primary feminist concern for revolutionary agency (Moi 1985). Feminists cannot afford to lose sight of the political character of their intervention in history: it is this which commits them to engage actively with traditional histories and belief systems in order to subvert their apparent 'truths'.

A necessary development from the project of decoding images of women in dance is the complementary task of a feminist rewriting of its history in terms which situate gender relations as a key determinant in cultural production and signification.

13.4   OUR DANCING FOREMOTHERS: TOWARDS A WOMAN-CENTRED DANCE HISTORY

The notion of giving women a 'voice' and making them visible within history has been a primary focus for the feminist historical project. Feminist historians have sought to install female creators within the mainstream canons of artistic production as well to assert the presence of an alternative canon. The first measure is a reformatory approach as it seeks to adjust the history of a particular discipline to consider the achievements of women as female creators, the assumptions of this endeavour being that the history of art as we know it is the history of art by men. The second measure involves the radical reconstruction of art history according to the notion of a female tradition of artistic production. Such an approach cuts across and undermines patrilineal traditions of culture through its primary consideration of women's relation to artistic production.

Despite women's visibility within dance history as icons or images, there has been, at least until the twentieth century, a dearth of historical analysis of their achievements as its choreographers and inventors. The presence of women as image or symbol within dance history, and their absence as creator both reflect and reinforce the passive/active, subject/object dichotomies of gender relations within patriarchal society. Any feminist intervention within dance history, as a preliminary strategy, needs to reclaim women's creative role in the production of dance, be that as choreographer, director or dancer, in order to affirm their agency within its history.

Feminist theorists have challenged the dominant representation of artistic creativity as an essentially male attribute. Christine Battersby (1989) in her survey of conceptions of artistic genius throughout western history considered its Romantic formulation as particularly harmful to women. Accordingly a great artist was associated with certain kinds of masculine personality-types, certain masculine social roles and certain kinds of masculine energies. This has meant that women creative geniuses have frequently been characterized either in relational terms to husbands, brothers or male mentors, whose influence is presumed to invest them with the essential qualities of creativity, or alternatively to be unwomanly in some way, their qualities of character and body type being aligned more in the stereotypically masculine, than the feminine, order of gender. Both of these characterizations of creative genius in its female form are articulated in Robertson and Hutera's description of Nijinska:

> Never a beauty, Nijinska's stage presence relied on strength and intelligence rather than delicacy. In later years she took to wearing a tuxedo, and even danced the title role in her own 1934 version of *Hamlet*. . . . Nijinska's choreographic identity is closely linked to her brother's revolutionary ideals. . . . His mental breakdown served as a catalyst for her own talent: she admitted that she began making dances in an attempt to further his ideas.
>
> (Robertson and Hutera 1988: 53)

Nijinska's desire to further her brother's ideals can be viewed not only as a result of familial affiliations but also as a way of ensuring her work would gain the exposure and attention it deserved. To confine an assessment of her contribution to dance history to its tangential relation to Nijinsky's 'superstar' status is to retrench the historical record. Though Nijinsky was forced to retreat from the ballet world in 1919 owing to mental illness, his sister continued a successful career as a choreographer and teacher of ballet, an art form then as now dominated by men, up until her death in 1972.

According to Battersby (1989), a feminist history which evaluates and acclaims the achievements of great, individual women artists such as Nijinska appropriates the category of genius *for* women and locates the individual within a matrilineal tradition. However, we need to be cautious of such an approach. Whilst there is a certain value in identifying a matrilineage of women's choreographic production, there is also a danger in locating this outside mainstream practices. Although some women may share certain experiences and attributes as women, this does not mean that their cultural forms and modes of signification can be celebrated as creativity in its female form. To claim otherwise is to risk the dangers of an essentialist position whereby feminine creativity is directly related to female biology.

The feminist project for dance history needs to consider not only the achievements of individual women choreographers, whose work is marginalized or silenced by mainstream history and criticism but also the role of female dancers in contributing to the choreographic process. Feminists forgo patriarchal culture's investment of authority in the 'author' as source, origin and articulator of meaning for the 'text' (Moi 1985). Within the practice of dance this means redrawing the categories of investigation to account for the role, not only of the choreographer and librettist in the production of meaning but also of the performer in her various guises, be that as principal dancer, member of a corps or company performer. For what is frequently overlooked in approaches to history which rely on a genealogy of distinguished, artistic creators is the role of the dancer in shaping choreographic production. Subject/object dichotomies prevail in discussions on dance which rely on notions of the body as the medium or instrument of expression, which the choreographer shapes to suit 'his' creative vision. But dancers are not neutral surfaces awaiting masterly inscriptions, they exist as highly trained and articulate experts of movement who colour the choreographic process with their own subjectivities. In relinquishing the hierarchical relation between choreographer and dancer, the process of artistic production can be realigned to consider the inventiveness of the dancer as interpreter and articulator of the 'text'.

Much of the work of British choreographer Rosemary Butcher has relied on a choreographic process which encourages the creative contributions of her performers, in both rehearsal and performance (Jordan 1992). Cynthia Novack (1990) in her study of contact improvization in the USA has documented the spirit of co-operation and egalitarianism that was intrinsic to this movement. Collective modes of production, widespread in the 1970s, have, however, lost much of their popularity. The difficulties of collective work, where no one person has overall control, are compounded by the constraints imposed by an industry which relies on the promotion and funding of individual 'names', reflecting and reinforcing capitalist modes of production. In order to align categories of analysis with a feminist praxis, historians would need to rescind conventional classificatory systems which rely on the notion of a gifted individual and alternatively examine the social production of art (Wolff 1981). Such a shift would necessitate a redefining of the categories of analysis by substituting terms like creation with production, and reception with consumption.

Christy Adair (1992) goes some way towards addressing the history of women's production in the performance and choreography of ballet but, as she herself admits, any account which remains committed to positive historical evidence is restricted to the role of the female 'greats' such as Camargo, Taglioni, Pavlova and Fonteyn, because so few records remain for consideration of the history of those 'other' women, the corps who were generally illiterate, frequently prostitutes and regarded as something of a backdrop to the main event, the ballerina. New approaches to history which attend to the discursive formation of cultural artefacts are more likely to uncover the hidden stories of these neglected 'mistresses' of the dance (Carter 1993).

By positioning the female dancer, historically and socially, as an autonomous subject rather than a contingent object, we can bypass the naturalizing of gender dichotomies, so much a feature of androcentric thought. Such an alternative history would make Fanny Cerrito's choreographic output much more than an addendum to the cataloguing of her 'feminine charms' as a ballerina: it would account for the regime of training she undertook in order to make her talent appear as an 'innate gift' (Gautier 1977: 89) whilst acknowledging the importance of her role in shaping the balletic tradition through the imparting of her knowledge to other dancers. For what is significant about dance is that it is one of the few arenas of artistic production in which women have claimed a vital role for themselves. We need to ask why it is that women have excelled to such a degree within dance when such success has eluded their, often restricted, endeavours in other fields.

The valorization of women's past achievements in dance emphasizes their autonomy by accrediting them with power. As a necessary stage in the feminist project, attempts to reclaim women's creative endeavours from the past correct the biases of traditional history and enlarge the subject area for the historian. The danger of such an approach, however, is its tendency towards an uncritical celebration of a feminine past. What this emphasis neglects to account for are the structures of dominance within social, economic and political systems and how these impinge upon the subject and the production and consumption of her work.

13.5   CHALLENGING ESSENTIALISM: MATERIALIST APPROACHES TO FEMINIST DANCE HISTORY

A materialist approach to feminist dance history would shift attention from the study of works according to notions of individual creativity and style to a consideration of how sexual differences are constructed within dance as a cultural practice. Materialist feminism divorces itself from radical conceptions of woman as an ahistorical essence. Alternatively it can be seen as a category of feminist thought which seeks to examine the cultural construction of sexuality, that is, how sexual identities are arrived at through their demarcation within social relations and institutional systems. Its conception of art as socially produced avoids the essentialist trap of distinguishing between men's and women's artistic production whilst acknowledging that women's cultural and social experiences are arrived at differently from men's.

The materialist feminist approach seeks to explain representations as producers of meaning and as shaping the construction of social subjects. The apparatus of representation, according to this view, functions by hardening ideologies into objects and images, and sustaining these are real, normative presences. It undermines the authority of representations by critiquing their capacity to encode as permanent, or natural, what may be temporary or learnt (Pollock 1988).

Such an approach would prove particularly useful in analysing the ways in which gender stereotypes are 'naturalized' within specific periods and genres of dance. A feminist dance history project could, for instance, analyse the systems of power which condone the re-presentation of certain kinds of female bodies whilst suppressing others. Elizabeth Dempster (1988) examines how the dancing body encodes and reproduces the social, cultural and political values of the period and genre within which it originated. She explains how a historical analysis of the construction of the dancing body, through participation in the discourse of classes, rehearsals and performances particular to a genre, generates a political history of corporeality. In thinking through the body in its various constructions throughout dance history, feminist analyses of dance come closer to an under-standing of the dynamic of history as a process, one which is constantly realigning the meanings of the dancing body according to the con-ditions of the production and the varying discourses, social, political and economic, within which it operates.

Any study of dance which attempts to acknowledge and incorporate the insights of cultural and feminist theories needs to exist within a double frame. First, the material specificity of dance as a practice needs to be systematically analysed in terms of its modes of production, distribution and reception as well as its forms of training, the codes and rhetorics of its genres, and the levels of competence and expertise of its practitioners. These phenomena are in turn interdependent for their meaning and apprehension upon a range of discourses and social practices. This second frame of analysis considers how dance practices interrelate with other discourses such as social relations, economies, cultural knowledge, media systems etc. This simultaneity of textual and institutional analyses within feminist history is of particular value to dance which has often, in the past, been marginalized owing to its self-enclosure within the celebratory rhetorics of the 'gentleman scholar'.

13.6   SPEAKING FROM THE MARGINS: DANCE, POST-STRUCTURALISM AND HISTORY

There is positive potential for a feminist dance history which embraces a post-structuralist approach since post-structuralism transforms the possibilities for feminist historical analysis. It values experiential knowl-edge concentrating on traces, such as oral history and autobiography, and, working through interrogation and deconstruction, critiques in-fluential historical works. By working with a variety of sources, post-structuralists create texts within the histories they write. They openly acknowledge their intervention as contingent, partial and particular to the social context in which they operate. Furthermore the accidents of survival or erasure of historical traces are accounted for and considered as an essential part of the historical assessment (Thom 1992).

Dances by their very nature embody a fluidity of authorship as it is virtually impossible for a choreographer to transpose exactly her or his movement on to another body. From muse to collaborator the most acclaimed ballerinas of the twentieth century are invariably coupled with their male choreographers: Lynn Seymour with Kenneth Mac-Millan, Margot Fonteyn with Frederick Ashton and Suzanne Farrell with George Balanchine (Robertson and Hutera 1988). This, combined with the fact that as a performative art it is constantly in process, signifies dance's resistance to being fixed as a stable, unitary object. The marginality of dance in relation to other art forms is seen to result from its ephemeral nature, but within post-structuralism its temporary, fleeting presence locates it as a privileged site for the exploration of fractured and fragmentary identities. Post-structuralists such as Foucault (1979) prove that categories of self or author are not as straightforward as conventional approaches to history would have us believe. Feminists working in this way expose the fault-lines that mark identities as fragmentary and oeuvres as resisting cohesion. In doing so they retrieve the dispersed traces of marginal experiences, locating them in their own narrations which remain open-ended.

Historians, in dealing with present traces of the past, that is represent-ations, engage in the production of meanings or narrations through interpretation. To deny this process is to fetishize the archive, making it into a substitute for what no longer exists, the past. Dance historians concerned with their role as the 'narrating figure' of their (hi)story need to acknowledge their mediation in its composition. For to deny their own existence is to fail to admit to the act of imposition in ordering the present traces of the past. For feminists who adopt this position the long-standing tradition of history which masquerades as 'truth' is ruptured through a radical reformulation of knowledge.

13.7   FEMINIST STRATEGIES FOR WRITING DANCE HISTORY

Feminist scholarship fundamentally challenges the dominance of mas-culine value systems in culture and in the history of artistic production. It serves a corrective role in rearranging the values, categories and con-ceptual structures of any field of enquiry, whilst expanding the field of knowledge to account for and accommodate female existence. In radic-ally altering the focus of history from an unacknowledged bias towards men in favour of being *for* women, feminist scholarship restores the role of the female artist by establishing her reputation within the established canon. Furthermore in foregrounding women's contributions to history feminists generate new areas of research, expanding the discourse of dance by privileging what has been previously silenced or left out.

Whilst most feminists admit to the political character of feminism, there is no common agreement as to the shape that this thinking should take. Political pluralism runs through all of feminism's manifestations within academic and artistic disciplines, hence the need to consider the specific potential of different kinds of feminist thought in relation to dance history. Several approaches towards writing feminist dance history have been outlined here: the decoding of 'images of women'; the celebration and appraisal of the achievements of individual women; the construction of sexuality within dance discourse; and the challenges of post-structuralism in refiguring identities and subjectivities as fragmentary and contradictory. Each of these positions is strategically located within contemporary feminist debates about culture, and needs to be considered within this context.

Given that patriarchy has been theorized as a 'universal' system of oppressive and exploitative relations in which women are subordinate, it is important to emphasize the many paths of resistance available to feminists (Humm 1989). A useful strategy to employ in the initial encounter with a dance text or image is one of 'reading against the grain' (Moi 1985). This involves a 're-tracing' of the meanings and significance of an image or piece of writing through an 'engaged vision', one which attempts to negotiate the feminine/feminist identities and experiences of the female subject by situating her within the prevailing discourses of her day. By refusing to respect or acknowledge the intentions of the choreographer the feminist critic posits her own perspective on the dance by revealing the ideologies which underpin its construction. Such an approach to the interpretation of a ballet may, for instance, allow for the female heroine's resistance to, as well as collusion with, the stereotypes of passive femininity to be revealed. One way to enter into such an analysis is to operate John Berger's (1972) exercise of switching the sex, while maintaining the body language and expression, of images of women and men. As an alternative to comparing images of women, the substitution of an image of a woman with that of a man discloses the kinds of meanings implied within the politics of a particular representation (Pollock 1987).

Dance is a relatively new academic discipline with a high ratio of women scholars. It is not to be assumed, however, that the dominance of women as practitioners and researchers of dance guarantees a feminist orientation. There is no necessary correlation between gender and political attitude and no guarantee that women scholars/teachers will be feminist. Yet feminism provides history with an enormously improved understanding of how women's lives are punctuated differently from men's, and how this divide is also a structure of dominance

(Campbell 1922). It is important not to lose sight of this in the search to discover more and more about the lives and artistic production of women, for feminism, being fundamentally political in character, seeks to change the world.

REFERENCES

Adair, C. (1992), *Women and Dance: Sylphs and Sirens*, London: Macmillan.
Allen, J. (1986) 'Evidence and silence: feminism and the limits of history', in Pateman, C. and Gross, E. (eds), *Feminist Challenges: Social and Political Theory*, Sydney: Allen & Unwin: 173–89.
Battersby, C. (1989), *Gender and Genius*, London: The Women's Press.
Beaumont, W. (1930), *A History of Ballet in Russia*, London: C. W. Beaumont.
Beauvoir, S. de (1988), *The Second Sex* (1949), London: Picador Classics, Pan Books.
Berger, J. (1972), *Ways of Seeing*, London: Penguin.
Bovenschen, S. (1985), 'Is there a feminine aesthetic?', in G. Ecker (ed.), *Feminist Aesthetics*, London: The Women's Press: 23–50.
Brown, C. (1993), *Feminist Issues in Choreography* (Ph.D. research in progress, University of Surrey).
Campbell, K. (1992), 'Introduction: matters of theory and practice – or, we'll be coming out the harbour', in K. Campbell (ed.), *Critical Feminism*, Buckingham and Philadelphia: Open University Press: 1–24.
Carter, A. (1993), *Winged and Shivering: Images of Women in the Alhambra and Empire Ballets 1884–1915* (unpublished Ph.D. thesis, University of Surrey).
Cohen, S. J. (ed.) (1977, 1991), *Dance as a Theatre Art*, London: Dance Books.
Coltheart, L. (1986), 'Desire, consent and liberal theory', in Pateman, C. and Gross, E. (eds), *Feminist Challenges: Social and Political Theory*, Sydney: Allen & Unwin: 112–22.
Copeland, R. (1982a), 'Towards a sexual politics of contemporary dance', *Contact Quarterly*, spring/summer: 45–50.
—— (1982b), 'Why women dominate modern dance', *The New York Times*, Sunday 18 April: 1, 22.
—— (1990a), 'In defence of formalism: the politics of disinterestedness', *Dance Theatre Journal*, 7, 4 (February): 4–7, 37–9.
—— (1990b), 'Founding mothers: Duncan, Graham, Rainer and sexual politics', *Dance Theatre Journal*, 8, 3 (autumn): 6–9, 27–9.
Daly, A. (1987), 'The Balanchine woman, of hummingbirds and channel swimmers', *The Drama Review*, 31, 1: 8–21.
—— (1987/8), 'Classical ballet: a discourse of difference', *Women and Performance*, 3, 2, 6: 57–66.
—— (1992), 'Dance history and feminist theory: reconsidering Isadora Duncan and the male gaze', in L. Senelick (ed.), *Gender in Performance: The Presentation of Difference in the Performing Arts*, Hanover: University Press of New England: 239–59.
Dempster, E. (1988), 'Women writing the body: let's watch a little how she dances', in S. Sheridan (ed.) *Grafts: Feminist Cultural Criticism*, London: Verso: 35–54.
Duncan, I. (1928) 'The dance of the future', in *The Art of the Dance*, edited by Cheney, New York: Theater Arts.
Elton, G. R. (1967), *The Practice of History*, Melbourne: Fontana.

Foucault, M. (1979), *The History of Sexuality*, London: Allen Lane.

Gautier, T. (1977), Reviews of Fanny Cerrito and Marie Guy-Stéphan, from *La Presse* (1846, 1853), in Cohen (1977): 86–90.

Goodwin, N. (1992), 'Gambling on drama', *Dance and Dancers*, March: 16–17.

Guest, I. (1977), *The Dancer's Heritage: A Short History of Ballet*, London: The Dancing Times.

—— (1986), *Gautier on Dance: Théophile Gautier*, selected, translated and annotated by I. Guest, London: Dance Books.

Gross, E. (1986), 'Conclusion: what is feminist theory?' in C. Pateman and E. Gross (eds) *Feminist Challenges: Social and Political Theory*, Sydney: Allen & Unwin: 190–204.

Grosz, E. (1987), 'Notes towards a corporeal feminism', *Australian Feminist Studies*, 5 (summer): 1–16.

Harding, S. (1987), 'Introduction: is there a feminist method?, in S. Harding (ed.), *Feminism and Methodology*, Bloomington, Ind.: Indiana University Press and Milton Keynes: Open University Press: 1–14.

Hartstock, N. (1983), 'The feminist standpoint: developing the ground for a specifically feminist historical materialism', in S. Harding and M. B. Hintakka (eds), *Discovering Reality: Feminist Perspectives on Epistemology, Metaphysics, Methodology and Philosophy of Science*, Dordrecht and London: D. Reidel: 283–310.

Humm, M. (1989), *The Dictionary of Feminist Theory*, Hemel Hempstead, Herts: Harvester, Wheatsheaf.

Jordan, S. (1992), *Striding Out: Aspects of Contemporary and New Dance in Britain*, London: Dance Books.

Kelly-Gadol, J. (1987), 'The social relation of the sexes: methodological implications of women's history', in S. Harding (ed.), *Feminism and Methodology*, Bloomington, Ind.: Indiana University Press and Milton Keynes: Open University Press: 15–28.

Kristeva, J. (1974), *La Révolution du langage poétique*, Paris: Tel Quel.

Layson, J. (1983), 'Methods in the historical study of dance', in J. Adshead and J. Layson (eds), *Dance History: A Methodology for Study*, London: Dance Books: 15–26.

—— (1991), 'Dance history methodology', in C. Brack and I. Wuyts (eds), *Dance and Research: An Interdisciplinary Approach*, Proceedings of the International Congress 'Dance and Research', Louvain: Peeters Press: 3–10.

Lloyd, G. (1989), 'The man of reason', in A. Garry and M. Pearsall (eds), *Women, Knowledge and Reality: Explorations in Feminist Philosophy*, Boston: Unwin Hyman: 111–28.

Mies, M. (1983), 'Towards a methodology for feminist research', in G. Bowles and R. Duelli Klein (eds), *Theories of Women's Studies*, London and New York: Routledge & Kegan Paul: 117–39.

Moi, T. (1985), *Sexual/Textual Politics: Feminist Literary Theory*, London and New York: Methuen.

Novack, C. (1990), *Sharing the Dance: Contact Improvisation and American Culture*, Madison, Wis.: University of Wisconsin Press.

Parry, J. (1992), 'Judas cast as a Docklands navvy', *The Observer*, 22 March: 61.

Pollock, G. (1987), 'What's wrong with images of women?', in R. Betterton (ed.), *Looking On: Images of Femininity in the Visual Arts and Media*, London: Pandora: 40–8.

—— (1988), *Vision and Difference: Femininity, Feminism and the Histories of Art*, London and New York: Routledge.

—— (1993), 'Rewriting the story of art', *Women's Art*, 50 (Jan./Feb.): 4–7.

Riley, D. (1988), *'Am I that Name?': Feminism and the Category of Women in History*, Basingstoke and London: Macmillan.

Robertson, A. and Hutera, D. (1988), *The Dance Handbook*, Harlow, Essex: Longman.

Stimpson, C. R. (1988), 'Nancy Reagan wears a hat: feminism and its cultural consensus', *Critical Inquiry*, 14, 2: 223–43.

Thom, D. (1992), 'A lop-sided view: feminist history or the history of women?', in K. Campbell (ed.) *Critical Feminism: Argument in the Disciplines*, Buckingham and Philadelphia: Open University Press: 25–51.

Thompson, J. (1986), 'Women and political rationality', in C. Pateman and E. Gross (eds), *Feminist Challenges: Social and Political Theory*, Sydney: Allen & Unwin: 99–111.

Wolff, J. (1981), *The Social Production of Art*, London: Macmillan.

—— (1992), 'Foreword' to Adair (1992): xi–xii.

Part III
Studying and writing dance history

Chapter 14

Pathways to studying dance history

Janet Adshead-Lansdale

The purpose of this chapter is to discuss ways in which the dance student learns to become a dance historian. Part II is used as a source since its contents are typical of research papers that both the lecturer and the student might be expected to become familiar with at conferences and in dance research journals. Reflection on the approaches and content of the preceding chapters suggests fruitful pathways for the development of dance history teaching and learning. The basic principles and methodologies of dance history that are discussed in Part I serve to underpin this review of the historical process and the fundamental skills that need to be acquired. The material in Part I can be employed in an exemplary way when initiating undergraduate and postgraduate students in a critical review of the dance history literature.

A further purpose here is to challenge traditional stereotypes of history teaching in general and dance history teaching in particular. These stereotypes are of dull, boring sessions in which so-called 'facts' are recounted, in which indigestible quantities of information are gathered, culled from more or less respectable secondary sources but presented in a manner totally devoid of any spark of involvement on the part of student or teacher. A much better introduction, however, can be found in sharing the excitement of dealing with 'raw' materials and, in so doing, developing a sense of the period and the social and artistic context of the time. Practical exercises based on actual sources can generate both enthusiasm and insight, while old narratives, however well-respected the author, may often simply deaden the experience and suggest that history is indelibly written, fixed in tablets of stone. The idea that history can be continually rewritten is a much more exciting and challenging one to convey to students.

By inviting students to make comparisons between sources and to analyse interpretive accounts in secondary texts, critical skills can be developed and lively debate encouraged. Exercises in discriminating between types of sources enhance perception, enable the student to

understand historical method and enliven the learning process. Identifying gaps in historical accounts may offer opportunities to explore an
alternative interpretation, for instance from a feminist position (see
Carol Brown's Chapter 13). Investigation of current local dance culture
can be another point of entry encouraging the student to see the
relevance of history and to begin independent research. Patricia Mitchinson's Chapter 6 on the dance of Harrogate is just such an example.
Choosing appropriate topics that match students' interests is also crucial.
While a study of the history of ballet across eighteenth-century Europe
might seem the right beginning for the ballet history teacher it is at best
remote and possibly irrelevant for the student of late-twentieth-century
dance forms, irrespective of her or his experience in ballet.

A major consideration for the dance history teacher is how to judge
the breadth and depth of investigation that is appropriate for students
at different stages of their development. Dance history taught to the
mature, interested ballet-goer is a very different proposition from the
brief outline that may be right for the young dancer whose primary
interest is in performance. Different again are the interests and requirements of undergraduate or postgraduate university students.
Motivation, reasons for study and the relationship to practical dance
experience are all relevant in the preparation of programmes of dance
history teaching.

One of the reasons why 'history' can be both unpopular and infre-
quently taught well in universities and colleges lies in the relationship
between history and other aspects of the dance programme. The
common practice of isolating history teaching in content, and history
teachers in person, from the live performance and choreographic
elements of the dance programme can only serve to raise questions in
the minds of some students about its relevance.

History, taught in an integrated manner, alongside both choreography and repertoire, offers the chance to demonstrate how traces of
the past exist in the present.[1] Thus if it is arranged that a choreography
class uses models, or examples, from a variety of works made in
different periods, it can have many purposes. One might be to acquaint
students with their chosen subject more thoroughly, a second to
demonstrate that the 'new' is often a re-working of ideas long known, a
third to locate the student's own ideas within the stylistic range of the
genre. Inevitably, a sense of the relevance of the historical dimension of
dance is conveyed by these means.

The different devices employed by choreographers can be explored
with an eye to their location in particular periods. While none of this is
new for the enlightened choreography or dance history teacher, it can
be enhanced by a more explicit recognition of the complex web of
relationships evident within the heritage of dance and between that

heritage and current practice. At another level the teaching of choreo-graphy itself can make a contribution to the history-making process. How choreography is taught to the next generation can be viewed historically in a reflexive manner. One obvious benefit of using repertoire extracts is that in learning the dance the problems of giving an 'authentic' rendering can be explored. Debate around the relation-ship of the work as originally performed to its current manifestations can prove endlessly fascinating in the teaching of both history and repertoire.

To perform a dance, whether of the here and now or from a previous era, demands an understanding of the changes in technique that have taken place over time, that is, an appreciation of the way fragments of the past remain, merge and change their character in the present is necessary. Thus a historical perspective is required.

This present text is in written, not choreographic, form, but this does not diminish its usefulness. Chapters 4–13 cover a range of dance genres and it is obvious that each is written from a particular perspective. Even within a related field, the three chapters which deal with tradi-tional or social dance forms, for example, use substantially different approaches and operate within very different parameters. These are worth noting as potential models. Theresa Buckland's focus in Chapter 4 is on methods for research across the diverse field of English traditional dance and is in contrast to Patricia Mitchinson's tighter focus in Chapter 6 on specific social dances in Harrogate, a north of England spa town, in the eighteenth century. Patricia Mitchinson illustrates the difficulties of research in practice, giving the student a good idea of the problems likely to be encountered and ways of dealing with them, while Theresa Buckland's text is of help in setting up a research project in the first place, giving guidance on how the para-meters of the investigation might be designed. In general terms, the broader and less defined the research, the less satisfactory will be the outcome. Time spent refining the logic of the project before embarking on the collection of a mass of information will be well spent. The detailed methodology in Theresa Buckland's chapter is of great value as a model for the student researcher. One area given as an example here is her examination of the modes of transmission of dances. Traditional dance forms are passed from generation to generation without refer-ence to national or international standards.

On the other hand much of the transmission of theatre dance, while also primarily oral in character, is distinguished by the reference to external, and often historically remote, standards. Roles in the classics clearly take their standards from previous versions of the work in a manner that is very different from the inheritance of traditional dances. In focusing on the process of transmission, questions of change and authenticity immediately arise. Whether the dance should be conceived of as a museum piece or as part of the living heritage is a constant debate and one which the student historian has to address in gathering information, analysing it and presenting it. This question is of crucial importance in reconstruction, and Kenneth Archer and Millicent Hodson in Chapter 7 reflect cogently on the decision-making process in such activity.

Patricia Mitchinson's account has as its purpose to find out what dance activities typified the spa town of Harrogate, thus defining certain parameters to direct this study of a period in local history. With the growing interest in popular dance forms and in redeeming one's heritage, a study of local traditions may be of rather more topical interest than the dance history of distant cultures for some students. Such a project also offers much that is relevant to the historian in developing detective skills of dance history in the investigation of library and newspaper sources, in seeking publications which are no longer thought to be extant and conveying something of the struggle to locate materials. It also demonstrates the attempt to develop a hypothesis: that social dance at Harrogate in this period took a form that was similar to the dance in other places. This turns out not to be the case, a perfectly valid conclusion, from this judicious assessment of the available materials.

The focus on the dance is matched by building up a sense of context, of Harrogate in the eighteenth and nineteenth centuries. The flavour of the time is conveyed in part through quoted sources, and this practice raises useful questions of interpretation simply from the recognition of differences in the use of language and in the form of expression. Awareness of changes in the use of language about dance might take the student to a wider study of the literature of the period.

The issue of language is crucial for the debate about how far we can understand the dance of other eras and places. The extent to which language itself inscribes concepts rather than acting as a pointing device to things outside itself is emphasized in postmodern thinking and in some earlier Wittgenstein-derived work (see Best 1975). Poesio (1993) illustrates the point in pursuing his research on the Italian ballet mime, drawing on the original French and Italian texts of the nineteenth century but commenting on them in modern English. The complexities of language-use are legion in the act of translation and re-interpretation, problems which are exacerbated by writing in another era.

The challenge is not only to language but to the construction or creation of the historical account (see Chapters 1 and 15). Hutcheon's (1989) challenge to the creation of a 'narrative' in history makes the budding historian question the attempt to make a unified text, with all the implications that this carries of possible distortion. The temptation for the historian to do this is obvious since writing itself demands structure, and the investigation has to be limited in some way if it is not to become incoherent. Students and teachers, similarly, have traditionally felt the need for structures and stories, a beginning and an end. Educational packages tend to be divided into time-determined slots which provide the learner with a structured environment. Simultaneously remaining open to ambiguity is problematic not just theoretically but both practically and educationally.

The excitement of postmodern approaches for the dance history student and teacher arises from grasping this same principle: that history-making, by constructing narratives, is an intensely human process which imparts not only order but meaning. While in one sense this is self-evident, and is something of which any historian would be aware, it serves to direct the researcher's attention to a number of difficulties in distinguishing history writing from fiction writing.

The question to keep in mind throughout the research and writing process is the relationship between inventing an account and discovering the 'truth'. The formulation of the title 'Re-presenting the past' (Hutcheon 1989: Chapter 3) highlights the role of re-creation in the interpretation of the past and the possibility of the emergence of a series of differing accounts. The style of writing of much dance history reveals little consciousness of this creative role and dance students should become aware of it.

Indeed, it is not just the narrative aspect of history that may be questioned but the very existence of 'facts'. Is it an arbitrary process by which 'events become facts', Hutcheon asks (1989: 78). Some are chosen for narration, others are not, as revealed in recent research on the corps de ballet of early-twentieth-century ballets in London whose history has been largely erased (Carter 1993).

The difficulties of establishing a 'text' of the dance, with the uncertainties that the interpretation of fragmentary data carries, the exposing of subjective positions in this process, the decisions that are taken about how an audience of the present will respond and therefore how the dance is inflected (even changed for current production) all provide excellent examples of the problems facing the historian in practice. These concerns need to be elevated to greater awareness so that questions such as those the postmodernist theorist explores, about the creation of a narrative, can be addressed directly (see Chapter 1 above). A view of dance structure and of dance writing as consisting of a series of interrupted narratives, which are inherently ambiguous, challenges the traditional drive for a beginning, a middle and an end.

Foucault's writing (see Foucault 1972 and Chapter 1 above) questions not only historical methodology but also the concept and status of a 'document'. A 'document' is seen to be not just a piece of evidence, such as a programme or a photograph, but something created here and now; wherever dances are devised new 'documents' are created. In this sense the historical process is seen to be very similar to the choreographic process, in that there are analogies with dividing movement up, distributing it, ordering it, arranging it in many levels, creating series, describing relations. Hence the relevance of teaching choreography and performance with an eye to history, and history with an eye to choreography and performance.

Theresa Buckland (Chapter 4 above) offers the chance to speculate on the character of the 'fact' in her analysis of previous scholarship and the differing contributions of previous theorists and collectors of dances. This promotes speculation on the importance for dance of what is recorded and in what mode. The importance of the selection process for the historian should not be underestimated.

The question of what is to count as a fact is raised again in Jane Pritchard's study (Chapter 9 above) of the Rambert Dance Company Archive. Archives are highly variable collections: they may be major, minor, small or large collections of sources. For companies without a theatre-base it is unusual to find an archive of any kind. The selective process of creating sources or 'facts' is made very evident in this case since it explicitly revolves around the Rambert Company's life, certain materials are collected and not others. It opens up questions for the dance history student because of this, since it is comprehensive (for that Company's purposes) but highly selective. The companies with which Rambert shares an artistic life are less well represented in the archive, and neither is the wider context addressed. The actual materials collected by any company also reflect what is thought to count as relevant and important in its history. The decisions about collecting policies are made with reference to the works and lives of individuals and other organizations. The materials cited by Jane Pritchard include posters, photographs and other visual images of works, some of which are now lost, others fortunately captured on video, and in notation. Costumes, designs, production notes and accounts of meetings are also retained. It is possible that other sources could be identified and valued as part of the life of the Company. The challenge to the archivist is in deciding what to collect and what to omit and for the historian in interpreting the decisions of previous collectors.

The detective work of the historian is well illustrated by the difficulty of identifying photographs and programmes if unattributed in name or date. Thus the possibility of establishing an undisputed document of factual material is seen to be inherently problematic. More revealing still is material relating to crucial decisions in the history of a company based on political, economic or artistic change. These policy decisions themselves constitute a significant narrative and the historian, sub-sequently, might be tempted to see issues solely from that company's perspective if other material is not also consulted and placed in relationship to it.

In stark contrast Georgiana Gore's writing on dance in West Africa (Chapter 5 above) privileges the oral source above the written source. This is not just a matter of the lack of written accounts affecting the collection of data but a recognition of the eclectic nature of this process. The anthropological questioning of the relative values of eye-witness accounts and pre-existing written accounts is worth addressing. Alter-native processes of authenticating information may be required, and any attempt to reach a universal truth about the nature or function of a dance might be seen to be seriously misleading. Part of the strength of such work is in learning to recognize that many views of a dance can co-exist depending on different participants' and observers' positions. Discussion of these issues need not be limited to the dances of West Africa since these points about the direct engagement of any participant or observer necessarily affect the outcome of any research.

Where evidence conflicts there is a real question of how sources are to be balanced and how far to place reliance on them. This opens up further the possibility of questioning the evidence in recognition that documents may be simply misleading, apparently well-informed or otherwise, tampered with or genuine (see Chapter 2 above). In other words, by virtue of the voice that is heard there may be not one truth but several different positions to be understood. These questions might be brought directly to the attention of the dance history student and raised in the teaching of dance history courses so that the significance of the student's and teacher's own positions are understood.

The writing of a narrative which gives a coherent account of a new set of practices in dance is revealed in Michael Huxley's study (Chapter 10 above) of European early modern dance, where he describes distinctive features of dances created by western European choreographers in the period between 1910 and the late 1930s. Changing views of expres-sionism emerge as he traces the rise of a consensus of meaning in naming new types of dance in this period. A late-twentieth-century consciousness of how the political events leading to the Second World War affected the ideological situation of dance is evident in his writing but rarely present in earlier, more strictly genealogical, accounts. The importance of a wider perspective than that of western European dance is illustrated in this first acknowledgement of Russian experiments of a similar kind between 1913 and 1935.

Dance history is opened up in a manner sympathetic to postmodern thinking through Huxley's stress on the importance not only of theatre dance forms but of their amateur, or social counterparts, the 'lay dances' of the German movement choirs. The juxtaposition of so-called high art and popular culture is explored at some length.

The presence in a dance history text such as this of commentaries dealing with social and traditional dance forms beyond the western European tradition to that of parts of Africa is significant in the same sense. Most dance history writing privileges conventional theatre forms in a far more obvious way without recognizing that what is written is but the narrow history of the so-called 'art' forms of a small minority of the white western world.

The story of Expressionism is one of the metanarratives of the white western world in the twentieth century and thus can bear more detailed exploration. It is the sub-text (with abstraction or formalism) of many dance history courses. Any investigation of expressionism and the expression of emotion in dance reveals typical terminological ambiguities and stimulates valuable discussion of the impossibility of legislating for common use. Simplistic attempts at definition have long been challenged (Best 1975) but the predominant thrust of much student dance history can still be to seek this kind of 'clarity' rather than to recognize that many readings are possible with the correspondingly rich potential this offers for promoting further understanding. As a theory of art, Expressionism can be seen to relate very specifically to certain times and circumstances, notably the German Expressionist period in theatre and the visual arts. In dance there are at least two sets of referents; the same concept of expressionism and, in addition, a recurrent notion of the 'innate' Expressiveness of the human body and human movement which is not tied specifically to the Expressionist period. Movement, it is commonly said, irrespective of time, place and genre, speaks of the human condition.

The implications of failing to distinguish between the art movement of Expressionism and the expressiveness of dance more generally is revealed, as Deborah Jowitt points out, in her discussions of Merce Cunningham's work (Chapter 11 above). The oft-repeated view is that Cunningham is totally unconcerned with expression which, Jowitt suggests, is to assume that the choreographer's restraint in imposing his own feelings results in work that is inexpressive. The work may not answer to Expressionism (with a capital E), indeed it may run entirely counter to it, but it can still remain utterly expressive of human moods and states.

One of the many ways in which Deborah Jowitt's work might act as a model for the student dance historian is to highlight the process of untangling some of these problems. In addition, the support that she gives for her statements is exemplary, often being drawn from the choreographic detail of the movement. When she writes of Humphrey's *Two Ecstatic Themes* (1931) she demonstrates the 'precariousness of her equilibrium' (p. 172) through description of the curve and its dynamic phrasing. An extreme version of expressionist phraseology is revealed in her description of Sokolow's gestures 'stretching out shivering fingers' (p. 173). Procedures to be learnt en route to becoming a historian include the vital need to offer support for statements and to acquire the ability to explain the significance of sources while maintaining the expressive flow of language in writing.

Deborah Jowitt's work in tracing the attitude of successive dance generations to the idea of 'expression' follows a traditional historical methodology; looking for change through time. Attention to the individual case, a particular dance, a particular instance, a particular juxtaposition of events, gives the support that is necessary to challenge received wisdom, as, for example, in her discussion of Rainer's *Trio A*. What emerges is a shifting concept of 'expression'. This corresponds to recent theory, which draws attention to the character of the discourse that operates in discussion of dances. The analysis of discourse shows how a set of rules that any one way of speaking puts into operation is both relevant specifically to that field and irreducible to any other set of practices.

In Roger Copeland's writing (Chapter 12 above) it is clearly evident that theoretical positions, just as much as dance forms, are themselves the product of time and place, and that they represent a specific view of the world. The timing of Cunningham's rejection of the expressionist theory of modern dance is not insignificant. Roger Copeland's exploration of the relationship between chance and choice in Cunningham's work avoids the simplification of many standard history texts and reveals the extent of Cunningham's control over his output. Detailed analysis of the dance indicates very clearly the fundamental philosophical positions held by the group of collaborators of which Cunningham was part. The debates are seen to have shifted from 'natural expressiveness' to perceptual freedom, in response to the concerns of the artists. Thus artistic discourse is not just responsive to the activity but a vital part of it. The very rejection of language, which is embodied in expressionism, can only be revealed in the language of rejection. The lesson to be learnt from Copeland, as from Jowitt, is to seek support for arguments, both in the use of example and in elaboration of an argument.

The conceptual shift that is required to conceive of Cunningham's work as being about 'interference . . . and . . . the habits of attention one needs to cultivate in an urban environment of unceasing sensory overload' (p. 185) is shown to be clearly at odds with the preferences of critics such as Croce and Siegel. To approach Cunningham's work from the perspective solely of dance, rather than from a more holistic arts perspective (as Copeland argues) may produce a view that is, at least, limited and, at worst, positively misleading. An inappropriate discourse is seen to be at work. Copeland's tracing of Cunningham's relationship to the Graham aesthetic, and that of his collaborators to the spirit of abstract expressionism, demonstrates history in its explanatory mode, history which identifies changes in concept, for example, arguing that when 'one can no longer view the unconscious (and/or the 'primitive') as a source of inviolable purity' (p. 191) the rationale for expressionism is challenged.

This examination of expressionism in the twentieth century is in line with modern historical method in which an attempt is made (maybe fruitlessly) to reveal the larger movements of accumulation. Latterly, however, attention has turned away from vast unities like periods and centuries to the phenomena of rupture, or discontinuity, suggesting that 'beneath the persistence of a particular genre, form, discipline, or theoretical activity, one is now trying to detect the incidence of interruptions' (Foucault 1972: 4). The focus narrows from the larger periods, or groups, or schools, to the smaller and highly particular text.

Asking questions about the codification of dance steps and their subsequent imperviousness to change is part of Poesio's method in Chapter 8 above. Here he is discussing Cecchetti, but he also incidentally addresses bigger questions. By re-examining historical evidence and provoking discussion of the years Cecchetti spent in Russia, the significance of three spheres of influence, indeed three eras, can be revealed. In other words, several potentially competing explanations of Cecchetti's role arise from his relationship to the Italian *ballo grande*, the Russian Imperial Ballet and to Diaghilev's Ballets Russes respectively. The problematic nature of the sources is also explored since they sometimes assume a ghostly absence rather than a presence, being held in private, often inaccessible, archives. The analysis of documents, however, has but one end, the postmodernists and the traditionalists agree, the reconstitution of the past.

Archer and Hodson in Chapter 7 above rightly raise the question of what this search for the past is for and adumbrate the pressure for 'authentic' revival that is revealed with each work that they 'reconstruct'. Archer and Hodson make reference to methods which necessarily differ from work to work in the process of becoming familiar with the specificity of each discourse. Their chapter is rich with examples of the importance of the researchers' own conception of events allowing them to make sense of information that the informant could not necessarily see as relevant in the same way. The subjectivity of the response is made clear as in feminist readings of dances (see Carol Brown's Chapter 13 above).

The instability of history as seen through postmodern eyes raises questions of how courses in dance history should be taught as well as rendering problematic the procedures that the traditional historian should employ both in doing research and in writing about it. Irrespective of recent theorizing in postmodern and poststructuralism, however, the question still has to asked: is it possible or desirable to try not to 'suppress, repeat, subordinate, highlight, and order those facts' to create a 'certain meaning' (Hutcheon 1989: 67)? What would be left?

While the construction and presentation of chronological accounts of dance are the most usual way of teaching dance history there is much to be said for exploring the possibility of teaching from the present, from where the student is, to generate questions about how traces of the past exist in the present and how these can be used to enlighten a view of the past.

Further, to start a history course with the exploration of current dance forms is probably a sound choice in terms of generating genuine interest and motivation. Although current ballet and modern dance forms can be traced far back in time, the early versions of these forms may appear somewhat remote today. They may lack the immediate appeal of live theatre that brings most students to dance, and history teaching which fails to recognize this can become divorced from practice in dance and from the rest of the dance programme.

Many approaches to dance history are possible, ranging from a focus on the structure of the dance itself and its change through time to projects based on aspects of the social and historical conditions of groups of artists.

The biggest challenge in relating postmodernism and cultural theory to dance teaching lies, perhaps, in this area of dance history and dance appreciation. The early-twentieth-century emphasis on abstraction and the allied theories of the autonomy of the art work has finally been dislodged by a consciousness of the locatedness, the situatedness, of all art works. This being the case, appreciation, itself integral to choreography, cannot be taught without a historical and cultural dimension. The very language in which analysis is conducted and the concepts which are used to inform interpretation, derive from culturally located practices in art (see Adshead 1988).

Advocating the use of historical method to inform current practice in the studio is a way of demonstrating the importance of history for understanding current choreographic and reconstruction practices. The same can be argued for teaching performance, technique or production. This does not deny the integrity of dance history itself but underlines its confidence in taking on new theory and in applying itself to the heart of the matter, the making of dances.

NOTE

1 The B.A. (Hons) Dance in Society course at the University of Surrey is planned on this principle.

REFERENCES

Adshead, J. (ed.) (1988), *Dance Analysis: Theory and Practice*, London: Dance Books.

Best, D. (1975), *Expression and Movement in the Arts*, London: Lepus.

Foucault, M. (1972), *The Archeology of Knowledge*, London: Routledge.

Hutcheon, L. (1989), *The Politics of Postmodernism*, London: Routledge.

Carter, A. (1993), *Winged and Shivering: Images of Women in the Alhambra and Empire Ballets 1884–1915* (unpublished Ph.D. thesis, University of Surrey).

Poesio, G. (1993), *The Language of Gesture in Italian Dance from Commedia dell'Arte to Blasis*, (unpublished Ph.D. thesis, University of Surrey).

Chapter 15

Writing dance history

June Layson

15.1   INTRODUCTION

This chapter is concerned with the act of writing dance history. To write is just one aspect of creating and communicating since dance history commentary or outcomes may well take other forms such as oral or video presentations or actual performances.[1] However, since this book is itself a written text on the study of dance history it is the processes culminating in writing, together with the presentation of the various written forms, which are discussed here. Even so, much of what is stated is highly relevant to other modes of communicating about dance history. Outcomes may differ but most of the procedures for dealing with dance history are common.

Writings on dance history may cover a wide range. Typically, at school and college level these may be students' descriptions or accounts of selected dance history topics based on secondary sources and more designed to demonstrate the writers' understanding and grasp of major historical events and themes rather than to make a valid contribution to dance history knowledge itself. Nevertheless, such accounts need not be in the form of partially digested information culled from a few sources and presented in an uncritical fashion. Even if there is no opportunity to use primary source material (and at a local level this may be partially compensated for since photocopies of original documents, such as theatre programmes, can be made available) student writers should be encouraged to exercise their powers of discrimination and to discuss and evaluate their material. First encounters with the task of writing dance history can be imbued with the notion, proposed and elaborated upon in the opening chapter of this book, that the subject is essentially open to interpretation and re-interpretation and is far removed from being merely a catalogue of dates and blocks of inert knowledge to be learned and accepted without the active participation of the learner.

At college and first degree level, written work in dance history may take the form of summaries or overviews of dance types, genres and styles within particular periods. These may or may not be based on primary sources, although working with some first-hand material is always desirable, but it is unlikely that the results will constitute original research. Nevertheless, the hallmark of such writing should be a growing ability to adopt a critical stance and the mode of presentation should ideally raise questions, point to ambiguities, and, generally, convey the authors' understanding of and active involvement with the topic.

At graduate, postgraduate level and beyond the defining characteristics of dance history writing are the scholarly use of primary sources and unpublished materials. The sources may not in themselves be 'new' (in the sense that others have previously referred to them) although dance historians are fortunate, compared with most other historians, in that much extant material is to be found in a 'pristine' state. Written outcomes at doctorate and postdoctorate level should be academic discourse of the highest calibre and may well merit publication in some form. To ensure the future development of dance history as an academic subject such writings need to be rigorous, with meticulous documentation providing the bedrock for hypotheses to be tested, critical judgements and evaluations to be made, insights to be offered, and, above all, knowledge and understanding of the area to be furthered.

15.2 PROCEDURES

The procedures usually adopted by the dance student and the dance scholar are basically similar even though individual topics may require adaptations to the norm. Here a typical process is laid out as a series of consecutive stages although in practice the work in hand at any one time often embraces two or more steps.

The main 'literary forms' discussed in the sub-sections which follow are: description (often termed 'narrative' in general history writing), analysis, interpretation and evaluation. These are traditional modes in so far as they are characteristic of the vast majority of dance history literature. The innovative forms which take a neo- or latter-day Marxist approach, or range from a traditional to a radical feminist theory base, or are derived from 'new' criticism and postmodern theories, are not specifically referred to. This is because first, there are as yet few 'new' examples to present[2] and, second, as these fresh approaches gain ground it seems likely that, as in history writing generally, they will inform traditional practice rather than immediately fostering fully-fledged radical alternative structures. In this way, for example, the act of interpretation might become increasingly open to a creative engagement on the part of the writer instead of, as the 'new' history would claim, perpetuating a traditional pseudo-scientific format in a quasi-objective manner. However, it is clear that within the next few years dance history writing is likely to encompass several styles as new approaches become increasingly accepted.

In the final analysis, whatever school of thought is in ascendance and influences the mode of writing dance history, it is the outcome which is judged on the grounds of whether it is good of its kind.

15.2.1 Selection of study area

The topic or area of study may be given, as in an assignment, or selected, as when a student is free to choose the focus of a project or dissertation within certain requirements. The historical period, type of dance, contexts to be considered and so on may be specified and there will almost certainly be a completion date together with lower and upper word limits. Occasionally, the area of study eventually crystallizes itself. The term 'eventually' is apt since it is not uncommon for Ph.D. students to start work based on an earlier research proposal only to find, after further extensive preliminary reading and much reconsideration, that the proposed point of departure is untenable. This may be simply because it begs prior questions or is based on assumptions that now, with hindsight, seem contentious. In such cases it takes time to determine what is essentially the focus of the study and its inherent starting point.

By whatever means the topic is selected, the prime need, if the written outcomes are to be successful, is that it should be sharply focused. Initial work with source materials for both beginner and experienced scholar often leads to the opening-up of a large and potentially unmanageable area. Therefore, the selection of the topic and the necessity to refine it as the work gains momentum is crucial.

The three-dimensional model proposed in Chapter 1 as a means of characterizing dance history as a subject of study can also be applied to the process of clarifying a topic area. The 'time', 'type' and 'context' dimensions can be used to determine the parameters of a study.

Thus the time parameters should be clear in terms of historical epochs, periods, centuries or decades. Any actual dates used may, for example, be dictated by the life-span of the prominent personality under scrutiny[3] or reflect socio-political contexts or events which shaped the dance being studied.[4] What is essential in terms of the time delineation of the topic area is that it enables changes and developments which occur through time to be identified and articulated.

The type of dance to be written about may well be given in an assignment or reflect the interests of the writer or both. Nevertheless, it is crucial to clarify exactly what kind of dance is to the forefront of the study. If the focus is a global dance type such as social or traditional dance then there may well be a need to state exactly what is meant by the use of such terms. Current definitions of terminology from respected sources may be quoted and used. Sometimes it is necessary for the writer to deal with contemporary problems of definition, vital characteristics of the dance and so on, in order to give the reader a firm basis from which to understand the text.[5] Occasionally an agreed terminology and accepted definition of terms may not exist (in which case this in itself could provide the focal point of a study) and then it may be necessary to propose 'stipulative definitions'[6] of dance types so that the study can proceed on an explicit basis.

However, many studies are less concerned with an over-arching dance type than with one or more selected aspects of it. Therefore, in studying western theatre dance, for example, it is usually necessary to specify genre (ballet, modern, postmodern) and often style as well, as in 'early modern dance'. From this clarification of the dance type parameters the next step might be to identify further dance preoccupations of the study in, for example, its concern with particular practitioners within that field, such as choreographers, critics, managers, performers, etc., or coherent groups, such as audiences, companies and organizations.

The context of the dance under scrutiny also needs to be stated unequivocally. As discussed in Chapter 1, the contexts which can be related to both the time and dance type dimensions are numerous and varied. This means that in the selection of an area for study it is essential to consider a range of contexts. It is likely that some contexts will be particularly relevant to certain dance types. For example, the prevailing concerns of the arts generally are likely to influence and to interact with theatre dance while contemporary social mores are often implicitly or explicitly embedded in social dances. Any historical studies undertaken in these areas and devoid of at least an acknowledgement of such vital contexts would almost inevitably be the poorer and, possibly, even invalid.

Therefore, it is important to recognize that while the writer can often select the preferred time and dance type parameters the contexts for these are often contingent, that is, they are necessarily dependent and are not a matter of choice. By the same token, if a specific contextually-rooted concern itself becomes the initial impetus for study, such as gender relationships in dance, then it may well result in particular time and dance type parameters being identified in order to highlight and to analyse different socio-psychological examples and practices.

The selection of the study area is a crucial process. While clear parameters do not in themselves guarantee successful outcomes it follows that if the time considerations are unclear, the dance types largely unstated or minimally characterized and the relevant contexts mainly ignored then it is unlikely that the study will either absorb the full interest and capabilities of the writer or have any appeal to the reader. Good historical communication depends initially on the focus and parameters of the study area being clearly and decisively stated.

15.2.2   Identification and location of sources

If a study area is to be selected then of necessity the process will entail early interaction with source materials. However, when the topic is pre-determined the first step towards writing a dance history paper is to gain further information about the area and to identify sources.

In both cases the most profitable way to do this is to consult some of the widely available general and specific dance bibliographies, diction-aries, encyclopedias and similar texts (see Appendix B for a com-prehensive, annotated listing of reference books). Typically, these provide brief overviews of important and related areas, define terms, chart significant events, list prominent people and seminal works and suggest further reading.

Where it is available a highly rewarding entry point is via the New York Public Library (NYPL) Catalogue and Bibliographic Guides, now avail-able in print, on-line and CD-ROM forms (see Appendix B for full reference). This is a valuable source which is organized as an alphabetical listing of a comprehensive range of dance materials.[7] Most entries are followed with a list of cross-references to related items in the catalogue and guides which gives an immediate impression of the field of study available. The organization of the items into 'works by' a person (which includes written and choreographic output as appropriate) and 'works about' a person or other subject matter is particularly useful, as is the categorization of 'visual works' and 'audio materials'.

This initial foray into the topic area by means of textual guides is important because such secondary sources offer not only numerous starting points but also enable the student to plan the work ahead.

Armed with lists of potential sources the next stage is to locate them. For many students it is the availability and accessibility of source materials that, because of time, travel and financial constraints, deter-mines what items are used. However, in fully developed research work the imperative to track down most, if not all, extant material or to generate unique material or both often necessitates prolonged periods of searching, extensive travel and, invariably, considerable expense.

However, if it can be assumed that most students have access to local or campus libraries with at least basic dance collections and, possibly, the opportunity to consult regional or even national collections or can obtain photocopied material where a visit is precluded, then the next procedure is straightforward. First, the list of desirable sources is checked against what is available. Following this choices need to be made based on several criteria. These are the balance between the primary and secondary sources to be used, the ratio of written to visual to sound sources to be consulted and whether there is a need to gener-ate additional material, through conducting interviews, administering questionnaires etc. In short all the factors discussed in Chapter 2 come into play at this stage as sources are accessed, scrutinized and evaluated in terms of the nature of their testimony, authenticity, reliability and status and their value and relevance to the study area.

Some sources may at this early stage be deemed so vital to the study that they need to be acquired on a permanent rather than a temporary loan basis. For example, a dancer's autobiography, a collection of key critical texts of the period, a drawing or photograph may need to be in constant use throughout the study period. When it is not possible to own such materials, photocopies of the whole or part are useful substitutes.[8]

Should time allow at this juncture it is often worth considering whether source materials relating to all elements of the proposed topic are available for use. If more details are needed in particular areas it might be profitable to make a further search of specialist journals and periodicals (see Appendix C.) Similarly, a decision may be made to use a dance archive or collection in order to consult sources not immediately available locally.[9]

The identification and location of sources can be both exciting and frustrating in terms of what is available. It also usually acts as a means by which the study area is further clarified and delineated. In essence though, this stage functions as the first encounter with the study area and as such constitutes the early, vital steps in writing dance history.

15.2.3   Documentation

This is the process in which the various disparate materials and sources are collated to form a related whole. It provides the basis for the more conceptually orientated stages that follow.

The traditional method of documentation is by means of one or more card indexes, hand-written notes, diagrams, tables and so on. However, the use of personal computers has considerably enhanced this process. To begin with, the need to make multiple card index entries relating to one item is eliminated. More importantly, though, new software offers many time-saving opportunities such as automatic alphabetical listings, fast cross-referencing of files etc. as well as various facilities for generating sophisticated diagrams, models and other means of presenting detailed data.

Nevertheless, whether it be manual or computerized, a system has to be devised whereby not only all the information gained can be brought together in a coherent manner but also any one item can be easily retrieved. Much of this process is common to all dance scholarship and not the sole province of dance history but in the latter the amount of source material to be dealt with usually necessitates the setting-up of a comprehensive documentation system. Each topic will invariably require particular documentary techniques, some of which may have to be devised en route; even so there are common procedures.

The prime concern is that each source used should be clearly annotated in terms of its provenance. That is, it needs to be identified fully with all details concerning authorship, dates, publication, origins or location together with any other relevant information. The immediate reason for establishing this element of 'good practice' is for ease of identification, particularly when subsequent reference is made to an item, since it is unlikely that any source material is used only once. Later, such annotation is significant in giving credibility to the written outcomes and in imparting supplementary information to the reader. The documentation of written sources is usually carried out in accordance with one of several internationally recognized formats (see section 15.3.1). However, the important point to note here is that in the setting-up of a documentation system each source, whether it be written, visual or sound, is clearly identified in all respects and entered into the system at the point of first usage.

As well as the careful documentation of individual items it may be appropriate to bring together material from various sources. For example, it might be advantageous to draw up an annotated ongoing list of eminent people or key works in the topic area. In this instance a system has to be adhered to whereby as new information and evidence is obtained so it is entered, along with its provenance, under appropriate headings and cross-references indicated.

However, whereas some sources can be documented immediately, as in writing a short description of the subject and provenance of a photograph, other, usually written, sources require more prolonged scrutiny. Reading is, therefore, intrinsically bound up with the documentation of written sources. This seems an all-too-obvious point to make but if reading can be regarded as the forerunner to documentation then it becomes focused and structured, and leads to either concurrent or subsequent note-taking.

Assuming that the full reference for each source will be automatically recorded, it is important that all notes made should, in addition, be clearly marked to indicate whether they constitute a paraphrase, summary or quotation. In paraphrasing, the intention is to restate the original in different words, usually in order to clarify a point, so that it is essentially a reworking of the selected source. A summary is a brief account of a longer passage in the original text with the main points or argument being made clear. A quotation is the exact replication of the original in both words and punctuation. This is often selected because it is apt, illustrates a point succinctly and, more importantly, states a concept or gives a description which is unlikely to be bettered by rewriting. Paired quotations may also be chosen because they encapsulate contradictory statements or are examples of the polarities of an argument or simply stand as ambiguous statements which might be typical of a section of dance history writing. A quotation may, therefore, be noted as a key segment of a source text and identified for possible inclusion in the final written outcome. However, whether notes take the form of paraphrases, summaries or quotations it is essential that the page numbers of the source text are recorded.[10] In the first two cases this ensures that reference can be made back to the original for further information. When a quotation is used in any written work it is accepted scholarly practice to give page numbers as well as author and date details and it saves time during the writing stage if all such necessary information is readily to hand.

In cases where photocopies of texts have been obtained it is often more practicable to highlight or underline important passages and words rather than to make notes. When audiotape recordings have been made these need to be transcribed and a special numbering system devised so that they can be referenced and included alongside other types of source materials.

Since it normally provides the basis for, rather than the whole substance of, the written work, most of the documentation will not appear as such in the final outcome. However, occasionally it may be worthwhile to include an element of the documentation in the written outcome either in the main text or, more usually, as an appendix. The use of chronologies (sequences of events arranged in strict order of occurrence) and choreochronicles (lists of choreographers' part or complete oeuvres in order of première dates) can provide important supporting evidence to the written text. A chronology can present information in a brief easy-to-assimilate form which would otherwise take up several pages of text. As well as giving basic information on a choreographer's output, a choreochronicle can be used to show ancillary material ranging from production details to frequency of performance and duration in the repertoire, all in a succinct form. The particular format of a chronology or choreochronicle will need to be devised according to the material being used. If a chronology or choreochronicle of a hitherto undocumented work has been culled from primary sources and authenticated by reference to other primary source materials then it can make a substantial contribution to the development of dance knowledge.

Other documentation can be included in the written work as tables and charts. These have the merit of presenting facts and figures in an immediate manner. The use of a pie chart[11] to show, for example, the components of an audience, or a histogram[12] to demonstrate the introduction rate of new social dances in the 1920s can make a visually telling impact not easily achieved by words alone.

The aim of the documentation process is to gather as much relevant information as possible from a wide variety of sources. Documentation needs to be carried out in a systematic and scholarly manner in which the content of the sources used is understood, related and brought together as a coherent whole based on an easily retrievable system. Such documentation can then form the bedrock for the next and more sophisticated stages in the process of writing dance history.

15.2.4   Description[13]

When the bulk of the documentation has been carried out, the writing of the dance history paper commences. Judging the most appropriate time at which to start writing, however, is not easy. There is often an understandable reluctance to begin this next stage until the documentation is 'finished'. Even so, in one respect the documentation is never complete.[14] More importantly, the process of writing is a key public mode in which both student and scholar come to terms with the study area; therefore, writing should always be begun sooner rather than later. Making a start for the novice dance historian is easier if it is acknowledged that the earlier writing will inevitably be descriptive in nature and that the potentially more difficult handling of conceptual concerns cannot take place until the grounds for the discussion and analysis have been sufficiently set out.

It is important to note that the move from documenting to writing has additional significance because it involves a change of stance from one of being reactive to the source materials to one of becoming proactive and using them as the basis for the written work. This is not to deny that good documentation demands thought and discernment but the point at which the dance historian, with command of the source materials, makes the move into the public domain to begin the process of communication needs to be appreciated. Furthermore, the dance historian is endeavouring to make sense of the source materials and to give them a coherent structure. This involves not only a sustained conceptual process but also an appreciation of the many possible ways of construing facts and information. Choices have to be made and reasons offered and arguments put forward to justify such selections.

Much of the early part of any written dance history is presented as a straightforward descriptive account. This enables the topic area to be laid out and the defining characteristics and main features to be delineated. From this it does not follow that in writing in a descriptive mode any ambiguities and points of contention encountered are ignored. Indeed, it is often the ideal place to identify and to raise such issues and to signal to the reader their importance and the detailed discussion of them that is to follow. However, by making the early sections of a written paper mainly descriptive the scene is set in an unambiguous manner so that the rest of the study can be developed upon this groundwork.

In focusing on description the writer is endeavouring to present the case, or what is generally assumed to be the case, rather than putting forward personal viewpoints. Of course, in one very real sense the description is personal since it is how the field is perceived by one person at a particular time. Similarly, a general assumption is just that, a shared view held by many. Nevertheless, the intention at this stage is to describe the widely-accepted state of knowledge of the study area based on sound documentation. This is a basic necessity prior to embarking upon the debate where an argued and defended and, possibly, a more personal stance is more likely to be taken.

The first part of any historical study with its concerns to introduce overview and expound, and characterized here as being entirely or mainly descriptive in character, has an important function within the whole written communication. It allows the writer to demonstrate an understanding of the topic area, to show awareness of the main issues entailed and to do this within a thoroughly-grounded, source-based familiarity with the field. Description at its best is not a cobbling together of disparate facts but an imaginative blending of diverse materials and sources to make a coherent, apprehendable whole.

In turn, this sanctions, as it were, the student's or scholar's rights to analyse, to argue, to be critical and to make the attempt to advance the debate and to contribute to knowledge of the area. Furthermore, if presented well, the first part of a written paper can give the reader security in the writer's grasp of the topic area and, from this, a willingness to be fully engaged in the next and possibly more contentious parts of the written communication.

15.2.5   Analysis

The move from description to analysis is just as significant as the earlier shift from documentation to description. For, whereas description is a way of imparting facts, mainly in a propositional manner, in analysis and the two stages that follow there is a more immediate interaction with the material, which itself becomes the subject of close scrutiny.

In analysis the focus is towards sorting out constituent parts, seeking the smallest comprehensible units and, generally, trying to unscramble complex issues and events. The aim is to achieve clarification and understanding. Sometimes analysis is mistakenly regarded as a destructive process since it is seen to be akin to dissection and, therefore, irreversible. However, the sorting out and isolating of elements is far from embarking upon a 'demolition job' because it provides the basis for synthesis and the combining of basic units in different relationships. This in turn can lead to new ideas and fresh insights being generated.

In the study of dance generally, analytical procedures have either been adapted from other disciplines, as in textual analysis and criticism, or have been especially developed, as in choreographic analysis.[15] Both these techniques can be adopted in specific circumstances for use in dance history writing. For example, a study of a critic's body of writing, perhaps over one important decade, would enable the reviews to be studied in a systematic manner and, as a result, such factors as changes in perception and judgements through time might emerge.[16] Similarly, a choreographic analysis of a choreographer's complete oeuvre carried out in a broad time-orientated manner would be likely to produce hitherto unrecognized features such as prevailing concerns, cyclic elements and so on.

In the study of history per se, analysis is regarded as one technique among several, such as narrative, description, explanation etc., which together constitute the main procedural tools used by the historian. In dance history there is, as yet, scant interest and little consensus on what form a systematic analysis might take although it is hoped that this book might provide a basis for future discussion. In the absence of an agreed, tried and tested analytical framework dance historians usually devise their own processes, possibly comparable to the procedures outlined here, but tailor-made to suit the chosen study area.

It is the complex events, the seemingly intractable problems and inexplicable issues which are most likely to be the subject of analysis in dance history. They need to be disentangled or unravelled and their constituent parts teased out so that, for example, a complicated situation is revealed to be composed of many interacting factors each one of which can be identified and its relationship to the whole established. Such an analytical process helps to distinguish the important from the trivial, the magical from the mundane and so on. In analysing a multi-layered contextual concern the aim might be, for example, to distinguish between main and subsidiary influences, to trace the origins of crucial events, to ascertain the links between cause and effect, to seek connections and disjunctions or to expose any relationships underlying parallel but apparently distinct developments.

Analysis, therefore, can equip the dance historian with a powerful tool. Used to the full it can provide both the impetus and the basis for the subsequent stages of interpretation and evaluation.

15.2.6   Interpretation

It is pertinent to reiterate at this juncture that for the purpose of this text and the need to make the various procedures in writing dance history distinct, the act of interpretation is separated here from description and analysis as well as the later stage of evaluation. However, in specific instances it may be more convenient, preferable, profitable or even necessary to combine analysis and interpretation, for example, so that the latter would proceed alongside the former.

Interpretation focuses on such matters as intrinsic issues and problems and attempts to explain and offer reasons for their existence. The process is one of clarifying, of giving reasons and seeking meanings and understanding significances. Essentially then, interpretation is to do with explanations and it goes beyond the facts to 'open up' areas for discussion and elucidation and in so doing, reveals inherent contradictions and ambiguities and the possibility of different 'readings'.

In dance history, theories or points of view are often established that gain evidence over time but later, with hindsight (in essence an ability to understand or interpret after an event), are seen to be misleading or even untenable.[17] In other instances, popular profiles of eminent people in the dance world are gradually built up and become the accepted view. It is the role of the dance historian to re-examine such characterization and, if appropriate, to re-interpret the evidence and to proffer a more rounded or even alternative profile.[18]

Just as important as interpretation and re-interpretation of the long-gone past is the need to address the immediate past and its links with the present and this can be undertaken using the same procedural tools. The intention is not to pre-empt the interpretations of later generations of dance history scholars by endeavouring to 'fix' recent history with definitive accounts, since this is palpably impossible, but to try to explain and to interpret these current developments that have their roots in the immediate past. Such a process can present a rational alternative viewpoint or a counter-balance to the popular myth-forming or simplistic labelling which inevitably takes place.[19]

The style of writing in an interpretative mode is one of debate and reasoned argument, of testing points of view, challenging hypotheses and offering explanations. It demands considerable clarity of thought and a secure grasp of conceptual concerns. As the process of interpretation and re-interpretation proceeds it can give rise to revelation and insight and suggest 'new' maps of 'old' territories of dance history knowledge. Interpretation reinforces the notion of the open and essentially-contested nature of dance history.

15.2.7   Evaluation

This is the final main stage in writing dance history, even though the various forms of written papers often require further end-matter such as summaries, conclusions etc. (see section 15.3.2). Evaluation is to do with making appraisals, assessments and judgements.

As a procedure, evaluation has elements in common with the stages which precede it but it is, nevertheless, distinct and in one sense is the culmination of all that has been written before. Making judgements is similar to the later stages of description where a broad picture of the study area is presented and the writer steps back from the topic area and sees it as an entirety. Similarly, the process of arriving at an assessment also resembles that of analysis and interpretation in the close engagement with fundamental concerns and issues.

In many instances evaluation is a holistic process since the intention might be to bring together all the separate considerations arrived at in the earlier stages of writing and to make over-arching judgements about them. Such judgements might concern the success or failure of a particular dance style or an assessment of the value of an eminent person's contribution to a specific area of dance or the relative importance of an innovatory dance technique. Appraisals might also be highly specific and focus on one particular key dance performance and its impact at the time and subsequently or on a narrowly defined thematic concern such as the significance of one building in the development of dance in a small locality. Nevertheless, whatever judgements are arrived at, the bases for them, in terms of the particular collection of materials used and the specific analytical mode employed, would need to be acknowledged.

In Part II of this text all the chapters have different characteristics and outcomes and yet each is concerned in one respect or another with evaluation. Those chapters which focus on methodology, as in the choice and use of source materials, [20] or the importance of articulating contexts,[21] also contain evaluations, since the authors offer advice about the most profitable ways to start and to proceed with dance history study in their areas of specialization. This advice is based on experience but, more importantly, on judgements well supported by cogent reasons.

In the chapters more concerned with product rather than process, that is, where the methodology per se is subservient to the outcomes, the writing culminates in evaluation. These chapters are presented in the form of dance history polemic such that the prime concern is with an argument or controversy which is embedded in a fundamental dance belief or doctrine and seen to demand evaluation. It is the case, of course, that the topic area is firstly clearly defined and described, sources acknowledged (often en route rather than en bloc) and the various threads of the main argument analysed and interpreted. Nevertheless, the whole thrust of the discussion is one in which the stances of the various authors cited are examined, sifted and assessed for their relative merits and judged in terms of their veracity and viability. In this way a stated hypothesis is probed and proved or nullified.[22]

The process of evaluating inevitably has connotations of the subjective and the personal: indeed it is unlikely that the writer will be totally uninvolved or uninterested in the topic or outcome. However, in making judgements the procedure is, firstly, to acknowledge any interests or commitment and then to endeavour to conduct the debate in a logical and open manner. There need be no tension between caring passionately for a dance cause or topic and being able to make reasoned argument and to arrive at tenable judgements about it. Indeed, putting forward a hypothesis and testing it to the full is an academic device by which judgements can be made, although the writer has to entertain the possibility of surprising and unlooked for outcomes.

Evaluation in dance history and the strengthening and validating of such work by detailed, objective argument and reason is vital to the development of dance history knowledge. It is the means by which events, personalities and all the complex interactions that make up the fabric of the area are placed in perspective, judged in relation to each other and the whole and the field of study given structure, meaning and viability.

15.2.8   Summary

The concern in this section is with the procedures for writing dance history and the laying out of the successive stages likely to be followed may be summarized in a dynamic model (Figure 15.1).[23] The term 'dynamic' is used to emphasize the essential ongoing nature of the process and 'model' is used in the sense of representing the described structure diagrammatically rather than setting a rigid pattern to be complied with. The vertical solid arrows indicate the sequence of the separate stages although one or more may be combined for particular purposes. The horizontal and vertical broken arrow lines acknowledge the fact that as the writing progresses and the study develops so there is usually a need to return to earlier stages in order to rework material or to rethink intransigent problems. This is especially so with documentation where often a preliminary first-level consultation will suffice. However, as new ideas emerge it usually becomes necessary to return to the sources and subject them to much closer scrutiny than before. This second or even third interrogation of source materials is invariably more robust and focused than the first because there is a greater familiarity with the topic area, the search is targeted and information previously unrecognized as such or overlooked can now be gleaned.

This section has not dealt with other processes concomitant with writing dance history such as reading, conceptualizing and studying as

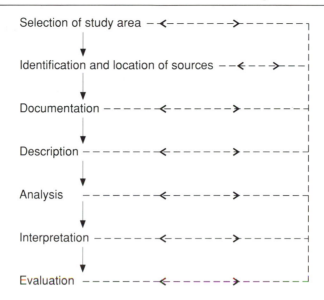

Figure 15.1

a whole. These are in the nature of study skills and are discussed at length in the various specialist texts on the area.

Writing dance history is a technique which can be learned both by practice and by reading the writings of dance history scholars established in their fields. Chapter 3 and Appendix A evaluate dance history books according to several stated criteria including that of good communication. It would be of value for dance history students with little experience of writing about their subject to read such texts on the basis of the procedures covered in this section.

15.3   PRESENTATION

15.3.1   Style guidelines

The presentation of a dance history paper is invariably in a format prescribed by college, university, or editorial board of a journal or publisher. These formats encompass matters such as upper and lower word limits, page size and layouts, order of contents, typeface and spacing for general text and quotations, presentation of text, diagrams, tables, references, bibliographies and so on. Often these requirements are grouped together under a 'style sheet' or 'house-style guide'. As a general rule the more public the written outcome the more precise are the guidelines and the higher the expectation that authors will conform to them.

There are good reasons for promoting style guidelines. One is to achieve uniformity in presentational style so that the reader is not distracted from content by idiosyncratic or unsystematic layouts. Another is that the reader can extract information with ease, such as reference to a text recommended for further study, and have confidence that the full publication details given will ensure its location elsewhere.

Several systems for references and bibliographies exist. That used by Routledge, the publishers of this book, is the Harvard or author-date system, so-called because of its origins and, as a quick check of any chapter will reveal, the format whereby the author and date of publication are always given in tandem in the text. This means that for knowledgeable readers the author and date is sufficient to identify the source; alternatively it can easily be found in the full list of references or in the bibliography. Although the main reference systems are universal, it is important to realize that different academic disciplines have different conventions. For example, in the sciences the latest edition of a text is usually cited simply because up-to-date knowledge is prized, whereas in dance history it is more important to give the first date of publication, as well as subsequent editions or reprints, in order to state historical provenance. In cases where a system does not appear to cover the citation of a publication the rule is to give as much information as is necessary for a reader to follow up the reference.

The use of chapter or paper endnotes (footnotes are now largely obsolete) can be problematic. Some style guidelines are quite specific about such usage. Generally, though, endnotes provide the opportunity to give further information which, while of relevance and interest, might well intrude upon the main text. Endnotes are often in the nature of digressions whereas in the main text the writer is concerned with the progression of the topic area.

15.3.2   Structure

The different kinds of writing, from description to evaluation, are discussed in section 15.2, but the structure of the written communication is as important since it provides the framework for presentation. Most written outcomes are divided into sections or chapters according to length. Typically the plan is developmental although for particular purposes sections may be amalgamated or further divided.

Structure of a typical written historical study
   Title page
   Abstract
   Table of contents
   Introduction
   Plan of study
   Methodology

Overview of sources
Main part of study (sub-divided and titled to reflect the principal
stages of discussion)
Summary
Conclusion
Appendix or Appendices
References or Bibliography or both

There are many student manuals which cover the planning and
writing of essays, papers, dissertations and theses and these should be
consulted for general guidance. Here the intention is to highlight the
main dance history concerns.

Titles are important. As the likely first point of contact with the
reader they need both to inform and attract attention. Ideally a dance
history title should be explicit in terms of the time, dance type and
context parameters and, where appropriate, also contain a short pithy
phrase which epitomizes the study area. Several of the books cited in
Appendix A achieve this, such as Ruyter, N. (1979), *Reformers and
Visionaries: The Americanisation of the Art of Dance*, and Banes, S. (1980),
Terpsichore in Sneakers: Postmodern Dance.[24]

An abstract is, literally, a highly condensed version of the whole
written work and, therefore, is invariably the last section to be completed. It rarely extends beyond one page and so demands very explicit
writing devoid of redundancy. Abstracts provide entry points for scholars
and, as such, constitute a special kind of written communication.

The contents table signals, in a different manner, the scope of
the work by the laying-out of the structure. It follows that the
main historical concerns should be clear in section and sub-section
titles.

It is a convention that most written work begins with an introduction.
This is, literally, to introduce the reader to the topic area in terms of its
focus and parameters (that is, what is being studied), the particular
points of interest or hypotheses being pursued (that is, why the topic
has been selected) and the various methodologies employed (that is,
how the study is carried out). It may also be appropriate to include in
the introduction statements about the plan or structure of the paper.
Similarly, if particularly innovative methodologies have been used (as in
the generation of special source materials), this would also need to be
elaborated upon in the introduction. However, in longer written
outcomes it is likely that both of these areas would require separate and
extended sections. The length of the introduction clearly depends
upon the total length of the written paper but it needs to encompass all
the necessary preliminaries without running into areas properly covered
by later sections.

The introduction is normally followed by a section which is often loosely termed 'an overview of the literature'. In dance history writing it is usual for the source base to extend beyond the written word. Therefore, this section becomes an overview of all the sources used and all the evidence gained. In essence the purpose of an overview is to present a comprehensive account of the range, type, status and value of the sources consulted and by virtue of this, to offer an exposition of the study area as it can be constructed and construed from these sources.

Following on from the source overview, although occasionally juxtaposed, is the main part of the written paper. This may take many forms. It may be based on a chronological structure or take a thematic approach or have elements of both, but primarily it is an exposition. In dance history it is the arena in which the writer comes to terms with the subject area. Depending upon the topic and the manner in which it is addressed the writing may range through the descriptive, analytical, interpretive and evaluative modes discussed in section 15.2. Essentially though, it will be discursive in nature and, characteristically, concerned with reason and argument. The central sections should, therefore, progress from the outlining of issues and the stating of problems through informed discussion and analysis to the point where proposals can be made and solutions offered. Generally the overall aim is to move forward the current debate on an area and this, although unlikely to be totally conclusive or definitive, given the nature of dance history, is of value in itself.

A summary is the point at which a brief overview is given of the total discussion and, in this sense, it complements the introduction by summing up the main thrust of the text. In conclusions, which are different in focus from summaries, the outcomes or findings of the study are stated. These are arrived at only through discussion and argument and, by definition, thoroughly supported with evidence and reasons. It is in this section that the opportunity can be taken to suggest further areas of enquiry and research. In its attempts to answer questions and to solve problems much scholarly work achieves at least partial success and in so doing is likely to raise yet more questions. In dance history study the academically verified knowledge base is of recent origin and has, as yet, hardly begun to do justice to the bulk of dance history. Therefore, the identification of further areas for debate and research is important.

Matter which is not essential to the main text but supports it is included in one or more appendices. The use of these for presenting documentary evidence is noted in section 15.2.3. In writing dance history it is often helpful to refer the reader to an appendix item such as a choreochronicle, an illustration or a photocopy of a letter, in order to substantiate the point being made.

Reference and bibliography formats are usually covered by style guides or in-house requirements. However, since these listings are sometimes consulted separately by readers in order to gain an impression of the scope and nature of the text and the literature underlying it or to obtain references for further reading, the rules of accuracy and detail are paramount in their presentation.

15.4   CONCLUSION

There are many ways of writing dance history, probably at least as many as there are writers of dance history. Each topic area will suggest different approaches to different people. But among the great diversity are discernible common features and it is these which are the concern of this chapter. The procedures discussed are not immutable either in themselves or collectively. However, they constitute many of the elements of good practice and it is to this that the best writing of dance history aspires. High-calibre dance history writing cannot be prescribed but the rudiments of it can be learned and honed, and individual styles developed.

Matters of punctuation, spelling and grammar have been omitted from this text simply because at undergraduate level and beyond they should not pose any problems in writing dance history. However, would-be dance history writers who have deficiencies in this respect need to remedy them. A high standard of writing necessarily entails proficiency in this regard and it is not a coincidence that well-written communication is associated with clarity of thought.

Given that there is no such phenomenon as private knowledge, writing dance history is one way in which knowledge of the subject can be brought into the public domain and, in the process, refined and fully understood. Communication is essential if dance history, as a subject of study, is to flourish and writing is clearly one important mode of communication.

NOTES

1   For example, see Kenneth Archer and Millicent Hodson (Chapter 7 above). The outcomes sought are authentic reconstructions. Of the three phases of reconstruction discussed, that is, research, documentation and, ultimately, rehearsal and production, the first two are congruent with the stages that any valid mode of dance history communication must encompass. This is particularly the case if the term 'research' is used in its widest and non-specific sense as discussed in Chapter 1.

2   See Carol Brown (Chapter 13 above). Her bibliography is eclectic but it is evident that the literature which deals specifically with feminist dance history is sparse.

3   For example, see Giannandrea Poesio (Chapter 8 above). Although the introduction leads into the historical account with a brief mention of other comparable figures in the world of ballet, all of whom predate Cecchetti,

and, later, the influences upon those who in turn influenced Cecchetti are considered, the study is essentially concerned with Cecchetti's life and work. Therefore, his birth and death dates provide the main time parameters.

4 For example, see Michael Huxley (Chapter 10 above). In the discussion on pp. 156 and 158 the reasons underlying the choice of dates in relation to other studies of European early modern dance are given. It is of particular significance that 1933, a date highlighted by Huxley, does not 'refer to a specific dance event: . . . [but] marks both the end of the Weimar Republic and the seizure of complete political power by the Nazi party in Germany' (p. 156). This is an extreme case of a momentous national socio-political event which had a profound and lasting effect upon one theatre dance genre of the time. Consequently, acknowledgement of it would be crucial in any historical account of the dance of this period.

5 For example, see Theresa Buckland (Chapter 4 above). The introduction is almost totally concerned with explaining the use of terms in the text and identifying those key characteristics of the dances which allow various groupings and categories to be proposed.

6 A 'stipulative definition' is one in which the author offers a reasonable and concise statement of the meaning of words or phrases used and, in so doing, acknowledges that this usage is only for the purpose of the study. Occasionally, such definitions may, if particularly apt and useful, attract a wider currency and over time gain credence and acceptance within the general dance literature.

7 Although the NYPL Dictionary Catalogue and Bibliographic Guides itemize only the contents of the NYPL Dance Collection this is the premier world holding in terms of quantity and scope. It is, therefore, not surprising that Giannandrea Poesio (Chapter 8 above) notes the significance of the NYPL Dance Collection for the study of Cecchetti, particularly in its acquisition of the Cia Fornaroli private archives.

8 See the discussion in section 2.3 on the status of photocopied materials.

9 For example, see Jane Pritchard (Chapter 9 above). The scope and nature of a typical dance company archive is described in detail and advice given to any would-be visitor, particularly in terms of prior preparation.

10 Unambiguity in the use of paraphrasing, summarizing and quoting and the scrupulous noting of page numbers will avoid unwitting plagiarism, that is the appropriation of an author's ideas and or words without acknowledgement but also without the intention to pass such work off as original. Witting plagiarism is, of course, totally unscholarly and indefensible in the academic world.

11 This is a circular diagram with the various proportions shown as 'slices' of the whole.

12 Also termed a bar graph, this shows frequency distribution by means of contiguous vertical rectangles. In the example given the horizontal dimension would indicate the individual years of the decade while the vertical would show the number of dances introduced.

13 The term 'description' is used in its basic and traditional sense. However, this is not to deny the value of what is held in the field of 'new' criticism to be finely-observed, detailed description or the 'close reading' of art works. Such procedures go beyond the characterization of description given in this chapter and are somewhat akin to the processes of interpretation and the engagement of the writer in more than surface details.

14 For example, see pp. 101–2 below where Kenneth Archer and Millicent Hodson describe the last-minute emergence of vital evidence in the re-

construction of *La Chatte* (Balanchine, 1927) and *Le Sacre du printemps* (Nijinsky, 1913).

15 For example, see Adshead, J. (ed.) (1988), *Dance Analysis: Theory and Practice*, London: Dance Books.

16 For examples of textual analysis see Deborah Jowitt (Chapter 11 above) and Roger Copeland (Chapter 12 above). Both authors use an analytically-based technique in their discussion of dance critics' writings.

17 For example see pp. 46–7 above where Theresa Buckland cites the theory of 'cultural survival' which was highly regarded at the end of the nineteenth century in Britain and subsequently influenced generations of folklorists. Current traditional dance scholarship questions such stances and their outcomes and, as Buckland explains, this has led to different inter-pretations, new collecting policies and so on.

18 For example, much of Giannandrea Poesio's argument (Chapter 8 above), which is based on a wide variety of source material not normally brought together, is towards a re-interpretation of Cecchetti's work and influence so that a more detailed and balanced profile than hitherto emerges.

19 For example, see Chapter 12 above, in which Roger Copeland examines many of the current widely-held assumptions about Cunningham's choreo-graphy. Copeland's thesis, that the meaning of Cunningham's so-called 'liberated choreography' is misunderstood, is argued on an aesthetics-based examination of Cunningham's collaborations with composers and visual artists within what is termed 'the particular "dance historical" context of the 1950s' (p. 183). In this respect Copeland's chapter is an example of a sustained process of interpretation.

20 For example, see Georgiana Gore (Chapter 5 above). Here the range and type of the various source materials (which are very different in kind from those normally used in European or North American dance history studies) are described in detail and their usefulness to the study of traditional dance in West Africa assessed.

21 For example, see Patricia Mitchinson (Chapter 6 above). The importance of context is stressed throughout the text together with the need to consult a wide variety of disparate sources and, at the same time, to make judgements as to their particular veracity and value to the study.

22 For example, see Deborah Jowitt (Chapter 11 above). The hypothesis 'the human body . . . can never be a neutral artistic medium' (p. 169) is stated in the second paragraph and provides the lode star for the chapter. The argument is historically contextualized but throughout the focus is on the evaluation of the evidence and counter-evidence as the hypothesis is tested and, ultimately, judged.

23 Earlier published versions of this model served slightly different purposes; for example, see Layson, J. (1990), 'Dance history methodology: dynamic models for teaching, learning and research' in *The Fifth Hong Kong International Dance Conference Papers*, vol. II: 56–65. In the current text the opportunity has been taken to refine the terminology and to include more detailed reference to the early stages of writing dance history.

24 Nevertheless, a scrutiny of all the titles in Appendix A reveals that not many encapsulate the time, dance type and contexts considerations of their respective contents.

Appendix A

Dance history texts annotated

Janet Adshead-Lansdale

Appendix A is designed to complement Chapter 3 in summarizing and offering a brief evaluation of the contents of many of the texts described there. The books selected are standard works which are generally available through bookshops and libraries. Appendix B gives a longer and more comprehensive list of books, journals, bibliographic sources, dictionaries, encyclopedias, etc., with shorter annotations of a rather different kind.

Seven categories of texts are presented here listed in publication date order and the orientation and main concerns of each are outlined. In the first column of the tables the full title and publication details can be found. In the second and third columns the time-span and geographical range is noted so that its coverage is clear. In the fourth column the overall scope of the work and its major aims, purposes and concerns are identified. The sources on which it is based are characterized in column five and its structure and content in column six. The seventh column contains an evaluation of the book based on criteria for good historical communication and the usefulness of the text for the dance history student.

1 General histories of dance spread widely over time and place

The main feature of a general history of dance text is its long time-span. It also likely to range widely across North American and western European cultures and to give more attention to theatre dance than to other forms. Where a text limits its scope to one century or to a particular kind or function of dance, for example social dance, greater depth is possible. This might produce a more detailed account of the function of dance in that period, while still retaining the breadth of a general historical account.

2   General histories of an era and/or a type of dance

In these texts the breadth of the area of study is limited in different ways: by time-span, by the function of the dance (e.g. as a social form), by genre (e.g. jazz dance) and by political and ethnic concerns (e.g. black dance).

3   Dance histories which cover a limited period

These studies of a specific type of dance within a clearly defined era in dance history usually relate to smaller geographical areas. Both the time and the geographical span are governed by significant events.

4   Accounts of the emergence of new forms of dance

These texts have in common the desire to document and explain the beginnings of new dance styles and genres. The time-span is fairly short, the focus is on one emerging form of dance.

5   Accounts of the life and work of notable figures in dance history

These texts are typical of a substantial body of literature which focuses on the life and contribution of centrally important choreographers, dancers and, less frequently, critics and theorists.

6   Collected writings of choreographers, performers and theorists

Some of these texts consist solely of the written output of choreographers and/or dancers while others embrace theoretical writings on dance. There is some overlap with the following section, which deals exclusively with the collected writings of critics since an extract of a critic's writing may be included in a more broadly-based collection.

7   Collected writings of dance critics

These are brought together separately from the texts in (6) since they constitute a rather special collection of sources, namely, eye-witness accounts of dances, often recorded immediately after their first performances. They are all of recent origin illustrating, in their collected form, the development of a new kind of dance history literature.

A bibliography containing all these texts is presented in the normal way, in author name order at the end of the charts.

1   General histories of dance spread widely over time and place

Title	Time-span	Geographical range	Scope and major concerns	Sources used
Sachs., C., *World History of the Dance*, New York: Norton, 1933, trans. 1937	Antiquity– present	Worldwide	History of the dance worldwide, illustrating themes common to the dance and its movement characteristics	Standard C19 anthropological theories, travellers' tales, mainly primary sources
Sorell, W., *Dance in its Time*, New York: Doubleday, 1981	C12–1960s	Europe and USA	Socio-historical view of theatre dance; accounts for the development of dance in terms of the artistic, social and political climate	Standard histories e.g. Sachs, mainly secondary sources, but covering the context as well as the dance
Kraus, R., *History of the Dance in Art and Education*, Princeton, N.J.: Prentice-Hall, 1969	'Primitive' times to 1960s	Europe and USA	History of the cultural roles of dance, illustrates the emergence of contemporary theatre dance and dance in education	Secondary, derived from standard accounts, e.g. Sachs, Lawler, Backman, appropriately acknowledged. Primary sources on education in the USA
Quirey, B., *May I Have the Pleasure?*, London: BBC, 1976	Prehistory to 1976 mainly C17th–C20th	Western Europe, narrows to England	History of popular dancing written to accompany TV programmes, describes the dances and the style of performance with some socio-historical background	Original writings of dancing masters, pictorial, verbal, musical and dance notation sources, as well as general histories
Backman, F. L., *Religious Dances in the Christian Church and in Popular Medicine*, Westport, Conn.: Greenwood, 1952, 1972	Antiquity– C19th	Asia/Europe, narrows to W. Europe including Scandinavia	History of religious and therapeutic uses of dance, traces outbreaks of dancing and relates them to theological dogma and medical practice	Original European and Scandinavian sources: theological, literary, legal and musical
Kirstein, I., *A Short History of Classical Theatrical Dancing*, New York: Dance Horizons, 1935, 1942, 1969	Prehistory– 1942	Western world, narrows to USA	History of theatrical dancing, traces growth of dance in this context	Secondary sources in three languages used to illustrate detailed points. Primary, first-hand account of the early part of the C20th
Au, S., *Ballet and Modern Dance*, London: Thames & Hudson, 1988	C16th– mid-1980s	Europe & USA	History of theatre dance in the Western world	Secondary sources, sound historical accounts by well known scholars. Many illustrations

Structure and content	Evaluation
Common characteristics of dance, by types and themes Chronological account of dances from the Stone Age to the C20	*The* standard dance history. Its generality gives rise to misconceptions because of its unsubstantiated theoretical basis A broad picture of the multiplicity of dance forms emerges clearly
Chronological but under thematic headings e.g. C12th–C14th dance, 'The long awakening', 'Balletomania', 'Dance criticism and the era of Gautier'	A useful example of a socio-historical account with little emphasis on the structure of the dance. General themes, parallels across forms emerge within a total picture of the dance A good introductory text
Chronological account from 'primitive' times, covering a wide variety of dance styles and relating dance to other arts Two major sections on contemporary dance in the theatre in America and on dance education, a review of its aims, current practice and problems	A readable history, well illustrated which provides a good overview of the history of dance and of standard sources of information One of the few accounts of dance in education in C20th America and very useful from this point of view A good introductory text
The validity of evidence used in reconstructing dances of the past General historical overview C17th–C20th dances in detail, with descriptions of the steps and style of performance Brief chronology of events; occupants of the thrones of England and France	A short book which provides a useful starting point, particularly for courses in dance history which have a practical element Reconstruction and interpretation are emphasized as is the consideration of the evidence upon which this is done
Chronological account but thematic within the broad structure, e.g. 'The prohibition of religious dances', 'The dance and the dead', 'Choreomania and heresy'	Detailed but readable account of the religious and therapeutic role of dance. Uncovers many strands of this complex area of study, demonstrates interwoven threads of myth, medical and religious dogma An original, well researched source
Chronological account emphasizing the theatrical context of dance through myth and ritual of Rome and Egypt, the Middle Ages, the Court ballet, to C20th classical dance	A valuable source for adult/student beginners in dance history, using authentic evidence to good effect The broad sweep leads to generalization and a certain bias towards ballet means comments on modern dance should be treated with caution
12 chapters arranged chronologically to cover theatre dance from the French court ballet to the experimental dance theatre of the 1980s Suggestions for further reading provided in an annotated bibliography	Written in a straightforward and clear style. A good introduction to theatre dance history, readable, and more comprehensive than many

2   General histories of an era and/or a type of dance

Title	Time-span	Geographical range	Scope and major concerns	Sources used
Rust, F., *Dance in Society*, London: Routledge & Kegan Paul, 1969	Brief early history, C13th–1969	England	History of social dance and society, analyses changes in the dance in relation to class; sex differences; economic change	Standard sources in dance history, some primary material reproduced at length Original sociological analysis based on questionnaires
Richardson, P. J. S., *The Social Dances of the Nineteenth Century in England*, London: Jenkins, 1960	C19th	England	Socio-historical account of social dances, describes origins and traces change correlated to the social life of the time. Focus on who danced and what they danced	General sources from the period, technical descriptions from primary sources and dancing manuals of the time
Stearns, M. &. J., *Jazz Dance: The Story of American Vernacular Dance*, London: Macmillan, 1964	Prehistory–1960s	USA	A history of dancing to jazz from its origins in Africa to present American forms, focus on genre and style from an analysis of steps	General histories, original material based on interviews with over 200 individuals Discusses problems of interpreting evidence and its validity Gives detailed notes
Emery, L., *Black Dance in the U.S. from 1619–1970*, Palo Alto, Cal.: National 1972	C15th–1970	USA (Caribbean)	Socio-historical account of black dance forms used by people of African origin	Detailed reference to previously unpublished primary material Extensive quotations

3   Dance histories which cover a limited period of time

Lawler, L., *The Dance in Ancient Greece*, London and Middletown, Conn.: A. & C. Black and Wesleyan U.P., 1964	3,000 BC–527 AD	Ancient Greece	History of all types of dance occuring during this period; examines characteristics and functions	Original Greek sources listed and use discussed whether archeological, literary, etc. Discusses problems of interpretation

Structure and content	Evaluation
Overview of historical function of dance from an anthropological point of view Functional analysis of different eras from C13th through Tudor and Elizabethan times to the C20th Discussion based on sociological hypothesis Report of original research study of attitudes to dance in contemporary society	Structural/functionalist analysis of dance within a historical framework. Dance presented as an integral part of culture, giving an indication of the many complex factors as they influence the dance A useful text for studying dance that has primarily a social function and for those contemplating any practical social study of dance forms
Description of the assembly rooms as special places for dance in the late C18th and early C19th The dances performed in them with particular emphasis on the period to 1865 American influences of the later C19th Characterization of steps and dance programmes The whole is within the context of C18th influences, relating change in social life to general issues	Presents the general proposition that change in dance is brought about by changes in social life and that new dances start with the ordinary people and rise through the social scale Detailed descriptions are combined with interesting anecdotes Some background knowledge probably required to make full use of this text It offers discussion about reconstruction and possibilities for further studies of a similar kind
Chronological tracing of major developments in style through minstrel, carnival, circus, roadshow, tin pan alley, Broadway, tap, acrobatics, etc. Basic movements given in notation	Substantial original study of a specific style of dance, well documented and entertainingly written Suitable as an example of a study of any kind of dance and particularly required for jazz and vernacular USA studies
Chapters range from the early slave trade through Caribbean dance 1518–1900, Juba; minstrelsy; dance hall; to concert dance of the 1930–70 period Uses meticulously referenced sources from contemporary accounts within the context of modern social and cultural theory	The social meanings of many forms of black dance are illuminated by reference to the societies in which they occurred A very useful and well researched study, invaluable as a guide to any serious investigation of black dance Exposes the bias of many accounts of slave owners and wealthy travellers
Chronological: prehistoric; Mycenean; pre-classical; transition to Middle Ages Then by types of dances; animal dances; dances at shrines; mystery dances; dance and drama; dance and the people Discusses types of dance and their function for that society	Excellent standard reference text for the period Research results presented in a highly readable manner Illustrates the problems of pursuing studies of this kind where the dance itself no longer exists

Title	Time-span	Geographical range	Scope and major concerns	Sources used
Hilton, W., *Dance of Court and Theatre: The French Noble, Style 1690–1725*, London: Dance Books, 1981	1690–1725	France	History of a particular style of dancing, the French Noble style; analyses style, technique, and notation	Original sources from Louis XIV's dancing masters Discusses problems of reconstruction from the various kinds of evidence available, i.e. verbal, pictorial, notation
Guest, I., *The Romantic Ballet in Paris*, London: Pitman, 1966	1820–47	Paris	History of a distinctive style within the genre of ballet, documents the emergence of ballet as a major theatre art in the Romantic Age	Based on the archives of the Paris Opera and on contemporary written sources in a number of languages Extensive notes; Appendix lists principal dancers 1820–47 and dances performed
Gautier, T., *The Romantic Ballet, as seen by Theophile Gautier*, trans. from French by C. W. Beaumont, London: Beaumont, 1932	1837–48	Paris	Collected reviews over eleven years of the major dance critic of the period	Original views and reviews of performances of new works and revivals
Garafola, L. *Diaghilev's Ballets Russes*, New York and Oxford: OUP, 1989	1909–29	Russia, W. Europe	History of the company, which attempts to rethink its significance in terms of the relation between art, business matters and the reception of the works	Based on British critics' first-hand accounts and other original sources New history methodologies inform the sources

4   Accounts of the emergence of new forms of dance

Ruyter, N. L., *Reformers and Visionaries: The Americanisation of the Art of Dance*, New York: Dance Horizons, 1979	late C18th– mid C20th	USA	A history of the emergence of a distinctively American form of dance in the theatre and in education	Major collection of primary Delsarte material in English published 1882–1913 Historical summaries based on primary sources

Structure and content	Evaluation
General background of court and theatre, place and type of dance, dancing masters and their publications Analysis of the noble style and its notation Appendices of Labanotation for the steps, exercises for performance style, chronology of political events Bibliography categorized into periods, countries; French, Italian, German and English sources both original and modern writings	An example of the depth of study that is possible both in the area of performance skills and interpretation of steps and in the problems of imagining/reconstructing a dance style of the past May be used as a manual of instruction for dances of the early C18th and as a theoretical analysis A crucially important, highly detailed study of a very short period in dance history
A chronological account of the emergence of the Romantic Style, from its origins in Noverre's work and taking account of the influence of notable artists in bringing about a more lyrical style Discusses the dances, technique, scenic design and music Gives a detailed assessment of individuals, e.g. Taglioni, Elssler	A valuable account of the socio-historical context of the arts and of the distinctive heritage of the classical ballet Detailed research source book for the period but also a highly readable text which give the lives of important individuals and stories of events The short time span allows detail to be presented
Account of Gautier's life from 1811 to 1872 by Beaumont, as poet, journalist, art and drama critic, writer of scenarios Principal notices of performances given in Paris 1837–48 with detailed descriptions of staging, costumes and dancers' physical attributes Gives both story lines and qualitative assessment of performance	A valuable original account of dance performed during this period, from the critic's point of view He places strong emphasis on the dancer rather than the structure of the dance but reveals the aesthetic prevailing at the time
12 chapters grouped around three major themes, art, enterprise, audience. Appendices of works created/produced by Fokine and Diaghilev Extensive bibliography Detailed index	Re-interprets familiar material (e.g. Buckle 1979) in the light of social history, new writings in dance criticism and feminism Valuable in its attention to the audience and to political and economic factors An excellent scholarly source for the modern historian

General historical account of early theatre dance in the American social scene of the C18th and C19th. Detailed accounts of ballet; Delsarte; and early modern dancers such as Isadora Duncan and Ruth St Denis General historical account of educational theory in the C18th and C19th. Detailed account of dance education and its early development through the work of e.g. Colby, H'Doubler Valuable bibliography	An interesting account of the entry of dance into the mainstream of respectable life in education and the theatre and its acquisition of status in middle-class culture The dance emerges through a study of personalities in two distinct manifestations, as art and as art in education A thematic study which would be best used after some background knowledge has been acquired

Title	Time-span	Geographical range	Scope and major concerns	Sources used
Kendall, E., *Where She Danced*, New York: Knopf, 1979	1845–1930	USA	A history of two major figures in modern dance, Ruth St Denis and Martha Graham, and through them the growth of a new dance form	Sources not directly attributed in the text, but the whole based on scholarly work Reference to late C19th sources valuable
Magriel, P. (ed.) *Chronicles of American Dance From the Shakers to Martha Graham*, New York: Da Capo, 1948, 1978	mid C19th–1940s	USA	A history of dance from religious to theatrical forms in a specifically American style	Primary sources, newspaper criticisms, and reviews, e.g. of *The Black Crook* 1866–8
Banes, S., *Terpsichore in Sneakers*, Middletown, Conn.: Wesleyan University Press, 1980, 1987	1960–80	USA	A documentation of the emergence of a new form of dance through the writings of those involved	Primary sources,writings of first-hand observers and those making the works
Mackrell, J., *Out of Line*, London: Dance Books, 1992	mid 1960s–1990	Britain	Emergence of British new dance	Based on professional practice as a dance critic Other sources not attributed
Jordan, S., *Striding Out: Aspects of Contemporary and New Dance in Britain*, London: Dance Books: 1992	mid 1960s–1991	Britain	An account of the evolution of later forms of modernism and postmodernism in dance in Britain	Interviews with leading figures Archival sources Journal articles

Structure and content	Evaluation
Ruth St Denis and her influence on health and beauty, the theatre, European art and Isadora Duncan Developments in dance on the West Coast from Salome to Denishawn and Hollywood Martha Graham's emergence as a major artist Valuable bibliography	A highly readable account of dance as popular entertainment, as spectacular extravaganza in balletic style and as a serious art form The very early period is particularly of value Useful in attempting to answer the question of what gave the protagonists of modern dance the courage to insist that they had found a new art form
Points to different precursors of the modern dance in religious forms (Shakers); show dance; minstrels; tap, theatrical spectacles; social dance academies; early ballet in the classic mode Focus on innovators of the early C20th e.g. Duncan, Fuller, Allan, Denishawn, Graham Valuable notes and bibliography	Through a collection of readings and research articles by different authors Magriel draws together a history from religious and puritan origins to tap and minstrel forms as a context for the emergence of major personalities in modern dance Each one presents an insight and a wealth of material for further study
Writings of major postmodern dance figures placed in detailed socio-historical perspective. Traces trends, general areas of agreement, etc. between such people as Brown, Halprin, Rainer, Monk, Dunn, King New introduction in 2nd ed. describes the emergence of distinct styles in this 20-year period. Offers an account of the evolution of postmodern dance	Illuminating attempt to give insight into the most recent developments in dance without imposing standards of judgement derived from earlier styles
Divides the text into '1. What is new dance?'; '2. History of the movement'; '3. Characteristics and concerns of new dance'; '4. Choreographers and works'; 5. 'Into the 90s'. The sections are uneven in length with Chapter 2 being the longest Written as a series of short essays on individuals, companies and themes	Covers the early stages of new dance in Britain in a readable, discursive style. Very valuable in spanning both the choreography, the organizations and the politics of creating and funding new work An accessible and interesting introductory text suitable for the general reader as well as the dance student
Structured in two parts, the first dealing with the organizations which established a second wave of contemporary and new dance (four chapters) and the second with four major choreographers: Alston, Davies, Butcher and Spink Extensive appendices documenting Strider, ADMA, Dartington Festivals and the works of the four choreographers above	Presents valuable information which is difficult for the student to acquire in any other way. A series of essays rather than a sustained historical account. The distinctive character of the work of the four exponents emerges clearly. These chapters provide a useful introduction to their work Very valuable source text on an as yet poorly researched area

5   Accounts of the life and work of notable figures in dance history

Title	Time-span	Geographical range	Scope and major concerns	Sources used
Lynham, D., *The Chevalier Noverre: Father of Modern Ballet*, London: Dance Books, 1972	Noverre's life 1727–1810	W. Europe	An account of Noverre's life and work as theorist and choreographer within the context of the ballet of the time	Original contemporary sources carefully annotated Details 80 ballets, 24 operas, 11 small works
Buckle, R., *Diaghilev*, London: Weidenfeld & Nicholson, 1979	Diaghilev's life 1872–1929	Russia W. Europe	An account of Diaghilev's life and work, with the hindsight of 40 years	Meticulous detail matching interviews, newspaper reports, correspondence, articles, theatre programmes, manuscripts Annotated with precision
Macdonald, N., *Diaghilev Observed by Critics in England and the United States 1911–1929*, London: Dance Books: 1975	Diaghilev's USA and London visits 1911–29	England USA	The presentation of major reviews of the works of the Diaghilev companies over a 28-year time-span	Contemporary first-hand accounts of performances from the *Daily Mail, The Times, The Lady, Vogue*, etc. selected to present a range of views Original illustrations
Shelton, S. *Divine Dancer: A Biography of Ruth St Denis*, New York: Doubleday, 1981	St Denis's life 1878–1968	USA	An examination of St Denis's aspirations and her work both personally and professionally	Use of many original newly discovered sources Indicates British sources that could be followed up
Sorell, W. (ed., trans.), *The Mary Wigman Book*, Middletown, Conn.: Wesleyan U.P., 1973, 1975	Wigman's life 1886–1973	Central Europe visits to USA	A translation and presentation of some of Wigman's writings as choreographer, theorist, dancer and poet	Her own writings, correspondence, poetry, views and reviews American response to her work Hanya Holm's first-hand account of Wigman's work compared with contemporary US work

Structure and content	Evaluation
Chronological account of his life and work followed by an assessment of his contribution to the ballet Uses Noverre's own writings and descriptions of his ballets Appendices include translated scenarios; details of known productions, both first and later performances Index subdivided by subjects, e.g. ballets, composers, librettists, etc.	Noverre's aesthetic and compositional theories outlined and placed in the context of prevailing ideas as well as his own productions A very readable introductory text based on a sound scholarly use of sources
18 chapters arranged chronologically under general headings, e.g. 'The Early Years', 'The Movement West', 'The Fokine–Nijinksy' period Accounts by and about collaborators from all artistic disciplines provide a vivid day-to-day view of his life and work	Relevant for any student of the life of an artist or animateur and as an example of detailed research and the balancing of sources of evidence A very important resource book for the period and for the works and the artists involved
Press notices grouped chronologically in relation to first performances of works Changing reaction to particular dances can be monitored through time Information about the creation of the works provides the context for the reviews and links the sections Long quotations used for the summary of his life and for accounts of earlier Russian performances	Invaluable as a reference book for the choreography and subsequent performances of Diaghilev's works Major works and critics represented An excellent example of this type of study, a life through the eyes of the critics, and also as an account in its own right of the period
A chronological account of Ruth St Denis's life and work in which the social and historical context from which she emerged is linked with the existing dance of the time Detailed descriptions of some of her dances provide a rare and qualitative account Her own dance concerns are related to those of other dancers of the period Detailed bibliography	A useful critical biography which presents her life, her romances, motivations, etc., in conjunction with her work Attempts to explain the origins of, and to characterize, her style, the stages of her choreographic and personal development
Basically chronological but under titles of 'Reminiscences of early work with Laban'; 'Statements on the dance'; 'American tours'; 'Swastika years'; 'Post-war years'; 'Poetic and other writings' Sorell's contribution in the first part and his own comments on her work	Both a tribute to Wigman and a well-translated and researched presentation of her work, in its written form and in the memories of others Her theories of composition, of form and process, the use of music, etc., are of value in a study of the historical development of theories of composition in the art of dance

Title	Time-span	Geographical range	Scope and major concerns	Sources used
Vaughan, D., *Frederick Ashton and his Ballets*, London: A. & C. Black, 1977	Ashton's life since 1904	England, tours abroad	An account of the development of Ashton's choreography through over 80 ballets, films, musical and operatic works	Ashton's own writings and choreographic notes Newspaper and periodical reviews of his work. Letters, interviews. Critics', performers' and choreographers' views all represented
Servos, N. and Weigelt, G., *Pina Bausch: Wuppertal Dance Theatre or the Art of Training a Goldfish*, Cologne: Ballet Bühnen, 1984	Bausch's work 1969–84	Germany	An account of Pina Bausch's works with extensive illustrations	Author's observations of live performance Reconstructions
Siegel, M., *Days on Earth: The Dance of Doris Humphrey*, New Haven, Conn.: Yale University Press, 1987	Humphrey's life 1895 to date of text	USA	A critical biography of Doris Humphrey which focuses on her works	Uses film, videotape and live performances as source material to cover the span of her work 35 illustrations
Sorley Walker, K., *Ninette de Valois: Idealist without Illusions*, London: Hamish Hamilton, 1987	de Valois' life 1898–1987	Ireland England	An account of the career of Ninette de Valois as dancer, choreographer, teacher, artistic director	British journal and newspaper articles, company archives. Interviews with de Valois 63 photographs
Perlmutter, D., *Shadowplay: The Life of Antony Tudor*, London & New York: Viking Penguin, 1991	Tudor's life 1908–87	England USA	An account of Tudor's life and work	Bibliography reveals books only Secondary sources Some interview material
de Mille, A., *Martha: The Life and Work of Martha Graham*, London and New York: Hutchinson, 1992	Martha Graham's life 1894–1991	USA	Biography of Martha Graham	Author's experience of the subject over 70 years. Private correspondence and conversations
Kostelanetz, R. (ed.), *Dancing in Space and Time*, London: Dance Books, 1992	Cunningham's work from the 1950s	USA	Anthology on writings on Cunningham	Selection of mainly American dance critics Reviews with articles by Cunningham and Cage 11 photographs

Structure and content	Evaluation
Combines description and analysis of works with critics' comments in a chronological account of Ashton's life so far Structure of chapters relates to the amount of dance interest, i.e. one early chapter covers 22 years of his life while a later one covers a single year, 1934 Chronology Substantial bibliography subdivided Appendix comments on change in choreographic structure of *Les Rendezvous* over time	Not a biography in the usual sense since it concentrates on the works and their structure and not his personal life Ashton's way of working, his methods and the craft he employs become evident A very valuable scholarly resource for work in this period of British ballet as well as for the choreographer himself
Brief introduction by Jochem Schmidt & philosophical excursion by Servos on the nature of Bausch's work. Works from *Rite of Spring* (1975) onwards described with photographic material presented. Four interviews with Bausch reported Biography includes index of works	Valuable in being the first and only text in English to present a collection of sources on Bausch's work Critical in character rather than historical, provides the reader with useful material and a consistent critical perspective
A chronological account of Doris Humphrey's works with greater attention given to her mature period Changing context in the growing popularity of modern dance exposed Chronology, filmography, notes	Doris Humphrey's humanism and craftsmanship emerge in this pioneering attempt to recapture an entire choreographic output Ability to group the mass of information and then to write thematically provides an impressive example of the critic/historian at work
Fifteen chapters with 5 interviews with de Valois Chronological Notes and references Appendices including list of choreography 1918–73	No chapter notes so Sorley Walker's organizing principles are not explicit. Interrelationship of ideas, choreography, management. Highlights de Valois' many-sided strengths as dancer, choreographer, teacher, artistic director, writer A very useful chronicle of the work of this central figure in the development of British ballet
Chronological account in 40 chapters which integrates the life and work. A psychological study Bibliography Source notes Choreographic chronology	First book-length biographical study of Tudor to emerge since his death. An informal account, few sources cited. Highly speculative in character. A personal story that attempts to reveal Tudor's deepest thoughts and motivations If used critically could demonstrate the many problems for the historian in using this approach
Chronological structure over 30 sections. Titles reflect different emphases – influential people, e.g. Ruth St Denis; personal life; places, e.g. Bennington; works, e.g. *Episodes* Appendices include a listing of the dances and the dancers	Personal account of a great choreographer by a contemporary practitioner. Valuable for the insights this kind of account offers It is rather more about personalities than about the dances Readable and informal in style
Chronological presentation of articles by 30 authors including Croce, Denby, Johnstone, King, Macaulay, Tomkins, Vaughan. Symposium of the Dance Critics Association (USA) presented. Chronology of works 1942–92 Selected bibliography of reviews	Many of these articles have become 'classics' on Merce Cunningham so this collection provides a useful source text Fairly short articles, little explanation of why this selection is made

6   Collected writings of choreographers, performers and theorists

Title	Time-span	Geographical range	Scope and major concerns	Sources used
Cohen, S. J. (ed.), *Dance as a Theatre Art, Source Readings in Dance History from 1581 to the Present*, 1st edn New York: Dodd Mead, 1974, 2nd edn London: Dance Books 1977, 1991	1581–1974	Europe USA	An anthology of primary sources, the writings of major choreographers, performers and theorists in the history of dance	Original technical manuals, statements of theory, discussion of performances. Some new English translations
Steinberg, C. (ed.), *The Dance Anthology*, New York: Plume, 1980	1558–1978	Europe USA	Collection of essays by those involved in dance and in theorizing about it, also provides a guide to the dance literature	Original primary sources, writings of dancers, etc. Essays on dance from first-hand observations and original theoretical discussion
Brown, J. M. (ed.), *The Vision of Modern Dance*, London: Dance Books, 1980	C20th	USA	Presentation of the writings of important dancers and choreographers in the history of modern dance	Original primary sources, writings of these individuals
Livet, A. (ed.) *Contemporary Dance*, New York: Abbeville, 1978	1960–78	USA	Anthology of lectures, interviews and essays by and about choreographers, dancers, critics and scholars of dance	Original writings and photographs The latter capture historic moments both of the dance and of design for it
Cunningham, M. and Lesschaeve, J., *The Dancer and the Dance, Merce Cunningham in conversation with Jacqueline Lesschaeve*, London: Boyars, 1985	Merce Cunningham's life 1919 to date of text	USA Europe	Tracing the development of a new dance language in the evolution of Cunningham's work	Interview material: Merce Cunningham talking to Jacqueline Lesschaeve 1977 onwards Archival sources covering entire career Film & video collections 38 photographs Chronological drawings and diagrams

Structure and content	Evaluation
Writings presented with brief introductions from a wide historical period, from The Court Ballet e.g. Caroso C18th e.g. Weaver Romantic Era e.g. Bournonville Russia e.g. Petipa Modern dance e.g. Duncan Classical e.g. Balanchine Recent rebels e.g. Cunningham	Essential student source text of primary source material for theatre dance from the late C16th to mid C20th Relevant pithy introductions by this major American dance historian
Introduction to each of three sections draws historical threads together Dance as a collaborative art e.g. Nijinksy, Benois Dance aesthetics and theory e.g. Denby, Langer, Martin History of dance from courts to modern dance e.g. Beaumont, Sorell, Crisp Selective chronology; family trees; guide to literature including notation guides and references to related arts	Useful source text for essays about dance as movement; as drama; its links with design and music; its role in society and theories of art related to it
Arranged chronologically with four main sections The forerunners, e.g. Duncan, Fuller, Wigman The four pioneers, i.e. Graham, Humphrey, Weidman, Holm The second generation, e.g. Cunningham, Limón, Nikolais, Hawkins The new avant-garde, e.g. Halprin, Rainer, Brown, Dunn J. & D. Bibliography sectioned under 'artists' and topics such as 'choreography', 'criticisms', etc.	Very useful source text for modern dance and later developments. One of the most up-to-date collections of writings not otherwise easily available Introductions to each section link the whole historically
Introduction places writings in the US historical context in the growth of the post-modern dance Writings by e.g. Brown, Childs, Farber Writings by critics e.g. Jowitt, Kirby Writings by historians e.g. McDonagh Highly detailed but selective chronology 1902–78 of performances, particularly detailed from the 1960s	Invaluable reference to dates and places of performances and collaborative works in the post-Cunningham period Major influences and developments since modern dance traced
Roughly chronological. Dance titles, e.g. *Torso*, *Locale*, used as headings but interspersed with themes, e.g. *Energy & positions: Clarity of the dances.* List of choreography with production details up to 1985 Films and videos, list of dances and dancers. Brief chronology of career	Invaluable compilation of original material, written in the form of the interview Open-ended questions and free-ranging answers reveal in fascinating detail the philosophy and working methods of a crucial figure in C20th dance Vital source text

7   Collected writings of dance critics

Title	Time-span	Geographical range	Scope and major concerns	Sources used
Coton, A. V., *Writings on Dance 1938–1968*, London: Dance Books, 1975	1938–68	Europe USA	To analyse the critic's function and to present 30 years of reviews of dance from Jooss to classical ballet and Graham works	Author's reviews for the *Daily Telegraph* 1954–68 and other publications from 1938 First-hand critical accounts of performances and discussion of new trends
Denby, E., *Looking at the Dance*, New York: Horizon, 1949, 1968	1930s–40s	USA	Collected reviews of performances of modern ballet and modern dance	Author's reviews for *N.Y. Herald Tribune*, *Dance Index, Dance Magazine*, etc., written in the 1930s and 40s
Buckle, R., *Buckle at the Ballet*, London: Dance Books, 1980	1940–75	Europe USA	A historic collection of selections from Buckle's critical output	Author's reviews mainly for the *Sunday Times*, some date back to the 1940s First-hand critical accounts
Croce, A., *Afterimages*, London A. &. C. Black, 1978	1966–77	USA	Collected reviews of Croce's work	Author's first-hand accounts written for *Ballet Review, The New Yorker, Dancing Times* and others
Jowitt, D., *Dance Beat: Selected Views and Reviews 1967–76*, New York: Dekker, 1977	1967–76	USA	Critical reviews of dance performances selected to demonstrate 'the liveliness and variety of the N.Y. dance scene'	Author's reviews for *Village Voice, N.Y. Times, Art in America, Dance Calendar*, etc. First-hand accounts with later additions on further viewings
Jowitt, D., *The Dance in Mind*, Boston: Godine, 1985	1974–83	New York USA	Collected reviews and profiles primarily of performances of American modern/ postmodern dance. Continues from *Dance Beat* (1977)	Author's profiles & reviews originally published in *The Village Voice* 1976–83 with one exception, *New York Times* 1974 Selected to reveal the diversity of dance in New York. Introductions to each section written by the author

Structure and content	Evaluation
Comments on the critic's function Reviews from the 1943 and 1945 seasons, then 1961 Reviews under headings of 'English ballet'; 'Foreign ballet'; 'Modern dance', grouped together Chapter on 'What's the use of critics?'	One of the few critics to state clearly what their role might be and to argue for an objective, historically located method of criticism Focus on principles and themes Excellent example of critical writing and of change of views through time
Reviews grouped under headings such as 'Meaning in ballet'; 'Ballets in recent repertoire'; 'Dancers in performance'; 'Notable events'; 'Ballet music and decoration'; 'Modern dancers'; 'Dancers in exotic styles'	Points to the critic's functions as animating perception, ranges widely in discussion Very valuable first-hand accounts by this major American dance critic of the early period, including reconstructions of Duncan's works
Chronological sections deal with America 1959–60 Russia 1961–2 Royal Ballet 1963–5 Classics 1966–8 Western Europe 1969–71 New trends in Britain 1972–5 with additional reviews from other periods	Humorous, perceptive portrayal of many facets mainly of the ballet world, although some accounts of Graham and British modern dance Excellent reference work for criticisms of the period
Different types of writing for different publications clear from the division of the text into weekly articles 1973–7 monthly articles 1969–71 quarterly essays 1966–72 occasional pieces Ranges from classical ballet to the postmodern dance	Very informative collection of writings recording well-argued views of contemporary performances Very good reference work for American performances, an example of reaction to works through time and in relation to emerging genres
Preface on the role of the critic and use of language; her own preconceptions Sections divide into: ballets, mostly new; 'Sunday' pieces; modern dance, pioneers and 2nd generation; 3rd generation, mostly rebels; ancient festivals; reports on revivals of early modern dance works	Delightfully descriptive collection of reviews, accepting a wide range of activity under the heading of 'dance' Open style captures the fleeting moment Very good reference work for American performances and for the appraisal of works over several viewings
Reviews and profiles grouped. *Some masters* e.g. Robbins, Balanchine, Cunningham, Graham *Iconoclasts of the Sixties & Seventies* e.g. Brown, Gordon, Monk *The past rekindled* revivals e.g. Duncan, Bournonville, Fokine *The new generation* e.g. Armitage, Reitz, Wiener, Boyce *Modern, traditional and very popular* e.g. Nikolais, Hawkins, Béjart, MacMillan *Traditions of other countries* e.g. Aboriginal, Bolero, Nigerian Hand Puppets *Some other vistas* e.g. Western ballets, Trocadero	Points to the critic's role in conjuring up 'vivid images of dancers and what they are doing on stage' (p x) Examples of highly informative, informal writing that is detailed and lively Seeking the 'essence', inherent qualities and the focus on conveying the experience of seeing the dance Open to many kinds of performance, makes her own preferences evident

Title	Time-span	Geographical range	Scope and major concerns	Sources used
Guest, I. (trans., ed.), *Gautier on Dance*, London: Dance Books, 1986	1836–71	Paris France	Compilation of Gautier's reviews to present a view of the Romantic ballet	Gautier's press reviews. Mainly ballet at the Paris Opera. Written in French Selected, translated & annotated by Guest 88 photographs
Croce, A., *Sightlines*, New York: Knopf, 1987	1981–7	New York USA	Collected reviews covering a short time-span. Continues from *Afterimages* (1979) and *Going to the Dance* (1982)	Author's articles mainly published in *The New Yorker*
Acocella, J. and Garafola, L. (eds), *André Levinson on Dance: Writings from Paris in the twenties*, Middletown, Conn.: Wesleyan U.P., 1991	1922–30	Paris France	Selected reviews presented	Fourteen reviews from Levinson's Paris writing 25 photographs from Taglioni to Dalcroze and Joséphine Baker
Siegel, M., *The Tail of the Dragon: New Dance 1976–82*, Durham, NC: Duke University Press, 1991	1976–82	New York USA	Collected reviews with photographs by Nathaniel Tilston focusing on the Judson and other 1960s revolutions. Continues from *At the Vanishing Point* (1972), *Watching Dance Go By* (1979)	Author's own writing on performances 1976–1982 Compiled from newspaper, journal and other sources

Structure and content	Evaluation
Covers the Romantic period from Taglioni & Elssler in the 1830s to *Coppelia* in 1871. Introduction gives a brief account of Gautier's life Reviews structured chronologically with accounts from every year except 1857 and 1859–62	Very valuable collection of reviews recording this most famous of dance critic's experiences of a critical period in the history of ballet Unique compilation of primary sources on the French Romantic ballet Careful annotation providing fascinating insight into the work of the historian
Collection of reviews covering the musical, ballet (NYCB & ABT) mainly of the US companies in NY but also Kirov in Paris, Rambert in NY	Not divided into sections so the logic of the order (if any) has to be deduced Useful as a source on new works and revivals of the period Insightful writing, prejudices in favour of and against certain styles of dance very evident
Biographical introduction, notes, bibliography provided by editors Review articles by Levinson e.g. Diaghilev's Ballets Russes Articles of more general interest, e.g. 'The spirit of the classic dance' & covering a variety of forms e.g. Javanese & Spanish dance Bibliography of Levinson's writings	Valuable for the exposition of a formalist approach to dance criticism Very useful collection of reviews of an important period in the history of ballet Clear preferences for traditional dance forms is evident in this writing
Introduction explores the concerns of the critic with transitional moments – the here and now, in particular between the early 1960s and the late 1980s Principally concerned with Cunningham, Tharp, Brown, Gordon, but also with a wide range of experimental art forms and with some European performances Arranged by years 1976–7, 1977–8 etc. List of available films	Chronological sections allow the reader to monitor change in the dance scene and in Siegel's perception of it From counter culture to a media dominated art, Siegel captures the changing moment

BIBLIOGRAPHY

Acocella, J. and Garafola, S. (eds) (1991), *André Levinson on Dance: Writings from Paris in the Twenties*, Middletown. Conn.: Wesleyan University Press

Au, S. (1988), *Ballet and Modern Dance*, London: Thames & Hudson

Backman, E. L. (1952, 1972), *Religious Dances in the Christian Church and in Popular Medicine*, Westport, Conn.: Greenwood

Banes, S. (1980, 1987), *Terpsichore in Sneakers*, Boston: Houghton Mifflin

Brown, J. M. (ed.) (1980), *The Vision of Modern Dance*, London and New York: Dance Books and Dodd, Mead.

Buckle, R. (1979) *Diaghilev*, London: Weidenfeld & Nicholson

—— (1980), *Buckle at the Ballet*, London: Dance Books

Cohen, S. J. (ed.) (1974, 1977), *Dance as a Theatre Art*, London: Dance Books

Coton, A. V. (1975), *Writings on Dance 1938–68*, London: Dance Books

Croce, A. (1978), *Afterimages*, London: A. & C. Black

—— (1987), *Sightlines*, New York: Knopf

Cunningham, M. and Lesschaeve, J. (1985), *The Dancer and the Dance*, Merce Cunningham in conversation with Jacqueline Lesschaeve, London: Boyars

de Mille, A. (1992), *Martha: The Life and Work of Martha Graham*, London and New York: Hutchinson

Denby, E. (1949, 1968), *Looking at the Dance*, New York: Horizon

Emery, L. (1972), *Black Dance in the U.S. from 1619–1970*, Cal.: National

Garafola, L. (1989), *Diaghilev's Ballets Russes*, New York and Oxford: Oxford University Press

Gautier, T. (1932), *The Romantic Ballet* as seen by Théophile Gautier, trans. from French by C. W. Beaumont, London: Beaumont

Guest, I. (1966), *The Romantic Ballet in Paris*, London: Pitman

—— (trans., ed.) (1986), *Gautier on Dance*, London: Dance Books

Hilton, W. (1981) *Dance of Court and Theatre: The French Noble Style 1690–1725*, London: Dance Books

Jordan, S. (1992), *Striding Out: Aspects of Contemporary and New Dance in Britain*, London: Dance Books

Jowitt, D. (1977), *Dance Beat: Selected Views and Reviews 1967–76*, New York: Dekker

—— (1985), *The Dance in Mind*, Boston: Godine

Kendall, E. (1979), *Where She Danced*, New York: Knopf

Kirstein, L. (1935, 1942, 1969), *A Short History of Classic Theatrical Dancing*, New York: Dance Horizons

Kostelanetz, R. (ed.) (1992), *Dancing in Space and Time*, London: Dance Books

Kraus, R. (1969), *History of the Dance in Art and Education*, Princeton, N.J.: Prentice Hall

Lawler, L. (1964), *The Dance in Ancient Greece*, London and Middletown, Conn.: A. &. C. Black and Wesleyan University Press

Livet, A. (ed.) (1978), *Contemporary Dance*, New York: Abbeville

Lynham, D. (1972), *The Chevalier Noverre: Father of Modern Ballet*, London: Dance Books

Macdonald, N. (1975), *Diaghilev Observed by Critics in England and the United States 1911–29*, London: Dance Books

Mackrell, J. (1992), *Out of Line*, London: Dance Books

Magriel, P. (ed.) (1948, 1978), *Chronicles of American Dance from the Shakers to Martha Graham*, New York: Da Capo

Perlmutter, D. (1991), *Shadowplay: The Life of Antony Tudor*, London: Viking Penguin

Quirey, B. (1976), *May I Have the Pleasure?* London: BBC

Ranger, T. O. (1975), *Dance and Society in Eastern Africa 1890–1970,* London: Heinemann

Richardson, P. J. S. (1960), *The Social Dances of the Nineteenth Century in England,* London: Jenkins

Rust, F. (1969), *Dance in Society,* London: Routledge & Kegan Paul

Ruyter, N. L. (1979), *Reformers and Visionaries: The Americanisation of the Art of Dance,* New York: Dance Horizons

Sachs, C. (1933, trans. 1937), *World History of the Dance,* New York: Norton

Servos, N. and Weigelt, G. (1984), *Pina Bausch: Wuppertal Dance Theatre or the Art of Training Goldfish,* Cologne: Ballet Bühnen

Shelton, S. (1981), *Divine Dancer: A Biography of Ruth St Denis,* New York: Doubleday

Siegel, M. (1987), *Days on Earth: The Dance of Doris Humphrey,* New Haven, Conn.: Yale University Press

—— (1991), *The Tail of the Dragon: New Dance 1976–82,* Durham, NC: Duke University Press

Sorell, W. (ed., trans.) (1973, 1975), *The Mary Wigman Book,* Middletown, Conn.: Wesleyan University Press

—— (1981) *Dance in its Time,* New York: Doubleday

Sorley Walker, K. (1987), *Ninette de Valois: Idealist without Illusions,* London: Hamish Hamilton

Stearns, M. & J. (1964), *Jazz Dance: The Story of American Vernacular Dance,* London: Macmillan

Steinberg, C. (ed.) (1980), *The Dance Anthology,* New York: Plume

Vaughan, D. (1977), *Frederick Ashton and his Ballets,* London: A. & C. Black

Selected list of reference texts

Judith Chapman

This a selected list of reference sources for dance which are mainly, though not exclusively, written in the English language. Titles are grouped to facilitate ease of finding. The annotations are descriptive rather than evaluative.

1 Anthologies
2 Bibliographies
3 Catalogues and directories
4 Dictionaries/encyclopedias
5 Film/video catalogues
6 Guides to periodicals
7 Repertory guides
8 Research listings
9 Technical manuals
10 Terminology manuals
11 Yearbooks

Currently the most extensive tool for finding information about dance is: New York Public Library (1974), *Dictionary Catalogue of the Dance Collection* (10 volumes) with annual supplements entitled *Bibliographic Guide to Dance*. In addition to traditional print form this dictionary catalogue is now available on CD-Rom.

1 ANTHOLOGIES

Brown, J. M. (ed.) (1980), *The Vision of Modern Dance*, London: Dance Books. Dancers statements about their philosophies spanning the early development of modern dance in the USA through to the 1970s. Includes bibliographies on each artist and on a range of topics.

Cohen, S. J. (ed.) (1974, 1977), *Dance as a Theatre Art: Source Readings in Dance History from 1581 to the Present*, New York: Dodd Mead. A selection of primary source writings chosen to give an overview of the history of theatre dance in Europe and America. Includes a comprehensive introduction to each of seven sections and a bibliography.

Copeland, R. and Cohen, M. (eds) (1983), *What is Dance? Readings in Theory and Criticism*, Oxford: Oxford University Press. Sixty essays which examine key issues in dance aesthetics, selected to represent scholarship in America and Europe.

Fancher, G. and Myers, G. (eds) (1981), *Philosophical Essays on Dance*,

Brooklyn, NY: Dance Horizons. A collection of essays which were originally presented at the American Dance Festival at Duke University in Durham, North Carolina in 1979.

Kreemer, C. (1987), *Further Steps: Fifteen Choreographers on Modern Dance*, London: Harper & Row. Edited transcripts of interviews carried out in 1979, and subsequently, with choreographers about their approach to movement and choreography. Includes chronologies and bibliography.

Livet, A. (ed.) (1978), *Contemporary Dance*, New York: Abbeville. An anthology of lectures, interviews and essays from key American choreographers, scholars and critics. Includes a chronology of modern and postmodern dance works and a bibliography.

Magriel, P. (ed.) (1948, 1978), *Chronicles of the American Dance: From the Shakers to Martha Graham*, New York: da Capo. A collection of essays culled from *Dance Index* covering the artists who created the basis of theatre dance in America and including the history of negro dance, the ballet pantomimes and American ballerinas of the eighteenth century, as well as the pioneers of modern dance in America.

Nadel, M. H. and Miller, C. N. (eds) (1970, 1978), *The Dance Experience*, New York: Universe Books. Forty-five articles in nine sections: the nature of dance; the creative personality and the choreographic process; forms of dance; the language and literature of dance; dance and the other arts; dance criticism; the dance artist; problems in dance; facets of dance education.

Preston-Dunlop, V. and Lahusen, S. (1990), *Schrifttanz: A View of German Dance in the Weimar Republic*, London: Dance Books. Selected articles from *Schrifttanz*, a major journal of the German expressionist dance published 1928–32. Includes translated articles, commentaries, lists of contents of *Schrifttanz*, bibliography and details of dance journals of the period.

Sorell, W. (ed.) (1951, 1966), *The Dance has Many Faces*, New York: World, New York: Columbia, revised edition 1992, New York: a cappella Books. A small number of articles is included in each edition alongside a changing selection of other articles so that overall the three editions constitute an implicit history covering four decades of dance writings.

Steinberg, C. (ed.) (1980), *The Dance Anthology*, New York: Plume. A comprehensive collection of essays grouped into sections with introductions to sections by the author. Includes a chronology and a family tree of dance and a guide to the dance literature.

Taplin, D. T. (ed.) (1979), *New Directions in Dance*, Oxford: Pergamon. A collection of conference papers organized under the headings of: aesthetics and criticism; history; the application of science; notation; policy and education.

—— (ed.), (1982) *Dance Spectrum: Critical and Philosophical Enquiry*. University of Waterloo, Canada: Otium Publications/Parsons Press of Trinity College, Dublin. Seven essays ranging across the changing image of dance; the vocabulary of dance; the aesthetic value of dance for creator, performer and viewer; definitions of dance as performed art and the felt experience of dance.

2   BIBLIOGRAPHIES

Au, S. (1979), 'Resources for dance historians: a selected list of bibliographies published since 1960', *Dance Research Journal*, 11, 2 & 3: 76–8. A list of sources from outside the main dance literature. Sections include: guides to reference sources; guides to periodicals; guides to books and periodicals; guides to academic research; some bibliographies in books.

Adamczyk, A. (1989), *Black Dance: An Annotated Bibliography*, London: Garland Publications. A first attempt to compile published material documenting black dance in all of its forms. Includes some material written by Europeans travelling or living in the Americas.

Beaumont, C. W. (1929, 1963), *A Bibliography of Dancing*, London: Dancing Times. Lists books in the British Museum. (Note: several of the items listed were destroyed during the 1939–45 war.)

—— (1966), *A Bibliography of the Dance Collection of Doris Niles and Serge Leslie. Part 1: A–K*, annotated by Serge Leslie, London: Beaumont. An annotated bibliography of a private collection. Contains reference to criticism, essays and belles-lettres relating to all forms of dance but especially to ballet. Includes a subject index.

—— (1968), *A Bibliography of the Dance Collection of Doris Niles and Serge Leslie. Part 2: L–Z*, London: Beaumont. Completes the annotation of the Niles–Leslie collection.

—— (1974), *A Bibliography of the Dance Collection of Doris Niles and Serge Leslie. Part 3: A–Z, Mainly 20th Century publications*, London: Beaumont. Additions to the items listed in the first two volumes.

Benson-Talley, L. (1985) 'Annual international bibliography of dance history: the Western tradition. Works published in 1979. Part III', *Dance Research Journal*, 17, 1 (spring/summer): 43–51. Continuation of the work begun in 1978 and compiled by Nancy Lee Ruyter. Additional category on music in relation to dance.

Davis, M. (1972), *Understanding Body Movement: An Annotated Bibliography*, New York: Arno Press. Contains original abstracts of published and unpublished literature on body movement style; facial expression; gaze behaviour; symbolic actions; gestures; postures; movement interaction. Majority of titles date from 1900 to June 1971.

Davis, M. and Skupian, J. (1982), *Body Movement and Nonverbal Communication: An Annotated Bibliography 1971–1981*, Bloomington Ind.: Indiana University Press. Different from the earlier work in that it includes published work only; also foreign titles.

Derra de Moroda, F. (1982), *The Dance Library: A Catalogue*, Munich: Wolfie. The catalogue of a private collection given to Salzburg University. Covers books on all aspects of dance; musical scores and libretti; prints; programmes; posters and manuscripts.

Fletcher, I. K. (1954), *Bibliographical Description of Forty Rare Books Relating to the Art of Dancing in the Collection of P. J. S. Richardson, 1977*, London: Dance Books. Brief but detailed descriptions of books dating from the fifteenth to the nineteenth century.

Forbes, F. R. (1986), *Dance: An Annotated Bibliography 1965–1982*, New York and London: Garland Publishing. Compiled through use of on-line databases and therefore representative of their coverage. Includes sections on aesthetics; style and the art of dancing; anthropology; education; history; literature; physiology; psychology; sociology; an author and subject index.

Forrester, F. S. (1968), *Ballet in England: A Bibliography and Survey, c. 1700–June 1966*, London: Library Association. Includes books, periodicals and newspaper articles; the result of a systematic search through a range of collections and indexing and abstracting tools.

Hodgens, P. (1985), *Dance: A Selected and Annotated Bibliography of Philosophical Readings in Art, Aesthetics and Criticism*, Guildford: National Resource Centre for Dance, University of Surrey. Sections include: art; art and dance; interpreting art works; evaluating art works; dance–interpretation and evaluation; criticism; dance and criticism; aesthetics; dance and aesthetics; collections and bibliographies; index.

Kaprelian, M. H. (1976), *Aesthetics for Dancers: A Selected Annotated Bibliography*, Washington D.C.: American Alliance for Health, Physical Education and Recreation. Lists sources to be found in books and journals. Includes references to books with further bibliographies relating to aesthetics.

Kuppuswamy, G. and Hariharan, M. (1981), *Indian Dance and Music Literature: A Select Bibliography*, New Delhi: Biblia Impex. About 800 books and 3,000 articles listed by author. Includes a short subject index.

Leslie, S. (annotator) (1974), *A Bibliography of the Dance Collection of Doris Niles and Serge Leslie. Part IV: A–Z, Mainly 20th Century Publications*, London: Beaumont. In addition to completing the bibliography of the collection, this volume is notable for the extensive listing of articles by C. W. Beaumont, editor of the earlier three volumes.

Magriel, P. D. (1936), *A Bibliography of Dancing: A List of Books and Articles on the Dance and Related Subjects*, republished 1974, New York: H. W. Wilson. A list of reference works on many forms of dance. Divided into eight sections: general works, history and criticism; folk, national, regional and ethnological dances; art of dancing; ballet; mime and pantomime; masques; accessories. Includes many works not generally available.

New York Public Library (1974 and supplements), *Dictionary Catalogue of the Dance Collection 1974 with Annual Supplements entitled Bibliographic Guide to Dance*, New York: G. K. Hall. Initial ten volumes published in 1974 provide a catalogue to the Dance Collection at Lincoln Center, New York. Each annual supplement, consisting of one or two volumes, lists materials catalogued during the past year by the Dance Collection. Covers all aspects of dance. All types of material are listed and some 8,000 subject headings provide entry points. Extensive cross-referencing links headings. A single reference source to a comprehensive archive. In addition to traditional print form this dictionary catalogue is now available on CD-Rom. Internet users can also access the catalogues on-line through telnet. (Access enquiries FAX – (212) 247–5848, Voice (212) 621–0648.)

Osterreich, S. A. (1991), *The American Indian Ghost Dance, 1870–1890: An Annotated Bibliography*, New York: Greenwood. Covers a range of sources on the ghost dances and, through sectioning of contents, indicates various paths of enquiry.

Ruyter, N. L. (1980), 'Annual international bibliography of dance history: the western tradition. Works published in 1978. Part 1', *Dance Research Journal*, 12, 2 (spring/summer): 28–30. Books and articles divided into sections: bibliographies and bibliographic information; reference works; historical sources; methodology; historical studies; biographical, historical and evaluative material on individuals and their work; historical and evaluative material on dance companies; studies and material on dance works; reports; general and miscellaneous. Indexes.

—— (1984) 'Annual international bibliography of dance history: the western tradition. Works published in 1978. Part II', *Dance Research Journal*, 16, 1 (spring): 41–50. Books and articles divided into sections: bibliography; reference works and information; historical sources; historical studies; biographical, historical and evaluative material on individuals and their work; historical and evaluative material on dance companies; studies and material on dance works; reports; general and miscellaneous. Indexes.

Schwartz, J. L. and Schlundt, C. L. (1987) *French Court Dance and Dance Music: A Guide to Primary Source Writings, 1643–1789. Dance and music series No. 1,* Stuyvesant, New York: Pendragon Press. Covers printed matter relating to social and theatrical dance of the French royal court from the reign of Louis XIV to the French Revolution, its music, its practitioners in France and its imitators abroad.

Senelick, L., Cheshire, D. F. and Schneider, U. (1981), *British Music-hall, 1840–1923: A Bibliography and Guide to Sources with a Supplement on European Music-hall,* Hamden, Connecticut: Archon books. Articles, caricatures, books, records; information on other collections and sources.

Wenig, A. R. (1983), *Pearl Primus: An Annotated Bibliography of Sources 1943 to 1975,* Oakland, Cal.: Wenadance Unlimited. Includes book, periodical and newspaper references, publications by Primus, plus audio and visual materials and programmes.

Zile, J. van (1973), *Dance in India: An Annotated Guide to Source Materials,* Providence, R.I.: Asian Music Publishers. Includes reference to various dance traditions in India as well as theatrical forms in which dance plays a role.

3   CATALOGUES AND DIRECTORIES

Berry, I. (1986), *Benesh Movement Notation Score Catalogue,* London: Benesh Institute. An international listing of Benesh movement notation scores of professional dance works recorded 1955–85.

Connolly, T. (ed.) (1991), *The Mentor Dance Directory,* London: Mentor. Sections include information on UK dance companies, organizations, clothing and equipment and dance schools. One section provides a detailed guide to courses at colleges, polytechnics and universities in the UK. Includes information on types of dance studied, time devoted to different aspects of dance study, and details of facilities and performances.

Warner, M. J. (1984), *Notation Scores Catalogue,* New York: International Council for Kinetography Laban. Includes scores in institutional and private collections in North America and Europe. Covers dance and non-dance transcriptions, unfinished manuscripts in addition to completed scores.

4   DICTIONARIES/ENCYCLOPEDIAS

d'Albert, C. (1913, 1921), *The Encyclopedia of Dancing,* London: Middleton. A glossary of terms which also gives instructions for some dances.

Chujoy, A. and Manchester, P. W. (1949, 1967, 1977), *The Dance Encyclopedia,* New York: Simon & Schuster. A collection of brief and extended entries on many forms of dance worldwide. Includes a bibliography of books published in England and the USA between 1940 and 1948.

Clarke, M. and Vaughan, D. (eds) (1977), *The Encyclopedia of Dance and Ballet,* London: Pitman. Just over 2,000 entries covering both ballet and modern theatre dance. Extensively illustrated.

Cohen-Stratyner, B. N. (ed.) (1982), *Bibliographical Dictionary of Modern Ballet,* New York: Dance Horizons/Schirmer and London: Collier Macmillan. Entries for *c.* 2,000 performers and choreographers, composers and artists spanning four centuries in Europe and America.

Gadan, F. and Maillard, R. (1959), *A Dictionary of Modern Ballet,* London: Methuen. Approximately 650 brief accounts of artists, performers, ballets and institutions which have contributed to the development of ballet from the Diaghilev period onwards.

Koegler, H. (1977, 1982, 1987) (original German language edition 1972), *The Concise Oxford Dictionary of Ballet*, London and New York: Oxford University Press. Approximately 5,000 entries, mainly though not exclusively on ballet. Includes choreographers, companies, composers, dancers, designers; ballets, theatres, ballet schools and technical terms.

Mezzanotte, R. (1979, 1980, 1981), *Phaidon Book of the Ballet*, Oxford: Phaidon Press. Chronicles 500 ballets from the sixteenth to the twentieth century according to date of first performance.

Raffe, W. G. and Purden, M. E. (eds) (1964), *Dictionary of the Dance*, London: Yoseloff. Approximately 5,000 entries aiming at comprehensive coverage of dance through time. Includes a bibliography, a geographical index and subject index.

Reyna, F. (1974), *Concise Encyclopedia of Ballet*, Glasgow: Collins. An account of the history of ballet including chapters on France, Germany, England, the Soviet Union. Illustrated. Includes an index of ballets and persons.

Robertson, A. and Hutera, D. (eds) (1988), *The Dance Handbook*, Harlow, Essex: Longman. Approximately 200 entries each dedicated to a choreographer, dance work, company or dancer. Entries provide biographical or production details, with a brief appraisal of their place in dance history. Glossary.

Wilson, G. B. L. (1957, 1974), *A Dictionary of Ballet*, 1961, London: A. &. C. Black. Entries are chiefly concerned with ballet though reference is made to modern dance, Spanish and Indian dance.

5   FILM/VIDEO CATALOGUES

Braun, S. and Kitching, J. (compilers) (1974, 1980), *Dance and Mime Film and Videotape Catalog*, New York: Dance Films Association. Lists *c.* 1,100 works on film/video covering all areas of dance; experimental film and video; includes some mime.

Chapman, J. A. (ed.) (1982), *Dance Film and Video Catalogue*, supplement 1985, new edition 1992, Guildford: National Resource Centre for Dance, University of Surrey. The new edition lists by title *c.* 700 videos or films which are available in the UK for purchase or for hire; technical details and notes about each item. Indexes to choreographers, companies, dancers and dance titles; directory of distributors and sales outlets.

Mueller, J. E. (*c.* 1979), *Dance Film Directory: An Annotated and Evaluative Guide to Films on Ballet and Modern Dance*, Princeton, N.J.: Princeton Book Company. A directory, mainly of 16mm films and some videos that feature ballet and modern dance performances and excerpts. Indexes to film distributors, choreographers, dance works, dancers and an alphabetical list of films.

Parker, D. L. and Siegel, E. (1978), *Guide to Dance in Film: A Guide to Information Sources*, Detroit: Gale Research. A list of US professional productions including dance sequences with names of dancers, choreographers, directors. Some films listed pre-date the turn of the century.

Penman, R. (1987), *A Catalogue of Ballet and Contemporary Dance in the BBC Television Film and Videotape Library, 1937–1984*, London: BBC Data Publications. Comprehensive guide to holdings of ballet and contemporary dance materials which, because of copyright and contractual limitations, were at the time unavailable for purchase or hire. (Note: Since publication of the catalogue the Society for Dance Research London has negotiated with the

BBC and the British Film Institute and made arrangements for viewing copies of selected materials from the BBC Archive at the National Film Archive, London.)

Towers, D. (1991), *Dance, Film and Video Guide*, Pennington, N.J.: Princeton Book Company. A listing (including dances, duration, format and distributor) of over 2,000 dance films and video, updating the 1986 edition. Indexes to choreographers, composers, dance companies, dancers, directors and subject, plus a directory of distributors.

Unesco (1968), *Catalogue: Ten Years of Films on Ballet and Classical Dance*, Paris: Unesco. A catalogue with brief entries on dance in the theatre.

6   GUIDES TO PERIODICALS

Belknap, S. Y. (ed.) (1959–63), *A Guide to Dance Periodicals*, Gainsville, Fl.: University of Florida Press. Volume I covers 1931–5; volume II, 1936–40; volume III, 1941–5; volume IV, 1946–50; Volume V, 1951–2 and thereafter issued biennially. Includes mainly American journals with small number of UK dance and theatre journals.

Chapman, J. A. (ed.) (1983 to present), *Dance Current Awareness Bulletin*, Guildford: National Resource Centre for Dance, University of Surrey. Indexing and abstracting tool published three times per year. Main section covers contents of about 35 periodicals, includes summaries of major articles grouped under subject headings. Further sections list new publications (books, periodicals, video and multi-media) and forthcoming conferences and courses.

Getz, L. (1981 to present), *Attitudes and Arabesques*, Menlo Park, Cal.: Getz Dance Library. Lists contents pages of journals, new and forthcoming books and recent additions to the Getz Dance Library.

7   REPERTORY GUIDES

Balanchine, G. (1954), *Complete Stories of the Great Ballets*, 1968, New York: Doubleday. A collection of the narratives of contemporary ballets.

Balanchine, G. and Mason, F. (1954, 1968, 1975, 1977, 1978), *Festival of Ballet*, New York: Doubleday. Narrates the plots of 404 classic ballets; sections on how to enjoy ballet, a brief history and chronology.

Beaumont, C. W. (1937, 1949 and 1951, 1956), *The Complete Book of Ballets: A Guide to the Principal Ballets of the Nineteenth and Twentieth Centuries*, London: Putnam. Comprehensive reference work. Libretti, dates of first performance, details of original cast, contemporary critics' reactions to the performance.

—— (1942, 1945, 1952), *Supplement to the Complete Book of Ballets*, London: Beaumont and London: Putnam. The first supplement covers 57 ballets. When reprinted in 1945 and 1952 an index was added.

—— (1954), *Ballets of Today: Being a Second Supplement to the Complete Book of Ballets*, London: Putnam. Comments on 42 ballets produced during the previous decade.

—— (1955), *Ballets Past and Present: Being a Third Supplement to the Complete Book of Ballets*, London: Putnam. Brings up to date the information about ballets produced in recent years and also includes sections on Robert Helpmann, Soviet ballets and notes on six additional ballets of previous centuries not included in the *Complete Book of Ballet*.

—— (1980), *Ballet and Dance: A Guide to the Repertory*, Newton Abbot: David & Charles. Synopsis and commentaries for over 130 dance works from the Romantic era to the contemporary repertory.

Clarke, M. and Crisp, C. (1981), *The Ballet-goer's Guide*, London: Michael Joseph. Synopses of ballets together with accounts of different productions by major companies world-wide. Includes glossary of dance steps and biographic information on selected artists.

Crosland, M. (1955), *Ballet Carnival: A Companion to Ballet*, London: Arco Publishers. An introduction for young people. Includes sections on the people, the stories, vocabulary and the music.

Kahn, M. C., Lasselle, N. and Simmonds, H. (1983) *Choreography by George Balanchine: A Catalogue of Works*, New York: Eakins Press. A first chronological listing; includes first performance details, note of major revisions, a record of stagings for each work Balanchine created from his student days up to and including June 1982.

McDonagh, D. (1976, 1977, 1990), *Complete Guide to Modern Dance*, New York: Doubleday. Brief biographies of choreographers and entries about selected works by major figures in the early years of American modern dance.

Reynolds, N. (1977), *Repertory in Review: 40 Years of the New York City Ballet*, New York: Dial Press. Documents the New York City Ballet with details of 237 of its works. Includes articles on Balanchine and the School of American Ballet.

Reynolds, N. and Reimer-Torn, S. (1991), *Dance Classics: A Viewer's Guide to the Best Loved Ballets and Modern Dances*, Chicago: a cappella Books. First published in 1980 under the title *In Performance: A Companion to the Classics*. Major sections include: traditional ballets; early ballet rebels; modern and contemporary dance. Glossary. Index.

Robert, G. (1946, 1947, 1949), *The Borzoi Book of Ballets*, New York: Knopf. Draws on Beaumont's *Complete Book of Ballets* and other sources for more recent works. Includes a glossary and index.

Studwell, W. E. and Hamilton, D. A. (1987), *Ballet Plot Index: A Guide to Locating Plots and Descriptions of Ballets and Associated Material*, New York and London: Garland Publishing. Indexes plots and descriptions of ballets, plus associated materials. Includes ballet and composer index but omits names of choreographers.

Terry, W. (1976), *Ballet Guide: Background, Listings, Credits and Descriptions of More than 500 of the World's Major Ballets*, Newton Abbot: David & Charles. Each ballet is listed with choreographic, musical and scenic credits, plus titles of companies which produced them with dates, places and principal dancers for the first performance. Synopses of all major ballets and historical comment.

8   RESEARCH LISTINGS

American Alliance (formerly Association) for Health, Physical Education and Recreation. National Section on Dance (1964), *Compilation of Dance Research 1901–1963*, edited by E. E. Pease, Washington D.C.: AAHPER. List of all available dance research completed at graduate level.

—— Dance Division (1968), *Research in Dance I*, Washington D.C.: AAHPER. Supplement to the compilation of *Dance Research 1901–1963* and, in addition to graduate level research, includes a list of projects, reports and related research.

—— Dance Division (1973), *Research in Dance II*, Washington D.C.: AAHPER. Not available for annotation.

—— Dance Division (1982), *Research in Dance III*, Washington D.C.: AAHPER. Covers research completed since 1971. Some inclusions for earlier years if not already reported.

Overby, L. Y. and Humphrey, J. H. (eds) (1989), *Dance: Current Selected Research*, New York: AMS Press. A collection of articles, anthropological, educational, historical, philosophical, sociological; surveys of research literature.

—— (1990), *Dance: Current Selected Research, vol. 2*, New York: AMS Press. As above, a collection of research articles on a range of issues.

9   TECHNICAL MANUALS

Beaumont, C. W. and Craske, M. (1930), *The Theory and Practice of Allegro in Classical Ballet (Cecchetti Method)*, London: Beaumont. Explanation of Cecchetti work with tables for weekly practice.

Beaumont, C. W. and Idzikowski, S. (1922, 1932), *A Manual of the Theory and Practice of Classical Theatrical Dancing (Méthode Cecchetti)*, London: Beaumont. Concise manual of classical ballet technique. Revised edition includes a directory of publications.

Cohan, R. (1986), *The Dance Workshop*, London: Allen & Unwin. Introductory sections on the elements of dance, followed by basic, development and jazz workouts. Illustrated.

Craske, M. and Derra de Moroda, F. (1956, 1979), *The Theory and Practice of Advanced Allegro in Classical Ballet (Cecchetti Method)*, London: Beaumont. A record of daily classes written from authors' notes.

Golovkina, S. (1991), *Lessons in Classical Dance*, translated by Nigel Timothy Coey and edited by Joan Lawson, London: Dance Books. Lessons by Golovkina, Bolshoi Theatre ballerina and Director of the Moscow Academic Choreographic School.

Hammond, S. N. (1982), *Ballet Beyond the Basics*, Palo Alto: Mayfield. The stated aim of the book is to provide a reference source for intermediate students of ballet for their continuing technical development.

Messerer, A. (1976) *Classes in Classical Ballet*, translated by Oleg Briansky, London: Dance Books. Outlines the background to a Messerer class and provides a series of classes and exercises. Biography of Asaf Messerer.

Royal Academy of Dancing (1984), *Ballet Class*, London: Ebury Press. Describes the Royal Academy of Dancing classes, grades 1–4 and senior grade.

Stuart, M. (1952), *The Classic Ballet: Basic Technique and Terminology*, New York: Alfred Knopf. The technique and terminology used are those of the Imperial Dancing Academy in St Petersburg and continued in the School of American Ballet in New York since 1934.

Vaganova, A. (1946, 1953, 1969), *Basic Principles of Classical Ballet: Russian Ballet Technique*, New York: Kamin Dance Publishers; London: A. & C. Black; New York: Dover. Vaganova's system is the development and continuation of the traditions of the Russian school of ballet. First appearing in Russian in 1934, the book has been translated into several languages. Illustrated.

10   TERMINOLOGY MANUALS

Books in this section are not annotated since titles are, for the most part, self-explanatory.

Baum, E. L. (1932), *Dictionary of Ballet Terms*, Chicago: no publisher.

Beaumont, C. W. (1931), *A French–English Dictionary of Technical Terms used in Classical Ballet*, London: Beaumont.

Grant, G. (1950, 1967, 1982), *Technical Manual and Dictionary of Classical Ballet*, New York: Dover.

Kersley, L. and Sinclair, J. (1952, 1973, 1977), *A Dictionary of Ballet Terms*, New York: da Capo.

Love, P. (1953), *Modern Dance Terminology*, New York: Kamin Dance Publishers.

Mackie, J. (1973, 1980), *Basic Ballet*, Leeds: Blackburn.

Mara, T. (1966), *Language of Ballet: An Informal Dictionary*, New York: Dance Horizons.

11   YEARBOOKS

Where a yearbook has ceased publication a date is given to indicate the years it covered. In all other cases the yearbook is available currently. Yearbooks are listed by title since the name of the editor may change while the title continues.

Ballet Annual (1947–63), London: A. & C. Black. Eighteen volumes containing articles by a range of contributors on ballet in the UK and abroad. Illustrated, sometimes includes chronologies for the year.

British Performing Arts Yearbook (first published 1991), London: Rhinegold. Guide to venues, performers, arts centres, festivals, supporting organizations and services for the arts profession.

Dancing Yearbook (including The Ballroom Dancing Yearbook) (first published 1958), Brighton: International Dance Teachers Association. Lists international organizations, festivals, calendar of events, championships, scholarship winners, ballroom teachers' directory and a bibliography.

Dans Jaarboek (first published 1983/84), Amsterdam: Nederlands Instituut voor de dans. Articles about dance in the Netherlands, details of new productions and a contacts list.

The Folk Directory (first published 1965), London: The English Folk Dance and Song Society. Includes contacts lists and clubs; conferences; archives; festivals, venues, promoters, agents; radio, television; arts administration and management courses.

Performing Arts Yearbook for Europe (first published 1991), London: Arts Publishing International. Ministries of culture and funding agencies; supra-national organizations and networks; national organizations and resource centres; opera, ballet, dance companies, orchestras, puppets, mime; festivals, venues, promoters, agents; radio, television; arts administration and management courses.

Stern's Performing Arts Directory (first published 1967), New York: Dance Magazine. Dance, music, resources; lists performers, teachers, schools, organizations, financial services, sponsors in the USA.

World Ballet and Dance (first published 1989), London: Dance Books. International yearbook providing coverage of classical and contemporary dance companies. Includes critical appraisals of the season's activities, on repertoire and personnel and information on major dance archives.

Selected list of periodicals

Judith Chapman

This is a selected list of dance periodicals almost all currently in print and, in most instances, commonly available. The selection is mainly of English language periodicals though a small number of titles in other languages has been included in order to give at least some coverage of sources and scholarship in different countries. Where a publisher is indicated, the information given is correct to January 1993. Publisher's addresses are given only for periodicals currently in print.

1 About the House (UK)

The Journal of the Friends of Covent Garden (UK). Address: The Royal Opera House, Covent Garden, London WC2E 9DD, UK. Text in English. First published in November 1962. Published four times per year. Initially an in-house magazine but now generally available. Articles and photographic essays on ballet and opera productions by the companies resident at the Royal Opera House, London.

2 Action! Recording! (UK)

Address: Labanotation Institute, Department of Dance Studies, University of Surrey, Guildford, Surrey GU2 5XH, UK. Text in English. First published in January 1976. Published three or four times per year. Brief articles; conference reports and news of forthcoming events and developments in Labanotation.

3 Ballet (UK)

Text in English. First published in 1939. Ceased publication in 1952. In October 1948 the title became *Ballet and Opera*. In January 1950 the title reverted to *Ballet*.

4   Ballet Review (USA)

Address: Dance Research Foundation Inc., 150 Claremont Avenue, New York, NY 10027, USA. Text in English. First published in 1965. Published four times per year. Scholarly articles on dance history in addition to interviews, catalogues of exhibitions and photographic portfolios.

5   Ballett International (Germany)

Address: Ballett International Verlags-GmbH Buerozentrolle, Richard-Wagner Strasse 33, PO Box 270 443, W-5000, Cologne 1, Germany. Text in English and German. First published in 1978. Published monthly with occasional variations. Gives international information on a range of events in dance (ballet, mime, dance theatre, performance art) with substantial essays and interviews covering the history of dance as well as current cultural issues.

6   Ballett Journal/Das Tanzarchiv (Germany)

Address: Ulrich Steiner Verlag, Kielsberg 60, 5063 Overath, Germany. Text in German. First published in 1953 under the title of *Das Tanzarchiv*. Published approximately five times per year. Reviews: ballet, music. Biographies, interviews. Calendar of events.

7   Choreography and Dance. An international journal (UK)

Address: Harwood Academic Publishers, c/o STBS Ltd, ONE Bedford Street, London WC2 9PP, UK. Text in English. First published in autumn 1988. Published irregularly. Studies of choreographers, choreographic methods, training, relation of choreography with other components of dance performance such as music.

8   Contact Quarterly. A vehicle for moving ideas (USA)

Address: Contact Collaborations, Inc., PO Box 603, Northampton, MA 01061, USA. Text in English. First published in 1980. Published four times per year. Dance/movement journal with focus on movement studies, performance art and body therapies.

9   Dance and Dancers (UK)

Address: Dance and Dancers Limited, 214 Panther House, 38 Mount Pleasant, London WC1X OAP, UK. Text in English. First published in 1950. Published monthly. Reviews of performances; book and video reviews; interviews with figures in the dance world; calendar of events.

10   Dance Australia (Australia)

Address: Publications Pty. Ltd., Room 16–17, City Road, South Melbourne, Vic 3205, Australia. Text in English. First published in 1980. Published bi-monthly. Brief articles on people and topics on interest in Australian dance.

11   Dance Chronicle: Studies in Dance and the Related Arts (USA)

Address: Marcel Dekker Inc., 270 Madison Avenue, New York, NY 10016, USA. Text in English. First published in 1977. Published approximately twice per year. Scholarly, lengthy articles on dance and dance history.

12   Dance Connection (Canada)

Address: Dance Connection, #603, 815 1St. SW Calgary, AB T2P 1N3, Canada. Text in English. First published in 1983. Published five times per year. Articles about dance in Canada, both historical and current. Conference reports, interviews and performance reviews.

13   Dance Gazette (UK)

Address: The Royal Academy of Dancing, 36 Battersea Square, London SW11 3RA, UK. Text in English. First published in 1930. Published three times per year. Originally conceived as an in-house magazine but now generally available. Historical articles; ballet; RAD news to members; RAD syllabus developments and courses.

14   Dance Journal (UK)

Address: Imperial Society of Teachers of Dancing, Euston Hall, Birkenhead Street, London WC1H 8BE, UK. Text in English. First published 1924. Ceased publication in 1991. Mainly a voice for the Imperial Society and its teachers but also includes articles of general historical interest. Re-titled *Dance* in 1986.

15   Dance Research. The Journal of the Society for Dance Research (UK)

Address: Oxford University Press, Walton Street, Oxford OX2 6DP, UK on behalf of The Society for Dance Research, 9 Cecil Court, London WC2N 4EZ, UK. Text in English. First published in 1983. Published bi-annually. Scholarly articles, series on dance archives worldwide; book reviews; international and inter-disciplinary.

16   Dance Research Journal (CORD) (USA)

Address: Congress on Research in Dance, Department of Dance, State University of New York College at Brockport, Brockport, New York, NY 14420, USA. Text in English. First published in 1969. Published bi-annually. Scholarly articles, book reviews, list of books and journals received, reports of scholarly conferences, archives and other projects of interest to the field. Formerly *CORD News*, vols I–VI.

17   Dance Theatre Journal (UK)

Address: Laban Centre, Laurie Grove, London SE14 6NH, UK. Text in English. First published 1983. Published four times per year. Reviews – performances, books and video; brief scholarly articles on new dance, performance arts and issues of current interest in experimental dance. Calendar of events.

18   Dancemagazine (USA)

Address: Dancemagazine, 33 West 60 Street, New York, NY 10023, USA. Text in English. First published in 1926. Published monthly. Articles of current interest written for an audience interested in topical and popular issues. Reviews – books, performances and film/video. Details of college dance courses and education/training in North America.

19   Dancing Times (UK)

Address: Clerkenwell House, 45–7 Clerkenwell Green, London EC1R 0BE, UK. Text in English. First published in 1910 (new series). Published monthly. The title was first used in 1894 'as the name of a house journal published in connection with the Cavendish Rooms. The title was acquired by the present proprietors in 1910'. From then until 1956, all kinds of dance were covered. In 1956 a new title, *The Ballroom Dancing Times* came into being, leaving *The Dancing Times* to focus its coverage on a range of forms of theatre dance. Reviews of performances, books and video; historical articles; biographies and interviews.

20   English Dance and Song. Journal of the English Folk Dance and Song Society (UK)

Address: English Folk Dance and Song Society, Cecil Sharp House, 2 Regent's Park Road, London NW1 7AY, UK. Text in English. First published in September 1936. Published four times per year. Brief articles and news about folk dance and song in Britain. Section on library acquisitions. Supersedes *English Folk Dance News* which was last published in June 1936.

21   Hungarian Dance News (Hungary)

Address: Office of International Music Competitions and Festivals, H 1366, Vorosmaty ter 1, H-1051, Budapest, Hungary. Text in English. First published in 1978. Published three to six times per year. Brief articles and news items.

22   Israel Dance/Ma Hol Be-Yisrael (Israel)

Address: Israel Dance Library, Bialik Street, Tel Aviv, Israel. Text in Hebrew with abstracts in English for selected articles. First published in 1975. Published irregularly. Annual bilingual publication with articles by Israeli and American dance writers about dance in Israel; biographies, photographs; all forms of dance.

23   Movement and Dance. Journal of the Laban Guild (UK)

Address: The Laban Guild, c/o 2 Brockham Warren, Box Hill Road, Tadworth, Surrey KT20 7JX, UK. Text in English. First published in 1947 under the title *Laban Art of Movement Guild News Sheet*. Also known formerly as *The Laban Art of Movement and Dance Magazine*. For several years published bi-annually but now published annually. Articles by and about Laban based work and theories. Course/conference reviews and books reviews.

24   Music, Theatre, Dance (UK)

Address: Middlesex University, Bramley Road, Oakwood, London N14 4XS, UK. Text in English. First published in 1990. Published irregularly. Scholarly articles, mainly historical and socio-political, with reviews of performances and books.

25   Pour la Danse. Chaussons et petits rats (France)

Address: Societe Rivanova, 51 rue de Belleville, 75019 Paris, France. Text in French. First published in 1975. Published irregularly. Articles on theatre dance in France. Book reviews.

26   Studies in Dance History (USA)

Address: Dance History Scholars at Princeton Periodicals, PO Box 380, Pennington, NJ 08534-6380, USA. Text in English. First published in 1989. Published bi-annually. Each issue contains a single long article or a collection of articles on one topic (by one or more authors) in the form of new research, important out-of-print titles, primary sources, bibliographic or other reference material.

27   Tanechni Listy (Czechoslovakia)

Address: Ministerstvo Kultury Ceske Socialisticke Republike, Panorama, Halkova 1, 120 72 Prague 2, Czechoslovakia. Text in Czech. First published in 1963. Published irregularly.

28   UCLA Journal of Dance Ethnology (USA)

Address: UCLA Dance Ethnology Association, Dance Dept, UCLA, Los Angeles, CA 90024, USA. Text in English. First published in 1977. Published annually. Scholarly articles by authors who are generally faculty or students of UCLA.

29   York Dance Review (Canada)

Address: Department of Dance of York University, 4700 Keele Street, Downsview, Ontario, M3J 1P3 Canada. Text in English. First published in 1973. Ceased publication in 1978. Scholarly articles on dance, historical and contemporary, social and in the theatre.